The Economics of Climate Change

The impact of climate change is arguably one of the most significant challenges facing the world today. Mitigating this impact will require profound changes in many economic, business, political and industrial spheres.

This book provides a rigorous analytical assessment of the key issues at the heart of the economics of climate change such as:

* the economics of the Kyoto Protocol;
* Cost-Benefit Analysis and climate change;
* developing countries and climate change.

With contributions from recognized international authorities in their respective disciplines, this readable, salient book will be appreciated by academics and postgraduate students with an interest in environmental economics, climate change and energy economics. The book will also appeal to environmental consultants as well as policy makers.

Anthony D. Owen is Associate Professor in the School of Economics at the University of New South Wales, Australia. **Nick Hanley** is Professor of Environmental Economics at the University of Glasgow, UK.

Routledge explorations in environmental economics
Edited by Nick Hanley
University of Glasgow

The Economics of Climate Change

Edited by Anthony D. Owen
and Nick Hanley

WITHDRAWN

Routledge
Taylor & Francis Group

LONDON AND NEW YORK

Dedicated to
Jackie, Catherine and Rhys (A.D.O.)
Fiona, Rose, Charlie and Finn (N.H.)

First published 2004
by Routledge
11 New Fetter Lane, London EC4P 4EE

Simultaneously published in the USA and Canada
by Routledge
29 West 35th Street, New York, NY 10001

Routledge is an imprint of the Taylor & Francis Group

Typeset in Perpetua by Wearset Ltd, Boldon, Tyne and Wear
Printed and bound in Great Britain by Antony Rowe, Chippenham,
Wiltshire

British Library Cataloguing in Publication Data
A catalogue record for this book is available from the British Library

Library of Congress Cataloging in Publication Data
A catalog record for this book has been requested

ISBN 0-415-28724-3

Contents

Figures

Tables

Boxes

Acknowledgements

The editors would like to thank Kevin Brennan who proofread the entire manuscript from a student's perspective and made many useful suggestions.

The editors acknowledge the International Energy Agency for permission to reproduce copyright material; the Intergovernmental Panel on Climate Change for permission to reproduce Figures 2.1, 2.2, 2.5 and 2.6; and John Wiley & Sons (for Belhaven Books) for permission to reproduce Figure 2.3, from Goodess *et al.* (1992) *The Nature and Causes of Climate Change: Assessing long-term futures*.

Contributors

Joanna Depledge is Sutasoma Research Fellow at Lucy Cavendish College, Cambridge University. She holds a PhD from University College London, in which she researched the climate change negotiation process, along with a Masters in Development Studies from the London School of Economics. Joanna is a former staff member of the UNFCCC Secretariat, where she was closely involved in the negotiations on the Kyoto Protocol and subsequent decisions.

Jane Ellis is a policy analyst in the Environment Directorate of the Organisation for Economic Co-operation and Development (Paris). The focus of her work since 1998 has been on the Kyoto Protocol's project-based mechanisms, in particular on establishing ground rules for project baselines and monitoring, and on developing standardized baseline methodologies in different sectors. Her previous experience at the International Energy Agency focused on policy linkages between energy and climate change, in particular on renewable energy and on emissions inventory issues. She is a member of the CDM Executive Board's advisory panel on methodologies ('Methodology Panel').

Brian S. Fisher was first appointed ABARE's Executive Director in 1988. He was appointed to the chair in Agricultural Economics at the University of Sydney in 1985, and became Adjunct Professor of Sustainable Resources Development in 2003. He has published over 220 papers and monographs, and has been involved in climate change research since the early 1990s. Dr Fisher was one of the experts appointed to the IPCC Second and Third Assessment Reports, and is currently engaged in scoping work for the Fourth Report. He has played an integral role in international climate change negotiations as economic adviser to Australia's negotiating team. Dr Fisher was awarded the Public Service Medal in 2002 for 'outstanding public service in the field of agricultural and resources policy development'.

Michael Grubb is Visiting Professor of Climate Change and Energy Policy, at Imperial College, London, and Senior Research Associate at the Department of Applied Economics, Cambridge University. He is also Associate Director of Policy at the UK Carbon Trust. Formerly Head of the Energy and Environmental Programme at the Royal Institute of International Affairs, he is author of seven books and numerous research publications on international and domestic energy and environmental problems. He has been a lead author for several reports of the Intergovernmental Panel on Climate Change addressing the economic, technological and social aspects of limiting greenhouse gas emissions and has advised a number of governments, companies and international studies on climate change policy. He is editor-in-chief of the journal *Climate Policy* and is on the editorial board of *Energy Policy*.

Kirsten Halsnaes is an international expert on the economics of climate change and sustainable development implications of climate change policies. She has played a leading role in several international projects on economics perspectives of climate change policies in developing countries and has authored several key international publications on the economics of climate change mitigation, Kyoto flexibility mechanisms, as well as more general development perspectives of climate change policies. A major work is a recent book, *Climate Change and Sustainable Development – Prospects for Developing Countries*, co-authored with Anil Markandya. Kirsten has been among the internationally leading economists in the work of the Intergovernmental Panel on Climate Change, IPCC.

Nick Hanley is Professor of Environmental Economics at the University of Glasgow. He was previously Professor of Natural Resource Economics at Edinburgh University, and Reader at the University of Stirling. His main areas of research are environmental valuation, cost-benefit analysis, the economics of sustainable development, and the economics of non-point pollution control.

Jochen Hauff holds a Diploma in Economics from Tübingen University, Germany, as well as a MSc in Environmental Science and Policy from the Central European University in Budapest. His academic work is in the area of environmental economics and transformation processes in Central and Eastern Europe. His Master thesis focused on the applicability of a domestic emissions trading system to Poland in 1999. Since 2000, he has been employed as a management consultant at A.T. Kearney, working mostly with clients in the European energy sector. In this capacity he is actively involved in the discussion on how companies may prepare themselves for the challenges of the European Union's emissions trading system.

Mike D. Hinchy is a senior economist at the Australian Bureau of Agricultural and Resource Economics. During the past ten years he has specialized in the economics of climate change, writing numerous papers on emission trading schemes and general equilibrium modelling of the impacts of policies to combat climate change. He has been a contributing author to the Second and Third Assessment Reports of the IPCC. He has published over 60 papers and research monographs. He holds a bachelor of economics (honours) from the University of Sydney and a master of science from Cambridge University.

Anil Markandya is Professor of Quantitative Economics at the University of Bath and Lead Economist at the World Bank. He has written widely in the field of environmental economics, including a number of contributions on the issue of climate change. He is co-author of *Climate Change and Sustainable Development* (Earthscan) and was coordinating lead author of the IPCC's *Climate Change 2001: Mitigation*.

Warwick J. McKibbin is Professor of International Economics and Director of the Centre for Applied Macroeconomic Analysis at the Australian National University. He is also a Professorial Fellow at the Lowy Institute for International Policy, a non-resident Senior Fellow at the Brookings Institution in Washington D.C., and a Board member of the Reserve Bank of Australia. Professor McKibbin has been a visiting scholar or consultant for many international agencies and governments on issues of macroeconomic policy, international trade and finance and greenhouse policy issues. He is a Fellow of the Australian Academy of Social Sciences. He has published widely and is internationally renowned for his contribution to multi-country economic modelling through his development of the MSG multi-country model and the G-Cubed series of multi-country models, which are used in many countries by policy makers, corporations, financial institutions and academics.

Fanny Missfeldt-Ringius is Energy Economist at the World Bank. Before joining the World Bank she worked for the United Nations Environment Programme (UNEP) Centre on Energy and Environment, Denmark, and the Royal Institute for International Affairs, England. She has also been a consultant to the United Nations Framework Convention on Climate Change (UNFCCC) Secretariat. Her PhD from the University of Stirling, Scotland, is in environmental economics. Her academic work has considered game theory approaches to addressing the global commons, greenhouse gas emissions trading, and renewable energy sources.

Dr Ian Moffatt is a Senior Lecturer in the School of Biological and Environmental Sciences at the University of Stirling, Scotland UK. He was Senior Visiting Research Fellow at the Australian National University 1990–1993 and a member of the Northern Territory Government Greenhouse Advisory panel, Australia. His research interests are into measuring and modelling sustainable development from environmental, economic and social perspectives.

Anthony (Tony) D. Owen is Associate Professor in the School of Economics at the University of New South Wales (UNSW), Director of the UNSW Energy Research Development and Information Centre (ERDIC) and Joint-Director of the UNSW Centre for Energy and Environmental Markets (CEEM). He has a PhD in Econometrics from the University of Kent (UK) and has held visiting appointments at the Universities of British Columbia, Colorado, Exeter and Leeds, the International Energy Agency, the Organization for Economic Cooperation and Development, and the UK Department of Energy. Tony is a Fellow of the Royal Statistical Society and President (2004) of the International Association for Energy Economics. He serves on the International Editorial Boards of *Energy Policy* and *Energy Economics*.

Jason Shogren is the Stroock Distinguished Professor of Natural Resource Conservation and Management, and Professor of Economics at the University of Wyoming. His research focuses on the behavioural underpinnings of private choice and public policy, especially for environmental and natural resources. Before returning to his alma mater, he taught at Iowa State and Yale. In 1997, he served as the senior economist for environmental and natural resource policy on the Council of Economic Advisers in the White House during the run up to Kyoto. Currently, he serves on Wyoming's Environmental Quality Council, and Western Governors' Association's Enlibra advisory board.

Dugald Tinch is a researcher in the Economics Department at the University of Glasgow, working with Nick Hanley on a two-year project on the impact of climate change in Scotland. He gained his masters degree in environmental economics from the University of York, having studied economics at Strathclyde University previously. His research interests include environmental valuation, energy economics and biodiversity.

Peter J. Wilcoxen is Associate Professor of Economics and Public Administration, the Maxwell School, Syracuse University, and a non-resident senior fellow in the Economic Studies program at the Brookings Institution, Washington D.C. He is internationally renowned for his contributions to environmental economics, public finance and economic modelling.

Abbreviations

AAU	Assigned Amount Units
AEEI	Autonomous Energy Efficiency Improvement
AGCM	Atmospheric General Circulation Model
AIJ	Activities Implemented Jointly
AOGCM	Atmospheric Ocean General Circulation Model
AOSIS	Alliance of Small Island States
A/R	Afforestation/Reforestation
BAU	Business As Usual
BP	Before (the) Present
C	(degrees) Celsius
CBA	Cost-Benefit Analysis
CDM	Clean Development Mechanism
CEEC	Central and Eastern European Countries
CER	Certified Emission Reduction
CFCs	Chlorofluorocarbons
CGE	Computable General Equilibrium (model)
CH_4	Methane
CIS	Commonwealth of the Independent States
CO_2	Carbon Dioxide
CO_2e	Carbon Dioxide equivalent
COP	Conference of the Parties (of the UNFCCC)
EC	European Commission
ECU	European Currency Unit
EE	Eastern Europe
EITs	Economies in Transition
EMIC	Environmental Model of Intermediate Complexity
EPRI	Electric Power Research Institute
ERU	Emission Reduction Unit
ERUPT	Emission Reduction Unit Procurement Tender
EU	European Union

FSU	Former Soviet Union
g	grammes
GDF	Geophysical Data Facility
GDP	Gross Domestic Product
GEF	Global Environment Facility
GERT	Greenhouse Gas Emissions Reduction Trading Program
GHG	Greenhouse Gases
GIS	Green Investment Scheme
GISS	Goddard Institute for Space Studies
GJ	Gigajoules
GWP	Global Warming Potential
HCFC	Hydro-Chloro-Fluoro-Carbon
HFC	Hydro-Fluoro-Carbon
ICAO	International Civil Aviation Organization
ICLEI	International Council for Local Environmental Initiatives
ICCEPT	Imperial College Centre for Energy Policy and Technology
IEA	International Energy Agency
IETA	International Emissions Trading Association
IMAGE	Integrated Model to Assess the Greenhouse Effect
IPCC	Intergovernmental Panel on Climate Change
IR	Infrared
IVMVP	International Performance Measurement and Verification Protocol
JI	Joint Implementation
K	(degrees) Kelvin
kW	Kilowatt
kWh	Kilowatt hour
LCA	Life Cycle Analysis
LDCs	Least Developed Countries
LEC	Levelized Electricity Cost
MIT	Massachusetts Institute of Technology
MITI	Ministry of International Trade and Industry (Japan)
MOP	Meeting of Parties
MSB	Marginal Social Benefit
MSC	Marginal Social Cost
MSG	McKibbin-Sachs Global (model)
MSU	Microwave Sounding Unit
Mt	Million tonnes
MtC	Million tonnes of Carbon
$MtCO_2(e)$	Million tonnes (of) Carbon Dioxide equivalent
MW	Megawatt
NCAR	National Center for Atmospheric Research (USA)
NGCC	Natural Gas Combined Cycle

NGGIP	National Greenhouse Gas Inventories Programme
NGO	Non-Governmental Organization
N_2O	Nitrous Oxide
NO_x	Nitrogen Oxides
NPV	Net Present Value
ODA	Official Development Assistance
OE	Operational Entities
OECD	Organisation for Economic Cooperation and Development
OGCM	Oceanic General Circulation Model
OPEC	Organization of Petroleum Exporting Countries
OSI	Oil Supply Insecurity
PCF	Prototype Carbon Fund (of the World Bank)
PERT	Pilot Emissions Reduction Trading (of Ontario)
ppbv	Parts per billion by volume
ppmv	Parts per million by volume
PV	Photovoltaic
PV	Present Value
PVLC	Present Value of Lifecycle Costs
RAO UES	Russian Joint Stock Company 'United Energy Systems'
RCM	Regional Climate Models
RMU	Removal Unit
SBI	Subsidiary Body for Implementation
SBSTA	Subsidiary Body for Scientific and Technological Advice
SD	Sustainable Development
SO_2	Sulphur Dioxide
SWF	Social Welfare Function
t	Tonnes
TJ	Terajoule
TWC	Three-Way Catalyst
UK	United Kingdom
UKMO	United Kingdom Meteorological Office
UN	United Nations
UNCED	United Nations Conference on Environment and Development
UNCTAD	United Nations Conference on Trade and Development
UNEP	United Nations Environment Programme
UNFCCC	United Nations Framework Convention on Climate Change
UNGA	United Nations General Assembly
USOSTP	United States Office of Science and Technology Policy
VER	Verified Emission Reduction
VOC	Volatile Organic Compound
VSL	Value of Statistical Life
WBCSD	World Business Council for Sustainable Development

WMO	World Meteorological Organization
WRI	World Resources Institute
WTP	Willingness to pay
WWF	World Wildlife Fund

1 Introduction

Anthony D. Owen and Nick Hanley

The impact of climate change is one of the most significant environmental challenges facing the world today. Mitigating this impact will require profound changes in energy production and use, since emission of greenhouse gases from combustion of fossil fuels is the dominant human contribution to climate change. In the short-term, a range of emission reduction strategies is available. For example, both opportunities for enhanced levels of energy efficiency and for fuel switching (from high to low carbon content fuels) are readily available in all sectors of the economy. However, a long-term solution is possible only if technological development receives the appropriate price signals to enable it to proceed in a climate friendly manner.

In the context of environmental economics, three important characteristics make the study of climate change unique:

- it is global in nature;
- its impacts are of an unusually long-term character;
- understanding of both the nature of climate change itself and the effects of policies designed to mitigate it remain deficient.

The global nature of climate change arises from the fact that irrespective of where on earth greenhouse gases are emitted they are rapidly absorbed into the atmosphere and spread around the globe. The consequences of the resulting global climate change, however, are projected to be far from uniform, with some countries expected to suffer far greater adverse impacts than others. In addition, unilateral action by any one country could not alter this situation significantly. It therefore requires concerted remedial cooperative action at the international level to address the problem.

The long-term nature of the impacts of climate change arises from the fact that greenhouse gases comprise a stock in the atmosphere that is continually augmented by new emissions. The natural rate of breakdown of this stock varies from a few decades for short-lived gases such as methane, to hundreds of years (for carbon dioxide), through to thousands of years (for longer-lived gases such as perfluorocarbons). Thus, impacts induced by these emissions, such as global average temperature increases and rises in sea level, will be progressive over long time horizons. These long time lags will also influence remedial measures, where the risks of climate change in the future have to be offset against the costs of undertaking mitigating action today.

The ultimate physical impact of climate change has yet to be determined with a realistic degree of precision. Although this is true for other pollutants, uncertainty over climate change impacts involves a huge scale and breadth of possibilities worldwide. As a consequence, there is uncertainty about the magnitude of damage costs associated with changing weather patterns, changing agricultural patterns and numerous other effects. This makes policy options difficult to determine and encourages decision makers to delay their response until stronger scientific evidence of potential damages becomes available.

In evaluating future emission reduction options economics can play an important role, for example in terms of:

- assessing the cost-effectiveness of alternative measures;
- estimating the impacts on economic growth and sustainable development;
- modelling impacts on social equity.

This book aims to provide a sound analytical environment for assessing these issues. It also aims to show how the general principles of environmental economics can be applied to serious real-world environmental problems.

The structure of this book

In the next chapter, Ian Moffatt provides a concise guide to the science of climate change, with a focus on the construction of climatic data, the causes of climate change and the growth rate of greenhouse gases, and climate change modelling methodology. He concentrates upon climate change over the last two centuries, a period short enough for astronomical and geological processes of climate change to be assumed constant. Thus attention can be focused on the climatic impact of the changing composition of greenhouse gases in the atmosphere over this time-frame. The science underpinning climate change models is illustrated by means of a simple thermodynamic model of the greenhouse effect. More sophisticated models are then discussed, together with the related degree of uncertainty associated with such complex processes. Finally, he examines scenarios exploring possible climate futures, their associated physical impacts, and alternative policy issues and options.

At the 1992 Earth Summit in Rio de Janeiro, the United Nations Framework Convention on Climate Change (UNFCCC) was adopted by more than one hundred nations in order to develop an international coordination framework for addressing climate change. In Chapter 3, Joanna Depledge explores the evolution of the climate change regime over the ensuing 12-year period. After outlining the history of the regime, she focuses first on the Convention and the further development of its rulebook. The chapter then turns to the Kyoto Protocol, looking at its provisions and rulebook, before offering some remarks on the road ahead.

In the following chapter, Jason Shogren discusses what insights economics can offer policy makers in the debate over rational climate protection policy. These include identification of market failure, the costs and benefits of pursuing action (or inaction) for climate protection, risk reduction strategies and the creation of economic incentives that will assign a price to climate protection. However, the fundamental longer-term economic insight identified by Shogren is the evaluation of risk and associated hedges against uncertainty at local, national and global levels.

In Chapter 5, Michael Grubb gives an overview of the economics of the Kyoto Protocol. The intention of the agreement is to tackle the threat of climate change by establishing an efficient regulatory framework that sets an international 'price' on emissions of CO_2 and other greenhouse gases. The core mechanism for achieving this is quantified emission commitments, that are given market-based flexibility through the use of emissions trading and other international economic instruments, and with negotiations on subsequent period commitments mandated to follow. Grubb provides an explanation of the basic structure of the Protocol, illustrated with respect to some of the key debates that went into its formation. He then examines the practical economic consequences of the final agreement as elaborated at the Marrakech COP 7 conference, including the economic consequences of withdrawal by the Bush administration. He concludes with some thoughts on the future of the Kyoto system.

Carbon taxes and emissions trading are both policy instruments that in a competitive and transparent market setting are capable of bringing about desired levels of greenhouse gas emissions reductions at the lowest cost. In Chapter 6 Fanny Missfeldt and Jochen Hauff show that both instruments can reach a given emission target at minimum cost in the context of a perfectly competitive, fully transparent and static market. However, when discussing the actual introduction of tradable permits as a policy tool, it is essential to analyse their properties under more realistic assumptions. Issues examined in this chapter include uncertainty, market power, and transaction costs which all make the case for the cost-effectiveness of a tradable permit approach less clear-cut. The authors then address the issue of carbon taxes, at both the international and domestic levels, and highlight the constraints that have restricted their implementation to date.

Cost-Benefit Analysis (CBA) is widely used as a tool for policy and project analysis. In order to improve the quality of decision making using Cost-Benefit analysis, attempts have been made to incorporate the environmental impacts of projects and policies. Many technical problems persist, however, in applying CBA to environmental issues. In Chapter 7, Nick Hanley and Dugald Tinch address some major problems in applying the CBA method to decisions over climate change, and question the appropriateness of CBA in this instance as a way of informed social decision-making. They point out that the costs of a policy must be lower than the perceived benefits for it to be adopted and non-adoption indicates that the costs are thought to be higher than the benefits. It therefore seems rational to suggest that decision makers should be informed by some quantifiable measure of the size of costs and benefits, rather than relying on implicit notions of what these costs and benefits are.

In the following chapter, Warwick McKibbin and Peter Wilcoxen outline the role that economic models have played in the climate change debate. They argue that economic models can play a very useful role but need to be used carefully to form the core of a structured debate rather than the source of definitive answers. Models are particularly useful for analysing the myriad of issues arising in the debate on greenhouse policies because it is impossible to solve the many interdependencies without using a framework that captures these interdependencies transparently. The ultimate usefulness of an economic model is not so much in the numerical magnitudes it produces (although these are very useful in placing debates in context) but in improving our understanding of the key underlying mechanisms that determine any set of numbers. As an illustration of how models are structured and used, they present an outline of the G-Cubed multi-country model and summarize the key insights from this model and others in the climate change debate to date. These insights include issues about baseline projections as well as the evaluation of the costs and benefits of alternative greenhouse policies.

Policies that target energy prices (either directly through taxes/subsidies or indirectly through emission caps) are likely to play an important role in any effort to combat global climate change. Although there has been considerable research effort into the impacts of possible energy pricing policies, there remains a number of unresolved issues and a need for continuing research. In Chapter 9, Brian Fisher and Mike Hinchy summarize the long standing disagreement between proponents of bottom up and top down models over the appropriateness of assumptions and plausibility of results from respective types of these models. In the specific case of the removal of fossil fuel subsidies, the main uncertainty is the size of the second-order repercussions of such a move. It is possible that the reduction in global carbon dioxide emissions could be smaller than suggested by the analysis of first-order impacts.

The Kyoto Protocol created the Clean Development Mechanism (CDM) and Joint Implementation (JI) to generate emission reduction credits that can be used to offset domestic emissions in Annex I countries. In order for the credits generated from CDM or JI projects to be credible, projects have to show that emission reductions they generate are 'additional' to any that would occur in the absence of the certified project activity. Further, the emission baselines against which a project performance is compared need to be environmentally sound, and project monitoring needs to be rigorous. In Chapter 10, Jane Ellis examines issues related to assessing a project's additionality, setting baselines, and monitoring and verifying the emission mitigation effect of projects. She also suggests means to achieve the appropriate balance between environmental integrity and practical feasibility.

Historically, developing countries have been relatively minor sources of GHG emissions and, with just a few exceptions, are likely to remain so for the foreseeable future. Yet they are likely to suffer disproportionately more than developed countries as the impacts of climate change are realized. In Chapter 11, Anil Markandya and Kirsten Halsnaes look at the present and projected share of GHG emissions of developing countries, what different GHG emission allocation rules would mean in economic terms, and evidence on the possible impacts of climate change on developing, in contrast to developed, countries. They then discuss how climate policies are determined, the role of self-interest in the negotiations, and how developing countries have been included in the agreements. Finally, they review mechanisms that have been created specifically to assist developing countries adopt low carbon technologies, whilst simultaneously providing low-cost abatement credits for developed nations.

In the final chapter, Tony Owen reviews life cycle analyses of alternative energy technologies in terms of both their private and societal (that is, inclusive of externalities and net of taxes and subsidies) costs. The economic viability of renewable energy technologies is shown to be heavily dependent upon the removal of market distortions. In other words, the removal of subsidies to fossil fuel based technologies and the appropriate pricing of these fuels to reflect the environmental damage (local, regional and global) created by their combustion are essential policy strategies for stimulating the development of renewable energy technologies in both the stationary power and transportation sectors. However, a number of non-quantifiable policy objectives are also of significance in the planning of future technology options. Currently, the most important of these would appear to be security of oil supplies and their associated transportation and distribution systems.

We hope that this collection of essays will prove helpful both to individuals working in climate change and to those entering the area and seeking insight into the current directions of research and policy. We also hope that the book illustrates the advantages and limitations of environmental economics as a discipline through which environmental problems can be understood, and by which appropriate responses can be chosen.

2   Global warming

Scientific modelling and its relationship to the economic dimensions of policy

Ian Moffatt

Introduction

Global warming is considered by many scientists to be the major environmental problem confronting life on Earth.[1] Whilst it is well established that the Earth has a *natural* greenhouse effect concern is over the anthropogenic alteration to the composition and quantities of atmospheric greenhouse gases. The anthropogenic alteration of the climate is known as the *enhanced* greenhouse effect or, more commonly, global warming. In order to understand the processes underpinning global warming a massive scientific programme of research has been undertaken over the past three decades. Several major monographs on the scientific and social responses to global warming have already been produced and vitally important scientific research continues.[2]

Simultaneous to this research, the last two decades have witnessed increasing political and economic discussions over the ways of reducing greenhouse gases or, at least, exploring ways of adapting to the predicted climatic changes. The Kyoto Protocol, for example, is part of this on-going political and economic debate.[3] Clearly, global warming has the potential of impacting directly or indirectly on every sentient being on Earth. Hence, many political leaders, together with the rest of humanity, are concerned over the likely impacts that global warming will have on society and the environment as well as the costs and benefits of coping with this human made threat. The scientific and policy debates continue.

The purpose of this chapter is to focus on scientific modelling of global warming and discuss its relationship with the economic dimensions of policy. In this chapter our attention is focused mainly on climate change over the past 200 years (i.e. short-term change) and we examine some probable changes caused by human activities that will occur by 2050 or 2100.

In the following section a concise guide to the science of global warming is presented. We begin by describing the types of data used in constructing climatic data. Next, the different causes of climate change and the temporal and spatial scales over which they operate are described. This then leads into a brief account of the growth rates of greenhouse gases that represent the basis for one theory of short-term climate change.

We then focus upon the ways in which scientists can model climate change. The basic thermodynamics of climate change are described as a simple one-dimensional dynamic model. Such models were developed in the 1960s but, whilst the thermodynamics are captured in these models, other details of the ter-restrial and oceanic environment were not. More recent atmospheric general cir-culation models (AGCMs) have been developed as a way of representing our knowledge of the processes underpinning global warming. These models also contain some uncertainties and these are described. Despite these uncertainties these sophisticated dynamic models give reasonable simulations of past climatic change over the last 100 years. Generally, these models are then run forward to give alternative scenarios of possible future climate change. It will be argued that until the 1990s the early AGCMs were able to capture the temporal variation in global climatic change but were unable to capture the detailed regional variations associated with global climatic change. Current research, however, has developed models that give more detailed regional descriptions of atmospheric pressure, precipitation and temperature.[4] These new regional models can provide useful information for politicians, economists and environmental man-agers (along with other interested people) and are important tools for assessing local and regional effects of global warming. Some of the recent research into models of greater complexity is also noted.

The final section of this chapter examines the relationship between scientific research and policies on global warming. Several scenarios generated by AGCMs giving some possible future changes in the Earth's climate are presented. These scenarios are not scientific predictions (the latter depend on natural laws and con-trolled experimental conditions) nor are these scenarios mere weather forecasts. AGCMs' scenarios are exploring possible climate futures and as we move further into the future the uncertainties grow and hence the forecasts become less reliable. Using a series of different, but realistic, scenarios, alternative types of policies and economic instruments are briefly considered. This then leads into a brief discus-sion on the relationship between scientific activity and the on-going political-economic debate on the policies to be used to counteract global warming.

The science of global warming – a concise guide

Climate change is an important scientific issue and has been examined in various publications (IPCC 1990 *et seq.*; Schneider 1989). Climate change can be defined as change which is attributed directly or indirectly to human activity that alters the composition of the global atmosphere and which is in addition to natural climate variability observed over comparable time periods (IPCC 1996: 59). The

purpose of this section is to provide a concise guide to some of the major problems in describing and explaining climate change.

Climate is a statistical average of meteorological data

At the outset it should be realized that climate is simply a statistical concept based
on the averaging of meteorological phenomena (such as solar radiation, precipitation, temperature and atmospheric pressure) over a 35-year period. Obviously, a
long consistent record of meteorological data is required for climatic statistics to
be calculated. It should be noted that the land based meteorological records tend
to be less reliable the older the record. This is, in part, due to different means of
measuring the meteorological data. Reliable records for instrumented observations also vary spatially. We have, for example, very little cover of meteorological conditions at sea or over lakes which together cover approximately 70 per
cent of the Earth's surface.

If we want to reconstruct past climates than we need to use non-instrumented
measures of climate change. These methods include the use of tree rings and
sea level rises as well as the more reliable measurement of methane and
carbon dioxide trapped in air taken from ice cores in Antarctica.[5] Using non-
instrumented data we can get an idea of the way in which climate has changed
over the last 160,000 years in the Quaternary period (Figure 2.1). The research
indicates that the Earth's mean surface temperature was closely related to the
concentration of carbon dioxide and methane in the atmosphere.[6]

Using a mixture of instrumented and secondary data it is possible to illustrate
the changing climate. The changing climate as measured by mean surface temperature for the Northern and Southern hemispheres as well as for the global mean
surface temperature for about 200 years has been calculated (Jones 1985a and b).
It will be observed (Figure 2.2) that there has been a 'real warming of the globe
of 0.3 degrees C to 0.6 degrees C over the period 1861–1989'. The pattern of
climate change has differed in both timing and across geographical space. With
regard to timing of global warming much of the warming has occurred in two
periods – 1920–1940 and then 1980–2000. In particular the last decade of the
twentieth century had the warmest years of the entire century.

Geographical variations in the pattern of warming are important. The Northern hemisphere cooled between 1940s and the early 1970s whilst Southern hemisphere temperatures stayed nearly constant. As will be shown later, regional
patterns of climate change are likely to differ considerably from the global
average.[7] The investigation into the regional patterns of climate change is an
important aspect of current climatic research. These regional forecasts are very
important for environmental managers as well as for local policy decision
making.

It should be noted that there are scaling problems associated with the captur-

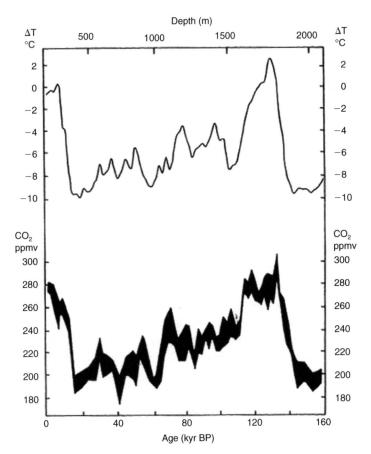

Figure 2.1 CO_2 concentrations (bottom) and estimated temperature changes (top) during the last 160,000 years, as determined on the ice core from Vostock, Antarctica.

Source: IPCC (1990).

ing of geographical distributions of precipitation and surface temperature. Often the data is recorded at local scales and has to be upscaled to represent regional and global variation in the climate. When satellite and other remote sensing data are used then the problems of downscaling are also involved. Current research is attempting to develop even more robust methods to ensure that there is reasonable empirical validation for regional and local models based on global simulations and for validating global and regional models based on locally collected data.[8]

Despite the methodological problems concerned with data collection and scaling, by 1991 the scientific community could write with confidence: 'There is a natural greenhouse effect which already keeps the Earth warmer than it would be otherwise be' and, further:

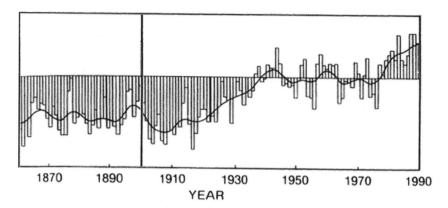

Figure 2.2 Global mean combined land–air and sea-surface temperatures, 1861–1989, relative to the average for 1951–1980.

Source: IPCC (1990).

that emissions resulting from human activities are substantially increasing the atmospheric concentrations of greenhouse gases: carbon dioxide, methane, chloroflurocarbons (CFCs) and nitrous oxide. These increases will enhance the greenhouse effect, resulting on average in additional warming of the Earth's surface temperature.[9]

By 1996 attempts to quantify the human influence on global climate had been made (compared to 1990) and it was noted that 'the balance of evidence suggests that there is a discernible human influence on global climate'.[10] The enhanced greenhouse effect or global warming is now accepted by the vast majority of the scientific community as a matter of fact rather than as a hypothetical conjecture.

Causality of climate change: temporal and spatial scales

The nature and causes of climate change operate at different temporal and spatial scales.[11] Over the last 4.5 billion years the Earth's history has witnessed changes in the energy flowing from the sun.[12] Alterations in the orbit of the Earth around the sun have also had an impact on the Earth's climate.[13] Similarly, the formation, distribution and movement of the Earth's plates (including the continents) alter both the oceanic currents and mountain chains. The changing composition of the atmosphere has also contributed to the earth's changing climate. Clearly, there are many processes involved in explaining the climate change. These different processes operate at different temporal and spatial scales, and often occur simultaneously, which makes any modelling effort extremely difficult – even if we could obtain reliable and detailed records. Wigley (1981), for example, has

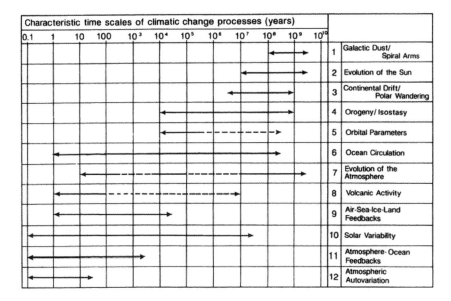

Figure 2.3 Major mechanisms of climate change and their time scales of operation.

Source: Goodess *et al.* (1992).

shown some of the characteristic time scales of climate change processes in years (Figure 2.3).

The climatic changes associated with the Quaternary and Holocene periods have been the subject of intensive palaeoclimate reconstruction and modelling.[14] The data for such palaeoclimatic reconstruction includes inferences made from archaeological records, varve clays, tree-rings, lichenometry and lake sediments as well as radiocarbon and thermoluminescence dating techniques. Overall reliability of using different types of data to record climatic change is often improved by use of several techniques together (Roberts 1989). By piecing together the relevant data sets and exploring extreme climatic conditions such as those experienced 21,000 years BP and 6,000 years BP an opportunity to evaluate how models of climate change respond to large climatic forcings has been simulated.[15] These simulations of past extreme climatic conditions are useful for evaluating how models of climate respond to large forcings, and ultimately provide a key credibility test for modelling future changes to the Earth's climate.[16]

Despite the progress in this area of palaeoenvironmental reconstruction it should be noted that the study of past climatic change is only analogous to the current situation. In particular the major difference between the past period and today is the inclusion of additional greenhouse gases into the atmosphere from human activities. These human activities include changes in agricultural practices, the large-scale human modification of the world's ecosystems and burning of fossil fuels. This set of activities is causing concern amongst scientists and policy makers as they are definitely damaging the life chances of many other living species[17] and may lead to our own extinction[18] or, at least, impose significant costs on humans.

The remainder of this chapter will focus upon climate change over the last 200 years and will also examine the ways in which scientific modelling inter-relates with the economic dimensions of policy-making. At this scale of resolution (i.e. short-term) the astronomical and geological processes of climate change can be assumed constant and attention can be focused on short-term changes associated with the changing composition of greenhouse gases in the atmosphere.

Greenhouse gases

The greenhouse effect is a natural phenomenon that has been operating for millions of years and without it the Earth would be too cold to support life as we know it. It is well established in both theory and measurement that the greenhouse gases (carbon dioxide, methane, nitrous oxide and chloroflurocarbons (CFCs)) in the atmosphere keep the Earth's mean surface temperature at an average of 15 degrees C. Without the greenhouse effect, the mean surface temperature would be −18 degrees C. The mean surface temperatures of Venus, Mars and Earth (477, −47 and 15 degrees C respectively) are in agreement with those calculated on the basis of the greenhouse theory of climate change. The current concern over anthropogenic changes to the greenhouse gases in the Earth's atmosphere has resulted in a long debate over the human activities and their influence on global warming which are added to the natural phenomenon of the greenhouse effect. This sub-section briefly describes the theory and evidence for the enhanced greenhouse gases which contribute to global warming.

As a cause of climatic change, the greenhouse gas theory has a relatively long lineage.[19] In 1827, for example, Fourier[20] suggested that the heat could be retained by the atmosphere and described the effect as acting in a manner similar to a hot house (greenhouse). In the 1860s Tyndall[21] measured the capacity of water vapour, carbon dioxide and other gases to absorb heat. It was first suggested that carbonic acid (carbon dioxide) could influence the thermal properties of the atmosphere by about 4 degrees C in 1896.[22] Later, in 1938, Callendar[23] demonstrated that carbon dioxide could account for a warmer climate. Subsequent laboratory experiments, simulations and field observations have corroborated this theory of global warming.[24] It should be noted that carbon dioxide is not the only greenhouse gas − water vapour, nitrous oxides, methane and other gases are also greenhouse gases. Each greenhouse gas has a different thermal warming potential.

The difference in the Earth's mean surface temperature from −18 to 15 degrees C results from the presence of an atmosphere, and in particular to the suite of gases that are called greenhouse gases. The term greenhouse gas implies that the gases are radiatively active. The sun emits most of its energy at wavelengths between 0.2 to 0.4 micro-μ, primarily in the ultraviolet, visible and near-infrared wavelengths. As the Earth is much cooler than the Sun it re-emits the energy it absorbs back to space and thereby maintains an energy balance. Much of this emission takes place at wavelengths longer than those for incoming solar radiation, generally from 4 to 100 micro-μ – these are termed long wave or infra-red radiation. Although water vapour, carbon dioxide and other greenhouse gases are inefficient absorbers of solar radiation, they are strong absorbers of long wave infra-red radiation. These greenhouse gases re-emit the absorbed long wave radiation in all directions as a function of the difference in local air temperature, which tends to be cooler than the Earth's surface temperature. Obviously, some of this radiation is lost to space, but the remainder is emitted downwards, leading to a net trapping of long-wave radiation and hence a warming of the surface.[25] The mixture of greenhouse gases and aerosols (airborne particles) that make up the Earth's atmosphere is, therefore, central to understanding the short-term climatic changes of the Earth.

Whilst the greenhouse effect is a naturally occurring phenomenon it is anthropogenic changes to the composition of greenhouse gases that has caused concern in the scientific community, the public and policy makers. In particular the increase of some greenhouse gases from economic activity has caused many to ponder the ways in which we are altering the Earth's climate. It is possible to measure the increase in the atmospheric concentrations of the more important greenhouse gases. Over the period 1975–1985 the following increases occurred: carbon dioxide (CO_2) 4.6 per cent; methane (CH_4) 11.05 per cent; nitrous oxide (N_2O) 3.5 per cent and man-made chlorofluorocarbons (CFC-11 and CFC-12) 103 per cent and 101 per cent respectively.[26] The main sources of these gases have been identified as energy production (CO_2 and CH_4); industrial activities (CO_2 and CFCs); agriculture (CO_2, N_2O and CH_4); and land clearances (CO_2 and N_2O). The concentrations of greenhouse gases are small, often measured in parts per million (ppmv) or per billion (ppbv) by volume, but the proportion of their warming effect is important (Table 2.1). Clearly, economic activity is adding 'fuel' to the natural processes of the greenhouse effect and causing global warming.

If we examine the changes in the greenhouse gas composition over the last century then it is possible to show the trend in many of these gases and point to possible causes. Observations into the changing composition of greenhouse gases in Mauna Loa and at Cape Grim, Tasmania, show an upward trend in all the major greenhouse gases (the exception being water vapour). Carbon dioxide and methane have risen from 325 ppmv and 1,450 ppbv respectively in 1972 and respectively to 345 and 1,680 by 1988. It will be observed that both gaseous concentrations show an annual cyclical change due to the slowing down of the

Table 2.1 1987 greenhouse gas concentrations, trends and degree of forcing relative to
         CO_2

Gas	Concentrations 1987	Observed trend per year 1990 (%)	Projected concentrations 2050	Existing radiative forcing relative to CO_2	Proportion of total warming (%)
CO_2	348 ppmv	0.46	400–600 ppmv	1	61.0
CH_4	1.68 ppmv	0.7–1.0	2.1–4 ppmv	21	15.0
N_2O	0.31 ppmv	0.2	0.35–0.45 ppmv	206	4.0
CFC-11	0.24 ppbv	*10.3	0.41 ppbv	12,400	2.0
CCFC-12	0.42 ppbv	*10.1	0.85 ppbv	15,800	7.0
CFC-113	38 pptv	4.2	0.14 pptv	158,800	1.5
HCFC-22	0.10 ppbv	6.2	0.94 ppbv	10,700	0.4
O_3	10–100 ppbv	0.0–1.0	15–50%	—	0.11
Others	—	—	—	—	8.2

Source: Moffatt (1992).

metabolism of plants and other organisms in the winter period. As the Northern
hemisphere has the most land cover this winter slow down overawes the Southern hemisphere summer production. The concentration of N_2O is more erratic
but also shows a growing trend as does the growth in the concentrations of
atmospheric CFCs (Figure 2.4).

The possibility of greenhouse gases warming the Earth is both theoretically
well founded and empirically demonstrated. Humankind's activities are altering
the natural vegetation cover of the Earth and these agricultural and urbanization
activities, coupled with the increasing use of carbon-based fossil fuels, have been
responsible for the dramatic rise in atmospheric greenhouse gases. The problem
confronting both the scientific community and policy makers is to estimate what
are the likely environmental, social and economic consequences of such unprecedented changes to the atmosphere greenhouse gases in recorded history and
devise a suite of policies to address these problems. One way of contributing to
these forward-looking activities is to develop models of the global warming
process. These models are calibrated and tested with relevant data; the models
are then run forward to give a series of scenarios indicating possible climate
change in the next 50 to 100 years (i.e. 2050 to 2100).

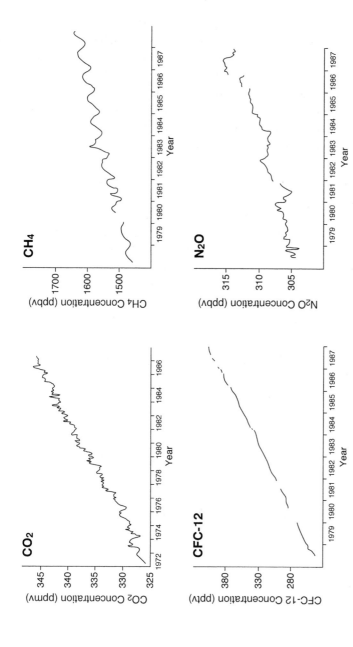

Figure 2.4 Concentrations of greenhouse gases measured in air at Cape Grim, Tasmania.

Source: Moffatt (1992).

Scientific models of the enhanced greenhouse effect

Modelling the Earth's solar energy balance

The Earth and all its surface ecosystems rely on energy from the sun. Much of this energy for atmospheric motions comes indirectly through radiative, sensible and latent heat transfers from the Earth's surface. As noted above the mixture of greenhouse gases that makes up the Earth's atmosphere is, therefore, central to our understanding of short-term climatic change. This solar derived energy drives the biogeochemical cycles such as the carbon, nitrogen and hydrological cycles. Solar energy also provides one of the vital inputs to the photosynthetic process. Without the inputs of solar energy life as we know it would not exist on planet Earth.

There are numerous models of the atmosphere and many of these are still undergoing further research and development. These models range from the very crude one-dimensional energy models of the 1960s through to the more complex three or four dimensional atmospheric general circulation models (AGCMs) currently used in scientific research and policy discussion. This section describes the science underpinning these models by developing a simple, thermodynamically sound model of the greenhouse effect. More sophisticated versions of modelling global warming are described in the following sub-section.

The solar energy flux just above the Earth's atmosphere is estimated as 1,372 W/m^2 – where 1 Watt = 1 Joule/second. This energy flow varies because of solar activity (sun spots), the Earth's distance from the sun and other variables. Nevertheless, despite these changes it is convenient to represent this input of energy as the solar constant:

$$W_s = 1372.\pi.R^2 \tag{2.1}$$

where W_s is the amount of energy per time period delivered from the sun and R is the radius of the Earth.

In 24 hours the energy is distributed over the entire spheroid of the Earth (assumed to be a sphere) with an area of $4.\pi.R^2$. Hence, the average flux of solar energy reaching the Earth is:

$$1372.\pi.R^2/4.\pi.R^2 = 343(W/m^2) \tag{2.2}$$

and this is the solar flux (Ω_s). This energy flux covers a large portion of the electromagnetic spectrum.

Not all the energy reaches the Earth's surface by absorption as the Earth also reflects some of the energy back into space. This reflected heat is referred to as the albedo and accounts for 31 per cent of all incoming solar radiation. The remaining 69 per cent of the energy is absorbed by the Earths' atmosphere and is usually re-radiated in the infra-red part of the electromagnetic spectrum.

Under steady-state conditions the Earth is in an energy balance: the amount of incoming solar flux is equal to the amount of energy reflected and re-radiated from the Earth:

$$\Omega_s = \alpha.\Omega_s + (1-\alpha).\Omega_s \qquad (2.3)$$
$$\Omega_e = \Omega_s - \alpha.\Omega_s = (1-\alpha).\Omega_s$$

where Ω_e (W/m^2) is the energy flux re-radiated from the Earth; Ω_s is the incoming solar flux (equation 2.2) 343 W/m^2 and α is the albedo of the Earth (0.31).

Under steady-state conditions we can apply the Stefan-Boltzmann Law of Black-Body radiation. This law states that the energy flux radiation for a black body is a function of the surface temperature of that body raised to the fourth power:

$$\Omega = \lambda.T^4 \qquad (2.4)$$

where Ω = energy flux (W/m^2); λ = Stefan-Boltzmann Constant (5.67 $\times$ 10^{-8} W/m^2/K); T = is the temperature in degrees Kelvin (to convert degrees Kelvin (K) to Celsius (C) use the formula K = C + 273.15). By combining equations 2.3 and 2.4 the Earth's average surface temperature is given as:

$$T = (\Omega_e/\lambda)^{1/4} = [(1-\alpha).\Omega_s/\lambda]^{1/4} \qquad (2.5)$$

By substituting the values of α = 0.31 and Ω_s = 343 W/m^2 then equation 2.4 yields a value of: T = 255K (or -18 degrees C).

The average temperature of the Earth would be too cold to support life. Fortunately, the real Earth surface temperature is not so low – it is approximately 33 degrees C higher than the temperature calculated by equation 2.4, or 15 degrees C. The discrepancy between the calculated and actual temperature is due, mainly, but not exclusively, to the presence of greenhouse gases.

Obviously, the model described in this section is very simple. It excludes, for example, any consideration of day and night, nor does it address seasonal changes. Similarly, the model does not incorporate different levels of the atmosphere with different cloud cover. The feedback loops between different surface cover (ice, vegetation and water) and the atmosphere are also omitted. It is possible, however, to develop this argument as a dynamic simulation model by including a set of feedback loops to represent changes in atmospheric CO_2.[27] It should be noted that this dynamic simulation model excludes any consideration of the dynamics of atmospheric general circulation which is another vitally important aspect of a realistic model of the Earth's changing climate. The model is, therefore, a highly simplified view of the greenhouse effect. Nevertheless, the model does indicate very clearly the role of greenhouse gases in increasing the mean surface temperature of the Earth.

The early energy based models were useful analytical devices but do not treat the world as a three or four dimensional (x, y, z and t (time)) entity and therefore cannot incorporate realistic land surface properties in anything but the crudest of ways. An accurate understanding and reliable prediction of the effect of the greenhouse gases requires consideration of the three dimensional nature of the Earth's surface together with the known dynamics of the atmospheric and oceanic circulation. A fully developed AGCM would incorporate oceanic atmosphere interactions; details of the gaseous transfers between different species of vegetation; details of the albedo effect from dry and wet surfaces (including ice); cloud feedbacks as well as perturbations from volcanic emissions. To describe these missing processes in more detail lead us into a description of the more complex models known as atmospheric general circulation models (AGCMs).

Atmospheric general circulation models

It is not the purpose of this introductory chapter to describe in detail the ways in which AGCMs function. Elementary accounts of the procedures involved can be read in several texts.[28] Nevertheless, it is important to comprehend some of the problems involved in building AGCMs especially when policy decisions may be based on a misunderstanding of the strengths and weaknesses of the models.

Atmospheric general circulation models (AGCMs) are based on the numerical formulations of the physical and chemical laws which govern the dynamics of the atmosphere and upper ocean. These laws are fed into a series of computer programs to try and simulate climatic changes on the assumption of changes (often simulated as a doubling) of carbon dioxide levels. The doubling of carbon dioxide really means that all the greenhouse gases are expressed as thermal equivalents to twice the current global carbon dioxide level.[29] The models sub-divide the Earth's surface into a set of blocks. These blocks vary in size, ranging from 3 by 3 degrees to 8 by 10 degrees; on average the blocks used in global climate models are approximately 300 by 500 km. At the surface of the Earth the ground temperature, water and energy fluxes are computed and stored in the computer's memory. Each block has a vertical atmospheric column which can contain as little as two, or as many as 19, levels. The interactions of wind vectors, humidity, cloud cover, temperature and altitude are computed and stored for each level for all the columns which cover the Earth. In addition to these calculations there are a set of interactions between adjacent cells, both horizontally and vertically between adjacent blocks. Often the interactions between the elements in each block are represented by non-linear differential equations. The equations are solved for an hourly or half-hourly time-step and the model can be run for a long simulated time (e.g. 400 years) with each set of equations being solved every half an hour for every day for the length of the simulation. The early models ran at a 'twilight', with incoming solar radiation flowing at a low intensity every 24 hours. Today, however, the AGCMs can include diurnal and seasonal variation in incoming solar energy which drives the atmospheric system. Clearly, current AGCMs are complex and current research includes further coupling of the atmospheric system with oceanic general circulation models (OGCMs) to produce atmospheric ocean general circulation models (AOGCMs). More advanced research is developing environmental models of intermediate complexity (EMICs) as part of scientific understanding of the atmosphere, biosphere, hydrosphere, cryosphere and human interactions.[30] Despite their complexity some EMICs do permit the evaluation of greenhouse gas mitigation proposals. The MIT integrated global system model, for example, permits an investigation into the multi-gas assessment of the Kyoto Protocol.[31] Similarly, the Integrated Model to Assess the Greenhouse Effect (IMAGE) model is explicitly developed to explore the impact of greenhouse gases and sea-level rising on The Netherlands.[32]

It should be stressed that any model is a simplification of real world physical, biological and chemical interactions. It should also be noted that different research groups of AGCM builders stress different interactions in their attempts to simplify, yet understand and predict, climatic changes due to increases in greenhouse gases. The feedback interactions between clouds and the Earth's surface, for example, can be modelled in different ways. Similarly, the interactions of water and vegetation and their effect on the albedo are important feedbacks. Despite the different ways both in which AGCMs are built, the major feedbacks incorporated and the methods used for estimating the numerical values of the parameters, they give broadly similar results with regard to the temporal patterning of climate change.

Many early AGCMs were simply coupled to a single deep ocean, and it was clear that the oceans sequester heat in such a way as to give a new equilibrium temperature at 2 degrees C or an upper equilibrium temperature of 5.4 degrees C by 2030.[33] Similar results using different AGCMs have indicated that when a fully interactive ocean is incorporated into an atmospheric oceanic general circulation model (AOGCM) then there is significant improvement in modelling global temperature changes than observed in the early 1980 models. The incorporation of greenhouse gases and aerosols in AOGCMs has resulted in reasonable simulations of global annual mean warming from 1860–1990 (Figure 2.5).

The important feature of these different model simulation runs is that the predicted global mean temperature curves statistically replicate the past empirical patterning of global temperature change. Further support for the temporal predictions of current (post-1990) AGCMs is given by the use of a

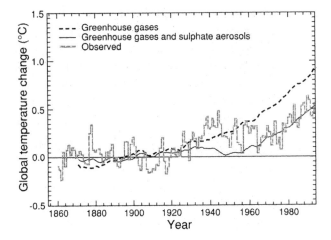

Figure 2.5 Simulated global annual mean warming from 1860–1990 allowing for increases in greenhouse gases only (dashed curve) and greenhouse gases and sulphate aerosols (solid curve), compared with observed changes over the same period.

Source: IPCC (1996).

satellite based Microwave Sounding Unit (MSU). By using an advanced AOGCM initialized with nineteenth century levels of CO_2 and driven (forced) by changes in both CO_2 and sulphur emissions it has been shown that 'there is no serious inconsistency between the most recent model predictions and MSU-based trend estimates'.[34] It should be noted that the MSU record is less than 20 years old and hence it is difficult to make a strong statement on the significance of any differences in trends on these time scales for climatic purposes.

Whilst the advanced models of climate change are capturing the temporal aspect of global climate change they are less successful in capturing the spatial variations in both temperature and precipitation. An analysis of five early (pre-1990) AGCMs covering Australia was undertaken in 1989. The five different AGCMs predict the pattern of temperature change in Australia for summer and winter under a doubling of CO_2 against the existing temperature in the same region. All the models show an increased warming throughout Australia by between 2 and 8 degrees C. When regional patterns are examined, however, there are significant regional differences in the predictions. During the summer season (December/January/February), for example, the GDF, GISS, NCAR and UKMO models' output all have areas of increased temperature in common – although there are important regional differences. When precipitation is examined all the models predict decreasing rainfall over some parts of Australia despite the fact all global models generally predict an intensification of the global hydrological cycle and a global increase in precipitation.[35] Again, more recent research has made great improvements in the accuracy of the geographical variations in the predicted precipitation, pressure and temperature regimes at regional levels.[36] These regional climate models (RCM) are based on 50 km grid squares and include 19 vertical levels. The Hadley Centre regional climate modelling system, for example, provides high resolution climate change predictions for a region generally consistent with the continental scale changes predicted in the AGCMs.[37] These regional simulations linked to the UKMO AGCM can be used to give an indication of the regional impact of global warming in small countries such as the UK when compared to the broad scale coverage of the earlier generations of AGCM.[38] It can be argued that regional climate models are now providing important information on the environmental impacts associated with global warming for use in regional planning – as long as the scenarios to be used in policy-making are cautiously interpreted.[39]

Scientists recognize that there are many uncertainties associated with the use of AGCMs for making scenarios of global warming. At least 17 broad classes of scientific uncertainties can be identified – 11 concern oceanic interactions and the other six are concerned with terrestrial ecosystem responses to a warmer Earth.[40] Some of these problems have been examined and although the magnitude of their impact is better understood some uncertainties still remain. The terrestrial uncertainties include the rate of biomass recovery after disturbance; the dynamics of carbon storage in terrestrial ecosystems including the boreal and tundra systems; the burying rate of organic matter in coastal areas and especially estuaries.

With regard to the oceanic component of the uncertainties in global models, it is clear that the earlier (pre-mid 1980s) models represented the ocean as a swamp rather than a tiered system of water and nutrients.[41] More recent research has developed the swamp conceptualization of the ocean into a detailed tiered circulatory system. This development of ocean general circulation models (OGCMs) since the 1990s give a better representation of the complex processes involved in the atmosphere oceanic feedback loops. Despite the enormous progress in this area of research it should be noted that the detailed effects of future climate change on oceanic circulation and the carbon cycle still require further investigation. If, for example, a warmer climate leads to further melting of ice sheets in the Northern and Southern hemispheres then it is possible that the global oceanic gyre system will break down. This gyre system is part of the complex pattern of circulation of heat through the Earth's oceans. One of the implications of such a radical change to the circulation system is on the regional climates. In north-west Europe, for example, these regions enjoy a warmer climate, especially in winter, due to the North Atlantic Drift (part of the gyre). If global warming continues with ice sheet melting in both Greenland and the Antarctica then the gyres will alter their circulatory flow pattern and we will find a much colder climate in winter months despite an overall global warming. The intricacies and uncertainties of the atmosphere-oceanic biosphere system (Earth system) are indeed complex and replete with uncertainties. Scientific research to further understanding of these feedback loop interactions is continuing.

The fact that uncertainties are identified is not a reason for delaying any policy prescriptions based on an inevitably incomplete knowledge of how complex systems interact. The physical-chemical conditions in the general circulation are reasonable well understood and the evidence of global warming is already observable. The longer we delay in making policy decisions then the greater the likelihood of global warming and, arguably, additional costs required to ameliorate the impacts of global warming. The recognition of the uncertainties and limitations of any model of global warming should be noted – as they are in the serious scientific literature and are acknowledged by many policy makers. Hence, in the development and use of scientific models, if we are not to mislead the public and its policy makers, eternal vigilance is required.[42]

Global warming: scenarios, potential impacts, policies and the economic debate

Scenarios and potential impacts

A scenario is not a scientific prediction based upon laboratory controlled conditions but simply a projection of a future state of a system given certain assumptions about its structure as embedded in a model of that system. As noted earlier there are several AGCMs and these are all in agreement over the fact that additional greenhouse gases, including aerosols (and changes to the Earth's ecosystems) are causing global warming.

In an attempt to explore the possible likely future consequences of global warming several scenarios have been developed using different AGCMs. The IPCC gives four basic scenarios. These are the business as usual (Scenario A) and three variants (Scenarios B, C and D) (Figure 2.6).

Scenario A is termed the business as usual scenario and is based on the premise that observed increases in the greenhouse gases will continue and effective CO_2 concentrations will double over the pre-industrial levels by 2020. This scenario gives a warming of 1.6 to 2.6 degrees C above pre-industrial levels at 2030, corresponding to a prescribed climate sensitivity of 1.5 to 4.5 degrees C. Scenarios B, C and D assume an effective doubling of CO_2 by 2040, Scenario C by 2050 and D by 2100. It will be noted that the last three scenarios all assume progressively increasing levels of control over the emission of greenhouse gases. The average rates of increase in global mean temperature are estimated to be about 0.2 degrees C per decade (Scenario B), just above 0.1 degrees C per decade (Scenario C) and about 0.1 degrees C per decade (Scenario D). It will also be

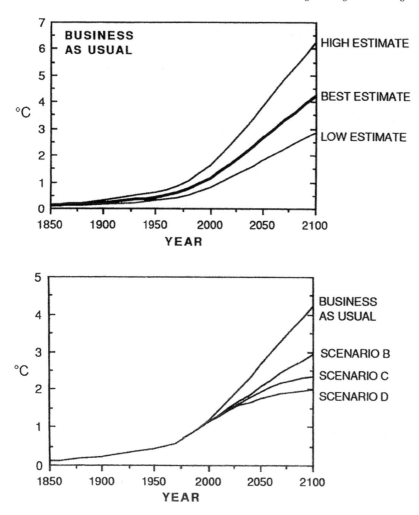

Figure 2.6 Four alternative scenarios of global warming.
Source: IPCC (1996).

noted that the changes in emission scenarios take some time to produce an effect, as a result of the slowness with which both the atmospheric gas concentrations and the oceans respond.[43]

More recently the IPCC has provided some 40 emission scenarios.[44] The scenarios are driven by complex changes in demography, social and economic development as well as energy technology. Four main 'story lines' (A1, A2, B1, B2) are presented as the basis of the forty scenarios. The A1 story line represents a world of rapid economic growth, a global population peaking in the mid twenty-first century then declining afterwards with the rapid introduction of efficient energy technologies. Story line B1 is similar to A1 with regard to population change but with the introduction of clean resource efficient technologies and rapid changes towards a service based economy with reductions in material intensity. Story line B1 also suggests global solutions to environmental, economic and social aspects of sustainable development. Story line A2 represents a heterogeneous world with self-reliance and preservation of local identities. Fertility patterns slowly converge and technological and economic change is primarily regional and fragmented. Story line B2 focuses upon local solutions to social, economic and environmental sustainability problems. Local and regional environmental protection and social equity are also included in scenarios generated from this story line. It should be noted that none of the scenarios assumes surprises in the response of socio-economic institutions or environmental systems to global warming. Additionally, it should be mentioned that the scenarios do not include any implementation of the proposed reductions in greenhouse gases as noted in the Kyoto Protocol.

The variations in the global carbon dioxide emissions and land use changes under the 40 scenarios are presented in Figure 2.7. It will be observed that most of the global carbon dioxide emissions are within the IS92 scenarios (A, B, C and D) but the land use changes associated with the new scenarios are well beyond the IS92 range. This raises some important policy issues that will be discussed in the following section.

The potential impacts of global warming under 'business as usual' scenarios can have environmental, economic and social consequences. Some of the possible negative and positive impacts can be noted. These include:

- rising sea-levels;
- salinity in water supplies;
- water shortages and, paradoxically, flooding in other areas;
- alterations to oceanic currents and fish supplies;
- increased intensity of tropical storms and wind damage to built structures and forests;
- changes to natural vegetation belts and to agricultural production;
- the risk of prolonged droughts in some areas is also possible, including areas where drought was not common e.g. eastern seaboard of UK;
- higher risk of fires in some regions;
- increase in ultra-violet exposure and risks of skin cancer;
- increase in malaria, dengue fever and other medical conditions including heat fatigue;
- more space cooling in some buildings and more heat required in higher latitudes and altitudes;
- reduction of skiing in some regions and alterations to patterns of tourism.

It should be noted that these environmental and socio-economic impacts will

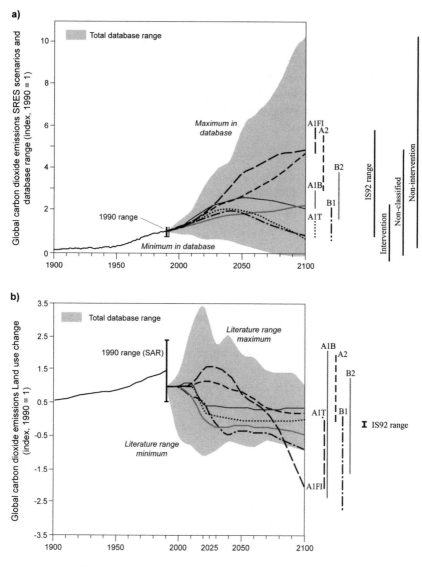

Figure 2.7 Global CO$_2$ emissions related to energy and industry and land use changes.
Source: IPCC (2000).

have a regional component and that the current regional climate models will be essential for assisting planning to prevent the worst impacts of global warming. It will also be noted that these changes may, in some areas, have positive advantages as well as negative impacts.

Whether we wait for better predictions of global warming and more empirical evidence or begin preventative measures is not the question. Rather we must begin preventative measures now based on our tentative understanding of the climate system. We must bear in mind that the full climatic response to our economic activities, both inadvertent and deliberate, will likely be delayed by several decades.[45] We have, however, a window of opportunity to develop and apply sensible policies to reduce global warming – or, at least, modify its impacts. The question is not whether we ought to adopt policies to combat or to adapt to global warming but rather to focus attention upon the type of policies we wish to implement.

Policy-making and economic instruments

Policy-making can be defined as an expression of intent to achieve certain objectives through the conscious choice of means and usually within a specified period of time. In liberal democracies public policy is distinctive in so far as it is normally open to public scrutiny and debate; it must proceed through formal channels of the constitutional process and is often codified by the sanction of law.[46] The lengthy on-going policy debate over global warming has broadly followed this description of policy. The global warming debate has, however, been played out on a world stage with a mixture of scientific, economic and political discussions alongside a background of pro- and anti-global warming lobbies from several business and NGO groups.

The management and regulation of atmospheric pollutants is not new. Ancient cities such as Rome or thirteenth century London suffered from air pollution problems. Today, however, many of the atmospheric pollutants are global in extent and need global agreement to ameliorate the problem. Such international agreements are difficult, but not impossible. In the case of regulating the emissions of CFC and HFC greenhouse gases the Montreal Protocol and subsequent meetings at Copenhagen and London were able to agree that the developed countries would stop production of these products.[47] The reduction to zero of these specific greenhouse gases is unusual in pollution control. Normally, some optimum level of pollution control (greater than zero) is approved. It should also be noted that even if there was a worldwide ban on these emissions their residence time in the atmosphere means that they will still have an impact on climate change. The remainder of this sub-section explores various strategic policy options concerned with reducing some of the rest of greenhouse gas emissions.

There are five possible responses to climatic change due to greenhouse gases. The first reaction would be to accept this as a matter of fact and do nothing. This ultra-conservative strategy tries to hide behind the untenable view that the signals of greenhouse warming are still hidden in the noise of normal climate change. Obviously, this conservative do-nothing strategy is one outcome of a political bargaining process.

Forced adaptation acknowledges anthropogenic climate change and that people will have to move immediately as they are unable to prevent the effects of the onset of global warming. For example a sea level rise with increased tropical storms can have potentially devastating impacts on low lying Pacific Islands. In Tuvalu, for example, steps are already being made to evacuate the population as the islands sink beneath the rising seas as a consequence of global warming.[48] Inhabitants of low lying Pacific islands are already witnessing the decline of their environment and culture as global warming kicks in. Earlier responses to reducing greenhouse gases would have prevented this tragedy. Will The Netherlands be the first European country to be seriously affected by sea level rises due to global warming?

We cannot prevent all greenhouse gas emissions, they are part of life, but we can limit their action or anticipate their impacts or limit them. Anticipatory adaptation is the third option and can be viewed as making strategic decisions to restrict types of land uses in areas of high environmental hazard risks. Obviously, permitting further building in river flood plains is to court disaster. Surprisingly, this is happening in some river basins. In other countries, e.g. Bangladesh, flooding by river and sea incursions is a perennial problem. Similarly, building near actively eroding cliffs on eastern England is another example of the lack of foresight in the face of climate change.

Positive responses to climate change can be anticipated and put into action. In areas of increasing water shortages building dams and reducing water consumption are sensible precautionary measures. Areas along eastern England and Scotland would benefit from this especially where the population growth in and around London and the south-east region is associated with drier, greenhouse induced conditions.

Prevention and limitation of greenhouse gas emissions

Some human made greenhouse gases such as the CFC family can be prevented. Unusually in pollution control the Montreal Protocol and subsequent amendments at London and Copenhagen were able to recommend and enforce a reduction to zero of CFC emissions in industrial countries. The weakness in this positive prevention policy was that developing countries were exempt from the proposals. Obviously, if CFCs are produced and used in the developing world this would only add to the greenhouse gas emissions and climate change.

Generally, however, with the exception of CFC and HCFC most greenhouse gases cannot be reduced to zero emissions. The most sensible greenhouse policies are either to restore and limit human use of natural ecosystems or to develop a greenhouse limitation strategy or combine both. It should, of course, be noted that any positive strategy to limit or ameliorate global climate change would carry economic costs and benefits.

Limiting human use of ecosystems

For the period 1860–1958 the increase in carbon dioxide has been mainly attributed to forest clearances and agricultural land use changes, whilst the increase since 1958 is due to the increased use of hydrocarbon based fossil fuels as energy sources.[49] Extending the time scale back to 1750 Gorshkov[50] has argued that our activities of altering land use has moved the climatic dynamic equilibrium of the planet into an unstable trajectory. Furthermore, he argues that to restore the Earth's climate back to a stable equilibrium we would need to alter our use of the terrestrial land cover and allow some 40 per cent of the land to revert back to native vegetation without any further direct interference from human activities. It should, however, be noted that the growing impact of human activities on ecosystems and the damage to species, as recorded in several major studies[51] would suggest that we are increasing our impact on the biosphere. On the basis of the recent evidence it may be worthwhile to re-examine Gorshkov's analysis. Clearly, even if Gorshkov's analysis is correct then this policy option would be difficult to implement.

Reducing greenhouse gas emissions

Reducing the emissions of greenhouse gases is the obvious and most direct way of managing global warming. The Kyoto Protocol eventually established some reductions in greenhouse gas emissions but the developing countries were exempt and the United States of America refused to ratify the Protocol. Within Europe there is a wide variation in the targets with some countries actually increasing their emissions and others reducing their emissions (Table 2.2). As in many political negotiations the table shows evidence of special pleading and horse-trading and O'Riordan[52] notes that the EU countries are pressing for as

Table 2.2 Currently proposed targets for 2010, based on 1990 CO_2 emission levels (pre-Kyoto in brackets)

Country	% change	Pre-Kyoto level	Country	% change	Pre-Kyoto level
Portugal	+27	(+40)	The Netherlands	−6	(−10)
Greece	+25	(+30)	Italy	−6.5	(−7)
Spain	+15	(+17)	Belgium	−7.5	(−10)
Ireland	+13	(+15)	United Kingdom	−12.5	(−10)
Sweden	+4	(+5)	Austria	−13	(−25)
Finland	0	(0)	Denmark	−21	(−25)
France	0	(0)	Germany	−21	(−25)
			Luxembourg	−28	(−30)

Source: O'Riordan (2000).

much to be achieved domestically by specific policy measures, rather than by flexible instruments such as tradable discharge permits.

The need to reduce the growth in greenhouse gas emissions has been noted in several studies. As in the cases of the reduction of CFCs via the Montreal Protocol the international community (scientists, NGOs, governments and businesses) have been locked into rounds of negotiations to agree on the need to make reductions and then agree on the best options to implement the chosen policy. As O'Riordan notes these debates enter an indeterministic policy area which will require 'politics of great vision and democracy that is more participatory than at present is the case'.[53]

Two economists[54] have suggested that 80 per cent of the variation of future projections of global atmospheric CO_2 emissions can be based on eight policy alternatives. These alternatives include the scope for alternative non-carbon fuels; efficiency of macroeconomic responses; substitution of energy for economic goods; the extent of joint implementation; the use of carbon tax revenues; the aversion to air pollution damage; the degree of climate change damage averted in the future and the size of the eventual CO_2 emissions reduction. In fact the new scenarios of global warming (A1, A2, B1 and B2) explicitly assume no Kyoto types of attempts as greenhouse reduction targets but they do include alternative non-carbon fuels as well the future size of the CO_2 atmospheric burden. If, however, we are to reduce the overall CO_2 burden (the IPCC recommends a 60 per cent reduction in greenhouse gases by 2010 compared to 1980 amounts) then some analytical approaches to reducing greenhouse gas emissions must be made.

It should be noted that some writers, such as Lomborg (2001), see little need to reduce greenhouse gas emissions. These arguments are based around the view of whether it is better to direct investment into developing countries rather than spend the same proportion of global world product to reduce anthropogenic greenhouse emissions. In this perspective the view of appropriate economic instruments to reduce greenhouse gases is supported by some economists.[55] Other economists and environmental scientists disagree with these policy prescriptions.

The Danish Ecological Council,[56] for example, has cast grave doubts over Lomborg's selective use of statistics and misquotations to support his own ad hoc opinions on global warming policy. In particular the estimate of optimal reductions in CO_2 emissions, as used by Nordhaus,[57] is very sensitive to the choice of the pure rate of time preference.[58] Similarly, Azar and Schneider,[59] for example, suggest that it is possible to reduce greenhouse emissions and simultaneously provide a better economic use of resources – even if it takes a few more years before the increased income levels are achieved.

Global warming: the ongoing debate over science, policies and economics

The scientific research into global warming has made massive progress over the last three decades. Improvements in the collection of data together with more advanced computing models of climate change have given a good understanding of the numerous, multi-disciplinary issues involved. Despite the uncertainties in modelling global warming it is clear that the scientific community has reached a consensus on the major impacts of global warming.

Furthermore, scientific groups and policy makers have been working together in an attempt to forecast likely impacts of global warming over the next century. By developing sets of scenarios based on different assumptions concerning greenhouse gas emissions and socio-economic responses some attention is now turning to the best set of practicable measure to combat global warming.[60] This important research is continuing.

As noted above there is a rich repertoire of policy strategies that can be chosen to reduce global warming. It should be noted that the scientific community are reasonably confident in their understanding of the basic science of global warming. It should also be noted that the AGCMs do produce similar scenarios of global climate change over the last century. The different AGCMs do, however, produce different regional scenarios. Current research is refining these regional models. The major problem, however, is in agreeing on the best policies to blend demographic, social, economic and technological changes that drive alternative scenarios. This is a major global political issue.

The detailed debate over the economic arguments underpinning some greenhouse policy issues will be examined in the rest of this text. This on-going debate revolves around the question of the reliability of the correct mix of policies to address the problem of global warming. It is, however, salutary to remind readers that greenhouse gas emission reduction policies are essentially best considered as a form of insurance. This insurance policy is one that safeguards the interests of future generations rather than one that makes the best returns to current generations and hence prematurely forecloses future opportunities.

Notes

1 Bolin *et al.* (1986).
2 See, for example, IPCC (2001) and Rayner and Malone (1998).
3 The evolution of debate is the subject of Chapter 3.
4 Hulme *et al.* (2001).
5 IPCC (1990, p.xv).
6 IPCC (1991).
7 See p.20.
8 See, for example, Zhang *et al.* (2002).

 9 IPCC (1991, p.23).
10 IPCC (1996, p.39).
11 Goodess *et al.* (1992).
12 Motz (1977).
13 Milankovitch (1941).
14 See COMAP (1988) and CLIMAP (1981).
15 Harrison (2002).
16 See Joussaume and Taylor (2000) and Gates (1976).
17 See UNEP (2002) and WWF (2000).
18 Leakey and Lewin (1997).
19 Plass (1956); Ramananthan *et al.* (1985); Ramananthan (1988); Jones and Henderson-Sellers (1990).
20 Fourier (1827).
21 Tyndall (1861).
22 Arrhenius (1896).
23 Callendar (1938).
24 IPCC (1990 *et seq.*).
25 Rayner and Malone (1998).
26 Ramanathan *et al.* (1985).
27 Deaton (1999).
28 For example: Henderson-Sellers and McGuffie (1987).
29 Manabe and Wetherald (1975).
30 Claussen (2000).
31 See, for example, Sokolov and Stone (1998) and Prinn *et al.* (1999).
32 Alcamo *et al.* (1994).
33 Henderson-Sellers and Blong (1989).
34 IPCC (1996, p.438).
35 Henderson-Sellers and Blong (1989), Moffatt (1992).
36 DEFRA (2001).
37 Ibid.
38 See Hulme *et al.* (2001).
39 Moffatt (1992), Moffatt *et al.* (2001).
40 Peng *et al.* (1990).
41 Hasselmann (1982).
42 Braithwaite (1959).
43 IPCC (1991).
44 IPCC (2000).
45 See, for example, Taylor and Grotsch (1990) and Moffatt (1992).
46 Jager (1988a and b).
47 O'Riordan (2000).
48 IPCC (1991, p.527).
49 Bolin *et al.* (1986) and Houghton *et al.* (1983).
50 Gorshkov (1995).
51 For example, UNEP (2002) and WWF (2000).
52 O'Riordan (2000).
53 O'Riordan (2000, p.206).
54 Repetto and Austin (1997).
55 See, for example, Nordhaus (1998) and Nordhaus and Boyer (1999).
56 Danish Ecological Council (2002).

57 Nordhaus (1998).
58 Schultz and Kasting (1997).
59 Azar and Schneider (2002).
60 Markandya and Halsnaes (2002).

Bibliography

Alcamo, J., Kreileman, G.J.J., Krol, M. and Zuidema, G. (1994) 'Modelling the global society-biosphere-climate system: part 1: Model description and testing', *Journal of Water, Air and Soil Pollution*, Special Issue IMAGE 2.0.

Arrhenius, S. (1896) 'On the influence of carbonic acid in the air upon the temperature of the ground', *Philosophical Magazine* 41:237–276.

Azar, C. and Schneider, S.H. (2002) 'Are the economic costs of stabilising the atmosphere prohibitive?', *Ecological Economics* 42:73–80.

Bolin, B., Doos, B.R., Jager, J. and Warwick, R.A. (1986) *The Greenhouse Effect, Climate Change and Ecosystems SCOPE 29*, Chichester: Wiley.

Braithwaite, R.B. (1959) *Scientific Explanation*, Cambridge: Cambridge University Press.

Callendar, G.S. (1938) 'The artificial production of CO_2 and its influence on temperature', *Quarterly Journal of the Royal Meteorological Society* 64:223–237.

Claussen, M. (ed.) (2000) *Table of EMICs – Earth System Models of Intermediate Complexity*. PIK. Online. Available at http://www.pik.org.doc (accessed 9 September 2003).

CLIMAP (1981) *Seasonal Reconstructions of the Earth's Surface at the Last Glacial Maximum*, Geological Society of America, Map Chart Series MC-36, Boulder, Colorado.

COMAP (1988) 'Climatic changes of the last 18,000 years: observations and model simulations', *Science* 241:1043–1052.

Danish Ecological Council (2002) *Sceptical Questions and Sustainable Answer*, Copenhagen: Danish Ecological Council.

Deaton, M. (1999) *Dynamic Modelling of Environmental Systems*, Berlin: Springer Verlag.

DEFRA (2001) *PRECIS: Providing Regional Climates for Impact Studies*, Reading: Hadley Centre.

Fourier, J.B.J. (1827) 'Memoire sur les temperatures du globe terrestre et des espaces planetaires', *Memoir de l'Academie Royale des Sueries de l'Institute de France* 1:569–604.

Gates, W.L. (1976) 'The numerical simulation of ice-age climate with a global general circulation model', *Journal of Atmospheric Science* 33:1844–1873.

Goodess, C.M., Palutikof, J.P. and Davies, T.D. (1992) *The Nature and Causes of Climate Changes: Assessing Long-term Futures*, London: Belhaven Press.

Gorshkov, V.G. (1995) *Physical and Biological Bases of Life Stability*, Berlin: Verlag, Man, Biota and Environment.

Harrison, S.P. (2002) *Palaeoenvironmental Data Sets and Model Evaluation in PMIP*, Proceedings of the Third PMIP Workshop.

Hasselmann, K. (1982) 'An ocean model for climatic variability studies', *Progress in Oceanography* 11:69–92.

Henderson-Sellers, A. and Blong, R. (1989) *The Greenhouse Effect: Living in a Warmer Australia*, Kensington: The University of New South Wales Press.

Henderson-Sellers, A. and McGuffie, K. (1987) *A Climate Modeller Primer*, Chichester: Wiley.

Houghton, R.A., Hobbie, J.E., Melillo, J.M., Morre, B., Peterson, B.J., Shaver, G. and

Woodward, G.M. (1983) 'Changes in the carbon content of terrestrial biota and soils between 1860 and 1980: a net release of CO_2 and the atmosphere', *Ecological Monographs* 53:235–262.

Hulme, M., Crossley, J. and Xiandu, L. (2001) *An Exploration of Regional Climate Change Scenarios for Scotland*, Scottish Executive Central Research Unit Environment Group Research Programme Research Findings 11:1–4, Edinburgh: Scottish Executive.

IPCC (1990) *Climate Change – The IPCC Scientific Assessment World Meteorological Organisation – United Nations Environmental Program*, Cambridge: Cambridge University Press.

IPCC (1991) *Climate Change: Science, Impacts and Policy, the IPCC Scientific Assessment World Meteorological Organisation – United Nations Environmental Program*, Cambridge: Cambridge University Press.

IPCC (1996) *Climate Change 1995 The Science of Climate Change, the World Meteorological Organisation – United Nations Environmental Program*, Cambridge: Cambridge University Press.

IPCC (2000) *Emission Scenarios Database SRES Scenarios Version 1.1*. Online. Available at http:sres/ciesn.org/final_data.html (accessed 9 September 2003).

IPCC (2001) Climate Change (2001) *Mitigation, The World Meteorological Organisation – United Nations Environmental Program*, Cambridge: Cambridge University Press.

Jager, J. (1988a) 'Anticipating climate change', *Environment* 30:30–33.

Jager, J. (1988b) *Developing Policies for Responding to Climate Change*, WCIP-1, WMO/TD No. 225, World Climate Impact Studies, Geneva: World Meteorological Organization.

Jones, M.D.H. and Henderson-Sellers, A. (1990) 'History of the greenhouse effect', *Progress in Physical Geography* 14:1–18.

Jones, P.D. (1985a) 'Northern hemisphere temperatures, 1851–1984', *Climate Monitor* 14:14–21.

Jones, P.D. (1985b) 'Southern hemisphere temperatures, 1851–1985', *Climate Monitor* 14:132–140.

Joussaume, S. and Taylor, K.E. (2000) *Status of the Palaeoclimate Modelling Intercomparison Project (PMIP)*, Proceedings of the Third PMIP Workshop.

Leakey, R. and Lewin, R. (1997) *The Sixth Extinction: Biodiversity and Survival*, London: Weidenfeld and Nicolson.

Lomborg, B. (2001) *The Sceptical Environmentalist*, Cambridge: Cambridge University Press.

Manabe, S. and Wetherald, R.T. (1975) 'The effects of doubling the CO_2 concentrations on the climate of a general circulation model', *Journal of Atmospheric Sciences* 24: 241–259.

Markandya, A. and Halsnaes, K. (eds) (2002) *Climate Change and Sustainable Development: Prospects for Developing Countries*, London: Earthscan.

Milankovitch, M. (1941) *Kanaon der Erdbestrahlungen und seine Andwendung auf das Eiszeitenproblem*, Belgrade (Pantic, N. (1998) *Canon of Insolation and the Ice Age Problem*, Alven Press (English translation)).

Moffatt, I. (1992) *The Greenhouse Effect: Science and Policy in the Northern Territory, Australia*, Darwin: Australian National University, NARU.

Moffatt, I., Hanley, N. and Wilson, M.D. (2001) *Measuring and Modelling Sustainable Development*, Carnforth: Parthenon Publishers.

Motz, L. (1977) *The Universe: Its Beginning and End*, London: Abacus.

Nordhaus, W. (ed.) (1998) *Economics and Policy Issues in Climate Change*, Washington, D.C.: Resources for the Future.

Nordhaus, W. and Boyer, J. (1999) 'Requiem for Kyoto: an economic analysis of the Kyoto Protocol', *The Energy Journal*, Special Issue: 93–130.

O'Riordan, T. (ed.) (2000) *Environmental Science for Environmental Management*, Essex: Prentice Hall.

Peng, T.H., Post, W.M., De Angelis, D.L., Dale, V.H. and Farrell, M.P. (1990) 'Atmospheric carbon dioxide and the global carbon cycle: the key uncertainties', in T.N. Veziroglu (ed.) *Environmental Problems and Solutions: Greenhouse Effect, Acid Rain, Pollution*, New York: Hemisphere Press.

Plass, G.N. (1956) 'The carbon dioxide theory of climate change', *Tellus* 8:140–154.

Prinn, R., Jacoby, H., Sokolov, A., Wang, C., Xiao, X., Yang, Z., Eckhaus, R., Stone, P., Ellerman, D., Melillo, J., Fitzmaurice, J., Kicklighter, D., Holian, G. and Liu, Y. (1999) 'Integrated global system model for climate policy assessment: feedbacks and sensitivity studies', *Climatic Change* 41:469–546.

Ramananthan, V. (1988) 'The greenhouse theory of climate change: a test by inadvertent global experiment', *Science* 240:293–299.

Ramananthan, V., Cicerone, R.J., Singh, H.B. and Kiehl, J.T. (1985) 'Trace gas trends and their potential role in climatic change', *Journal of Geophysical Research* 90:5547–5566.

Rayner, S. and Malone, E.L. (eds) (1998) *Human Choice and Climate Change* (Volumes i–iv), Ohio: Battelle Press.

Reppetto, R. and Austin, D. (1997) *Climate Protection Policies: Can We Afford to Delay?*, Washington, D.C.: World Resources Institute.

Roberts, N. (1989) *The Holocene: An Environmental History*, Oxford: Blackwell.

Schneider, S.H. (1989) 'The greenhouse effect: science and policy', *Science* 243: 771–781.

Schultz, P.A. and Kasting, J. (1997) 'Optimal reductions in CO_2 emissions', *Energy Policy* 25:491–500.

Sokolov, A.P. and Stone, P.H. (1998) 'A flexible climate model for use in integrated assessments', *Climate Dynamics* 14:291–303.

Taylor, K.E. and Grotsch, S.L. (1990) 'Observational and theoretical studies of greenhouse climate effects', in T.N. Veziroglu (ed.) *Environmental Problems and Solutions: Greenhouse Effect, Acid Rain, Pollution*, New York: Hemisphere Press.

Tyndall, J. (1861) 'On the absorption and radiation of heat by gases and vapours, on the physical connections of radiation, absorption and conduction', *Philosophical Magazine* (4th series) 22:169–194; 22:273–285.

UNFCCC (1997) *Kyoto Protocol to the United Nations Framework Convention on Climate Change*, Bonn: UNFCCC.

UNEP (2002) *Global Environmental Outlook 3*, London: UNEP/Earthscan.

Wigley, T.M.L. (1981) 'Climate and Palaeoclimate: what we can learn about solar luminosity variations', *Solar Physics* 74:435–471.

WWF (2000) *Living Planet Report 2000*, Gland: WWF International.

Zhang, X., Drake, N.A. and Wainwright, J. (2002) 'Scaling issues in environmental modelling', in J. Wainwright and M. Mulligan (eds) *Environmental Modelling: Finding Simplicity in Complexity*, Chichester: Wiley.

3 From negotiation to implementation

The UN Framework Convention on Climate Change and its Kyoto Protocol

Joanna Depledge

Introduction

This chapter focuses on the intergovernmental climate change regime through which governments have coordinated their response to the threat of human-induced climate change. The foundation of this regime is the UN Framework Convention on Climate Change, adopted in 1992. The first decade of the climate change regime has seen an intense period of 'rule-making' negotiations aimed at further developing its commitments and institutions. These negotiations have followed a twin-track. Along the first track, governments have elaborated in more detail on the Convention's provisions, building up an extensive 'rulebook' for its implementation. Along the second, more high profile track, governments have negotiated substantively new and stronger commitments, leading to the adoption of the Kyoto Protocol in December 1997 and to subsequent negotiations to define the Protocol's operational details. Both negotiating tracks culminated in agreement on the so-called 'Marrakech Accords' in October/November 2001, setting out a comprehensive set of rules for both the Convention and the Kyoto Protocol. The adoption of the landmark Marrakech Accords signals a shift in the focus of the climate change regime from negotiation to implementation, not withstanding the continued delay in entry into force of the Kyoto Protocol.

This chapter explores the evolution of the climate change regime over its first 12 years. After outlining the history of the regime, we focus first on the Convention and the further development of its rulebook. The chapter then turns to the Kyoto Protocol, looking at its provisions and rulebook, before offering some concluding remarks on the road ahead.

The history of the climate change regime

While the scientific history of climate change dates back over a century,[1] its political history is shorter. The UN General Assembly (UNGA) first took up the issue of human-induced climate change in 1988, in the face of new scientific findings, an unusually hot summer in the United States, increasing awareness of global environmental problems, and rising expectations over the ability of the international community to address those problems, following the successful negotiations on the 1987 Montreal Protocol on Substances that Deplete the Ozone Layer. Also in 1988, the World Meteorological Organization (WMO) and the UN Environment Programme (UNEP) jointly established the Intergovernmental Panel on Climate Change (IPCC), with a mandate to assess the available scientific information on climate change, including its potential impacts, and options for adaptation and mitigation. By 1990, the IPCC had produced its First Assessment Report on the state of climate change science, warning that, although there were many uncertainties, human activity was leading to increased atmospheric concentrations of greenhouse gases (GHGs) and rising temperatures. Later that same year, the UNGA formally launched negotiations on a framework convention on climate change. The decision to address climate change through a global treaty under UN auspices reflected the widely held view that the global nature of climate change, whereby all countries contribute to the problem and all will be affected by it (albeit to vastly differing extents), demanded a global response.

The UN Framework Convention on Climate Change was negotiated in just 15 months. It was adopted on 9 May 1992 and opened for signature later that year at the UN Conference on Environment and Development (UNCED) in Rio de Janeiro (the 'Earth Summit'). The Convention entered into force less than two years later on 21 March 1994, having received the requisite 50 ratifications. At the time of writing, there are 189 Parties to the Convention, and it is approaching universal membership.

The UN Framework Convention on Climate Change

The Convention provides the basic foundation for the climate change regime. It sets forth an objective and principles to guide the actions of Parties in responding to climate change, substantive commitments giving effect to those principles, and a set of institutions and procedures to enable continuing negotiations on the Convention's further development. We now examine each of these elements in turn.

Objective and principles

The cornerstone of the climate change regime is its ultimate objective, defined by the Convention as follows:

> to achieve . . . stabilization of greenhouse gas concentrations in the atmosphere at a level *that would prevent dangerous anthropogenic interference with the climate system* . . . within a time-frame sufficient to allow ecosystems to adapt naturally . . . to ensure that food production is not threatened and to enable economic development to proceed in a sustainable manner.
>
> (Article 2, emphasis added)

The level of GHG concentrations that might constitute 'dangerous' interference with the climate, however, is not quantified. The IPCC has broached the scientific dimensions of this issue, with analysis of the climate change impacts that might be expected for various GHG concentration levels,[2] but what might constitute an acceptable, or unacceptable, degree of climate change remains an ultimately political and unanswered – perhaps unanswerable – question in the regime.

The Convention goes on to outline a set of principles (Article 3) that are to guide parties 'in their actions to achieve the objective', including the 'precautionary principle', cost-effectiveness and the importance of sustainable development. Equity considerations feature particularly strongly, expressed through the principle of 'common but differentiated responsibilities', and the requirement for industrialized countries to 'take the lead in combating climate change and the adverse effects thereof'. This principle recognizes that, although all countries have a common obligation to respond to climate change, the industrialized countries bear a special responsibility to first modify the upward trend in their own emissions, on account of their much greater historical contribution to climate change, their generally much higher emissions per capita, and their more abundant economic, technological and institutional resources to address the problem. Industrialized countries account for just over two-thirds of the CO_2 accumulated in the atmosphere,[3] while the per capita CO_2 emissions from fuel combustion of the members of the Organisation for Economic Cooperation and Development (OECD) are nearly three times greater than the world average and more than ten times greater than the average in Africa or Asia (excluding China). Even China, which is the second largest aggregate emitter of CO_2 from fuel combustion after the US, has per capita emissions nine times smaller.[4] The emphasis on equity in the Convention also reflects the inherent unfairness of climate change, where the poorer developing countries who have contributed the least to the problem are also the most vulnerable to its impacts. These countries tend to be located in geographically vulnerable regions, suffer from existing environmental and economic stress, and lack the resources to take expensive adaptation measures, such as building sea defences.

Implicit in the Convention, however, is the understanding that, once industrialized countries have shown leadership and started to reduce their emissions, developing countries will follow their lead. This 'leadership paradigm' is not unique to the climate change regime, featuring also in the Montreal Protocol, where developing countries were given a 'grace period' before being required to follow industrialized countries in cutting their emissions of ozone-depleting substances.

The Convention's principles are of more than rhetorical importance, providing the agreed framework for addressing climate change at the intergovernmental level. They rest on a fragile consensus, however. The recent US repudiation of the Kyoto Protocol on the grounds, among other concerns, that it excludes developing countries from emission targets amounts to an implicit rejection of the principle of common but differentiated responsibilities and industrialized country leadership in the context of the climate change regime.

Substantive commitments

The principle of equity is operationalized in the substantive commitments of the Convention, which divide countries into two main groups. The 40 countries, plus the European Community, that are listed in the Convention's Annex I include those that were members of the OECD in 1992 and countries of the former Soviet Union and Eastern Europe, the so-called economies in transition (EITs). These are known as Annex I Parties (see Table 3.1). All other countries that have ratified the Convention are known as non-Annex I Parties.

All parties are under a general obligation to address climate change, for example, by preparing national climate change programmes, facilitating techno-logy transfer, cooperating in scientific research, and promoting education and public awareness on the topic (Articles 4.1, 5, 6). However, in accordance with the leadership paradigm, only the Annex I Parties are subject to a specific commitment to adopt policies and measures 'with the aim of returning' their emissions of CO_2 and other greenhouse gases to 1990 levels by 2000 (Article 4.2(a) and (b)). This is not a legally-binding emissions target; the commitment of Annex I Parties is to *aim* to return their emissions to 1990 levels by 2000, not necessarily to achieve that goal.

Table 3.1 Countries included in Annexes I and II to the Convention

Australia	**Austria**	Belarus*
Belgium	Bulgaria*	**Canada**
Croatia*	Czech Republic*	**Denmark**
European Community	Estonia*	**Finland**
France	**Germany**	**Greece**
Hungary*	**Iceland**	**Ireland**
Italy	**Japan**	Latvia*
Liechtenstein	Lithuania*	**Luxembourg**
Monaco	**The Netherlands**	**New Zealand**
Norway	Poland*	**Portugal**
Romania*	Russian Federation*	Slovakia*
Slovenia*	**Spain**	**Sweden**
Switzerland	Turkey	Ukraine*
United Kingdom	**United States of America**	

Note
* Countries with economies in transition.
Bold denotes countries also included in Annex II. Alone among Annex I Parties, Turkey has not yet ratified the Convention, but is expected to do so following agreement to remove its name from Annex II at COP7.

In addition, the OECD countries only, whose names are listed in the Convention's Annex II and are therefore known as Annex II Parties, have a commitment to supply financial resources to developing countries to help them meet their commitments under the Convention and adapt to the adverse effects of climate change (Articles 4.3, 4.4, 11). The Convention also calls on Annex II Parties to promote the transfer of environmentally sound technologies to both developing countries and EITs (Article 4.5).

All Parties are required to compile an inventory of their greenhouse gas emissions, and to report on the action they are taking under the Convention by submitting so-called national communications to the Convention secretariat. The reporting requirements for non-Annex I Parties, however, are less detailed than for industrialized countries, while the timetable for submitting their national communications is looser and contingent on the receipt of adequate funding.

An important dimension to the Convention is its recognition of the diversity of national circumstances, and the need to take this diversity into account in addressing climate change. The most extreme example of diverse circumstances lies in the opposed interests of the Alliance of Small Island States (AOSIS) on the one hand, and the Organization of Petroleum Exporting Countries (OPEC) on the other. The small island and low lying states represented by AOSIS are highly vulnerable to climate change, being threatened by sea level rise, salt water encroachment, storm surges and, for some, significant loss of land. For these countries, the costs of climate change dramatically outweigh the costs of mitigation action. OPEC countries view their situation very differently. All of them are highly dependent on oil exports and fear that climate change mitigation policies will adversely affect their economies. They are also high emitters of greenhouse gases due to their oil production industries, and do not generally consider themselves vulnerable to climate change. For OPEC countries, therefore, the costs of climate change mitigation action are seen to be much greater than the impacts of climate change itself. Both these groups of countries thus perceive themselves to be participating in the climate change regime to safeguard their (actual or economic) survival, yet on very different grounds and often with very different aims.

The global scope of the climate change regime, however, requires that both these contrasting national circumstances, and all those in between, be accommodated. The Convention's principles thus call for full consideration to be given to the specific needs and circumstances of both developing countries that are particularly vulnerable to climate change, and those that are likely to suffer disproportionately from climate change mitigation action. Article 4.8 lists categories of countries to which this might apply, such as those with low lying coastal areas and those whose economies are highly dependent on fossil fuels and energy-intensive products; in practice, it is difficult to identify any developing country that does not fall into at least one of the categories. The Convention also singles out the specific needs of least developed countries (LDCs), calling for special consideration for these countries in the provision of funding and technology transfer (Article 4.9). In addition, the Convention recognizes the difficult circumstances faced by EITs as a result of the political and economic upheaval they have recently experienced, and therefore grants them a 'degree of flexibility' in implementing their commitments (Article 4.6). Several EITs have exercised this flexibility by choosing a baseline earlier than 1990, that is, prior to the economic collapse which led to massive cuts in their emissions.

Accompanying its substantive commitments, the Convention includes a series of review mechanisms to ensure that its provisions can be strengthened over time as scientific knowledge on climate change increases and political will harden. The first of these review mechanisms triggered the launch of negotiations on the Kyoto Protocol, discussed below.

Institutions and procedures

The main decision-making body of the Convention is the Conference of the Parties (COP). It is assigned the general function of keeping 'under regular review the implementation of the Convention' and making 'the decisions necessary to promote [its] effective implementation' (Article 7.2). The Convention stipulates that the COP should meet annually and it has indeed done so since its first session, held in Berlin in March/April 1995. The presidency of the COP, along with its venue, typically rotates among the five official UN regional groups (Africa, Asia, Central and Eastern Europe, Latin America and the Caribbean, and Western Europe and others).

The two permanent subsidiary bodies of the climate change regime are the Subsidiary Body for Scientific and Technological Advice (SBSTA) and the Subsidiary Body for Implementation (SBI), which are required to provide advice to the COP on 'scientific and technological matters' and 'the assessment and review of the effective implementation of the Convention', respectively (Articles 9, 10). The subsidiary bodies meet more often than the COP, usually twice a year at the seat of the secretariat, to formulate recommendations to it.

Like the COP, both bodies are intergovernmental, that is, composed of government representatives, and are open-ended, which means that any delegate can participate in discussions. The climate change regime therefore differs from several other multilateral environmental regimes in not having limited membership bodies of scientific or technical experts within the regime itself. Instead, the Convention specifies that the SBSTA should draw on other 'competent international bodies' to obtain scientific and technical information. The IPCC has played the dominant role in this regard, acting as a 'contractor' body to the regime. Its major Assessment Reports of the state of climate change science, produced at roughly five-year intervals, have become the most authoritative and comprehensive source of knowledge on climate change for the regime. The 1995

Second Assessment Report, for example, which confirmed the detection of a 'discernible human influence on global climate', provided important added impetus to the negotiations on the Kyoto Protocol. In addition, the IPCC supplies specific information to the regime on request in the form of shorter technical papers and special reports. Negotiations on rules under the Kyoto Protocol for the treatment of the land-use change and forestry sector, for example, benefited from input from the IPCC in the form of a Special Report.[5]

Another contractor body is the Global Environment Facility (GEF), which operates the financial mechanism of the Convention, channelling financial assistance from Annex II Parties to developing countries. On adoption of the Convention, the GEF was designated operating entity of the financial mechanism on an interim basis only. This was due to the misgivings of developing countries over its governance structure at the time, whose voting system was weighted towards donor countries, and their unanswered calls for a specific climate change fund under the Convention. At COP 4 in 1998, however, following the restructuring of the GEF's governance system, the GEF's role in operating the financial mechanism was extended on an ongoing basis, although subject to regular review. The latest review, at COP 8 in 2002, confirmed and extended the GEF's mandate. The GEF is accountable to the COP for its climate change related activities and the COP gives regular guidance to it, detailing funding priorities and eligibility criteria for climate change projects. The GEF, in turn, reports annually on its activities to the COP.

A permanent secretariat provides support to the COP and its subsidiary bodies. It is administered under UN rules and regulations and its head, the Executive Secretary, reports to the UN Secretary-General. The secretariat is staffed by international civil servants who have a duty of impartiality, and is accountable to the COP in its work. Its core funding is secured through contributions from Parties, their shares being based on the UN scale of assessment. For the biennium 2003–2004, the core budget of the secretariat stood at over US$17 million per year, having risen steadily over the past decade, although much more slowly in recent years. This reflects the importance attached by governments to the issue of climate change, as well as the rapidly expanding rulebook of the regime, which requires ever greater support from the secretariat. The secretariat now employs some 110 staff, and is located in Bonn, Germany.

In addition to the institutional structure described above, the Convention outlines formal procedures that govern negotiation and decision-making under the regime. These are, in turn, elaborated further in the Convention's rules of procedure, which the COP was due to adopt at its first session. However, due primarily to disagreement over the voting rule for adopting substantive decisions, it was unable to do so. This disagreement has never been resolved and the rules of procedure remain unadopted. They are, however, 'applied' at each session of the COP and the subsidiary bodies as if they were in force, except for the rule on voting.

Given the absence of a voting rule, most decisions under the Convention can only be taken by consensus. While the definition of consensus is contested, it is generally taken to mean that there are no stated objections to a decision. This implies that a small group of Parties, or arguably even a single Party, could object to a decision that is agreeable to all others, and prevent its adoption. In practice, Parties to multilateral treaties have proved very reluctant to resort to a vote even when voting procedures are in place, and particularly so in the context of global environmental problems such as climate change, where global participation is deemed critical for an effective response. Nevertheless, the absence of a voting rule to which Parties could turn to as a last resort has strengthened the hand of small minorities in the climate change regime, notably Parties such as OPEC who fear strong mitigation action, and are able to implicitly or explicitly threaten blockage of decisions if their demands are not met.

The evolution of the climate change regime

We now turn to explore recent developments in the climate change regime, focusing on the Marrakech Accords. We examine first the evolution of the Convention's rulebook on several key issues, before turning to the Kyoto Protocol and its rulebook.[6]

The Convention's rulebook

Finance

The issue of financial assistance for developing countries – how much they should receive, for which activities and through what institutional structure – has been a major source of debate in the climate change regime ever since the negotiation of the Convention. It continued as such in the post-Kyoto negotiations leading up to the adoption of the Marrakech Accords.

Since 1991, the GEF has disbursed grants for climate change activities amounting to around US$1.6 billion, plus over US$9 billion leveraged through co-financing from bilateral agencies, recipient countries and the private sector. Over the most recent reporting period (June 2002 to June 2003), total project financing for climate change activities came to over US$1.1 billion, comprising approximately US$183 million in grant funding and US$933 million leveraged through co-financing.[7] GEF funds have been used to finance the formulation, development and implementation of climate change mitigation projects, along with the preparation of national communications and associated capacity-building. The COP has gradually extended the scope of activities eligible for funding, for example, in the area of adaptation. Although there has been some improvement in recent years, the relationship between the GEF and the climate change regime has often been awkward, with the GEF frequently accused by non-Annex I Parties of not paying sufficient attention to the COP's guidance and of excessive delays in releasing funds. Nevertheless, the confirmation of the GEF as operating entity of the financial mechanism has secured its central role in the climate change regime.

Significant advances were made on funding issues as part of the 2001 Marrakech Accords, with the establishment of three new funds:

- A *special climate change fund*, to finance projects relating to adaptation; technology transfer; climate change mitigation; and economic diversification for countries highly dependent on income from fossil fuels;
- A *least developed countries fund*, to support a special work programme to assist LDCs;
- An *adaptation fund*, which will operate under the Kyoto Protocol. It will be financed by the 'share of the proceeds' for adaptation coming from the Protocol's clean development mechanism (see below), as well as other sources.

Donor countries did not accede to developing country calls for the funds to operate independently under the climate change regime, and all three are managed by the GEF. Contributions to the funds are expected to be additional to those allocated to climate change activities under the GEF, and several industrialized countries, including the EU and Canada, have already pledged to collectively contribute US$410 million a year by 2005. The Marrakech Accords also call on donor countries to report on their financial contributions on an annual basis, addressing concerns expressed by developing countries at insufficient reporting on this issue.

Technology transfer

Technology transfer is a long-standing issue in the international arena, extending far beyond the boundaries of climate change. Debates on how to promote the transfer of climate-friendly technologies in the climate change regime have been characterized by the seemingly intractable disputes that have long shaped relations between industrialized and developing countries on this issue. On the one hand, industrialized countries point to the difficulties in transferring technology on a concessional basis when most lies in the hands of the private sector, and emphasize the need for developing countries to remove their own domestic barriers to technology transfer. On the other hand, developing countries insist on a greater effort on the part of industrialized countries to transfer the climate-friendly technology that could help them move away from a carbon-intensive development path.

There was some movement on this issue as part of the Marrakech Accords with the establishment of a new 'Expert Group on Technology Transfer'. The group, composed of experts from governments and international organizations, has been charged with analysing and identifying ways to advance technology transfer activities. It remains to be seen whether this institutional development can lead to a breakthrough in a debate that has often resembled a dialogue of the deaf.

Capacity-building

The risk that some developing countries might be left behind in the fast moving pace of the climate change regime has highlighted the importance of capacity-building. Many developing countries lack domestic institutional and human capacity to meaningfully respond to climate change or even to participate in the negotiations that determine their obligations. The adoption of the Kyoto Protocol and specifically its clean development mechanism, which opens up important opportunities for those developing countries that are able to seize them, under-lined the need for capacity-building to ensure that less well-resourced developing countries are not excluded. This new focus on capacity-building also attracted the attention of the EITs, who face similar problems of insufficient resources and weak capacity. In response, the Marrakech Accords set out a framework for pro-moting capacity-building in both developing countries and EITs. Additional guid-ance was also given to the GEF to fund a greater scope of capacity-building activities. As with technology transfer, the concrete results of this advance in rule-making on capacity-building is a matter for future assessment.

Special circumstances: adverse impacts of climate change, adverse effects of mitigation measures, and least developed countries

Highly contentious debates have taken place in the climate change regime on how to lend concrete meaning to the special consideration called for by the Conven-tion for countries that are particularly vulnerable to the adverse impacts of climate change or of climate change mitigation measures. This issue was thrust into prominence during negotiations on the Kyoto Protocol by OPEC states, who feared the potential economic impact of new emission targets for Annex I Parties, and proposed to establish a fund to compensate them for any economic losses. OPEC states secured support for their stance from the wider negotiating group of developing countries – the Group of 77 (G77) and China – by linking their concerns to those of countries vulnerable to the adverse impacts of climate change and proposing that these adverse impacts also be covered by the proposed compensation fund. An undertaking to launch negotiations on how to meet the concerns of both sets of countries, as well as LDCs, but without any mention of compensation, was critical to reaching agreement on the Protocol itself. While industrialized countries are generally sympathetic to the concerns of countries vulnerable to climate change and of LDCs, they balk at the idea of compensating OPEC for loss of oil export revenue.

A fragile solution was found as part of the Marrakech Accords. Countries vulnerable to climate change secured funding for adaptation through the special climate change fund and the adaptation fund, and guidance to the GEF was extended to cover a wider range of adaptation activities. LDCs gained their own fund, along with a new work programme to address the particular challenges that they face, especially in the area of adaptation. OPEC also did well out of the Marrakech Accords, obtaining several important concessions, most notably the eligibility under the special climate change fund of economic diversification activities in countries highly dependent on income from fossil fuels. In addition, the Marrakech Accords outline more stringent requirements for industrialized countries to report on how they are addressing the potential negative impacts of climate change mitigation measures on developing countries, while OPEC secured an undertaking from Annex II Parties to support technological development, such as non-energy uses of fossil fuels and cleaner fossil fuel technologies. This complex issue promises to remain on the agenda of the climate change regime for a long time to come.

Reporting and review

Reporting by Parties makes up the backbone of the climate change regime, indeed of most any regime. It is only through the reporting of information that the nature, causes and possible solutions to climate change can be properly understood, and that progress made (or not) in addressing the problem can be assessed and placed under public scrutiny. Before being required to compile an inventory of their greenhouse gas emissions under the Convention, most countries, including many in the OECD, simply did not know how much they were emitting and from what sources.

Reporting and review by Annex I Parties

National communications must be submitted by Annex I Parties according to an agreed schedule roughly every three to five years, with almost all Annex I Parties having submitted three so far (the fourth is due on 1 January 2006). Greenhouse gas inventories are due on an annual basis, by 15 April each year, covering emissions up to the last but one year. Annex I Parties must prepare their national communications and greenhouse gas inventories according to agreed guidelines. These are periodically revised, each time setting out in more detail the content, methodology and presentation of data required. The regular updating of reporting guidelines represents an important learning process aimed at improving the accuracy, comparability, transparency and completeness of information submitted by Parties.

The national communications of Annex I Parties are compiled and synthesized by the secretariat for presentation to the COP. They are also subject to in-depth review by a small group of experts, coordinated by the secretariat, which typically includes a visit to the country concerned. The purpose of the expert reviews is to provide a technical assessment of the national communications, ensuring the accuracy and completeness of the information. Technical reviews of annual greenhouse gas inventories were introduced in 2002. Once again, such technical reviews are designed to help improve the quality of data in emission inventories. This is especially important in the context of the 'flexibility mechanisms' of the Kyoto Protocol discussed below, whose effective functioning depends on the availability of sound emissions data.

The climate change regime enjoys a relatively good reporting record, although the submission deadlines are not always respected. The updating and improvement of the reporting guidelines have helped Parties to submit increasingly consistent and complete data, although challenges remain. Data on the land-use change and forestry sector, for example, is still incomplete or inconsistent for many Parties, which has complicated the negotiations on carbon 'sinks' under the Kyoto Protocol. Lack of capacity and resources in some EITs means that these face particular problems, especially in submitting annual greenhouse gas inventories according to the agreed guidelines. Developing countries have also expressed concern at reporting by donor countries on financial assistance and technology transfer, arguing that this is insufficient and not presented in a transparent manner.

Reporting and review by non-Annex I Parties

The submission rate of national communications by non-Annex I Parties has been slower than for Annex I Parties, as the requisite time frame is looser and the commitment to report is contingent upon receipt of financial assistance. The submission of national communications was also delayed by political struggles over their appropriate content, with industrialized countries wanting to see more detailed reporting on mitigation actions than did developing countries. This prevented agreement on reporting guidelines until COP 2 in 1996. At the time of writing, 111 non-Annex I Parties had submitted their first national communications, in varying degrees of detail, but some of the largest aggregate emitters, including China, India and Brazil, were not among them.[8] No deadline has yet been set for second national communications, although a small number of Parties have started to prepare these. Developing countries are not required to submit separate annual inventories.

The national communications of non-Annex I Parties are compiled and synthesized by the secretariat, in the same way as Annex I Party communications, but are not subject to in-depth review. This again was the subject of conflict between

Annex I and non-Annex I Parties, with industrialized countries arguing that developing country reports should be subject to a review process akin to their own, and developing countries fearing that this was not appropriate given their more limited capacities, and might open up new avenues for conditionality in the granting of financial assistance. Instead of an in-depth review process, a 'Consultative Group of Experts' was set up in 1999 to help improve the quality of non-Annex I Party national communications.

Although almost all eligible Parties have now received funding, a number of developing countries have experienced long delays in obtaining financial assistance from the GEF, and several have faced technical problems in compiling data. Still more, especially the largest emitters, are wary of submitting their national communications for fear that these might be used by industrialized countries to place pressure on them to take on specific emission commitments. Although important progress has been made in this area, ten years after the adoption of the Convention, officially sanctioned data on emissions in non-Annex I Parties, including the largest emitters among them, remains sparse.

Activities implemented jointly

A particularly controversial issue during the negotiations on the Convention was the possibility of 'joint implementation', whereby one Party could implement a climate change mitigation project in the territory of another Party, and gain credit for the resulting emission reduction to offset against its own emission target. Debates over joint implementation highlight the often-contrasting world views of industrialized and developing countries revolving around the concepts of efficiency and equity in the context of climate change. Industrialized countries have supported joint implementation on the grounds of efficiency, arguing that it makes sense to reduce emissions wherever it is cheapest to do so, usually in the less efficient developing countries or EITs. Joint implementation, however, has been opposed on equity grounds by developing countries, who fear that it might allow industrialized countries to avoid taking action at home and to poach the cheapest emission reduction opportunities in developing countries (the 'low hanging fruits'), as well as leading to the imposition of commitments on them 'through the back door'. Due to the opposition of developing countries, only veiled references to the possibility of joint implementation appear in the Convention.

At COP 1, a compromise was reached to launch a pilot phase of so-called 'activities implemented jointly' (AIJ) (a change in name was needed given the sensitivities stirred up by the term 'joint implementation'), whereby Parties could implement emission mitigation projects in the territories of other Parties, including developing countries, but without gaining credit for the emissions reduced. The pilot phase, due to conclude by 2000, was intended simply to build up experience in conducting such projects through 'learning by doing'.

By June 2002, 157 AIJ projects had been communicated to the secretariat, engaging just under a third of Parties to the Convention, either as investors or as host countries.[9] While the absence of crediting may have discouraged business involvement (in 1999, only 8 per cent of projects were being financed through the private sector[10]), interest in the AIJ pilot phase has steadily grown, especially since the adoption of the Kyoto Protocol. Most projects are in the renewable energy and energy efficiency sectors, although the largest projects involve forest preservation, reforestation or restoration. An important political challenge has been regional imbalance. Although the situation has improved, over 80 per cent of projects are still concentrated in the EITs (in particular the Baltic states) and Latin America and the Caribbean.

Experiences from the AIJ pilot phase (e.g. in establishing baselines) have fed into negotiations on the rules for the project-based flexibility mechanisms under the Kyoto Protocol, that is, the clean development mechanism and joint implementation with EITs, which are based on the same efficiency rationale as AIJ and allow crediting. The fate of the pilot phase, which was extended by COP 5 in 1999, and ongoing projects under it, is closely linked to that of the Protocol's project-based flexibility mechanisms. Once these mechanisms are operational, there will be little interest in AIJ with its absence of crediting. In this regard, an issue that remains unresolved is the extent to which existing AIJ projects will be allowed to convert into credit-generating projects under the Protocol's fully-fledged flexibility mechanisms.

The Kyoto Protocol

While the first track of regime development focused on elaborating a detailed rulebook for the Convention, it was clear that the commitments within the Convention would not be sufficient to attain its ultimate objective. At COP 1 in 1995, Parties therefore launched a new round of negotiations to agree on stronger commitments for industrialized countries. In accordance with the principle of equity and industrialized country leadership, Parties eventually agreed that no new commitments would be set for developing countries as part of this negotiating round. Highly complex and contentious negotiations took place over two and a half years, eventually resulting in the adoption of the Kyoto Protocol on 11 December 1997.

The Kyoto Protocol

Emission targets

The Kyoto Protocol sets a collective emission reduction target for all Annex I Parties of 'at least' 5 per cent by 2008–2012 from the baseline 1990 (Article 3.1). This collective target is divided up among the Annex I Parties, who each have their own individual commitment listed in the Protocol's Annex B (see Table 3.2). The individual emission targets were decided in Kyoto by each Annex I Party choosing the target it felt able to commit to, in the face of varying degrees of pressure from other Parties. Under provisions known as the 'bubble', the EU is permitted to redistribute its 8 per cent reduction target as it wishes among its member states (Article 4). Importantly, the Protocol's individual emission commitments, unlike those in the Convention, are legally-binding; the Protocol states that Annex I Parties 'shall ensure' that they do not exceed their targets, indicating obligation to achieve the targets and not just to try.

The Protocol's targets are modest compared to some of those proposed during the negotiations (e.g. −15 per cent by 2010 by the EU; −20 per cent by 2005 by AOSIS) and, by themselves, will not stabilize the concentration of greenhouse gases in the atmosphere at anything close to a safe level. Nevertheless, if implemented, the Kyoto Protocol's emission targets would represent a historic reversal of the persistent upward trend in emissions in most of the industrialized world since the industrial revolution, and would demonstrate the leadership needed to induce developing countries to take on their own emission targets. For many industrialized countries, whose emissions have continued to rise since the adoption of the Convention, significant effort will be required to meet their Kyoto Protocol targets. The main exception are the EITs, especially the Russian

Table 3.2 Individual emission targets for Annex I Parties under the Kyoto Protocol

Target (%)	Parties
−8	EU-15, Bulgaria, Czech Republic, Estonia, Latvia, Liechtenstein, Lithuania, Monaco, Romania, Slovakia, Slovenia, Switzerland
−7	US
−6	Japan, Canada, Hungary, Poland
−5	Croatia
0	New Zealand, Russian Federation, Ukraine
+1	Norway
+8	Australia
+10	Iceland

Note

Belarus and Turkey, which are included in Annex I to the Convention, do not have emission targets under the Kyoto Protocol as they were not Parties to the Convention when the Protocol was negotiated and adopted.

Federation and Ukraine whose targets simply to stabilize emissions at 1990 levels are widely acknowledged as very generous, given that their emissions declined so dramatically in the early 1990s, by over 35 per cent from 1990 to 1998 in the case of the Russian Federation.[11]

Flexibilities

The level of effort required of Annex I Parties to meet their emission targets, and therefore the costs of doing so, is eased by the many flexibilities in the Kyoto Protocol, in terms of time, content and place.

In terms of time, the Protocol defines a target period (known as a 'commitment period') rather than a single date, thus allowing fluctuations in emissions due to uncontrollable factors such as the weather or economic cycles to be smoothed out. The Protocol also permits 'banking' (Article 3.13), whereby a country achieving greater emission reductions than required during the first commitment period can carry over the excess reduction to offset against its target in the second period.

In terms of content, the Protocol's targets cover the six main greenhouse gases – CO_2, methane (CH_4), nitrous oxide (N_2O), hydrofluorocarbons (HFCs), perfluorocarbons (PFCs) and sulphur hexafluoride (SF_6). Parties may choose to use a baseline of 1995 for the latter three gases, in recognition of the great rise in their use since 1990 (Article 3.8); HFC emissions, for example, increased by 40 per cent between 1990 and 1995 in Annex I Parties due to their use as replacements for ozone-depleting substances controlled by the Montreal Protocol.[12] Parties may also count certain activities in the land use, land-use change and forestry sector that emit or sequester CO_2 against their targets. The Protocol limits such carbon 'sink' activities to afforestation, reforestation and deforestation, but states that additional activities may be added to this list (Article 3.3, 3.4), as indeed they were, by the Marrakech Accords (see below).

In terms of place, the Kyoto Protocol defines three unprecedented 'flexibility mechanisms' that essentially allow Annex I Parties to claim credit for emissions that they reduce in any part of the world. Joint implementation[13] under Article 6 allows Annex I Parties to implement emission reducing projects in the territories of other Annex I Parties and acquire the resulting 'emission reduction units' to offset against their own targets. Such joint implementation is likely to take place principally between OECD countries and EITs, where emission reduction opportunities are often cheaper.

The clean development mechanism (CDM) under Article 12 sets up a more elaborate system for similar projects among Annex I Parties and developing countries. The CDM is supervised by an 'executive board', and 'operational entities' (independent companies or other organizations) certify emission reductions achieved by projects. Part of the 'share of the proceeds' from the CDM will go to meet its administrative expenses and to assist particularly vulnerable developing countries in adapting to climate change. This more elaborate mechanism was devised in line with G77 and China demands that there be intergovernmental oversight as regards what amounts to the joint implementation with developing countries that they had always resisted. More stringent monitoring and verification is also needed given that developing countries do not have emission targets themselves and often lack basic emissions data.

The third flexibility mechanism is emissions trading (Article 17), whereby Parties who are able to reduce emissions at less cost may sell their excess emissions allowance to Annex I Parties who find it more difficult to meet their targets. For all three mechanisms, the Protocol stipulates that their use should be 'supplemental'[14] to domestic action, a concession to those groups of Parties, notably the EU and the G77 and China, who sought to ensure that the flexibility mechanisms would not allow Annex I Parties to avoid taking emission reduction action at home.

Credibility mechanisms, institutions and review mechanisms

Accompanying the flexibility mechanisms, the Protocol defines a set of 'credibility mechanisms' aimed at securing its environmental integrity. These credibility mechanisms include more stringent reporting and review requirements than in the Convention (Articles 5, 7, 8), as well as mechanisms and procedures to address cases of non-compliance with the Protocol's provisions (Article 18).

In terms of its institutions, the COP to the Convention will serve as the 'meeting of the Parties' to the Kyoto Protocol when it enters into force, and the Kyoto Protocol will also make use of the Convention's existing subsidiary bodies and secretariat.

Like the Convention, the Kyoto Protocol includes a series of review mechanisms to ensure that its commitments can be tightened in the future and expanded to a wider group of countries. Negotiations on emission targets for Annex I Parties for the second commitment period, presumably 2013–2017, must start in 2005 (Article 3.9). In addition, a comprehensive review of the Protocol is scheduled for the second session of the COP serving as the meeting of the Parties to the Protocol, probably around 2006, depending on when the Protocol enters into force (Article 9). The combination of these two review mechanisms provides an opportunity to negotiate emission targets for developing countries for future commitment periods, while also strengthening the commitments of Annex I Parties. In tandem with the Convention, the Protocol thus provides the foundation for a long-term response to climate change.

The Kyoto Protocol rulebook

The Kyoto Protocol was signed by 84 countries, including all but two Annex I Parties (Hungary and Iceland), indicating their intent to ratify. The Protocol will enter into force when it has been ratified by 55 countries, including Annex I Parties accounting for 55 per cent of CO_2 emissions in 1990 from that group. At the time of writing, 120 countries had ratified the Protocol.[15]

The negotiations on the Kyoto Protocol rulebook were conducted as a package with those on the Convention discussed above, culminating with the adoption of the 2001 Marrakech Accords. They were characterized by a tension between the need, on the one hand, to secure the environmental integrity of the Kyoto Protocol, and, on the other, to minimize costs in reducing emissions. Environmental integrity was emphasized in particular by the EU, which called for a 'concrete ceiling' to be placed on the use of the mechanisms and for limitations on the eligibility of carbon sink activities. Minimizing costs, in turn, was advocated most strongly by the so-called 'Umbrella Group',[16] which argued for unrestrained use of the mechanisms and a more expansive eligibility of carbon sinks. The Marrakech Accords represent an attempt to reconcile these two sets of concerns.

The flexibility mechanisms

Under the Marrakech Accords, no quantified limits will be imposed on the use of the flexibility mechanisms. Instead, Annex I Parties must provide information in their national communications demonstrating that their use of the mechanisms is 'supplemental to domestic action' and constitutes 'a significant element' of their efforts in meeting their commitments. This information may be assessed by the Protocol's compliance committee, but only by its non-punitive facilitative branch (see below). Any Party that is in compliance with its reporting commitments and has accepted the Protocol's compliance system will be eligible to participate in the mechanisms.

Regarding projects under joint implementation and the CDM, the Marrakech Accords specify that Parties 'are to refrain' from using nuclear power, while afforestation and reforestation projects are the only carbon sink activities allowed under the CDM for the first commitment period, and even then subject to further guidelines adopted at COP9 in 2003. Simplified procedures will be put in place to promote small-scale renewable energy and energy efficiency projects under the CDM. The CDM is already operational, with the first Executive board starting work in 2001.

On emissions trading, in order to address the danger that some countries might over-sell their emissions allowance and then be unable to meet their own targets, the Marrakech Accords require Annex I Parties to keep 90 per cent of their emissions allowance for the commitment period (or five times their most recently reviewed emission inventory, whichever is the lowest) in a 'commitment period reserve' that cannot be traded.

Land use, land-use change and forestry (carbon sinks)

The main concern in negotiations on the rules governing carbon sinks under the Protocol was to allow Annex I Parties to gain credit for genuine carbon sequestration while making sure that credit was not granted for naturally-occurring sequestration, and to address the great uncertainties involved in the land use, land-use change and forestry sector, again to avoid generating fictitious emission credits.

In essence, the Marrakech Accords allow Annex I Parties to also count forest management, cropland management, grazing land management and revegetation activities against their emission targets, in addition to the afforestation, reforestation and deforestation already included under the Kyoto Protocol, so long as these activities are human-induced and have taken place since 1990. The amount of credit that can be claimed through forest management is subject to individual limits, with each country given a cap that is listed in a table.

Compliance

The compliance system set forth in the Marrakech Accords consists of a 'Compliance Committee', itself composed of two branches – a facilitative branch and an enforcement branch. As their names suggest, the facilitative branch aims to provide advice and assistance to Parties, whereas the enforcement branch has the power to impose penalties on Parties not meeting their commitments. Consequences for not complying with emission targets include a requirement to make additional emission reductions in the second commitment period (at a rate of three units to each unit of excess emissions), development of a 'compliance action plan', and suspension of eligibility to sell emission credits under emissions trading. While the climate regime's compliance system cannot impose any 'hard' penalties (such as sanctions or fines), it promises to have considerably more 'bite' than compliance measures in force in many other environmental regimes.

Looking ahead: from negotiation to implementation

The adoption of the Marrakech Accords marked an important milestone in the development of the climate change regime. It forged a considerably more complex and elaborate regime and, by setting out the detailed rules of the Kyoto Protocol, provided the basis for its eventual implementation upon entry into force.

The US withdrawal from the Kyoto Protocol process (although not from the Convention) certainly throws a dark shadow over the climate change regime. It is clear that the current US Administration will not ratify the Protocol. However, its withdrawal seems to have galvanized almost all of the remaining 185 Parties to the Convention in support of the Kyoto Protocol, rather than turning them against it. Indeed, the ratification and entry into force of the Kyoto Protocol is almost certainly the most promising strategy for coaxing the US back on board, perhaps in time for negotiations on second period commitments, which may include developing countries and thus overcome one of the major US objections to the Protocol. At the time of writing, however, this strategy was being thrown into question by uncertainty over the future of the Protocol, in the light of vacillation by the Russian Federation over its ratification, which is needed for entry into force.

Although negotiations will continue in the climate change regime, the adoption of the Marrakech Accords signals a shift in its focus towards implementation. As this chapter has shown, the regime has, to date, been very successful in its rule-making and institutional development. Greenhouse gas emissions in most Annex I Parties, however, have continued to rise. Although Annex I Parties as a whole did meet the collective aim of the Convention to return their emissions to 1990 levels by 2000, this was due mostly, but not entirely, to the dramatic collapse of emissions in the EITs. Emissions in the EITs as a whole fell by 37 per cent, while emissions in the OECD countries taken together rose by 8 per cent. Germany and the UK were among the handful of European countries enjoying a downward trend, while Australia and the US, the two countries who have declared that they do not intend to ratify the Kyoto Protocol, experienced rises of 14 per cent and 18 per cent respectively.[17] Many countries have started to implement climate change mitigation policies, including innovative steps such as national/regional emission trading programmes,[18] but these will need to be strengthened in order to make a real difference to greenhouse gas emissions.

Up to now, there has not been a set of legally-binding targets to send a clear signal to governments, industry and the public that business as usual must change, and to provide incentives to trigger that change. If the Kyoto Protocol enters into force, however, such a set of legally-binding targets will be in place, along with an elaborate architecture of institutions and mechanisms to help countries meet those targets at the lowest possible cost. The climate change regime has scored important successes in negotiation and rule-making in its first ten years; as it now moves into its second decade, it will need to translate these advances into concrete implementation.

Notes

1 The existence of the natural greenhouse effect was postulated by Jean Baptiste Fourier as far back as 1827, while awareness of the possible effects on the climate of

fossil fuel consumption can be dated to Svante Arrhenius, publishing in the late nineteenth and early twentieth centuries.

2 See, for example, IPCC (2001).
3 See IPCC (1996, p.94).
4 See IEA (2000).
5 See IPCC (2000).
6 For the full text of the Marrakech Accords, see FCCC/CP/2001/13 and Add.1-4, Report of the Conference of the Parties on its seventh session.
7 FCCC/CP/2002/4, Report of the Global Environment Facility.
8 An updated list of non-Annex I Party national communications submitted to the secretariat can be found at www.unfccc.int/resource/natcom/index.html.
9 FCCC/SBSTA/2002/8, sixth synthesis report.
10 FCCC/SB/1999/5, fourth synthesis report.
11 FCCC/SBI/2000/11, Table B.1, Report on national greenhouse gas inventory data from Annex I Parties for 1990–1998.
12 FCCC/SBI/2000/INF.13, Figure 6, basic inventory data for Annex I Parties, 1990–1998.
13 The political sensitivity surrounding the term means it does not appear anywhere in the Protocol although it is commonly used as a convenient shorthand.
14 The language is different in the case of the CDM, which states that CDM projects can only be used to meet 'part of' the commitments of Annex I Parties.
15 For an update on ratifications, see www.unfccc.int/resource/convkp.html.
16 The Umbrella Group includes Australia, Canada, Iceland, Japan, New Zealand, Norway, the Russian Federation, Ukraine and the US.
17 For more on emission trends, see compilation and synthesis of third national communications, FCCC/SBI/2003/7 and addenda.
18 See, for example, articles in *Climate Policy*, Vol. 3, issue 1.

Bibliography

Agrawala, S. (1998) 'Structural and process history of the Intergovernmental Panel on Climate Change', *Climatic Change* 39:621–642.

Bodansky, D. (1993) 'The United Nations Framework Convention on Climate Change: a commentary', *The Yale Journal of International Law* 18:451–558.

Grubb, M., Vrolijk, C. and Brack, D. (1999) *The Kyoto Protocol: A Guide and Assessment*, London: Earthscan.

Gupta, J. (1997) *The Climate Change Convention and Developing Countries: From Conflict to Consensus?* Dordrecht: Kluwer Academic Press.

Hey, E. (2001) 'The climate change regime: an enviro-economic problem and international administrative law in the making', *International Environmental Agreements: Politics, Law and Economics* 1:75–100.

Intergovernmental Panel on Climate Change (2001) *Climate Change 2001: Synthesis Report*, Cambridge: Cambridge University Press.

Intergovernmental Panel on Climate Change (2000) *Land Use, Land-Use Change, and Forestry*, Cambridge: Cambridge University Press.

Intergovernmental Panel on Climate Change (1996) *Climate Change 1995: Economic and Social Dimensions of Climate Change*, Cambridge: Cambridge University Press.

International Energy Agency (2000) *Key World Energy Statistics*, Paris: OECD/IEA.

Mintzer, I.M. and Leonard, J.A. (eds) (1994) *Negotiating Climate Change: The Inside Story of the Rio Convention*, Cambridge: Cambridge University Press

Oberthür, S. and Ott, H. (1999) *The Kyoto Protocol: International Climate Policy for the 21st Century*, Berlin: Springer Verlag.

Review of European Community and International Environmental Law (2001), Focus on: Climate change. Vol. 7, No. 2.

Yamin, F. and Depledge, J. (2004) *The Climate Change Regime: Rules, Institutions and Procedures*, Cambridge: Cambridge University Press.

www.unfccc.int for all official documents on the climate change process.

www.iisd.ca/linkages for reports on negotiating sessions.

Climate Policy (www.climatepolicy.com) for analysis of climate change issues.

4 Climate protection

What insight can economics offer?

Jason Shogren

Introduction

Scientists warn our daily actions are affecting the climate around the globe – to humanity's detriment. They warn greenhouse gases (GHGs) emitted by converting land, raising livestock, and burning fossil fuels might be changing the planet's climate, and the consequences could be devastating. Their case rests on connecting two trends. The Earth has warmed 0.5 degrees C over the past century; and atmospheric concentrations of greenhouse gases have increased by 30 per cent over the past two centuries (see Chapter 2). The Intergovernmental Panel on Climate Change perceived enough correlation to conclude humanity is the likely culprit for current and future climate change (IPCC 2001b). As a consequence, many scientists and policy makers continue to advocate for a worldwide reductions in greenhouse gas emissions to reduce the risks to human and environmental health posed by unprecedented carbon concentrations. In international conferences held over the past five years, nations have tried to flesh out the details of who should, and how to, reduce GHG emissions.

The Kyoto Protocol is the standard agreement thus far (see Chapters 3 and 5). The Protocol requires leading industrialized countries to reduce their greenhouse gas emissions by an average of 5 per cent below 1990 levels by 2008–2012. These reductions are severe relative to current GHG emission rates and will be costly to achieve (e.g. Nordhaus and Boyer 1998). Since emissions reductions do not come for free, the desire to find cost-effective policy options has made climate protection an economic issue, not just a natural science issue. Both the demand for and supply of economic insight into effective climate protection strategy has grown steadily since over the last decade and shows no sign of abating (e.g. Kane 1996). Numerous economics studies supporting or challenging alternative policy options for slowing climate change have been undertaken by the United Nations, industrial nations like the United States, Japan, the European Union, developing nations like China and India, and non-governmental organizations. Protecting the climate reduces potential risks to people and the environment, and economics offers a unique perspective to better understand such protection. Economics address the consequences of policy actions that would imply restrictions that could touch the lives of everyone on the planet. Finally, the nations of the world are currently engaged in negotiations on policy targets and measures for developed and developing countries: these negotiations would benefit from economics to help frame the debate over the stringency and flexibility of policy options (Bohm 1998; Barrett 2003).

This chapter discusses what insight economics can offer policy makers in the debate over rational climate protection policy. We focus on six points:

1   defining climate change as a market failure;
2   framing climate protection by its costs and benefits;
3   identifying the set of mitigation and adaptation strategies societies can use to reduce risks;
4   designing effective climate policy instruments (e.g. taxes and tradable permits);
5   rationalizing international architecture;
6   addressing the political economy at work behind domestic and international climate policy negotiations.

We now briefly consider each in turn.[1]

Insight one: defining market failure

Climate change is a global public bad, in which both physical and economic actions and their feedbacks determine potential risks to humans and the environment. Economics makes precise the exact nature of why the market system fails to provide the socially desirable level of climate protection. Global public 'bads' exist when no market has emerged to provide protection because everyone benefits from one person's actions. Economics treats climate change as the classic example of a global stock externality – the flow of greenhouse gas (GHG) emissions accumulates into a global carbon stock that poses risks to humanity around the globe. These GHGs remain in the atmosphere for hundreds of years. GHG concentrations reflect long-term emissions; changes in any one year's emissions have a trivial effect on current overall concentrations. Even significant reductions in emissions made today will not be evident in atmospheric concentrations for decades or more. Economics asks a person to distinguish a *stock* from a *flow* pollutant. Stock pollution is concentration – the accumulated carbon in the atmosphere, like water in a bathtub. Flow pollution is emissions – the annual rate of emission, like water flowing into the tub.

Because risk comes from the total stock of carbon, policies should attempt to focus on projected concentration levels. Greenhouse gases remain in the atmosphere decades before they dissipate, so different rates of emission could generate the same concentrations by a given year. Policy makers have options regarding how fast and how hard they hit a given concentration target. People usually have judged the benefits of climate protection as the incremental reduction in human and environmental risks compared to the business as usual (BAU) baseline. Under BAU, modellers have estimated that carbon concentrations might be expected to double pre-industrial levels within the next half century, with mean temperatures predicted to rise by about 1 degree C by 2050, and 2.5 degrees by 2100. With current international policy suggestions, concentrations are still likely to double, with temperatures increasing by about 0.1 degrees C by 2050 and 0.5 degrees by 2100.

The public good nature of climate change implies it is the sum of all the carbon emitted around the globe that matters – all climate protection is non-rival and non-excludable. This is crucial because the major emitters of greenhouse gases will change over the next few decades. Today the industrialized world accounts for the largest portion of emissions, but soon developing countries such as China and India will be the world's largest emitters. International cooperation is key for effective abatement. But achieving meaningful international coopera-tion is a challenge. Even though nations have a common interest in climate change, many are reluctant to reduce carbon voluntarily. They realize they cannot be prevented from 'free riding': enjoying a better climate whether they contribute to it or not. Free riding is complicated further in developing countries where clean water and a stable food supply seem more urgent than climate change policy (see Chapter 11).

Insight two: confronting costs and benefits

For better public policy decisions, it is useful to evaluate the benefits and costs of climate protection actions or inaction is unavoidable. Economics frames climate protection in benefit-cost terms because scarce resources – natural, physical and human – make it so. By costs, we mean what society forgoes to pursue climate policy. By benefits, we mean the gains from reducing climate change risks by lowering emissions or by enhancing the capacity for adaptation (see e.g. Sohngen and Mendelsohn 1997). Benefits and costs assessment provides policy makers with data to make more informed decisions in setting the stringency of a mitiga-tion policy and deciding how much adaptation infrastructure to create (Chapter 7 takes this up in more detail). Some critics worry that economic benefit-cost analysis might downplay the need for climate protection. But in practice, decision makers use benefit-cost analysis in combination with other concerns about equity and fairness. Decision makers also bring their own judgments about the rele-vance, credibility and robustness of benefit and cost information and about the appropriate degree of climate change and other risks that society should bear.

The argument for considering benefits and costs is that policy deliberations are better informed if good economic analysis is provided.

The potential benefits from climate protection involves estimating what is avoided – more severe weather patterns, hobbled ecosystems, less biodiversity, less potable water, loss of coastal areas, rises in mean temperature, more infectious diseases such as malaria and cholera. Climate change might actually benefit agriculture and forestry with longer growing seasons and more fertilization. These gains (or losses) can be categorized into four broad sets of increasing difficulty to quantify: the avoided losses to market goods and services, non-market goods, catastrophes, and ancillary effects from less use of fossil fuels (e.g. less air pollution).

Researchers have estimated the impact on Gross World Product from climate change at around 1 or 2 per cent (see Shogren 1999). Even if we include the potential non-market damages, the market and non-market benefits might be at most about 2 per cent of GDP. These impacts are neither trivial nor likely to cause the next global depression. The most significant affect the benefits of protection would be to prevent a sudden catastrophe like a structural change in ocean currents or the melting of the Western Antarctic ice sheet that people cannot adapt to with enough speed.

Estimates of climate protection costs range from modest – 0.5 per cent loss of global GDP, to an 'economic disarmament' – 3 per cent of GDP. For example, the Clinton Administration estimated the costs to the US to meet current emission targets are 'likely to be modest' if reductions are efficiently pursued with domestic and international emissions trading, joint implementation, and the Clean Development Mechanism (a system in which developed nations can buy the carbon reductions in developing nations). By modest, the report means an annual GDP drop of less than 0.5 per cent (roughly US$10 billion dollars); no expected negative effect on the trade deficit; increased gasoline prices of about 5 per cent; lower electricity rates; and no major impacts on the employment rate. But other estimates suggest that the US GDP could take an annual hit of nearly 3 per cent, the trade deficit would increase by billions of dollars; gasoline prices would increase by 50 per cent; electricity prices would nearly double; and two million US jobs would disappear. The net global costs have been estimated at over US$700 billion, with the US bearing about two-thirds of those costs.

The benefits and costs of international cooperation depend on three key elements that underlie climate protection: the real risk of a catastrophe, the degree of flexibility and the origins of technological advance. If one believes catastrophe is imminent, emission reductions cannot come soon enough. If you do not, it is hard to justify the likely costs of emission targets without global emission trading. The degree of flexibility affects costs. Flexibility is determined by the emission trading system, the number of nations participating and whether carbon sinks are included. A stringent, inflexible carbon policy will induce greater economic burden than a loose, flexible policy, since more flexibility allows firms greater agility to search out the lowest-cost alternatives. Estimates suggest that any agreement without the flexibility provided by trading will at least double the costs.

Economic theory has also addressed the idea that the costs of climate protection might be amplified by the existing tax system (for example, Goulder 1995). Labour and capital taxes distort behaviour because they reduce employment and investment levels below what they would have been otherwise. If we add on a carbon tax that discourages consumption and production, we further reduce employment and investment, which then exacerbates the labour and capital tax distortions, maybe by as much as 400 per cent. One could reduce these extra costs by channelling the revenue from the carbon tax, if any existed, to reduce the labour and capital taxes.

The costs of climate protection also depend on the creation, adoption and diffusion of new low-carbon technologies. Engineers argue that many technologies exist today that would reduce emissions at low to no extra costs, e.g. 'no regret' technologies. Economists argue that while these technologies might exist, people will not adopt them if they are too pricey or if other factors feature in their choice beside low-carbon output. Even if new technologies are available, people do not switch unless a price change induces them to switch. People behave as if their time horizons are short, perhaps reflecting their uncertainty about future energy prices and the reliability of the technology. The high initial investment costs also slow down adoption, e.g. replacing all the lights in your house at once with low-energy bulbs.

Regarding the question of ancillary benefits note that reducing carbon emissions is an activity with joint products: protection from climate change *and* reduced emissions of local air pollutants (see e.g. Lutter and Shogren 2002). The value of one product, reduced emissions of local air pollutants, varies with the stringency and nature of other local pollution control measures. Optimal controls on carbon emissions also depend on such measures. As a result, the optimal geographic distribution of carbon emissions reductions cannot be determined by international markets for carbon emissions permits because these generally reflect only the market cost of reducing carbon, not the extent or value of the ancillary emissions reductions. The size of ancillary benefits depends critically on the flexibility and stringency of local air pollution regulations and international emission trading. In general, international carbon emission trading ignores the ancillary benefits that might arise from local pollutant emissions. Moreover, departures from optimality in local pollution control imply that restricting emissions trading can actually increase the welfare of some countries. And since local air pollution policies in the US appear to have marginal costs many times greater than marginal benefits, the optimal tariff on carbon permit imported into the US, if one wants to count ancillary benefits, could be hundreds of dollars.

Insight three: identifying risk reduction strategies

People can and will protect themselves from the risks posed by climate change through private and collective mitigation, adaptation and insurance markets. They work collectively to mitigate climate risk by curtailing greenhouse gas emission to lower the likelihood that bad states of nature occur; they adapt to climate risk by changing production and consumption decisions to reduce the severity of a bad state if it does occur; they insure themselves against financial loss due to gradual and, sometimes, catastrophic changes. Mitigation, adaptation and insurance jointly determine the degree of climate risks and the costs to reduce these risks.[2] And since people have some liberty to adapt and insure on their own, a decision maker should consider these other responses when choosing the optimal degree of public mitigation in some international treaty. Otherwise, policy actions will be more expensive than need be with no additional reduction in climate risk.

Decision makers recognize that adaptation affects the costs and benefits of mitigation, but this obvious point has been neglected in actual policy-making. Following from the Rio agreement and the Framework Convention on Climate Change, international climate policy has been pursed sequentially, and separate consideration of mitigation and adaptation has pervaded most thinking at top levels of decision-making; it is also reflected in research budgets and agendas (USOSTP 1999). This separation has persisted because climate change policy is fragmented – the focus has been on mitigation in the context of climate and adaptation in the context of natural hazards. The Kyoto Protocol, for example, is almost all mitigation, with limited adaptation. The signatories focus on mitigation targets and timetables without acknowledging how adaptation can affect these emission reduction efforts. But many rational decision makers keep repeating, at least informally, that a mitigation-only approach like Kyoto limits our options. Effective climate protection needs to use an integrated portfolio of mitigation *and* adaptation strategies.

Economic theory can formalize the mitigation-adaptation issue following the literature on the theory of endogenous risk.[3] Endogenous risk implies that nations can select its level of climate risk reduction through a mix of mitigation, adaptation and insurance markets. In economic theory, mitigation is commonly referred to as self-protection, and adaptation is called self-insurance (Ehrlich and Becker 1972). The theory provides a systematic framework to help organize how we think about the optimal portfolio of mitigation and adaptation; how this mix of strategies interacts across different sectors and regions; and how new information about climate variability, short- and long-term, affect this mix. Similar to integrated assessment modelling, careful consideration of endogenous risk necessarily engages cross-disciplinary communications because it challenges the traditional division of labour in the assessment and management of climate risk.

Standard practice places risk assessment in the domain of the natural sciences, and risk management in the domain of the social sciences. But when people adapt, they affect the efficacy of mitigation, and thus influence risk. Risk assessment necessarily involves social sciences.

Economics has contributed insight into understanding decisions to reduce climate change risk. Some researchers have explored a range of options that include both mitigation and adaptation responses (e.g. Nordhaus 1994). Integrated modelling efforts also have included adaptation components in the systems under study (e.g. Weyant and Hill 1999). Sectoral work in agriculture, forestry and coastal areas has looked at mitigation and adaptation strategies, sometimes identifying direct interactions (Rayner and Malone 1998). Overall, the integrated assessment literature has moved beyond the risk assessment-management bifurcation. These models portray future climate risks as dependent on the time path of mitigation. Integrated modellers have long argued that effective risk reduction strategies should address the optimal mix of adaptation and mitigation (e.g. Schelling 1992).

Endogenous risk is a formal organizing framework to link risk reduction strategies like mitigation, adaptation and insurance in modelling climate risk. The model allows researchers to gain insight into key interdependencies between production of mitigation and adaptation that occur both in time and space. The framework suggests which information on unmeasured empirical links might be most valuable to decision makers in the future. Integrative modelling can provide reasonable guideposts to better understand behaviour and direct policy research. The international community has and continues to invest enormous resources into understanding options to reduce risk from climate change. Assessments by the Intergovernmental Panel on Climate Change and discussions throughout the negotiations on the Framework Convention on Climate Change bear witness to the substantial efforts being expended to understand mitigation and adaptation options. These efforts can benefit from an economic framework that organizes one's thinking about an approach that links these two key policy strategies.

Insight four: creating economic incentives

Economics can show how to create explicit incentives to deliver cost-effective climate protection. Climate protection policies reflect the trade-off between the stringency of a target and the flexibility to meet the goal. Different policy tools inflate or attenuate the costs of hitting any given target. Inflexible policies inflate costs without additional reductions in climate risk; flexible policies lower the costs. Economic incentives can lower costs because they create a *market price* for carbon, which is otherwise treated as a free good (see for instance Fisher *et al.* 1996). This price creates tangible financial reasons to reduce carbon emissions and provides the means to do so at low cost. Taxes and tradable permit trading are two favourite tools that can be used to price carbon emissions (these are both investigated in more detail in Chapter 6). People respond to these new prices by switching to less-carbon-intensive fuels (e.g. natural gas for coal); increasing energy efficiency per unit of output by using less-energy-intensive technologies; adopting technologies to reduce emissions; reducing the production of high-cost, carbon-intensive goods; increasing the sequestration of carbon; and developing and refining new technologies (e.g. renewable energy resources).

Carbon can be taxed indirectly by taxing fossil fuels. Taxing fossil fuels works because their carbon content is easily ascertained, and no viable option for end-of-pipe carbon abatement (for example, scrubbing) currently exists. A fossil fuel tax could be collected in several ways: as a severance tax on domestic fossil fuel output, plus an equal tax on imports; as a tax on primary energy inputs levied on refineries, gas transportation systems, and coal shippers; or as a tax downstream, on consumers of fossil fuels. The more a tax is levied near the producers of fossil fuels, the less carbon leaks out through uncovered activities such as oil field processing. Implementing such a tax would be relatively straightforward in the United States and most other developed countries, given existing tax collection systems, but more challenging in developing countries that have less effective institutions for levying taxes and monitoring behaviour.

Emission trading, first described by Crocker (1966) and Dales (1968), allows regulated emitters to buy emission reduction efforts from other emitters – in effect, contracting other emitters whose abatement costs are less than their own to make reductions for them. Emission markets have several appealing properties over traditional 'command and control' regulation, and chief amongst them is the fact that market outcomes can theoretically result in emission reductions occurring at least cost to society. Domestic trading programmes indicate that realized cost savings could be substantial.

Trading of carbon permits is more complicated than a carbon tax. One has to decide where to assign property rights for carbon: downstream, upstream, or some combination of the two. In principle, a downstream approach encompasses all emissions. In practice, however, everyone who heats their homes with fossil fuel or who drives a car would be required to buy and sell carbon permits. Operating and overseeing such a market would be an administrative nightmare, with huge transactions costs. In contrast, an upstream system would be easier to administer because the number of market actors is smaller. Comprehensive policy would account for imported refined products and domestic fossil energy supplies. Rules for banking and borrowing carbon permits are another key component of a trading system. Banking lowers costs by allowing traders to hedge against risks in emissions patterns, and to smooth out fluctuations in abatement costs over time. Borrowing gives traders more flexibility to respond to unexpected short-term increases in abatement costs, and consequently spreads the financial risk of compliance across time.

In theory, trading carbon can be extended around the globe. Global trading generates mutual gains by allowing low-cost nations to profit from selling permits to high-cost nations. The Kyoto Protocol allows for both carbon trading among the Annex I developed countries and bilateral trading through the Clean Development Mechanism (CDM). Under the CDM, emissions reduction activities in non-capped, non-Annex I nations can generate emission reduction credits for Annex I nations. Annex I trading could involve tying together domestic emissions trading programmes or a project-level approach in which participants can generate emission credits from emission-reducing actions in other Annex I countries (so-called joint implementation). These various endeavours could be organized and financed by Annex I investors, the developing countries themselves, and international third parties.

The exact trading rules matter, especially on how to deal with enforcement and sanctions for nations that shirk on their emission commitments. The critical issue is who should be held liable for overselling permits beyond quotas – the seller or buyer country? Weak under-compliance penalties and ineffective monitoring methods create the incentive for selling nations to oversell permits and shirk on their emission responsibilities due to the magnitude of the potential permit revenues. The broad social goals of climate protection have made buyer liability the preferred alternative. Relatively rich buyer nations are responsible for any shortfalls in emission reductions made by the relatively poorer sellers. The working thesis is that buyer liability will cause greater climate protection, with markets forming due to the gains from trade available and reputation policing market behaviour.[4]

Economics can be used to evaluate the institutional design of such incentive systems like buyer-liability international emission trading. Godby and Shogren (2003) show using experimental economic methods that buyer liability under realistic weak international enforcement leads to the worst possible outcome – less climate protection at greater costs. Weak enforcement levels mimics the reality of international emissions trading, in which potential sanctions on sovereign nations are likely to be puny (e.g. see Cooper 1998). Godby and Shogren found that buyer liability lowers economic efficiency, distorts permit prices and market production patterns. These rules significantly worsen environmental performance through greater non-compliance. Adoption of buyer liability with weak enforcement renders emission trading inadequate by creating less climate protection at greater economic cost.

Insight five: rationalizing international architecture

Economics help make operational a rational coherent international architecture. A climate agreement should be voluntary and self-enforcing – all sovereign parties should have no incentive to deviate unilaterally from the terms of the agreement. But the problem of achieving effective and lasting agreements is that a self-enforcing deal is easiest to find when the stakes are small, or when no other option exists. Nations have a common interest in responding to the risk of climate change, yet many are reluctant to reduce GHG emissions voluntarily. They hesitate because climate change is a global public good – no nation can be prevented from enjoying climate protection, regardless of whether it participates in a treaty. Each nation's incentive to reduce emissions is limited because it cannot be prevented from enjoying the benefits of other nations' efforts. This incentive to free ride reflects the divergence between national actions and global interests.

By free riding, some nations can be better off refusing an agreement. The greater the global net benefits of cooperation, the stronger the incentive to free ride; therefore, a self-enforcing agreement is harder to maintain. A self-enforcing agreement is most easily maintained when the global net benefits are about the same magnitude as no agreement (e.g. see Hoel 1992; Carraro and Siniscalco 1993; Barrett 1994). If self-enforcement is insufficient, signatories who have on-going relationships can try to alleviate free riding on climate change policy by retaliating with threats such as trade sanctions. But the force of linkage and deterrence is blunted in several respects. A nation's incentive not to participate in reducing GHG emissions depends on the balance between short-term gains from abstaining relative to the long-term cost related to punishment. Participating nations must see a gain in actually applying punishment, otherwise their threats of retaliation will not be credible. Credibility problems arise when, for example, retaliation through trade sanctions damages both the enforcer and the free rider. Moreover, because many forms of sanctions exist, nations would need to select a mutually agreeable set of approaches.

Even if a self-enforcing agreement involved only two or three big emitting markets (for example, the United States and the European Union) and many small nations refused to agree, total emissions would probably remain higher than global targets. For their part, many decision makers in industrialized countries worry about the consequences to their economies of reducing emissions while developing countries face no limits. This situation could adversely affect comparative advantages in the industrialized world, whereas leakage of emissions from controlled to uncontrolled countries would limit the environmental effectiveness of a partial agreement. Estimates of this carbon leakage vary from a few per cent to more than one-third of the Annex I reductions, depending on model assumptions regarding substitutability of different countries' outputs and other factors (Weyant and Hill 1999).

A second concern illuminated by game-theoretic models is how to draw developing nations into a climate protection treaty. Developing nations have many pressing needs, such as potable water and stable food supplies, and less financial and technical capacity than rich countries to mitigate or adapt to climate change. These nations have less incentive to agree to a policy that they see as imposing unacceptable costs. The international policy objective is obvious, but elusive: finding incentives to motivate nations with strong and diverse self-interests to move voluntarily towards a collective goal of reduced GHG emissions. Equity is a central element of this issue, because differences in perceptions about what constitutes equitable distributions of effort complicate any agreement. No standard exists for establishing the equity of any particular allocation of GHG control responsibility. Simple rules of thumb, such as allocating responsibility based on equal per capita rights to emit GHGs and allocations that are positively correlated to past and current emissions are unlikely to command broad political support internationally.

Direct side payments through financial or low-cost technical assistance can increase the incentive to join the agreement. Incentive-based climate policies can help by reducing the cost of action for all countries. In particular, both buyers and sellers benefit from trade in emissions permits. Emission trading also allows side payments through the international distribution of national emissions targets. More reluctant countries can be enticed to join with less stringent targets while other countries meet more stringent targets to achieve the same overall result. These points often are lost when critics argue that emissions trading will weaken international agreement because a seller country can fail to meet its domestic target and export 'phoney' emissions permits.

Insight six: clarifying political economics

Economics help clarify the political economic realities underlying the future of climate protection. After inaction during the final years of the Clinton Administration, the Bush Administration officially announced its opposition to Kyoto in 2001. They opposed Kyoto because they believed the costs to meet the targets would be excessive without the global participation of the developing countries. While other nations were coming to terms with the idea that cuts to greenhouse gases had to be made, the US Administration was still trying to understand the Kyoto Protocol's potential impact on their fossil fuel industries. They worried those firms producing fossil fuels like oil would have to follow rules ignored by competitors in developing nations. Across the border in Canada, the Alberta government raised similar fears. Discounting claims of 'corporate blackmailing', Alberta officials argue that industries including oil refineries might choose to invest outside Canada due to the extra risk created by uncertain rules implied by Kyoto ratification. They fear that the extra risk could scare these billion-dollar investments to the Middle East or Venezuela, which would cost jobs in Canada. In 2002, the Bush Administration finally announced its climate policy – a greenhouse gas emission intensity goal. Emission intensity focuses on reducing tonnes of greenhouse gases per million dollars of output (GHG t/$mo).

The Administration's stated target is to reduce the US economy to 151 from 180 GHG t/$mo by 2012, about a 20 per cent improvement. The administration's plan promotes voluntary measures to meet unilateral non-binding target of about 100 million metric tonnes GHG abatement, or less if the economy grows faster than expected – about a 2 per cent rate of improvement in greenhouse gas emissions intensity over the next decade. While proposed policies to make operational the Bush plan are similar to the Clinton Administration's – tax credits, early emissions reduction credits, R&D funding, and voluntary consultations and agreements, the sticking point remains developing country participation. Many developing nations remain uncommitted because they wish to avoid stifling their rapid fossil-fuel-driven economic growth through carbon emissions controls. A Chinese delegate captured the sentiment underlying the opposition: 'what they [developed nations] are doing is luxury emissions, what we are doing is survival emissions'. The Bush administration continues to promote more effort in voluntary actions and carbon sequestration as a least-disruptive-to-the-economy approach to reducing overall carbon concentrations. If President Bush is re-elected in 2004, the current unilateral approach towards climate protection will continue. And even if a Democrat is elected President, the future of Kyoto in the US is unclear given the unanimous 97–0 Byrd-Hagel resolution that requires developing nation participation before the Senate will consider ratification of the Protocol. And while Russia and China have recently announced they have both 'signed' the Protocol, Kyoto's future in the US looks dim by any standard measure of success.

In the political economy of the world community, however, the Kyoto Protocol in particular and climate change protection in general have evolved towards the broader social target of sustainable development and poverty reduction. Climate change policy as revealed by the 2001 Third Assessment Report of the Intergovernmental Panel on Climate Change (IPCC) and the 2002 Earth Summit in Johannesburg focuses in on 'alternative development paths'. Climate change policies will affect and be affected by broader societal objectives aim at development, sustainability and equity. The stated challenge in the IPCC's Third Assessment Report Mitigation Report for addressing climate change is addressing the 'important issue of equity – the extent to which the impacts of climate change or mitigation policies create or exacerbate inequities both within and across nations and regions' (IPCC 2001a). This challenge goes beyond the relatively narrow question of find cost-effective methods to reduce climate risk to broader and normative question of global politics and equity. Climate protection now becomes an explicit political problem, in which policy amounts to a wealth transfer from today's industrial nations to the future generations in the developing nations. The benefits from Kyoto are most likely to accrue to the future generations in developing nations because their economies depend more on favourable climate for agriculture, forestry and fishing.

The open question is whether the Kyoto Protocol, or something like it, is the best tool to accomplish these broader objectives of global equity. In effect, the future of the Kyoto Protocol rests on what Thomas Sowell calls one's choice of vision. People with an unconstrained vision believe we all have an untapped morality buried within waiting to emerge with the right guidance. Solutions like the Kyoto Protocol to solve global ills are primary; the trade-offs involved are secondary. Costs are unfortunate, but not decisive. In contrast, people with a constrained vision weigh ideals against the costs of achieving them. Understanding the benefits and costs help frame the climate change debate by identifying the elements of Kyoto that inflate costs with no movements towards these ideals. This matters because wealth spent here is not spent somewhere else; and with reasonable policy, it is possible to provide more human and environmental health with less wealth. If climate change is about the developed world paying for benefits accruing to future generations in the developing world, other ways exist – more direct ways – than Kyoto or the IPCC.

Concluding remarks

Economics offers insight into effective climate protection. These include showing others how to define the precise nature of market failure, the costs and benefits of action and inaction, to identify the full range of risk reduction strategies, to create economic incentives that will price climate protection, to make operational rational international architecture for providing global climate protection and to identify the underlying currents of political economy within and between nations. Economics searches for methods that balance the costs and benefits of achieving reasonable targets. Economics also helps people assign a price that could induce the developing countries to come on board in a substantive fashion; refine the odds for catastrophe and surprise; and to assess the nature of carbon sequestration to sort out whether the costs of measurement, verification and enforcement exceed the gains. Economics can test bed studies on the feasibility of international and domestic incentives like global emission trading markets; construct real case studies to understand what institution-building exercises work across developed and developing nations; and consider the incentives for technological progress created by different climate policies over the long term.

Overall, the most durable insight from economics is that although it makes sense to invest resources into climate protection, a global catastrophe will have to be exceedingly likely for current policies like the short-term Kyoto Protocol to make sense from a cost-benefit perspective. In the future, economics can add additional knowledge about the key links between the climate-human system including feedbacks; evaluating the empirical scope of the links between mitigation and adaptation most helpful for different levels of risk reduction decisions at the local, national and global level; constructing national damage functions that account explicitly for adaptation; and evaluating the potential for transformation and shift of risks over time and place from climate protection policies.

Notes

1 See Stavins (2001) and Kolstad and Toman (2003) for excellent overviews of the economics of climate change policy.
2 See Wilbanks *et al.* (2003).
3 For example, see Shogren and Crocker (1991).
4 For example, see European Business Council for a Sustainable Energy Future (2000).

Bibliography

Barrett, S. (1994) 'Self enforcing international environmental agreements', *Oxford Economic Papers* 46:878–894.

Barrett, S. (1998) 'On the theory and diplomacy of environmental treaty-making', *Environmental and Resource Economics* 11:317–333.

Barrett, S. (2003) *Statecraft and the Environment: The Strategy for Environmental Treaty-Making*, New York: Oxford University Press.

Bohm, P. (1998) 'Public investment issues and efficient climate change policy', in H. Shibata and T. Ihori (eds) *The Welfare State, Public Investment, and Growth*, Tokyo: Springer-Verlag.

Carraro, C. and Siniscalco, D. (1993) 'Strategies for the international protection of the environment', *Journal of Public Economics* 52:309–328.

Chichilnisky, G. and Heal, G. (1993) 'Global environmental risk', *Journal of Economics Perspectives* 7:65–86.

Cooper, R.N. (1998) 'Towards a real global warming treaty', *Foreign Affairs* 77:66–79.

Crocker, T.D. (1966) 'The structuring of atmospheric pollution control systems', in H. Wolozin (ed.) *The Economics of Air Pollution*, New York: Norton.

Dales, J.H. (1968) *Pollution, Property and Price*, Toronto: University Press.

Ehrlich, I. and Becker, G.S. (1972) 'Market insurance, self-insurance and self-protection', *Journal of Political Economy* 80:623–648.

European Business Council for a Sustainable Energy Future (2000) 'Position for the COP 6, Nov. 11, 2000'. Online. Available at http://www.e5.org/pages/st-08e.htm (accessed 26 September 2003).

Fisher, B.S., Barrett, S., Bohm, P., Kuroda, M., Mubazi, J.K.E., Shah, A. and Stavins, R.N. (1996) 'An economic assessment of policy instruments for combating climate change', in J.P. Bruce, H. Lee and E.F. Haites (eds) *Climate Change 1995: Economic and Social Dimensions of Climate Change*, Intergovernmental Panel on Climate Change, Working Group III, Cambridge: Cambridge University Press.

Godby, R. and Shogren, J. (2003) '*Caveat emptor* Kyoto', University of Wyoming, working paper.

Goulder, L.H. (1995) 'Environmental taxation and the double dividend: a reader's guide', *International Tax and Public Finance* 2:157–183.

Hoel, M. (1992) 'International environmental conventions: the case of uniform reductions of emissions', *Environmental and Resource Economics* 2:141–159.

Intergovernmental Panel on Climate Change (2001a) *Climate Change 2001: Mitigation*, Cambridge: Cambridge University Press.

Intergovernmental Panel on Climate Change (2001b) *Climate Change 2001: Synthesis Report. A Contribution of Working Groups I, II, and III to the Third Assessment of the Intergovernmental Panel on Climate Change*, Cambridge: Cambridge University Press.

Jacoby, H., Prinn, R. and Schmalensee, R. (1998) 'Kyoto's unfinished business', *Foreign Affairs* 77:54–66.

Lutter, R. and Shogren, J. (2002) 'Tradable permit tariffs: how local air pollution affects carbon emissions permit trading', *Land Economics* 78:159–170.

Kane, S. (1996) 'Economics of climate change', *Encyclopedia of Climate and Weather*, Oxford: Oxford University Press.

Kane, S. and Shogren, J. (2000) 'Linking adaptation and mitigation in climate change policy', *Climatic Change* 45:75–101.

Kolstad, C.D. and Toman, M.A. (2003) 'The economics of climate policy', in K.G. Maler and J. Vincent (eds) *The Handbook of Environmental Economics*, Amsterdam: North-Holland/Elsevier Science.

Nordhaus, W. (1994) *Managing the Global Commons*, Cambridge: MIT Press.

Nordhaus, W. and Boyer, J. (1998) 'Requiem for Kyoto: an economic analysis of the Kyoto Protocol', *Energy Journal*, Special Issue: 93–130.

Rayner, S. and Malone, E. (eds) (1998) *Human Choice and Climate Change*, Washington, D.C.: Battelle Press.

Schelling, T. (1992) 'Some economics of global warming', *American Economic Review* 82:1–14.

Schelling, T. (1997) 'The costs of combating global warming', *Foreign Affairs* 76:8–14.

Shogren, J. (1999) *The Benefits and Costs of the Kyoto Protocol*, Washington, D.C.: AEI Press.

Shogren, J. and Crocker, T. (1991) 'Risk, self-protection, and ex ante economic value', *Journal of Environmental Economics and Management* 20:1–15.

Shogren, J. and Toman, M. (2000) 'Climate change policy', in P. Portney and R. Stavins (eds) *Public Policies for Environmental Protection*, 2nd edn. Washington, D.C.: Resources for the Future.

Sohngen, B. and Mendelsohn, R. (1997) 'Valuing the impact of large-scale ecological change in a market: the effect of climate change on U.S. timber', *American Economic Review* 88:686–710.

Stavins, R. (2001) 'Economic analysis of global climate change policy: a primer', in E. Claussen, V.A. Cochran and D.P. Davis (eds) *Climate Change: Science, Strategies, and Solutions*, Boston: Brill Publishing.

United States Office of Science and Technology Policy (1999) *Our Changing Planet: The FY 2000 US Global Change Research Program*, Washington, D.C.

Weyant, J. and Hill, J. (1999) 'Introduction and overview: the costs of the Kyoto Protocol – a multi-model evaluation', *Energy Journal*, Special Issue: vii–xliv.

Wilbanks, T., Kane, S., Leiby, P., Perlack, R., Settle, C., Shogren, J. and Smith, J. (2003) 'Possible responses to global climate change: integrating mitigation and adaptation', *Environment* 9:28–38.

5 The economics of the Kyoto Protocol

Michael Grubb[1]

Introduction

This chapter gives an overview of the economics of the Kyoto Protocol, the agreement that was adopted unanimously by government negotiators in December 1997 at the Third Conference of Parties (COP 3) to the UNFCCC. The Protocol was adopted against a background of hugely disparate perspectives on the issue of climate change concerning the urgency of action, the costs of limitations and the appropriate instruments. In the end, the view of the US administration prevailed that binding emission commitments for industrialized countries should be complemented by the use of a number of 'economic instruments' adopted for the first time at the international level.

From a purely economic standpoint, the aim of the resulting agreement is to tackle the threat of climate change by establishing an efficient regulatory framework that will change the previous rising trajectory of emissions and set an international 'price' on emissions of CO_2 and other greenhouse gases, initially focused upon industrialized countries with mechanisms for offsetting against projects in developing countries. The core mechanism for achieving this is quantified emission commitments (established for industrialized countries in Kyoto's first commitment period of 2008–2012), which are given market-based flexibility through the use of emissions trading and other international economic instruments, and with negotiations on subsequent period commitments mandated to follow.

This chapter analyses the economics of Kyoto in two main parts. The first section provides an explanation of the basic structure of the Protocol, illustrated with respect to some of the key debates that went into its formation. The next section then examines the practical economic consequences of the final agreement as elaborated at the Marrakech COP 7 conference, including the economic consequences of withdrawal by the Bush administration. Finally, conclusions offer brief thoughts on the future of the Kyoto system given the economic issues noted.

Economic structure of the Kyoto Protocol

Context and coverage

The main aim of the Kyoto Protocol is to contain emissions of the main green-house gases in ways that reflect underlying national differences in emissions, wealth and capacity, following the main principles agreed in the UN Framework Convention. As described in Chapter 3, these include the need for evolutionary approaches and the principle of 'common but differentiated' responsibilities, including leadership by the richer and higher emitting industrialized countries.

The large divergence of emissions between countries is illustrated in Figure 5.1, which shows the global distribution of CO_2 emissions in terms of three major indices: emissions per capita (height of each block); population (width of each block); and total emissions (product of population and emissions per capita = area of block).

This figure illustrates several relevant dimensions. Per capita emissions in the industrialized countries are typically as much as ten times the average in develop-ing countries, particularly Africa and the Indian subcontinent. This is one of the reasons why industrialized countries accepted the responsibility for leading climate change efforts in the UNFCCC and subsequent Kyoto negotiations: unless they can control their own high emissions there is little prospect of con-trolling emissions from developing countries that start from a very much lower base.[2] There are also large differences among the industrialized countries, with per capita emissions in the EU and Japan at about half the levels of the United States and Australia.

Following the agreed negotiating mandate,[3] in Kyoto the countries that took on quantified commitments for the first period (2008–2012) are the industrial-ized countries as listed in Annex I to the Treaty. These correspond roughly to those with annual emissions in 1990 of two tonnes carbon per capita (2tC/cap) or higher – the 'Other EIT' category and all to the left of it in Figure 5.1.[4]

At the same time, the currently low emissions and large population of the developing countries indicates the huge potential for global emissions growth, if and as their emissions climb towards anything like levels in the industrialized world. The Kyoto negotiations were marked by large tensions on this issue. In the final agreement, in addition to the provisions on national reporting and technology transfer, the Clean Development Mechanism is intended to provide a mechanism to start reigning in the rapid growth of developing country emissions without these countries themselves bearing the costs. The general intent in Kyoto is that developing countries will be brought into the system of quantified commit-ments over time, in subsequent negotiation rounds, if and as the richer countries fulfil their first round commitments. The implicit threat (or bargaining counter) is that industrialized countries will refuse to take on subsequent commitments unless there is progress in this direction.

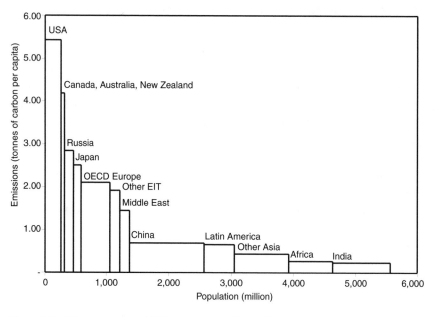

Figure 5.1 CO_2 emissions in 2000, per capita and population.

The quantified commitments in the Kyoto Protocol cover emissions of six greenhouse gases from identified sources that together account for almost all anthropogenic greenhouse gas emissions in the industrialized world (Table 5.1). The gases are taken together as a 'basket' compared on the basis of the 100-year 'global warming potentials' (GWP) estimated in the IPCC's Second Assessment Report for the first commitment period; the GWPs may be revised for any subsequent commitment periods.[5] On this basis carbon dioxide, principally from fossil fuels, accounted for over 80 per cent of greenhouse gas emissions from the industrialized world in 1990. Emissions of methane and nitrous oxide in many industrialized countries have declined during the 1990s, making the targets easier to achieve than would be case for just CO_2.[6]

The possible role of sinks – activities that absorb CO_2 from the atmosphere – formed one of the most technically complex issues in the entire negotiations. Proponents argued that CO_2 absorption should be directly offset against emissions (the 'net' approach) because, from an atmospheric standpoint, absorption is equivalent to reduced emissions. Opponents feared that this might allow countries to claim credit for the massive on-going naturally occurring absorption; that such sinks were inherently far too difficult to monitor accurately; that it would detract from the pressure to limit emissions; and that including sinks could give incentives to replace mature, old-growth forests with fast-growing monoculture plantations. In the end Kyoto included carbon sinks, but in ways carefully

Table 5.1 Greenhouse gases in the Kyoto Protocol

Gas	Qualifying sources	Emission trends since the late 1980s	Lifetime (years)	GWP–100	% GHG 1990, Annex I
Carbon dioxide (CO_2)	Fossil fuel burning, cement	EU static, increases other OECD, sharp decline EITs	Variable, with dominant component c.100 years	1	81.2
Methane (CH_4)	Rice, cattle, biomass burning and decay, fossil fuel production	Decline in most countries (big increase only in Canada, USA, Norway)	12.2 ± 3	21	13.7
Nitrous oxide (N_2O)	Fertilizers, fossil fuel burning, land conversion to agriculture	Varies, small increases in many countries, decline expected before 2000, decline in EITs	120	310	4.0
Hydrofluorocarbons (HFCs)	Industry, refrigerants	Fast-rising emissions due to substitution for CFCs	1.5–264, HFC 134a (most common) is 14.6	140–11,700; HFC 134a (most common) is 1,300	0.56
Perfluorocarbons (PFCs)	Industry, aluminium, electronic and electrical industries, fire fighting, solvents	Static	2,600–50,000	Average about 6,770; CF_4 is 6,500; C_2F6 is 9,200	0.29
Sulphur hexafluoride (SF_6)	Electronic and electrical industries, insulation	Increase in most countries, further rise expected	3,200	23,900	0.30

Source: adapted from IPCC (2001).

circumscribed to be linked to anthropogenic activities and measured as verifiable changes in carbon stocks.[7]

The Kyoto allocations

Timing and base year

The Kyoto allocations ('Assigned Amounts' in the formal terminology) specify allowed total national emissions for the period 2008–2012, subject to the adjustments that could be made through the international flexible mechanisms. As with everything else, this reflects a compromise between diverse considerations.

The EU pushed hard for a 2005 target, arguing that commitments that were outside the range of visible electoral cycles or typical industry financial horizons would be taken as an invitation to delay. The converse US concern was that early targets would prove costly to implement – also that they would leave insufficient time for the institutional and political developments required, particularly to get action through the domestic US legislature. US opposition was reinforced by (now largely discredited) economic studies that purported to show that it would be cheaper to defer abatement action, and do more later. Though the administration had rejected this view as a general principle, US industry – and in particular the electricity sector, which was concerned about the possible costs of being forced prematurely to retire its coal-based power stations – lobbied strenuously against early commitments and the Administration refused to consider anything before 2010.

This became the centre of a five-year averaging period (to allow for weather and economic cycles) in the final agreement, together with a modest requirement that the Parties show 'demonstrable progress' towards their target by 2005. The first binding point in the Protocol is thus in 2012, some 15 years after the agreement itself was adopted.

The United States in its original Protocol submission had proposed a second commitment period to follow the first, with an allowance for banking and borrowing of emission commitments between the two periods. The difficulties in negotiating – and even developing positions – on a single set of commitments were so huge as to make this impractical. Instead, the Protocol commits parties to open negotiations on a second commitment period no later than 2005, and countries that overachieve their commitments in the first period can 'bank' their unused allowances for use in the subsequent period. Suggestions that countries might 'borrow' emissions from subsequent periods were recognized as impractical, but the idea was transformed into part of the compliance package (see below).[8]

The negotiations never questioned that Annex I commitments should be defined in terms of changes from historic levels: proposals for other indices, such as defining emissions relative to population or GDP, remained confined to academic literature as they involved changes far greater than countries were willing to contemplate. The Convention had used 1990 as the base year for its non-binding aim – a date which had a huge significance as the year in which all governments, by endorsing the first IPCC report, formally recognized climate change as a serious issue, and launched the negotiations that led to the Rio Convention. The 1990 base year remains as the reference points for the Kyoto agreement: proposals to shift the base year for Kyoto forward to 1995 were rejected on the grounds that such a change would simply reward those countries that had done nothing to limit emissions since the Convention process was launched.[9] This has, however, led to varied problems discussed below, not least concerning the Economies in Transition.

Numerical allowances

The specific commitments, defined as percentage changes relative to base year emissions, are set out in Table 5.2. The fifteen countries of the EU accepted a collective 8 per cent reduction from 1990 levels, a commitment subsequently redistributed between its member states under the Protocol's 'bubble' provision (see below). When added together, the commitments equate to a 5.2 per cent reduction below 1990 levels for the industrialized countries taken together.

As with any major international negotiations, the numbers can only be understood as the outcome of a highly political process arising from the clash between competing numerical aims, structural visions and root conceptions of political imperative – all combined with the personal and political dynamics of the final days at Kyoto.[10] The dominant and almost obsessive focus in the negotiations was on how to distribute OECD commitments. Flat-rate emission targets appeared attractive because of their simplicity, and have indeed been a feature of the first round of several previous international environmental agreements, which have become subsequently more differentiated over time (Greene 1996). In addition, there was no specific logical basis upon which to agree differentiated commitments.[11]

In the central political dialogue between the United States and the EU there was a kind of logic to equal percentage cuts from 1990 levels. The United States, with per capita emissions almost twice those of most other OECD countries except Canada and Australia, was vulnerable to accusations that it had a huge potential for reductions and should cut back by more than other countries. Yet internal political pressures pointed in the opposite direction: the United States had the greatest difficulty in mustering any domestic support even for stabilizing emissions. Economic studies at the time varied in their estimates of which would bear the higher cost under equal reductions from 1990 levels. Equal reductions between the United States and the EU seemed the only safe solution in such a peculiar political context, and the most obvious way of keeping the US commitment 'in line' with the international community, in some basic psychological sense.

78   *Michael Grubb*

Table 5.2 Emissions and commitments in the Kyoto Protocol (from base year)

Country	Base year (1990 unless otherwise indicated)	Commitment (% change from base year emissions)	Non CO$_2$ emissions (% total in 1990)
Australia		+8	51.9
Canada		−6	18.4
European Union*		−8	20.3
Iceland		+10	25.6
Japan		−6	5.8
Liechtenstein		−8	—
Monaco		−8	0
New Zealand		0	68.7
Norway		+1	34.5
Switzerland		−8	17.8
United States		−7	15.2
EITs			
Bulgaria	1988	−8	28.8
Croatia	Tbc	−5	—
Czech Republic	1990	−8	13.9
Estonia	1990	−8	16.6
Hungary	1985–1998	−6	17.7
Latvia	Tbc	−8	16.9
Lithuania	1990	−8	—
Poland	1988	−6	14.6
Romania	1989	−8	30.5
Russia	1990	0	22.4
Slovak Republic	1990	−8	17.8
Slovenia	Tbc	−8	—
Ukraine	Tbc	0	—

Note
* The fifteen countries of the EU are listed as each having a target of −8. These targets were subsequently redistributed under the 'bubbling' provisions of Article 4; see Table 5.3.

From a wider perspective, flat-rate reductions were neither efficient nor feasible as a means of achieving emission reductions. As numerous studies showed, different countries faced very different costs of abatement. There was a danger that agreement could only be reached on a 'lowest common denominator target' which would require very little effort from some countries; or, if the pressures for greater resolutions were overwhelming, countries that faced insuperable difficulties might simply ensure that the agreement was full of loopholes. In the end, the negotiators agreed a small amount of differentiation among the dominant industrial powers, and wider differentiation for smaller countries.

In June 1998 the EU Council reached agreement, guided by a previous non-binding agreement of March 1997, and implemented the 'bubble' provision to define the emission commitments of its member states, as set out in Table 5.3.

Table 5.3 The internal distribution of the EU 'bubble'

Country	Internal commitment (% change from 1990 levels)
Austria	−13.0
Belgium	−7.5
Denmark	−21.0
Finland	0
France	0
Germany	−21.0
Greece	+25.0
Ireland	+13.0
Italy	−6.5
Luxembourg	−28.0
The Netherlands	−6.0
Portugal	+27.0
Spain	+15.0
Sweden	+4.0
United Kingdom	−12.5

These now form the legally binding commitments on member states in the EU instrument of ratification.

It was well understood at the time that countries were not expected to achieve these emission targets entirely domestically, and indeed that there was considerable room for flexibility arising from the various 'flexibility mechanisms' in the Protocol (discussed below) in particular when combined with the allowances granted to some of the Economies in Transition (EITs). Just how much flexibility this offered was not, however, appreciated at the time.

The context for the EITs was their transition from central planning to a market economy and the associated economic contraction which reduced their emissions considerably. These countries tended still to regard economy, energy consumption and emissions as intimately related, and having suffered such a dramatic decline they were in no mood to consider commitments that they feared might constrain their economic recovery. Most of the central and east European countries agreed to go along with the EU's commitment of 8 per cent below 1990 levels;[12] Russia and Ukraine however insisted on a right to return to 1990 levels. These lax targets, which (due to the trading possibilities) were also an important factor in the US's acceptance of a target stronger than many had expected, have created important difficulties which are considered later on in this chapter.

International flexibility mechanisms

Emissions trading

Emissions trading – the ability for two entities that are subject to emissions control to exchange part of their emission allowances – has evolved principally in a domestic context as a means for controlling industry sector emissions. In the Kyoto Protocol, it enables any two Parties to the Protocol to exchange part of their emission commitment, in effect redistributing the division of allowed emissions between them.

This proved to be one of the most controversial areas of the negotiations, though for different reasons in different quarters. Among the industrialized countries, Japan and some of the EU member states wanted to ensure that any such trading was competitive and transparent so as to prevent the United States using its political leverage to gain preferential access, particularly to the likely Russian surplus; the EU was also particularly anxious that trading should not enable the United States to avoid domestic action as the main agent. However, the developing countries objected more on basic principles, fearing the wider implications and that the US's overwhelming economic power would allow it to use the flexibility to its own advantage over the interests of weaker countries.

In the end, these objections were overridden, but the bare minimum of enabling language survived in the Protocol itself. Elaborating this into a workable structure governing international emissions trading took four years of further negotiations, to the COP 7 conference in Marrakech.

Joint implementation (JI) within Annex I

Article 6 of the Protocol enables emission savings or sink enhancement arising from cross-border investments between Annex I Parties to be transferred between them. This is joint implementation at the project level, in the sense that the term came to be used in the debates prior to Kyoto. However, because it occurs between countries that are both subject to legally binding constraints, it does not carry many of the political and technical complexities associated with joint implementation more widely. This establishes that JI projects between industries within Annex I may proceed and generate 'emission reduction units'. This necessarily involves private investment, but to have legal significance under the Protocol – and hence value to the governments concerned – it must be sanctioned by the governments of the participating industries.

Agreement must be reached on the emissions saved by the investment, as compared with what would otherwise have been emitted. At this point, the emission transfer between the Parties becomes equivalent to an international emissions trade, being deducted from the allowed emissions of the host country, and added to the

Box 5.1 Economic and crediting aspects of the Kyoto Protocol's project mechanisms

Between Annex I countries: 'Joint Implementation' (KP Article 6)
Any Party included in Annex I may transfer to, or acquire from, any other such Party emission reduction units (ERUs) resulting from projects aimed at reducing anthropogenic emissions by sources or enhancing anthropogenic removals by sinks of greenhouse gases in any sector of the economy, provided that:

1   Any such project has the approval of the Parties involved;
2   Any such project [reduces emissions or enhances removals by sinks], additional to any that would otherwise occur;
3   It does not acquire any emission reduction units if it is not in compliance with its obligations on [compilation of emission inventories and reporting];
4   The acquisition of emission reduction units shall be supplemental to domestic actions for the purposes of meeting commitments under Article 3.

Investments in developing countries: the Clean Development Mechanism (KP Article 12)
    Under the clean development mechanism:

1   Parties not included in Annex I will benefit from project activities resulting in certified emission reductions (CERs);
2   Parties included in Annex I may use the CERs accruing from such project activities to contribute to compliance with part of their . . . commitments under Article 3, as determined by the Conference of the Parties serving as the Meeting of the Parties to this Protocol (COP/MOP).

Emission reductions resulting from each project activity shall be certified by operational entities to be designated by the COP/MOP, on the basis of:

1   Voluntary participation approved by each Party involved;
2   Real, measurable, and long-term benefits related to the mitigation of climate change; and
3   Reductions in emissions that are additional to any that would occur in the absence of the certified project activity.

. . . a share of the proceeds [shall be used] to assist developing country Parties that are particularly vulnerable to the adverse effects of climate change to meet the costs of adaptation.
    CERs obtained during the period from the year 2000 up to the beginning of the first commitment period can be used to assist in achieving compliance in the first commitment period.

allowed emissions of the investing country. Because the combined emissions from the countries remain constrained, the accuracy of the estimated emissions savings is, from the standpoint of the environment and of the Protocol, of secondary importance; it is a matter for negotiation between the governments and industries concerned.

The clean development mechanism

In addition to these mechanisms for transfer between Annex I Parties, the Protocol establishes the 'clean development mechanism' which, in principle, enables activities similar to joint implementation to proceed with non-Annex I countries. The stated purpose of the CDM is to help developing countries to achieve sustainable development and so contribute to the ultimate objective of the Convention, and to 'assist Annex I Parties in achieving compliance' with their specific commitments. Project activities under the CDM shall 'benefit' developing countries, and generate 'certified emission reductions' which Annex I Parties may use to 'contribute to compliance with part of their quantified commitments'.

Emission reductions shall be certified on the basis of criteria including voluntary participation, 'real, measurable and long-term benefits' related to mitigating climate change, and emissions additionality ('reductions that are additional to any that would occur in the absence of the certified project activity'). The CDM is not a fund, but shall 'assist in arranging funding of certified project activities as necessary', and participation may explicitly involve private and/or public entities. In addition, 'a share of the proceeds from certified project activities' shall be used to cover administrative expenses as well as to assist particularly vulnerable developing countries to meet the costs of adapting to climate change. This clause, which was crucial in building sufficient G7 support for the CDM, represents an important novelty in funding sources, and starts to give concrete form to the Convention commitment in this area.

Other elements

The Protocol contains many other provisions, some of which build upon the UNFCCC provisions as discussed in Chapter 3. These include specific commitments relating to Policies and Measures, in accordance with the original Mandate of negotiations. Article 2.1 provides a wide list of measures, ranging from energy efficiency and subsidy reform through to technology research, development and dissemination. Generally, these were promoted by many and watered down by others, and as summarized in Box 5.2, the phrasing was almost entirely non-binding: countries were extremely resistant to anything that could intrude directly on national sovereignty over the choice of instruments adopted. However, these references could provide important pressure points, and hooks

---

Box 5.2 Elements of policies and measures in the Kyoto Protocol

2.1 Each Party included in Annex I . . . shall:

a   Implement and/or further elaborate policies and measures in accordance with its national circumstances, such as:

- enhancement of *energy efficiency* in relevant sectors;
- protection and enhancement of *sinks and reservoirs*;
- promotion of sustainable forms of *agriculture* in the light of climate change considerations;
- promotion, research, development and increased use of *new and renewable forms of energy*, of carbon dioxide *sequestration* technologies and of advanced and innovative environmentally sound technologies;
- progressive reduction or phasing out of *market imperfections* . . . that run counter to the objective of the Convention, and apply *market instruments*;
- measures to limit and/or reduce emissions . . . in the *transport* sector;
- limitation and reduction of *methane* . . . through recovery and use in waste management . . . and [provision of] energy.

Plus one catch-all sub-paragraph encouraging 'appropriate reforms in relevant sectors'.

b   Cooperate with other such Parties to enhance the individual and combined effectiveness of their policies and measures.

2.2 Pursue limitation or reduction of emissions . . . from *aviation and marine bunker fuels*, working through the International Civil Aviation Organization and the International Maritime Organization, respectively.

2.3 Strive to implement policies and measures . . . in such a way as to minimize adverse effects . . . on other Parties.

---

upon which to build subsequent negotiations on more specific actions including international collaboration under Article 2.1(b).

An important exception to the *laissez-faire* approach comes in the Article 2.2 requirement that parties *shall* (emphasis added) pursue limitation or reduction of emissions from aviation and marine bunker fuels, working through the ICAO and IMO, respectively (international bunker fuel emissions are not included in the Kyoto national allowances because of the complexity of allocating them to any particular country).

The Protocol contains many other provisions. A number of these place requirements on all countries (including developing countries) – for example, reporting on national emission inventories, and on policies and measures being adopted to tackle climate change. In addition, the provisions on technology trans-fer indicate increased attention to the importance of global diffusion of cleaner energy technologies. Many of these elements build upon provisions in the UNFCCC itself, extending and being more specific about the actions required (see Chapter 3 and Grubb *et al.* 1999).

In addition, the Protocol restates a principle of protecting countries from possible adverse effects of any of the policies and measures that may be adopted, 'including the adverse effects of climate change, effects on international trade, and social, environmental and economic impacts on other parties, especially developing country parties'. Reference is made to Articles 4.8 and 4.9 of the UNFCCC, which list categories of developing countries particularly at risk, including obvious ones such as small island countries or those with areas prone to natural disasters, but also including 'countries whose economies are highly dependent on income generated from the production, processing and export, and/or consumption of fossil fuels and associated energy-intensive products'.

Like most international treaties, the explicit consequences for non-compliance are weak compared to domestic law: the most concrete are that failure to meet the quantified commitments in the first period automatically disqualifies a country from participating in the mechanisms and will be penalized by deductions from allowed emissions in subsequent rounds with a 30 per cent penalty factor. Nevertheless, the compliance section was one of the most highly contested in the Marrakech Accords. The restatement of the principles that the commitments are legally binding, and the establishment of an enforcement branch in the compliance committee, make the compliance package considerably stronger than in most Treaties. Last-ditch Japanese attempts to water down the package (rejected) emphasized that most countries do not consider ratifying the Treaty and then abrogating its quantified commitments to be an option.

The Kyoto structure for the longer term

Although debate about Kyoto has tended to focus almost obsessively on the first period commitments, the basic intent is to provide the structure for a dynamic, evolving regime that can effectively tackle climate change over the course of the century. The current set of emission targets for the first commitment period represent the first concrete step in a much longer-term process of negotiating emission commitments over successive periods. Negotiations on second period commitments are due to start by 2005; it is generally assumed this would take the form of another five-year period, centred on 2015, though a different time-span would be legally possible.

The current first period emission targets are intended to meet the Convention requirement that industrialized countries should take the lead in tackling climate change by modifying their emission trends, and to provide a period of institutional development of the mechanisms, regime architecture (such as inventories) and national programmes for tackling emissions. The first period commitments

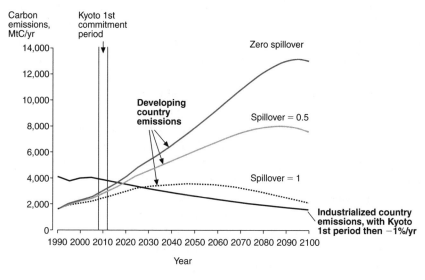

Figure 5.2 Kyoto first period commitments in context: global emissions dependence upon follow-up and spillover.

Source: Grubb, Hope and Fouquet (2002).

Note
The declining line shows emissions from industrialized (Annex I) countries, up to 2010 assuming that they *collectively* meet the Kyoto 1st period commitments and then follow with reductions averaging 1%/yr in subsequent Kyoto periods. Emissions from developing countries are modelled in terms of the assumed degree of spillover: a value of spillover = 1 means that aggregate developing country emission intensity (per unit GDP) tracks that of industrialized countries and converges over the century. Such spillover would be a combination of economic, technological and political spillovers, the latter including expansion of commitments to include more countries.

were never intended to provide the definitive solution to climate change, indeed a moment's thought reveals that no agreement reached in the 1990s could sensibly provide a one-step solution to such a massive and long-term problem.

Second and subsequent periods are likely to require more stringent emission commitments, and for a wider group of Parties, thus gradually 'ratcheting up' the Protocol and its resulting environmental effectiveness, as with the Montreal Protocol on CFC emissions. Figure 5.2 shows Kyoto's first period commitments in context, and underlines how the Protocol's ultimate impact will depend upon the degree and scope of follow-up to this initial action. The figure also shows that global emissions in the longer term cannot effectively be contained without emission controls in developing countries as well.

In the US particularly, the Protocol was widely condemned for 'not including' developing countries. In fact the Protocol is very much a global agreement, as is the Framework Convention on which it is based, but expecting developing countries to take quantified targets in the first period was never an option.[13] All parties, including developing countries, have a general commitment to adopt climate change mitigation policies and to report on the action they are taking. The Clean Development Mechanism (CDM) is intended to help disperse the effect of emission constraints globally, allowing industrialized countries (and their companies) to invest in emission reductions wherever it is cheapest globally.

That said, the North-South division embodied in the Kyoto Protocol (as well as under the UNFCCC) is undoubtedly a key problem area. There is an understanding that, if and as industrialized countries start to move their economies onto a less carbon intensive path, the developing countries must follow, and the Protocol stipulates that its provisions must be reviewed no more than two years after its entry into force. The structure of sequential negotiations provides a natural opportunity for engaging more countries in quantified emission caps over time, but the major developing countries would have to abandon their present refusal to take part in any debate about any possible future limits. However, the structure does offer a natural point of leverage in that the industrialized countries could simply refuse to take on stronger targets in the future unless more countries become so engaged over time.

Price and trading implications of the Kyoto–Marrakech first period commitments

Evolution of analysis

In the aftermath of initial agreement on the Kyoto Protocol, many economic modelling studies of the first period commitments, conducted under a programme of the Stanford-based Energy Modelling Forum, suggested that carbon prices under Kyoto could be several hundred dollars per tonne of carbon ($/tC) if emissions trading were impeded, or on the order of $100/tC ($= $27.3/tCO_2$) even with unrestricted trading amongst the industrialized countries (Weyant 1999).[14] Figure 5.3 shows results from the set of models covered in these studies, for the US and EU, for four cases: no trading (giving the marginal costs of achieving Kyoto targets domestically); full Annex I trading; a 'double bubble' in which there is no trade between the EU and the rest of Annex I but each bloc trades within itself; and full global trading, taken as crude approximation to maximal use of the CDM. Generally, increasing flexibility reduces prices as expected, but there is a huge range of prices across the models.

The main results from these modelling studies by country are reproduced in Chapter 6. The IPCC Third Assessment (IPCC 2001) numbers on the costs of Kyoto drew heavily on this set of studies, whilst noting that the models generally 'do not include carbon sinks, non-CO_2 gases, the CDM, negative cost options, ancillary benefits, or targeted revenue recycling'. This rather serious set of limitations goes some way to explaining the gulf between many of these

(a) United States

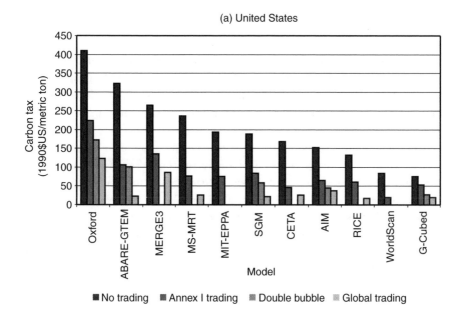

No trading   ■ Annex I trading   ■ Double bubble   ■ Global trading

(b) European Union

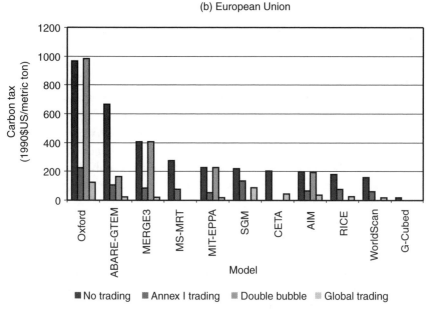

■ No trading   ■ Annex I trading   ■ Double bubble   ■ Global trading

Figure 5.3 Impact of international trading on abatement costs (EMF-16 studies) a US, b EU.

Note
'Double bubble' = trading separately within EU and within rest of Annex B countries. 'Global trading' is modelled as giving developing countries allowances equal to their business as usual emissions, but can also be considered as reflecting an economically highly idealized operation of the Protocol's Clean Development Mechanism.

modelling studies and the claims of some others even at that time that the Kyoto targets might be met at relatively low cost, perhaps even in the US (see literature review in IPCC 2001, also e.g. Yellen 1998).

A gulf away from modelling studies, a few nascent and speculative market trades did occur. In stark contrast to the projections of the EMF models, most such trades – discounted heavily by the uncertainty about future developments, and representing the first trades at the margin – were at a price of just a few \$/tC.

The tumultuous events of 2001 transformed the economic situation further due to at least three major factors explored further below: the withdrawal of the US, by far the largest source of potential 'demand' in the system; revision of Russian energy projections which greatly increased their projected allowance surplus; and the subsequent Bonn/Marrakech deal on carbon sinks. As a result, modelling projections of the price plummeted.

This section addresses the reasons for very divergent views about carbon prices, and the relationship between modelling studies and actual prices that might emerge under the Kyoto first period.

Survey of economic determinants and modelling results

The underpinnings of confusion about carbon prices under the Kyoto Protocol can be represented in terms of one diagram. Figure 5.4 represents the nearest thing to observable data on the potential supply-demand balance, using the most recent emissions for which comprehensive data are available (year 2000 emissions of industrial CO_2).[15] The main bars show the gap between countries' emissions and their Kyoto allocation. Thus, US emissions in 2000 were 300 MtC above their Kyoto allowance, and would have to be reduced by 19.3 per cent to get down to their original Kyoto allocation (7 per cent below 1990 levels). EU emissions had roughly stabilized at 1990 levels and the gap was only 70 MtC, whilst Canada faced a gap of around 40 MtC, the highest percentage of any due to its rapid growth since 1990.

In stark contrast, the bars on the right hand side of the graph illustrate that emissions of the Economies in Transition had declined since 1990 and were well below their Kyoto allowance (detailed data for EITs, with recent trends are given in the net section). This illustrates that the countries scheduled to join the EU in 2004 (the 'Accession countries') currently have an emissions 'headroom' about as large as the 'shortfall' in the present EU countries. The 'headroom' currently available to Russia and Ukraine (respectively, 200 MtC and about 90 MtC) is far larger than any of the individual shortfalls of OECD countries other than the US. In total, in fact, the sum of all these data indicate that the *aggregate* emissions of Annex I countries in 2000 were already below the *aggregate* Kyoto cap of −5.2 per cent, but with a huge east-west discrepancy in the distribution.

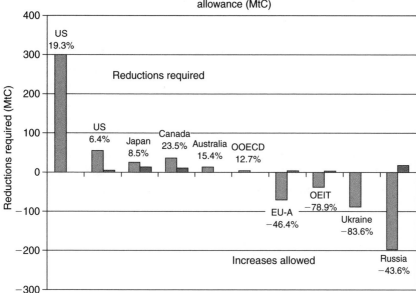

Figure 5.4 Kyoto commitments and trading potential.

Source: 2000 emission data: Energy Information Administration, USA.

Note
The main (single or larger) bars show the gap between 2000 emissions and Kyoto commitments for the principal countries/groups in Annex I. The smaller bars alongside show the maximum allowance that each can claim for carbon absorbed from managed forests under the Marrakech Accords (excluding the US which is not included in that agreement), which can in effect be deducted. Percentages show the per cent cut required to get from current levels to the Kyoto targets (negative numbers indicate the corresponding percentage growth from current levels for EITs).
Key: EU – A = the 10 EU candidate countries heading for early accession. OEIT = the 5 other countries applying for EU membership. OOECD = all other OECD countries. Data represents CO_2 total national emissions.

For two or three years after the Kyoto agreement, the usual economic perspective was that emissions in all these regions would rise substantially in the absence of strong action to limit domestic CO_2 emissions: growth of US and Japanese emissions would continue apace, the EU would 'recover' from the transitional effects of German reunification, the UK dash-for-gas, and its sluggish economy; and the emissions from the EITs would rise sharply as their economies recovered and began to grow apace. Consequently, economic models at that time mostly predicted that a high carbon price would be required if countries were to cut back emissions enough to comply, with the US and Japan facing the biggest gaps and bearing the biggest costs.

In addition to the fact that many of these models used already outdated data and neglected non-CO_2 gases and carbon sinks, three factors have served to completely reverse this perspective:

- Emissions of most countries, but especially the Economies in Transition, have failed to grow as many models predicted. The only exceptions were the New World economies (US, Canada, Australia). Emissions in Europe and Japan remain roughly static, and (even more significant) so did emissions from most of the EITs, where economic recovery was generally reflected in increased efficiency rather than emissions growth (see Table 5.5 below).
- The Marrakech Accords granted countries a certain allowance of carbon sinks from 'managed forests' as shown in Figure 5.4 – essentially a windfall gain, since many forests in industrialized countries are in practice managed in one way or another – and also allowed inclusion of afforestation and reforestation projects in the CDM.
- The Bush Administration's rejection of Kyoto removed by far the largest potential source of demand in the Kyoto system.

The result is to leave a large potential supply set against radically reduced demand. This has a dramatic impact on the results of economic models. Table 5.4 summarizes the results of various economic modelling studies conducted since the US withdrawal from Kyoto. Without exception, US withdrawal has a big impact in these models, which mostly assume a freely operating international trade in allowances – in some cases, pushing the price close to zero. Buchner *et al.* (2002) reviewed studies and found the impact of US withdrawal alone to result in more than a halving of the permit price in all studies except their own.[16] The conclusions do not only apply to European studies: the MIT group estimated a carbon price at about US$10/tCO$_2$ in the pre-COP 6 circumstances, and found this fell to a negligible level under the Marrakech agreement (without the US) with free international trade (Babiker *et al.* 2002). Springer (2003) reviews modelling results, unfortunately without comparing pre- and post-2001 results, and concurs that 'estimated prices fall dramatically, reaching values between 0 and $12/tCO$_2$'.

The relative influence of the three different factors varies between studies, and indeed the impact of revised emission projections is rarely carried out, presumably because the modellers are not so keen to illustrate just how wrong they were concerning past forecasts. Nevertheless, the withdrawal of the US is clearly an extremely big factor.

Kyoto realities: the context

Given the above, many economists have now totally reversed their assessment of a few years previously: no longer will Kyoto be too expensive, rather the international

Table 5.4 International carbon prices from economic models of the Kyoto system: impact of US withdrawal

Model / study	Includes Carbon sinks (managed forests / other)	Non-CO$_2$ gases	Equilibrium carbon price under Kyoto, $/tCO$_{2}$e With US	Without US	Price impact of US withdrawal (% decline)
Hagem and Holtsmark (2001)	N	N	15	5	66
Kemfert (2001)	Y/N	N	52	8	84
Eymans et al. (2001)	N	N	22	10	55
Den Elzen and Manders (2001)	Y/N	Y	37	13.6	63
Bohringer (2001)	Y/N	N	—	'Close to zero'	—
Babiker et al. (2001)	Y/partial	Y	10	Negligible	—

Note
The absolute numbers from different studies are not directly comparable as they may refer to different currency base years, as well as embodying different assumptions and base year emissions data used for 'reference' projections. However the impact of different currency and emission base years is small in relation to the impact of US withdrawal.

carbon price will be close to zero and hardly any action will be taken. In practice this is no more realistic than the former assessments, for three main reasons:

1   *The prioritization of domestic action.* Most countries are concentrating first on domestic action. For example, the EU and its member countries are taking a range of measures in all sectors to limit GHG emissions, and even its emissions trading directive is carefully confined to domestic action: whilst states retain the right to international trade under Kyoto, the Directive is clear that companies cannot themselves engage in international trading under the Directive. Climate mitigation policy in the EU already forms a patchwork of measures implicitly at widely divergent marginal costs, and existing policies in many areas (notably transport, in which existing excise duties already typically equate to over Euros $50/tCO_2$) will be insulated from competition with international carbon trading.

2   *Market power and other constraints on the operation of Kyoto as a fully competitive international market.* The international carbon price could be considerably higher because Kyoto will not operate as a fully competitive market. The project-based mechanisms will be inhibited by transaction costs, and international trading may be affected by the potential for major exporters to withhold supply so as to raise prices; they also have the option for holding any unused allowances over for use in the subsequent period through Kyoto's banking provisions.

3   *Buyer sovereignty.* Countries looking to import allowances have a sovereign right to choose from whom they buy and on what basis. For a whole variety of political and strategic reasons, elaborated below, countries are unlikely to seek to acquire allowances at least carbon cost.

These factors all involve considerations of political economy, particularly concerning the likely behaviour of sovereign states engaged in the Kyoto system. Kyoto is an intergovernmental agreement and the only entities that can be bound by it *directly* are governments. Value under Kyoto can only be accorded to private sector trades to the extent that these are endorsed, in one way or another, by governments. The Kyoto registries system requires the source of all units to be registered by a unique identifier, so that governments have the potential to be selective about the units they are willing to issue for trading, or to accept and use for their compliance assessment.

To understand how these factors may work, the next section explores the situation in the major countries involved.

The 'supply side': Economies in Transition and the developing countries

The biggest potential sellers in the international 'Kyoto market' are the Economies in Transition. The initial assumption has been that these countries would seek to sell all they could, providing they can comply with the Protocol's inventory and reporting requirements. In practice things are not so simple.

Russia and Ukrainian energy projections are still very diverse and their approach to selling has been cautious to avoid any possibility of having to buy back allowances if emissions growth is high. Also, there is emerging understanding of the trade-off between volume and prices. Figure 5.5 shows one estimate of the impact on permit prices and revenues to the EITs, as a function of the amount of their surplus allowances (relative to the 'business as usual' emissions in this

a Permit price as a function of the traded EIT surplus

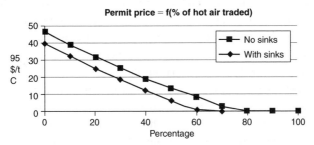

b Revenues of FSU and EEE as a function of the traded EIT surplus

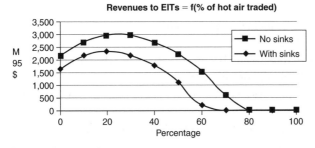

c Division between Former Soviet Union and other EITs

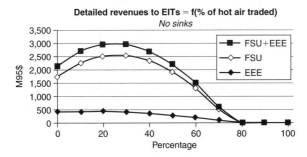

Figure 5.5 Impact of trading EIT emission surplus ('hot air') on permit price and EIT revenues.
Source: Criqui and Kitous (2001).

Note
Price Units: millions of US$/tC, at $1995. To express equivalent prices in current $ per tonne of CO_2, divide by about 3.5.

projection), more colloquially known as 'hot air'. In that study, the revenues to EITs would be maximized by trading only 20 per cent of their overall surplus, at a price in the region of $20–30/tC (*c.* $5–7/tCO$_2$) which would yield somewhat over US$2bn/yr; if more is traded, the collapse of price outweighs the increasing volumes. The review by Springer (2003) concludes that if all the EITs were a perfect cartel (obviously not a realistic assumption), they could maximize revenues by selling 10–60 per cent of their surplus at $5–22/tCO$_2$.

This in turn gives rise to the idea that the EITs could seek to maximize their revenues by operating a cartel on emissions supply. Again however things are not so simple – in part because it seems likely that the surplus will be larger and more widespread than originally anticipated. Table 5.5 shows emissions from the individual EITs, including recent trends. It shows that for all the EITs, with the single exception of Slovenia, emissions by 2000 were well below their base year levels, implying potential for a substantial surplus under Kyoto.

The Accession countries are for the most part more advanced in the transition process and it was widely predicted that their emissions would start rising as their economies recovered. As yet, there is little sign of this happening, though there is evidence of a 'bottoming out' by the year 2000. Resumed emissions growth cannot be ruled out, but there remain substantial inefficiencies in these countries and the Accession process (which requires *inter alia* removal of various subsidies, including continuing coal subsidies in many of these countries) may accelerate this.

The relationship between Ukraine and Russia, as the countries with by far the largest potential volumes of surplus to sell, is also important. This relationship is already complex not least because of on-going struggles over gas supplies and payments.

Cartels are notoriously difficult to hold together. In this case, close collaboration between EU Accession countries and other EITs seems implausible because of the former's close ties to the EU and the likelihood that they will be included in an EU-wide emissions trading scheme.

In addition, many individual actors in these countries are more concerned with *where* the money goes than with the overall flows. Of most direct relevance here, the Russian Ministries of Energy and of Economy are concerned to see that money flows into real investment to improve energy infrastructure. The reduced volume of money without US participation also increases the appeal of using the mechanisms primarily to try and leverage potentially much larger private sector flows.

This sets the context for the Russian proposal on a 'Green Investment Scheme', whereby revenues from emissions trading would be invested in environmentally-oriented projects, principally aimed at improving the efficiency of the energy sector, an idea explored in considerable depth by a recent international study (Tangen *et al.* 2002).

Table 5.5 Emissions from Economies in Transition: base year and recent trends

EIT countries	CO_2 emissions (excluding land use), MtC/yr			
EU Accession countries	In base year*	1998	1999	2000
Czech Republic	44.7	29.3	27.0	28.4
Estonia	10.4	2.3	2.0	1.9
Hungary (1985–1987)*	22.2	16.0	15.8	14.9
Latvia	6.4	2.1	1.8	1.9
Lithuania	10.8	4.8	3.4	3.6
Poland (1988)*	115.7	84.9	81.7	81.4
Slovakia	16.3	10.4	10.7	10.4
Slovenia	3.8	4.7	4.2	4.2
Malta**	—	—	—	—
Cyprus**	—	—	—	—
Total Accession	230.3	154.5	146.6	146.7
Other EU candidates				
Bulgaria (1988)*	28.3	15.3	13.7	15.0
Croatia	6.4	5.3	5.4	5.7
Romania (1989)*	53.4	27.2	24.0	24.7
Turkey**	—	—	—	—
Other Annex I EITs				
Ukraine	191.9	100.0	105.0	104.5
Russia	647.0	395.8	440.0	450.7

Source: base year emissions, UNFCCC (EIA for those with base years different to 1990); other emission years, Energy Information Administration, US DOE, Washington.

Note

Accession countries = the 10 countries officially accepted for EU Accession in 2004.

* Base year emissions are 1990 unless otherwise indicated, on the same basis as other data (i.e. energy-related CO_2 emissions). Emissions of the other GHGs collectively have generally declined by at least as much as CO_2 emissions, but full data for recent years are not available.

** Countries not in Kyoto Protocol Annex B, i.e. without emission targets, no emissions data shown as these countries are not relevant to the Kyoto first-period trading system.

Finally, the other 'suppliers' in the Kyoto market are the developing countries. They do not have a ready 'surplus' available to sell, but they can generate emission credits through CDM projects.

Views on the potential supply of credits from the CDM take one of two fundamental approaches. One consists of 'top down' assessments of potential, based on estimated marginal supply curves of the costs of the limiting GHG emissions in developing countries. Depending in part upon the price projections, the resulting estimates of CDM supply spanned a huge range, up to more than 500 MtC/yr (Table 5.6). The need for 'counterfactual' baselines (i.e. projections of what emissions would have been in the absence of the project) also leads

Table 5.6 'Top-down' estimates (prior to 2001) of the size of the CDM

Study	Cost ($billion)	Emission credits (cumulative MtC)	Implied Annex I emissions (% of 1990)
Haites	1–21	27–572	−4.7–+6.9
MIT	2.5–26	273–723	+0.5–+10.0
Austin	5.2–13	397–503	+3.2–+5.4
US administration	4.2–7.9	100–188	−3.1–−1.3
ITEA	3.3–3.9	67–141	−3.8–−2.3

Source: Grubb *et al.* (1999).

to the fear that credits could be generated spuriously (the additionality problem), with one study suggesting that such 'free riding' in the developing country power sector could lead to as much as 250–600 MtC of spurious credits over the first Kyoto period (Bernow *et al.* 2001).

The other approach focuses upon the various institutional and other obstacles to practical projects and the sheer number of projects that would be required. This results in far lower estimates of the CDM potential. Assessments of the scope for forestry similarly cast doubt on whether the volume of such projects in reality could ever reach even close to the 1 per cent cap in the time available (Bernoux *et al.* 2002; Forner and Jotso 2002). The lower prices and demand after the events of 2001, of course, will also depress CDM investments. A recent estimate of actual project flow suggests that projects in the pipeline as of early 2003 would only generate 3.35 MtCO$_2$e of CDM credits by 2005 (PointCarbon 2003), though rapid expansion could be expected as the institutions start to operate fully and if the first deal flows are successful.

The pricing aspect of the CDM is complex. Very low carbon prices are simply not big enough to make much difference to the economics of real projects; prices need to be several tens of $/tC before they are likely to make material difference to investors decisions on whether to proceed with complex, potentially difficult and risky projects in developing countries.

The main implication of all this is that Kyoto will be a 'buyers market', and the ultimate effect of the first period commitments will depend upon how the importing countries approach the international mechanisms.

The 'demand side': EU, Japan and Canada

The European Union

The EU's efforts are focusing first upon domestic implementation. Domestic programmes of member states are varied. Some are quite well developed: it is estimated for example that UK domestic programmes now give an annual incentive towards low carbon investments of about Euros 2bn/yr (Wordsworth and Grubb 2003). Germany, France, The Netherlands, Austria and the Scandinavian countries also all have substantial domestic programmes. In some others, efforts are still in very early stages (see review in Michaelowa 2003).

The most potent symbol of Europe's seriousness about domestic action was agreed in December 2002, with the adoption of a Directive on the European CO_2 Emissions Trading Scheme. This requires all member states – including the Accession countries due to join in 2004 – to implement, by 2005, emissions cap-and-trade regulations to cover the power and main industry sectors. In total the scheme will cover about 45 per cent of total European CO_2 emissions and will be at least ten times larger than the precursor US system on sulphur regulation.

In addition to this tendency to prioritize domestic action, EU reservation about unlimited use of the international mechanisms has a long history. At least three other factors will shape the EU's approach to the international carbon market under Kyoto:

1   *The politics of EU enlargement*. Economic and political considerations smoothing the path of Accession are likely to take precedence, so the 'price' in intra-Europe trading is unlikely to be allowed to fall to near zero.
2   *The EU-Russia energy dialogue*. Engagement with Russia and Ukraine will be set in an explicit context seeking political cooperation based largely around energy trade, and in particular east-west gas trade and the EU-Russia energy dialogue. Kyoto units are likely to be seen as a tool to be used in the context of this dialogue and its associated efforts to secure a stable basis for foreign investment in the Russian energy system.
3   *Political investment in Kyoto*. The EU was at the centre of political efforts to rescue the Kyoto Protocol. This involved convincing both developing countries and the EITs not only that it was the 'right' thing to do, but that they stood to benefit from the system. In addition, the EU has relatively strong ties with many developing countries, partly through ex-colonial links. The result is that the EU is bound (in both senses of the word) to factor political and strategic considerations in to any international trading under the Protocol.

All this will take expression in a diverse willingness to pay. For example, the EU might be willing to pay 'over the odds' to encourage CDM project in Africa, as compared to countries that are perceived to be less 'in need', or which are already attracting foreign investment. Indeed, the promise of international money flows form the glue behind the political consensus underpinning Kyoto. This implies a political need to do some international trading, but also to avoid a price collapse. The EU may be a buyer, but it cannot aim to be a least cost/lowest price buyer.

Japan

Japan has been ideologically even further from regarding Kyoto as a 'free market' than was Europe. Japan needs the flexibility, but at the same time the mechanisms are regarded as an instrument, at the sovereign disposal of 'Japan inc.' and not a market 'free for all'. As such, perhaps to an even greater extent than the EU, Japan will exercise buyer sovereignty over whom it wishes to trade with, and on what terms.

Against this background, the deep-rooted difficulties of Japanese relations with Russia – sustained since World War Two by the continuing dispute over the Kurile Islands – are highly relevant. When in 1998 MITI announced 20 'AIJ projects' with Russia it was seen as a breakthrough; the subsequent failure of any of these projects to materialize has reinforced Japanese scepticism about Russia being a reliable source of supply: Japanese implementation plans do not formally include *any* use of Russian allowances (Matsumura 2001). Japanese NGOs are also likely to demand, with influence, that emissions trading should be tied to environmentally legitimate investments – the only way in which transferring money to an old adversary is likely to be politically acceptable. Any Japan-Russia deals on JI or emissions trading will proceed cautiously, hesitantly, with conditions requiring monitorable environmental investments, and at a small scale as pilot programmes in building trust (Tangen *et al.* 2002).

Insofar as Japan needs emission units, it is likely to seek the bulk in the form of CDM credits from developing countries, and it may be willing to pay substantial prices, using this in part as a political instrument for maintaining good relations with its Asian developing country neighbours. Again, its behaviour will focus first upon domestic implementation, topped up by international access on carefully circumscribed terms.

Canada

Of all the countries in Kyoto, Canada probably has both an interest and an ideology inclined to treat Kyoto as a competitive international carbon market. In percentage terms, Canada probably faces an 'emissions gap' larger than Japan; and it may have less resistance to large-scale emissions trading with Russia.

Yet even for Canada, it is becoming apparent that reality will differ markedly from the models, for two big reasons. One is that environmental and international NGOs, which have a large influence in Canada (and the wider public), object strongly to the idea of giving Russia money for 'doing nothing', as indeed does the general public. In addition, Canadian industry has mixed interests. Those companies that have opposed Kyoto would nevertheless like to seek ways of benefiting from it, if Canada does go ahead. And the most obvious way they can do so is if foreign expenditure for emission units is directed primarily towards investments that involve Canadian companies – perhaps particularly for

Russia, where the similar range of climatic conditions makes Canadian expertise potentially valuable. Albertan companies, which have so fiercely opposed Kyoto, could be the first to line up in favour of linking emissions trading with Russia to real investments in the Russian energy systems – and at as high a price as possible, if they have prospects of being the main contractors.

Analogies with the oil market

How exceptional is the Kyoto 'market'? The above discussion suggests, at first sight, that it will be so far from the economic ideal of a least-cost market as to scarcely justify the term 'market', and that little insight could be gained from expertise with other market operations. Whilst Kyoto undoubtedly has many unique features, the behaviour sketched is not really so exceptional.

Consider the oil markets. Despite a century of evolution, international oil prices are generally maintained well above $20/bbl, despite the fact that the marginal production cost in Saudi Arabia is probably less than $5/bbl. Saudi Arabia's main influence is wielded through the OPEC alliance of exporting countries, yet even OPEC overall does not exert anything like monopoly control on supplies, whilst its members themselves have widely divergent interests according to their fiscal and reserve situations.

For Kyoto's first period, it is not hard to see Russia as the Saudi Arabia of carbon permits, and the EITs as OPEC. Nor is it hard to draw analogies with the 1980s oil price collapse, envisioning Russia trying to hold back supplies whilst the carbon price sinks lower and lower until it loses patience and threatens to flood the market. One potential feature of such markets certainly is their price instability, and dependence on political decisions and negotiations amongst suppliers. Similar features would hardly be surprising in the Kyoto first period system.

Yet a view of oil markets that focuses only on supply is also fundamentally misguided, or at least extremely dated. The oil price is maintained so far above its marginal production cost through processes that are to a large degree collaborative between producing and consuming nations and with industry. Such collaboration (mostly informal) is only possible because of a perceived common interest in maintaining prices that are stable, and at 'reasonable' levels, which is generally understood to mean in the range *c.* $20–25/bbl. Importing countries acquiesce (or even actively collaborate) to maintain prices an order of magnitude higher than marginal production costs, for a variety of complex reasons. These include the internal politics of their own oil industries, and long-term strategic calculations that oil is, ultimately, a highly valuable and (on strategic timescales) scarce resource. Higher prices do not only protect domestic investments in frontier non-OPEC production, and keep high-cost domestic oil companies in business; they also underpin efforts to reduce long-term dependence on imports through efficiency and diversification. Again, analogies with the carbon markets are not hard to draw.

Finally, much as the oil markets involve a high degree of government-industry interaction (though now somewhat less than formerly), the Kyoto system is bound to involve the same. Some governments at least wish to protect and support emergent industries that can deliver, and profit from, lower carbon futures.

Differentiation among the Kyoto units

The Protocol itself places no significant restrictions on the fungibility of the different units defined under Kyoto;[17] all can be added to bring a country into compliance.[18] Despite this effective lack of formal restrictions, there will be considerable price discrimination for the reasons set out in this chapter. Some such discrimination will come directly from the private sector in this nascent market. Especially in this formative stage, the value accorded to emission units by the private sector is strongly affected by both reputational and political risk considerations. Reputational considerations will make companies averse to large scale and potentially controversial projects, such as large scale agroforestry where land rights are disputed. Political risk considerations will include the risks associated with uncertainty about what kind of units home governments will ultimately accept.

With the Marrakech Accords establishing the fundamentals of project eligibility, the major governmental distinctions are likely to depend upon region – and corresponding mechanisms – but with important subdivisions according to project type (see Box 5.3).

Traded AAUs appear subject to the greatest political risk, and consequently the greatest discounting. Conversely however, AAU trading is likely to be an essential component of the compliance portfolio at least for Japan and Canada, simply because it is probably the only source large enough to ensure their compliance given the real-world constraints on project volumes. Within AAU trading, one can distinguish four possible components:

- 'Greened' trading, in which any revenues from trading are linked directly to environmental investment; this is likely to be the most widely favoured and attract the highest premium.

Box 5.3 Differentiation among the Kyoto project mechanisms

Project mechanisms. Credits from project mechanisms may attract a premium over AAUs from trading, principally because they can be seen on all sides to be associated with real project investments – real action and measured environmental gain – as opposed to paper trading. Supplementary reasons include the interests of domestic actors (e.g. within Russia) to use project credits to attract and leverage much larger overall investment to specific sectors and projects, as well as the sheer political difficulty of developing domestic corporate emission trading systems. However there is likely to be discrimination even within the project mechanisms.

CERs may attract a premium over ERUs for three reasons: they are more likely to be perceived as contributing to developmental needs in poor regions; the crediting can begin immediately (as opposed to being a forward transfer of credits projected from 2008); and they will pass through a more rigorous international procedure for accreditation. Amongst CERs, there may be preference for those generated from small-scale, renewable energy projects under the 'fast track' procedures agreed at COP 8, because of the general perception that renewable energy promotion is a good end in itself and because the COP 8 decision removes much political risk.[i] Detailed rules for accrediting other CDM project types have yet to be determined by the Executive Board. Discounting may be particularly large for some forestry projects, given both greater potential land-use conflicts, and the longer timescales likely to be involved in resolving rules for these (which are not scheduled to be resolved until COP 10, in 2004).

ERUs may be somewhat more homogenous, in part because of the smaller geographic and economic range of the source countries. However, there could clearly be a distinction between the 'mainstream' and 'track two' JI procedures. The former, for projects in countries that have fulfilled all relevant eligibility criteria, might give greater legal security about the credits, but for many EITs, full eligibility may imply a long delay, and the detailed project supervision is slight compared to CDM projects. 'Track two' procedures in principle could come on-stream quicker, but uncertainty still exists about the exact form and functioning of the Supervisory Committee.

RMUs (from carbon sink activities) may be more difficult to locate in the spectrum of perceived value. Carbon sink projects are frequently criticised on the grounds that the incremental emission savings are very hard to monitor and quantify, that they may displace 'better' land uses, and that the carbon stored might later be re-released (the problem of permanence). In these respects, the RMUs resulting from sink projects may be seen as less valuable than CERs and ERUs derived from energy sector investments. However, this perception of sink projects is also strongly disputed.[ii]

Notes

i FCCC/CP/2002/L.5, Report of the Executive Board of the CDM, Decision COP 8, Annex A: 'Draft simplified modalities and procedures for small-scale clean development mechanism project activities'. Such projects are defined as renewable energy project activities with maximum output capacity equivalent of up to 15 megawatts; energy efficiency improvement project activities which reduce energy consumption, on the supply and/or demand side, by up to the equivalent of 15 gigawatt hours per year; and other project activities that both reduce anthropogenic emission by source and directly emit less than 15 kilotonnes of carbon dioxide equivalent annually.

ii The idea that energy-sector emission savings are inherently 'better' than carbon sinks has been strongly disputed for certain kinds of land use projects. E.g. Chomitz (2002) argues that from a carbon perspective the differences between energy and land-use projects are far less clear and systematic than often supposed, and Pandey (2002) makes a strong case that agroforestry in developing countries could have large ancillary benefits for host countries.

- Trading from OECD countries that have exceeded their targets demonstrably due to domestic action may be considered next, and would provide a sense of diversity in the portfolio. The UK is one of few OECD countries likely to surpass its target, and international availability of such AAUs may depend in large measure upon the EU's wider progress towards compliance including Accession countries.
- AAUs could also be made available from EITs in a controlled manner through non-GIS-type routes: for example, EIT governments could develop some domestic trading schemes with allocation that is seen to have some degree of environmental credibility.
- Finally, wholesale transfers of AAUs without any such linkage would be legal under the Marrakech Accords, but for all the reasons discussed this is likely to be the option of 'last resort' and the most heavily discounted.

All this of course makes price prediction extremely difficult. However, various approaches, or influences, can be considered:

- *expert prediction* of those already engaged in real trading; these confirm strongly the hypothesis of wide price differentiation between projects and mechanisms;
- *sufficiency*, i.e. prices required to significantly affect investment behaviour; this implies prices around $/Euros 10–20/tCO$_2$ to be relevant in project economics;
- *financial flow constraints* arising from the desire to protect existing domestic policies on the one hand, but to constrain intergovernmental financial transfers on the other.

The last of these relates mostly to Canada, because of its likely high demand. Table 5.7 shows implications for Japan and Canada under combinations of extreme cases. If the need for allowance imports is low, and it is considered acceptable for international carbon allowance expenditure to reach 20 per cent of ODA expenditure, then Japan might accept international carbon prices about $20/tCO$_2$e, compatible with the other measures. Canada however, with a much higher proportion of carbon import needs relative to ODA expenditure, may find it hard to tolerate international AAU prices much above $5/tCO$_2$ even under relatively favourable conditions. Much more likely is that Canada will seek large volume international transfers of AAUs at prices well below this, and perhaps as low as $1/tCO$_2$e. Prices much above this are likely to run into varied political constraints: from the same domestic pressures that have curtailed ODA expenditure to the present levels; from domestic development aid constituencies, arguing that development is a far more pressing need for such large expenditures – and, indeed, from developing countries themselves, on the same grounds.

Table 5.7 International revenue flow constraints on carbon prices

	Current ODA expenditure (1998 data)		Likely volume of imports, MtCO₂e/yr		Price required for allowance trade to equal x% of ODA	
	US $bn/yr	% GNP	Low	High	20%	5%
Japan	10,640	0.28	100	200	21.28	2.66
Canada	1,691	0.29	50	100	6.76	0.85

These considerations underline why price differentiation is probably inevitable in the Kyoto system. Prices for project-mechanism credits that are high enough to be effective, in terms of influence on discrete projects, are likely to lead to unacceptably high financial transfers if applied to wholesale AAU trading. AAU transfers will generally be at much lower prices – but to avoid undermining the basic purpose of Kyoto and of domestic measures already in effect, they will be contained in application to those cases where such transfers are deemed necessary and acceptable to enable countries to comply.

This suggests a wide range of prices, differentiated according to the nature of the source, project and mechanism. Grubb (2003) suggests that prices for companies engaging in Kyoto-compliant projects in developing countries and EITs will be in the range £10–25/tCO$_2$ for the smaller-scale, widely-approved projects such as renewable energy investments, and £5–15/tCO$_2$ for more potentially controversial (and lower cost) projects including land-use, but also for example for large-scale boiler retrofitting or gas conversion. Prices for allowances themselves (AAUs) may be lower, but they may be seen as having lower value, and little or no co-benefits, except where they are visibly linked to environmental investments at prices that may push towards the level of project credits.

In turn, the prices for large-scale transfers of AAUs between governments may be lower still; but the private sector will not be given access to these. The reason for this, fundamentally, is that although emissions trading under Kyoto has been analysed as one instrument, in reality it will be used to fulfil two quite different functions. One is the traditional role of providing market flexibility and efficiency at the margin of project investments. The other is fundamentally a redistributional function, correcting the excessively lop-sided nature of the original Kyoto allocations. The cost of making such transfers at the 'market' price that would be required to sustain action effective action on climate change is politically tenable. Neither 'east nor west' has the market power to exact such a price, nor could the fledgling Kyoto institutions withstand the political pressures such transfers would generate. So, large-scale intergovernmental transfers, most notably for Canada, will occur at much lower prices – and domestic programmes, and the private sector, will be shielded from the malign influence that such low prices would otherwise exert on international efforts to initiate some real action under Kyoto.

Thus in the 'Kyoto market' there will be not be one uniform 'price of carbon', but many diverse prices at least in terms of implications for actual project economics. It may be that international trading facilities develop a 'carbon price' for Kyoto units, but not all sellers will make their units available at a flat price, nor will all buyers choose (as governments) to buy at such a price. Some will trade at a discount, some at a premium, because their value to companies for complying with domestic legislation will vary correspondingly.

This in fact is a characteristic of the nascent private sector market at present. Companies are more willing to pay for emission credits from projects that are perceived as very high quality and uncontroversial – projects to which hardly anyone is likely to object, and which seem likely to attract the approval of both governments and NGOs. Emission credits or allowances from other sources may be traded, but at a discount.

The Kyoto Protocol, as elaborated in the Marrakech Accords, will not in itself define 'the standard'. It may well do so for CDM project credits (CERs), though even for this, credits from renewable energy projects in the poorer countries may well be given a premium compared, for example, to forestry projects in some of the richer developing countries. The COP 8 decision on expedited procedures for small-scale CDM projects, indeed, could help to define the first real international carbon market component, and renewable energy credits generated under the CDM fast track procedures could emerge to be the 'marker' commodity in the carbon market.

The Marrakech Accords may also set market standards for JI project credits (ERUs) – but the Accords themselves create two tracks for JI. With 'track one' contingent upon meeting quite onerous national reporting requirements, and the value accorded to projects developed under 'track two' dependant in part upon choices yet to be made by the Supervisory Committee, ERUs are unlikely to generate a standard marker price in the near future; and the laxer the standards that may be set, the wider the differentiation of ERU prices may be.

For Kyoto's first period, price convergence, stability and greater homogeneity could only realistically be expected both as the institutions mature and if the supply overhand were somehow eliminated to make the market much 'tighter'.

Volume flows and potential carry-over of Kyoto units

As explained above, the international flexibility in Kyoto is not undermining the general impetus to domestic action in Kyoto countries; rather, the mechanisms are being developed as a 'reserve' to enable compliance when countries fall short of domestic targets. This, combined with recent emission trends, the carbon sink agreement, and US withdrawal, together have huge implications for the balance of supply and demand in the Kyoto first period. Table 5.8 shows two scenarios of

Table 5.8 Supply–demand balance in Kyoto system (MtCe/yr): limit scenarios

	Historical emissions		Low surplus (high demand, low supply)		High surplus (low demand, high supply)	
	1990	2000	% change 2000–2010	Carbon balance	% change 2000–2010	Carbon balance
Gross demand				220		53
EU carbon	911.4	895.5	7	120	−3	30
Japan carbon	305.3	313.7	10	58	−3	17
Canada carbon	128.6	158.0	15	61	0	37
+ Net other GHGs (+5, −5%)				12		−2
− Managed forest allowance				−30		−30
Supply				331		587
Russia carbon	647	450.7	20	106	0	196
Ukraine carbon	191.9	104.5	20	67	0	87
Accession 10 carbon	245.2	146.6	25	45	5	75
Other EITs	87.8	45.4	25	24	0	36
Other GHGs (10, 20%)				24		79
+ Managed forest allowance				40		40
CDM (MtC/yr equiv in Kyoto period)				15		50
Net surplus				110		530

potential volumes, that probably represent limiting high and low cases for the degree of surplus. These are constructed in terms of emission trends from the latest year's data, the year 2000, and taking account of underlying trends (such as high population and economic growth rates in Canada).

Under a 'low surplus' scenario that combines high demand with low supply, gross CO_2 emissions in the EU-15 might be about 120 MtC above its Kyoto allocation, and those from Japan and Canada might each be about half that (60 MtC/yr) in absolute terms. Assuming that Australia and the US remain outside the Protocol, and after taking account of other greenhouse gases and the managed forest allowance, the total demand from OECD countries might be about 220 MtC/yr. Under 'low supply' assumptions, in which emissions from the EITs grow 20–25 per cent from their levels in year 2000, the total supply from EITs might be about 330 MtC/yr, to which a minimum level of CDM investment might add the equivalent of about 15 MtC/yr. The result is a surplus of 110 MtC/yr – or a total over the five-year period of 550 MtC presumably 'banked' into subsequent commitment periods.

Under the 'high surplus' scenario, in which emissions from the EU and Japan decline 3 per cent below current (2000) levels and Canada stabilizes at 2000 levels, the potential demand (after taking account of the Marrakech forest allowances) is shrunk to only just over 50 MtC/yr. If emissions in the EITs follow their emission trend of the last three years – essentially flat at current levels in which economic growth is matched by equivalent gains in energy efficiency – then total availability of allowances from the EITs is likely to exceed 500 MtC/yr. If there is also greater take-up of the CDM, then the potential net surplus could be 550 MtC/yr.

These are limiting scenarios that combine extremes in opposite directions, particularly concerning the 'low surplus'. Far more likely is something more central; the actual surplus will probably be in the range 200–450 MtC/yr, or 1000–2250 MtC total unused from the first Kyoto period. For comparison, US CO_2 emissions in 2000 (and in 2001, in which emissions fell slightly) exceeded the US's original Kyoto allowance by about 300 MtC/yr.

Discussion and conclusions

The Kyoto Protocol stands out primarily for its unprecedented inclusion of a range of international economic instruments. Many of these ideas had been anathema a generation earlier; by the mid-1990s, when the Protocol's core ideas were born, they had become almost hegemonic in economic but not in environmental policy. The Protocol is essentially an agreement to extend economic globalization to environmental policy: to establish a global emissions market to counter the global environmental consequences of global economic growth. A great deal of work remained to be done to determine how such mechanisms might actually work and be governed in the international context, a task that took four years and culminated in the Marrakech Accords agreed at COP 7, generally dubbed the 'rulebook for implementing Kyoto'.

Politically, the most striking feature of the Protocol's design is the dominance of the US. The United States got virtually everything it wanted in respect of flexibility for Annex I commitments with the sole exception of 'borrowing' (which, in a different form, was finally embodied as part of the penalties for non-compliance after US withdrawal). The main policy objective of US strategy was to establish flexibility in all dimensions. This was a result of the country's confluence of political interest and economic ideology. Politically (and with good reason), the administration lacked confidence about what measures on CO_2 emissions could be ratified or implemented domestically, and it regarded the ability to meet any commitments through action on other gases, sinks and international mechanisms as a political imperative. Economically, US thinking was dominated by general equilibrium concepts which automatically imply that flexibility achieves the same environmental benefits at lower costs: hence, the more flexibility the better. That attitude, combined with US political dominance and the relative paucity of counter-arguments, largely determined the outcome of most of the key policy debates. As noted by the author elsewhere, 'to discover the source of most of the ideas in the Protocol, one only needs to read the US proposal of January 1997' (Grubb *et al.* 1999) – which makes the subsequent developments all the more ironic.

Economic fundamentals

In terms of its basic structure (abstracted from the specific numerical targets of the first period), the *fundamental economic issues* concern not so much the mechanisms, but the interface between uncertainties, technology, and the scope and evolution of commitments. There is no inherent 'right' answer to the issue of timescales. Long-term targets would maximize time for adjustment and technological change, but would suffer from huge uncertainty about their political credibility and give no room for learning in the interim. Shorter term commitments give politically plausible signals on timescales of immediate relevance, and allow scope for future commitments to be negotiated and expanded as knowledge accumulates. The balance struck in Kyoto, with a 15 year gap between the point of adoption in Kyoto and the first compliance point in 2012, seems not unreasonable, but its limitations in providing 'bankable' signals for longer term investment are becoming more apparent as time passes.

There are also deeper diverse perspectives about the relationship between targets and technology, and related issues of 'leakage' and longer term strategies. One perspective equates technical change largely with public R&D and proposes to focus on some kind of intergovernmental technology programme; from this perspective, the Kyoto targets are a premature and potentially costly distraction, and moreover subject to 'leakage' of emissions if some industries migrate to countries without emission caps (Barrett 2001). Most economists however remain sceptical about the utility of governments choosing and fostering technologies, and recognize that technical change is to an important degree fostered by market conditions (for a review with reference to modelling, see Grubb, Koehler and Anderson 2002). From this perspective, the Kyoto targets can be the impetus for investment in low carbon technologies, with the view that as the associated industries develop the technologies can diffuse globally (aided by Kyoto's CDM and technology transfer provisions, and subsequently by extension of commitments), thus bringing down emissions globally as well.

First period economics

This is one reason why the Kyoto Parties are focusing first upon domestic implementation, with the international mechanisms as a backup to aid compliance, rather than treating Kyoto as a free market. This, combined with the lop-sided nature of the initial allocations and the US withdrawal, has precipitated a 'buyers market' and the *first period economics* are subtle and complex. The over-arching role of governments, and the varied interests and mechanisms as sketched in this paper, have several implications. Governments are not cost-minimizing agents irrespective of geography: they exist primarily to represent their populations, who would far rather see money spent domestically than abroad, and far rather see it spent on 'good things' than on paper transfers. These are additional reasons why they are likely to be quite discriminating about the emission credits they use, making sure they are derived from projects they consider desirable and legitimate, or are otherwise linked to environmentally acceptable use of revenues. As a result, as explained, there will be considerable price divergence between different mechanisms and projects.

Kyoto may evolve towards greater price consistency over time, but price instability and discrimination between different kinds of emission units may be fundamental features of the early stages especially. As with other historical markets, the 'emissions market' is thus likely to evolve from the bottom-up, albeit in the global context set by Kyoto. The Kyoto/Marrakech Accords simply cannot in themselves set a definitive standard for the international trading of all the units potentially available, for the simple reason that this would lead the whole Kyoto system to collapse under a sea of meaningless paper transactions: the surplus of allowances available could be several hundred MtC/yr. Given the reality of such numbers, it is hard to see how a free and competitive market could emerge in the first period unless the US were to rejoin the system in ways that eliminate the huge supply/demand imbalance – not a prospect that seems likely at present.

Economics of the next step

In considering Kyoto's prospects, it is important to distinguish between the basic structure, and the specific first period allocations. Nearly all the criticisms have focused upon the latter. Obviously, the situation now arising from the first period allocations is neither desirable, nor not what was originally intended, and this has been used to claim the whole approach is flawed (e.g. Victor 2001).[19] If Kyoto does move to negotiations on a second commitment period, as mandated, there are three reasons for thinking that similar problems would not arise:

- the core problem in the first period allocations (apart from the US withdrawal) concerned allocations to the EITs that have proved excessive. This is a direct consequence of the transition from centrally-planned economies, and would not recur – even most developing countries now operating loosely on market principles, however imperfectly;
- countries would be immensely better informed and prepare much more carefully, in terms of understanding emission trends both for themselves and for others;
- second period negotiations would involve deciding allocations not as far ahead as the 15-year gap inherent in the Kyoto first period allocation, so the scope for major unexpected deviations would be more limited.

Nevertheless, the potential degree of carry-forward into the second period would exacerbate the difficulties, and in reality, little progress can be expected on developing country engagement unless and until after the US rejoins in some meaningful way.

Overall, Kyoto can be seen as a potent symbol of intent to control emissions, a basic regulatory framework with initial targets backed by a modest international price signal, and as a vast learning exercise. Through their national reporting requirements and implementation plans, countries are becoming familiar with what can be delivered in terms of emission reductions and the policies involved. Internationally, they are learning the fundamentals of developing efficient international responses including what is required to make international market instruments work. Whether or not the world draws on this investment, by proceeding to the next big step of negotiating second period allocations, remains to be seen.

Notes

1 This chapter draws upon Module 1 of the Kyoto-Marrakech Strategic Assessment project (Grubb 2003) for which the author is grateful for financial support from the governments of Sweden, Canada, Switzerland and the UK. Support from BP for a related project on future carbon prices under the Kyoto Protocol is also gratefully

acknowledged. In addition he would like to thank all those who made helpful comments on earlier drafts of the work. The views expressed are the responsibility of the author alone and should not be attributed to any of the supporting organizations.

2 Article 4.2 of the UNFCCC commits industrialized countries to adopt 'policies and measures that will demonstrate that developed countries are taking the lead in modifying longer-term trends in anthropogenic emissions consistent with the objective of the Convention', with the initial 'aim' of returning their emissions of CO_2 and other greenhouse gases to 1990 levels. This became the focus of attention in the years immediately after the Convention and the failure of key industrialized countries to move in this direction was a principal reason why Kyoto moved to binding commitments focused on the industrialized countries.

3 The COP 1 meeting agreed that the UNFCCC commitments were inadequate, and consequently to 'begin a process to enable it to take appropriate action for the period beyond 2000, including the strengthening of the commitments of Annex I Parties, i.e. the industrialized world', to 'elaborate policies and measures'; and 'set quantified limitation and reduction objectives within specified timeframes, such as 2005, 2010 and 2020. It was agreed that these negotiations 'should not introduce new commitments for developing countries', but should enhance the implementation of their existing commitments under the UNFCCC. Thus were launched the intensive negotiations that finally culminated in Kyoto.

4 Though the basis for the division is general UN categorization, and a few small non-Annex I countries such as Singapore also have high per-capita emissions.

5 Article 5, and Decision 2/CP-3. In the negotiations, technical concerns about the accuracy of monitoring became eclipsed by the economic and political arguments in favour of including a range of gases. If significant gases were excluded altogether, it would weaken the scope and impact of the Protocol. If they were included separately it would add yet more tracks of separate negotiations. But most important of all to the politicians, the inclusion of some other gases – especially methane, emissions of which are easier to control and in several countries were already declining – made it appear more cost-efficient and easier to adopt stronger emission targets.

6 In most countries the reverse is true for at least some of the three industrial trace gases emissions of some of which are increasing rapidly, and countries are allowed to take a 1995 base year for the three industrial trace gases.

7 The net changes in greenhouse gas emissions by sources and removals by sinks resulting from direct human-induced land-use change and forestry activities, limited to afforestation, reforestation and deforestation since 1990, measured as verifiable changes in carbon stocks in each commitment period shall be used to meet the commitments under this Article [they] shall be reported in a transparent and verifiable manner and reviewed in accordance with Articles 7 and 8. The subsequent Subsidiary Body meeting in June 1998 clarified this clause as meaning that Parties' assigned amounts should be adjusted by 'verifiable changes in carbon stocks during the period 2008 to 2012 resulting from direct human-induced activities of afforestation, reforestation and deforestation since 1 January 1990.

8 With 'borrowing' there would be no point in time at which a country could be assessed as being out of compliance, hence no point at which to apply any enforcement procedures – a strange interpretation of the term 'binding'. The United States recast its borrowing proposal in the form of a penalty for non-compliance (a deduction from allowances in the subsequent period) which was taken up in the subsequent Marrakech Accords.

9 A 1995 base year would have made life much easier for those, like Japan and the United States, whose emissions had risen since 1990, and it would have allowed a more impressive headline figure to emerge for these countries' commitments. Arguably, it would also put the economies in transition on a more comparable footing. But it would have created a whole new set of problems for handling EIT commitments, and rewarded inaction. The year 1990 remains as the official point of reference for when countries first accepted that climate change was a problem, and industrialized countries had already agreed under the UNFCCC to aim to return their emissions to 1990 levels as the demonstration of their commitment to lead the global effort.

10 The central clash was between the EU's aim of flat-rate reductions for all in the range 10–15 per cent below 1990 levels, and US and Japanese support for reductions of 0–5 per cent, with varied ideas about differentiation and flexibility, combined with Russian sensitivities and the special circumstances of some of the smaller countries. The United States traded percentage points for increases in the degree of flexibility (e.g. inclusion of sinks enabled them to add three percentage points; after Kyoto, the United States argued domestically that in reality it had only had to concede an additional two percentage points from its original negotiating position of zero, the rest being directly tied to increased flexibilities). Japan, the third party in the internecine OECD debates, was dragged reluctantly along to higher commitments than it had prepared. Russia started with zero and – annoyed by the EU's opening Ministerial reference to the importance of keeping the 'three major Parties' at the same level – refused to budge. All this was overlaid by root political objectives and perceptions that pegged some countries' numbers to those of others. EIT countries aspiring to membership of the EU or OECD wanted to align themselves with the EU's standard-setting commitment. Canada honoured its status as a G7 member by staying within the 'leading'; Australia, feeling no such constraint, simply insisted on being allowed a big increase.

11 Every country that supported differentiation had a different idea of how it should be calculated. Many different indicators were proposed, relating to GDP, energy intensity, carbon intensity, historical emissions, trade patterns, etc. Most 'differentiators' argued that low carbon intensity (i.e. low carbon emissions relative to GDP) in 1990 should be a basis for a weaker target; but Australia argued precisely the opposite, claiming that high carbon intensity showed an innate dependence upon fossil fuels that could only be broken at great expense. Almost the only common theme to emerge was that each country proposed indicators that would be most beneficial to itself.

12 At a late stage of negotiations, Poland and Hungary moved back to −6 per cent in protest at the weaker Russian and Ukrainian allocations.

13 Establishing quantified commitments for countries in early stages of development would not only have been politically impossible, it would also have faced huge uncertainties in their emissions data and growth trends. It is also questionable whether it would have been technically feasible from a negotiating standpoint, given the huge complexities of reaching agreement even amongst the 38 industrialized countries.

14 To conform with the emerging standard in the UNFCCC and the private sector, prices in this report are given per unit $MtCO_2$. The conversion factor between tC and tCO_2 is $44/12$.

15 Industrial CO_2 here refers to all CO_2 emissions from industrial activity, specifically energy-related activities. This accounts for about 80 per cent of the total GHG

emissions across all industrialized countries. Thus the absolute tonnes involved will be higher for the Kyoto basket in full than indicated in Figure 5.4. Every effort has been made to ensure that the 'emissions gap' calculation is derived from consistent comparison between the target as derived from 1990 emission levels, and actual recent emissions, i.e. both refer to CO_2 emissions from energy. Possible differences in trends of other greenhouse gases, and in carbon sinks other than the managed forest allowance as indicated, are not large enough to affect the main points derived from Figure 5.4.

16 This is due to the fact that the Buchner *et al.* model includes both cartelization of the market, and a feedback between prices and technological change. They argue that the low prices in the absence of the US will slow down technical change and lead to higher emissions in the rest of Annex I. In reality, it is hard to see how such an impact of induced technical change could operate so substantially on a timescale of just a few years, though the point, taken more generally, is pertinent.

17 Namely Annex I carbon sink projects (RMUs); CDM projects (CERs, from investments in developing countries under Article 12); JI projects (ERUs, from investments in other Annex I countries under Article 6); Trading of Assigned Amount Units (AAUs, acquired from another Annex I country through trading under Article 17).

18 There are restrictions on the volume of RMUs allowable (1 per cent of initial Assigned Amounts), though Jotzo and Michaelowa (2002) make a persuasive case that this cap could not be reached anyway. RMUs cannot be banked for use in subsequent periods, but their allowable and likely volume is sufficiently small that they can readily be used in the first period for compliance and other units banked instead. Similar remarks apply to ERUs and CERs, of which a maximum of 2.5 per cent of initial Assigned Amounts each can be banked.

19 Note however that Victor's proposed alternative structure is in many ways similar to Kyoto, being also based upon the fundamental core of sequentially negotiated national emission caps with emissions trading. The main differences are that he proposes restricting the system to CO_2 only, rather than the full set of gases, and to OECD countries only in the first instance to avoid many of the uncertainties and institutional difficulties associated with the transition economies.

Bibliography

Babiker, M.H., Jacoby, H.D., Reilly, J.M. and Reiner D.M. (2002) 'The evolution of a climate regime: Kyoto to Marrakech', Joint Program on the Science and Policy of Global Change, MIT.

Barrett, S. (2001) 'Towards a better climate treaty', *World Economics* 3:35–45.

Bernoux, M., Eschenbrenner, V., Cerri, C.C., Melillo, J.M. and Feller, C. (2002) 'LULUCF-based CDM: too much ado for a small carbon market', *Climate Policy* 2:379–385.

Bernow, S., Kartha, S., Lazarus, M. and Page, T. (2001) 'Cleaner generation, free-riders, and environmental integrity: clean development mechanism and the power sector', *Climate Policy* 1:229–249.

Böhringer, C. (2001) 'Climate politics from Kyoto to Bonn: from little to nothing?', ZEW Discussion Paper No. 01-49, Mannheim.

Böhringer, C. and Löschel, A. (2001) 'Market power in international emissions trading: the impact of US withdrawal from the Kyoto Protocol', ZEW Discussion Paper No. 01-58, Mannheim.

Buchner, B., Carraro, C. and Cersosimo, I. (2002) 'Economic consequences of the US withdrawal from the Kyoto/Bonn Protocol', *Climate Policy* 2:273–292.

Chomitz, K.M. (2002) 'Baseline, leakage and measurement issues: how do forestry and energy projects compare?', *Climate Policy* 2:35–49.

Criqui, P. and Kitous, A. (2001) 'POLES model and ASPEN software simulations', IEPE, Grenoble, France.

Den Elzen, M.G.J. and de Moor, A.P.G. (2001a) 'Evaluating the Bonn Agreement and some key issues', RIVM Report 728001016/2001.

Den Elzen, M.G.J. and de Moor, A.P.G. (2001b) 'The Bonn Agreement and Marrakech Accords: an updated analysis', RIVM Report 728001017/2001.

Eyckmans, J., van Regemorter, D. and van Steenberghe, V. (2001) 'Is Kyoto fatally flawed? An analysis with MacGEM', Katholike Universiteit Leuven, ETE Working Paper No. 118.

Forner, C. and Jotzo, F. (2002) 'Future restrictions for sinks in the CDM: how about a cap on supply?', *Climate Policy* 2:353–365.

Greene, O. (1996) 'Lessons from other international environmental agreements', in M. Patterson and M. Grubb (eds) *Sharing the Effort: Options for Differentiating Commitments on Climate Change*, London: RIIA.

Grubb, M. (2003) 'The "real economics" of the Kyoto-Marrakech System', Module 1 in Grubb *et al.*, *Strategic Assessment of the Kyoto-Marrakech System*. Online. Available at http://www.iccept.ic.ac.uk/a5-1.html (accessed 25 September 2003).

Grubb, M., Hope, C. and Fouquet, R. (2002) 'Climatic implications of the Kyoto Protocol: the contribution of international spillover', *Climatic Change* 54:11–28.

Grubb, M., Koehler, J. and Anderson, D. (2002) 'Induced technical change in energy/environmental modelling: analytic approaches and policy implications', *Annual Review of Energy and Environment* 27:271–308.

Grubb, M., Vrolijk, C. and Brack, D. (1999) *The Kyoto Protocol: A Guide and Assessment*, London: RIIA/Earthscan.

Hagem, C. and Holtsmark, B. (2001) 'From small to insignificant: climate impact of the Kyoto Protocol with and without US', CICERO Policy Note 2001:1, Oslo.

IPCC (2001) *Climate Change 2001: Mitigation*, Cambridge: Cambridge University Press.

Jotzo, F. and Michaelowa, A. (2002) 'Estimating the CDM market under the Marrakech Accords', *Climate Policy* 2:179–196.

Kemfert, C. (2001) 'Economic impact assessment of alternative climate policy strategies', FEEM Working Papers 86.01, Milan.

Manne, A.S. and Richels, R.G. (2001) 'US rejection of the Kyoto Protocol: the impact on compliance costs and CO_2 emissions', Working Paper 01-12, AEI-Brookings Joint Center for Regulatory Studies.

Matsumura, H. (2001) 'Japanese ratification of the Kyoto Protocol', *Climate Policy* 1:343–362.

Michaelowa, A. (ed.) (2003) 'Special Issue on European Implementation', *Climate Policy*, 3(1).

Pandey, D.N. (2002) 'Carbon sequestration in agroforestry systems', *Climate Policy* 2:367–377.

PointCarbon (2003) 'Killing CDM softly?' Online. Available at http://www.pointcarbon.com (accessed 25 September 2003).

Springer, U. (2003) 'The market for tradeable GHG permits under the Kyoto Protocol: a survey of model studies', *Energy Economics* 25:527–551.

Tangen, K., Korppo, A., Beidin, V., Sugiyama, T., Egenhofer, C., Drexhage, J., Pluzhnikov, O., Grubb, M., Legge, T. Moe, A., Stern, J. and Yamaguchi, K. (2002) 'A Russian Green Investment Scheme – securing environmental benefits from international emissions trading', Climate Strategies report. Online. Available at http://www.climate-strategies.org (accessed 25 September 2003).

Weyant, J. and Hill, J. (eds) (1999) 'The costs of the Kyoto Protocol: a multi-model evaluation', *Energy Journal*, Special Issue.

Wordsworth, A. and Grubb, M. (2003) 'Quantifying the UK's incentives for low carbon investment', in A. Michaelowa (ed.) 'Special Issue on European Implementation', Climate Policy 3(1).

Yellen, J. (1998) *The Kyoto Protocol and the President's Policies to Address Climate Change*, Washington, D.C.: US Administration.

Victor, D. (2001) *The Collapse of the Kyoto Protocol and the Struggle to Slow Global Warming*, Council on Foreign Relations: Princeton University Press.

Vrolijk, C. (2001) 'The Bonn Agreement – the world agrees to leave the US on the sideline', RIIA briefing paper: RIIA: London. Online. Available at http://www.riia.org (accessed 25 September 2003).

6   The role of economic instruments

Fanny Missfeldt and Jochen Hauff

What is a carbon tax and what is emissions trading?

Emissions trading and carbon taxes are two of several instruments a policy maker can choose from to reduce the emission of pollutants, including greenhouse gases. Along with subsidies, they belong to the class of economic instruments of environmental protection policy. As such, they contrast with the most common approach to pollution control, the 'command and control' measures, which include, for example, technical and emissions standards (Baumol and Oates 1988).

Pigou (1946) has been considered as the father of taxes imposed to limit negative environmental externalities, such as climate change. Accordingly, Pigouvian taxes are set at the level of the shadow price of the externality. The idea of emissions trading was first suggested by Crocker (1966) and Dales (1968). Its first practical application dates back to 1977, when the first emissions trading programme was adopted as part of amendments to the US Clean Air Act.

A carbon tax is a tax imposed on the total quantity of greenhouse gases emitted. If, for example, a tax rate, t, of 50 Eurocent per tonne of carbon emitted is imposed, and a company emits 40 tonnes of carbon per year, then the annual carbon tax payable by the company is 200 Euro. Carbon taxes are commonly limited to CO_2 emissions, but they can also be applied to other greenhouse gases such as methane or nitrous oxide.

Emissions trading involves the issuance of allowances or permits to emit a certain quantity (for example a tonne of CO_2) of greenhouse gases over a certain period of time (for example a year). For example, if the companies in a city emit a total of 2,000 tonnes of carbon per year, and the city council decides to limit emissions to a total of 1,400 tonnes of carbon, then 1,400 one-tonne allowances are allocated to the emitters of greenhouse gases. Say there are two emitters in the city, a cement factory and a bus and taxi company. The cement factory receives emission allowances of 600 tonnes of carbon per year. If the cement factory exceeds those 600 tonnes, it may buy the amount from the bus/taxi company, under the condition that the latter has generated emissions reductions in excess of its own target. Put differently, both companies can trade emissions rights. Box 6.1 gives an example from Poland that illustrates how such emissions trading can save costs.

In the case of greenhouse gas emissions, a tradable emission permit represents its owner's right to emit a certain amount of a greenhouse gas within a certain time period. In the case of a carbon tax, no such transfer of rights takes place and the 'polluter pays' principle applies.

As we have seen in previous chapters, greenhouse gases are uniformly mixed pollutants (Hanley *et al.* 1997). This means that emissions of greenhouse gases anywhere in the world add equally to the problem of climate change. Put differ-

---

Box 6.1 Saving costs through negotiated standards: the Chorzów project

Unlike what may be expected from a formerly centrally planned economy, Poland was one of the first European countries to experiment with the idea of emissions trading. In 1991, the Economics Department of the Ministry of the Environment initiated a project which attempted to show the potential of a tradable permit approach. Due to the absence of emission permits in Polish environmental legislation, the project took the form of negotiations of standards between a steel mill, a power plant, local small-scale heat producers and the local environmental administrator. The negotiations resulted in stricter standards for the steel mill, which had relatively low abatement cost, but looser emissions standards for the power plant, having only high-cost abatement options. Also, some of the local boiler houses were closed, and the power plant extended its heat deliveries instead. The firms and municipal agencies accepted this arrangement as the power plant paid additional fees for its increased emissions to the regional administrator. These funds were used to subsidize the introduction of abatement technology in the steel mill, enabling it to fulfil the stricter standard. The joint emissions of both firms fell significantly and much faster than they would have otherwise (Żylicz 1998).

While this project successfully showed the environmental benefits and cost saving potential of introducing flexibility into the standard system (Żylicz 1999), it was not a full blown test of a permit system. No trading took place between the firms due to the lack of a legal basis for such transfers. Instead, a deal was struck, involving the regulator who promised a subsidy to one enterprise while allowing the other one to emit more than previously intended and convincing other sources to close down. While this can be interpreted as a successful case of stakeholder negotiations in pollution prevention, the project could not be repeated, as it was not in all instances in compliance with legal procedures. A discussion of possibilities to establish a Polish emissions trading scheme for CO_2 is discussed in Hauff (2000) and Hauff and Missfeldt (2001). As Poland is an accession country to the European Union, it can be expected to adopt the European Trading scheme in the future.

ently, specific damages in one region cannot be linked to specific emissions in another region.[1] To prevent climate change, policy makers therefore focus on the regulation of emissions at source level, and not the distribution of emissions and attribution of damages.

Unlike SO_2 and NO_X, emissions of greenhouse gases are not commonly measured at the chimney or exhaust level, that is they are not commonly measured 'end-of-pipe'. Although this is technically feasible, policy makers both at the national and international level have commonly opted for an estimation of greenhouse gas emissions on the basis of emission factors attributed to processes and combusted fuels. For example, greenhouse gas emissions from combustion of diesel in motors and cars are calculated using a conversion factor. Such calculation does not take account of the efficiency of an underlying production process, which can affect the actual emissions significantly.[2]

In the next section we will consider the behaviour of both policy instruments in the context of a perfectly competitive, fully transparent and static market. We will mainly focus on the cost criteria and capacity to meet the environmental goals. Following this, we will extend our discussion to include more realistic economic settings, under which the remainder of the criteria listed above is addressed.

Why are carbon taxes and emissions trading least cost, and when?

Let us consider the example of two companies located in the same city. We assume that the mayor of the city has identified climate change as a serious environmental problem,[3] and that, together with the city council, she wants to address the problem. We assume that the city is operating within the framework of a transparent, certain, static and perfectly competitive market. There are two major emitters in the city: a cement factory and a local bus and taxi company.

In the absence of any regulation, the cement factory emits e_c^{Max}, and the local bus and taxi company emits e_b^{Max}. Total emissions in the city then add up to $E = e_c^{Max} + e_b^{Max}$. Costs of reducing emissions for both companies, $i \in \{c,b\}$, is zero for $e_i > e_i^{Max}$. If emissions are reduced to a level of $e_i < e_i^{Max}$, abatement costs $C_i(e_i)$ are incurred.

Costs of reducing emissions increase with the extent of pollution abatement undertaken. Put differently, the larger the emissions, the lower the abatement costs for all $e_i < e_i^{Max}$. This is reflected in the first order derivative of the abatement cost function, which is negative, thus indicating a negative slope:

$$C_i'(e_i) < 0 \qquad (6.1)$$

The absolute value of the first order derivative of the cost curve with respect to e_i is referred to as the marginal abatement cost. Commonly, the costs increase over-proportionally as emissions are reduced. This means that as the cheap options of reducing emissions are implemented first, the remaining options are increasingly more costly. This is reflected in the second derivative of the cost curve, which is positive:

$$C_i''(e_i) > 0 \qquad (6.2)$$

The welfare of the consumer j living in the city is negatively affected by the damage $D_j(E)$ that he incurs from these emissions. A standard assumption is that as emissions go up, damage will go up. Put differently, the first derivative of the damage function is positive:

$$D_j'(E) > 0 \qquad (6.3)$$

This is also referred to as the marginal damage of pollution and may be measured either in utility or monetary terms. Moreover, damage will increase at a higher rate, the higher the level of damage at its starting point. Put differently, the marginal damage of pollution is increasing:

$$D_j''(E) > 0 \qquad (6.4)$$

Total damages for all citizens are the sum of all damages as follows:

$$D(E) = \sum_{j}^{T} D_j(E) \qquad (6.5)$$

The damage generated by climate change could also affect the production of both firms, but we ignore this possibility here. Damage functions are very difficult to estimate for the case of climate change because damages from specific weather events cannot usually be directly linked to climate change, and because most damages will occur in the future.

As a first step, the mayor of the city wants to identify what an economically optimal solution to the reduction of greenhouse gases in his town would be. In doing so, she weighs up the total costs of reducing emissions against the total benefits as reflected in foregone damage. The objective function becomes:

$$\min_{e_c, e_b} W(e_c, e_b) = \min_{e_c, e_b} \{ D(E) + C_c(e_c) + C_b(e_b) \} \qquad (6.6)$$

First order conditions yield:

$$W_{e_c}' = D'(E) + C_c'(e_c) \overset{!}{=} 0$$

$$W_{e_b}' = D'(E) + C'_b(e_b) \overset{!}{=} 0 \qquad (6.7)$$

From this follows:

$$D'(E) = -C'_c(e_c) = -C'_b(e_b) \qquad (6.8)$$

Put differently, in order to reach the economically optimal solution, the marginal damage needs to equal the marginal costs of each individual firm in the optimum. The optimal level of emissions at this point is not zero, because marginal abatement costs at zero emissions are very high. Figure 6.1 shows the optimal level of emissions at e_i^* as the intersection of the marginal abatement cost curve and the marginal damage curve.

Let's call the emission levels at this economically optimal point e_c^* and e_b^*. How can this solution be reached?

Traditional command and control policy commonly implies the adoption of identical emission limits. In our case this would correspond to $e_{limit} = \frac{1}{2}(e_c^* + e_b^*)$ for each of the two emitters. This will only be efficient if the marginal abatement cost function of both (or all) firms is the same. If this is not the case, the social optimum would always lead to a solution where $e_c^* \neq e_b^*$. In our case, the cement factory has consistently higher marginal abatement costs, because CO_2 emissions stem from the process of producing cement. Investments in processes that reduce CO_2 emissions are lumpy and costly. Thus:

$$|C'_c(e_c)| > |C'_b(e_b)| \qquad (6.9)$$

for all levels of emissions. In the social optimum emission levels will therefore be

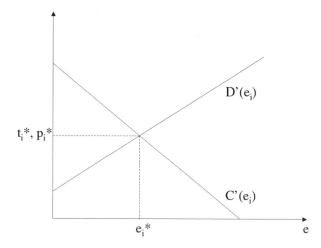

Figure 6.1 Economic equilibrium taxes and choice of permit quota.

$e_c^* > e_b^*$. The identical emissions limit on both firms thus leads to a solution that is unduly costly.

Let us assume that both the cement factory and the bus company are now subjected to a uniform carbon tax t. The total cost that both firms $i \in \{c,b\}$ are facing is now:

$$TC(e_i) = C(e_i) + te_i \qquad (6.10)$$

where t is the tax rate. Cost minimization leads to the following condition:

$$TC(e_i)' = C'(e_i) + t \stackrel{!}{=} 0, \text{ or } t = -C'(e_i) \qquad (6.11)$$

This implies that both firms will operate at equal marginal abatement costs:

$$t = -C'(e_c) = -C'(e_b) \qquad (6.12)$$

As we have seen above, this is the economically optimal solution for emissions abatement in our city.

If the mayor of our city has perfect information of the marginal costs of each of the firms, she can identify the optimal tax rate, t, on the basis of the equation above. If the mayor does not know the marginal abatement costs of these firms with certainty, she could use a trial and error method that would lead to the optimal tax rate. However, passing legislation on taxes is a lengthy political process, because the interest of many groups is involved. Thus in practice it may be difficult to embark on a trial and error approach for setting t.

In the case of emission permits, the mayor will make a quantity P of emission permits available, which correspond to the optimal emission level E^*. These permits can either be auctioned off or grandfathered. Grandfathering implies the gratis allocation of permits to emitting plant – often on the basis of historical emissions.

Let us assume initially that permits are auctioned off, and that the auction leads to a fully competitive result.[4] A market clearing price p for the permits will be established. Both of our firms will face costs:

$$TC(e_i) = C(e_i) + pe_i \qquad (6.13)$$

Cost minimization leads to:

$$TC'(e_i) = C'(e_i) + p \stackrel{!}{=} 0, \text{ or } p = -C'(e_i) \qquad (6.14)$$

Thus, marginal abatement costs are the same for all firms, thus bringing about the economic optimum.

To sum up, both taxes and emissions trading can bring about the economically optimal solution and meet the optimal limit $E^* = [e_c^*, e_b^*]$. Standards will bring about the economically optimal solution if the marginal abatement cost curves of both firms are identical. This, however, will only exceptionally be the case.

Although it may appear from the above discussion that carbon taxes and emissions trading are two instruments that require a decision either for the one or for the other instrument, they are actually quite complementary. Missfeldt and Requate (2001) show that at the national level a combination of carbon taxes and tradable permits does not distort cost efficiency, and may improve on the environmental outcome as emissions reductions can be targeted with greater certainty.

With each instrument likely to be able to capture different sectors or gases policy makers can exploit those synergies. For example, domestic households or the transport sector have many actors, which renders transaction costs for trading high. Thus, a tax can be employed in these sectors. For the industry and power sectors this does not apply as much, and these sectors may therefore more suitably be targeted by an emissions trading scheme. A practical example for the joint use of tax and emissions trading is the case of the UK emissions trading regime.

Beyond perfect competition

We have seen that under the assumption of perfect markets, complete information and no transaction cost carbon taxes and tradable permits are identical if it comes to achieving a set environmental goal at least cost. However, there are significant differences in the approaches when taking the view of an environmental agency or that of an affected enterprise.

The assumptions of perfect, static markets under certainty which were underlying the previous conclusions, made it possible to highlight some advantageous properties of carbon taxes and tradable permit systems. But when discussing the actual introduction of both instruments as a policy tool, it is essential to analyse their properties under more realistic assumptions. Issues examined in this section include uncertainty, market power, transaction costs, technological change, economic growth and instrument implementation.

Uncertainty

Uncertainty can exist with respect to the damage as well as the abatement cost curve. If there is uncertainty with regard to the marginal abatement cost curve, then there is a likelihood that the policy maker will either over- or underestimate the cost $TC(E)$ at which enterprises are able to abate emissions. In the case of the mayor in the city in our example above, the marginal abatement cost curve to be considered would be the sum of the marginal abatement cost curves of both the cement and the local bus and taxi company:

$$TC(E)' = C'(e_c) + C'(e_b) \qquad (6.15)$$

If the policy maker now implements a tax, the tax rate, t, will be chosen to equal the level of marginal abatement costs of the firms at the level of emission reduction target. If the marginal abatement costs turn out to be lower than expected, the tax rate will have been too high, and emissions are reduced beyond the emissions reduction target. If on the other hand marginal abatement costs are higher than anticipated by the policy maker, the tax rate will turn out to be too low. Then emissions will continue to exceed the emission limit E.

In the case of a tradable permit system it is possible to compare the emerging permit price p with the price the mayor expected based on her erroneous assumptions concerning abatement cost. If the policy maker overestimated actual cost of abatement, the resulting price of permits p will be lower than the initially expected permit price level. In the opposite case the permit price p will rise above the expected price level. The greenhouse gases would still be cut down to the level E, as the amount of permits in the system does not change. However, industry would have to bear a higher or lesser burden, depending on the emerging price.

Uncertainty in emissions trading is mainly related to the permit price. Unexpected spikes in permit prices can have harmful economic consequences as the case of the RECLAIM trading programme during the California energy crisis in 2000 showed. RECLAIM governs the trading of NO_X emissions from power plants in California. In late 1999, older power plants had to be started up as a result of power shortages in the state. While previously prices for NO_X had been around $2/kg, they shot up to $50/kg in mid-2000 at their highest level. In parallel, spot prices for power skyrocketed. Limited or no pass-through of wholesale costs to retail customers forced the two largest power companies to the verge of bankruptcy. Rolling power blackouts were mandated throughout the state at the end of 2000. Thus, RECLAIM contributed to rendering the power crisis more severe than otherwise would have been the case.[5]

An instrument to hedge against price risk is for the regulator to set aside a certain quantity of permits, which can be put on the market in situations of pronounced price increases. While such a set aside would leads to higher permit prices at the beginning of trading, it allows the policy maker to have an influence on the permit market. Such a set aside was included, for example, under the US SO_2 trading scheme (Title IV of the 1990 Clean Air Act Amendments). It has been identified as one of the factors contributing to the success of the SO_2 trading scheme (Sterner 2003: 283).[6]

A difference between expected price and actual price can have a negative impact on the least cost property of the permit system in case enterprises over- or under-invest in emission reduction equipment in anticipation of a certain permit price. Such inefficiencies can be dampened in systems which allow for borrowing and banking of emissions permits.

Finally, a higher than expected permit price can render the entry of new participants more difficult. It is here where a major difference with the tax solution is noteworthy. In the presence of a tax, the payment of the enterprises per unit of emissions would not change, however, the ecological aim would be missed.

When looking for a carbon tax or permit allowance that balances both damages and costs, the issue of uncertainty becomes considerably trickier. First, damage costs in the context of climate change are more difficult to evaluate, because damages will occur in the future. Moreover, damages from specific events can usually not be directly linked to climate change. Second, the combination of damage and cost curve offers many different ways in which uncertainty about information can play out.

Depending on the slope of the cost curves in relation to the benefit curves, the equivalence of permit versus tax solution no longer holds. It will depend on the specific slopes of the curves whether a tax or a permit system produces a result closer to the social optimum (Feess 1998). Stavins (1995) points out that the eventual superiority of a permits system versus a tax does in addition depend on the correlation between cost and benefit uncertainty.

Against the background of uncertainty, the choice of instrument will depend on whether the achievement of the environmental goal or the political risk connected with varying permit prices is a more important factor in the decision of the policy maker.

Market power

In the context of carbon taxes, market power is not relevant as no market is established. However, the issue of imperfectly competitive permit markets – that is the presence of a dominant enterprise or only few actors in a market – can lead to a situation where the least cost property of permit systems does not hold. This is due to the distorting influence a firm with market power can have on the price determination process in a market. Such a firm can, if in the position of a seller, keep the supply of permits low in order to gain monopoly rents, or conversely, if the firm has monopsonic power in the market, keep demand, and thus prices of permits, under the efficient level (Hanley *et al.* 1997).

Kemfert *et al.* (2003) compare estimates for the international price of tradable carbon permits in 2010. They find that carbon prices in fully competitive markets have been estimated at on average $2.50, while the average market price in markets with market power have been estimated at $11.60 on average.[7] Westkog

(1996) shows for international greenhouse gas trading with market power that efficiency losses occur with increasing market power and that the initial distribution of the permits affects the size of the efficiency loss.

Bohm (1998) concludes from a series of experiments that market design may remedy this efficiency problem. He shows that if market institutions are modelled according to stock markets, market power 'is unlikely to constitute an efficiency and cost distribution problem in an emissions trading market' (p.18). He argues that the players in the market have sufficient incentives to gather information on everybody's marginal abatement cost and are thus able to practice perfect price discrimination. Bohm shows that the number of players is less important to achieving the least cost property of a permit system, than is the difference in their respective abatement cost. Cost-savings are highest, when firms with a wide range of abatement cost participate, no matter how many firms are included.

Another concern is that firms could use a strong position in the permit market to raise strategic barriers against the entry of new firms (Hanley *et al.* 1997). This could occur in an auctioned permits system as well as in the context of grandfathered permit systems, where the argument is often discussed under the keyword of 'hoarding'. This refers to the behaviour of incumbents in a permit market who keep emissions permits in excess of their own emissions in order prevent a new competitor from being able to begin production (Feess 1998). Such behaviour is more likely in relatively shallow and/or narrow markets, where only few firms from only one sector (for example power plants) trade emissions permits.

Transaction costs

According to Stavins (1995) the following three sources for transaction costs exist in the context of both carbon taxes and emissions trading:

* search and information;
* bargaining and decision;
* monitoring and enforcement.

While the first two points mostly affect enterprises acting on a permit market, the issues of monitoring and enforcement also relate to carbon taxes. In the context of carbon taxes the first two types of transaction costs are only incurred during the period in which the tax system is being designed. Once implemented, the company simply pays the tax, and there is no cost from searching a trading partner, as the possibility of trading does not exist.

The issue of transaction costs in a tradable permit system was modelled by Montero (1997), who expanded the approach of Stavins (1995), and confirmed the result that in the presence of transaction costs and uncertainty, the resulting permit price will be higher than that of a least cost solution. This not withstanding, Montero (1997) shows for the case of NO_X abatement in the US, that despite considerable transaction cost, the cost-saving potential of a tradable permit system as compared with a command and control approach is substantial. Transaction costs for the carbon tax are commonly borne by the regulator, but may partially be rolled over to the taxpayer. In the case of emissions trading, the net buyers in the carbon market have to pay for the transactions costs via increased permit prices.

Technological change

A reduction or even stabilization of global greenhouse gas emissions depends, to an important degree, on the rate of technological change, that is to say, the rate at which present technology will be replaced with a less greenhouse gas-intensive capital stock. As Grubb (1997) points out, this is particularly true in the context of a growing world population and continuing economic growth, which goes along with naturally growing greenhouse gas emissions. Hence, any policy to combat climate change may be examined with regard to its ability to foster the development and introduction of greenhouse gas emission reducing technology over time.

Let us consider a simple static setting to illustrate the incentive for firm-level innovation. In Figure 6.2, $C_{TP}'(e)$ is the marginal abatement cost curve of an enterprise after having invested in new technology. Triangle e^{Max}, B, C represents the cost savings compared to the old marginal abatement cost curve shown as $C'(e_i)$. Under emissions trading, the incentive for the introduction of new technology thus consists of the saved cost for the abatement effort undertaken (triangle e^{Max}, B, A) and the profit from selling permits at price p (triangle A, B, C), which are freed up due to reducing emissions from e^* to e^*_{TP}.

The same effect would occur with a carbon tax approach. The original tax payment before technological change corresponded to square $0, e_i^*, B, t_i^*$. The new tax payment is reduced to square $0, e_{i,TP}^*, C, t_i^*$. The reduction in tax payment therefore corresponds to square $e_{i,TP}^*, e_i^*, B, C$. Of this square, the company has to pay the square $e_{i,TP}^*, e_i^*, A, C$ as abatement costs to reach the newly optimal emissions level $e_{i,TP}^*$. The total tax saving compared with the situation before technological change corresponds to the triangle A, B, C.

By comparison, under a command and control approach, the emissions standard e^* would have to be met by the enterprise. The incentive to introduce new technology would amount to triangle e^{Max}, B, A, that is would be restricted to the savings in abatement cost possible due to new technology. There would be no reward for abating more than the standard demands.

Alternatively, a technical standard could prescribe the introduction of new technology, eventually together with a stricter environmental standard e^*_{TP}. In

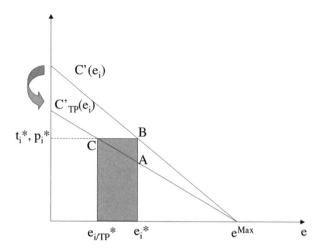

Figure 6.2 Incentive for innovation.

such a case, the enterprise would save triangle $e^{\mathrm{Max}}BA$ but would also have to bear the cost of additional abatement (area e^*,e^*_{TP},B,C) without being compensated for it by selling permits or reduced tax payments.

The discussion above is in line with the early results of the environmental economics literature, which shows that taxes and emission permits provide more incentives for firm-level innovation than standards.[8] Building on this, Milliman and Prince (1989) and Jung *et al.* (1996) show that incentives for innovation are greatest under auctioned emission permits, followed by emission taxes, followed by grandfathered permits.

However, as more assumptions have been released in the analysis of market instruments and technological innovation, a response to the question of what instruments generate most welfare gains and/or innovation has become less clear-cut. In a model with a vertical industry structure where a monopolistic upstream firm engages in research and development (R&D), Requate and Unold (2003) examines the possibility of strategic behaviour in the technology adoption decision of firms. He finds that in general, market-based instruments do not give higher incentives to innovate than command and control. This results from the fact that firms may free ride on the adoptive behaviour of competitors in the case of market-based instruments, while all firms have to comply with standards in the same way.

Fisher *et al.* (2003) incorporate the supply-side of the innovation market to examine welfare effects of environmental policies. They also include the possibility that firms can imitate patented technology, reflecting the inability of (patented) innovators to fully appropriate the rents of innovation. They conclude that under different circumstances either auctioned permits or taxes can induce larger amounts of innovation. Moreover, auctioned permits, taxes or grand-fathered permits may under different circumstances induce significantly greater welfare gains. The result depends on the scope for imitation of new technologies, the costs of innovation, the relative level and the slope of the marginal environ-mental benefit function and the number of polluting firms.

Fisher *et al.* therefore argue that 'an evaluation of the circumstances specific to a particular pollutant would be required in order to judge whether a case for the one instrument over the other two instruments can be made' (Fisher *et al.* 2003: 525).

In practice, widespread introduction of new technologies often occurs when newly introduced (environmental) legislation appears to be particularly onerous. This has in part been the case,[9] for example in the context of the 1990 US SO_2 trading programme, where permit prices were estimated to be \$750/tonne and where a penalty of non-compliance of \$2,000/tonne was put in place. Actual trading prices during the nineties were around \$150/tonne. To reduce costs, power producers switched to the use of low-sulphur coal (Sterner 2003: 282).

Economic growth

In a segment of the economy that is either subject to carbon taxes or to emissions trading, economic growth is reflected either by increased production of existing plants or by new entrants (companies) in that market segment.

Under a carbon tax increases in production and new entrants will be taxed at the same, unchanged tax rates, unless the tax rate is pegged to economic growth. However, stable emissions can only be achieved by newly estimating the marginal abatement costs and increasing the tax rate accordingly. Otherwise environ-mental standards would be watered down. Under a tax approach, economic growth thus necessitates administrative effort and unpopular political decisions.

Under emissions trading growth leads to a higher demand for permits and thus an increase in permit prices. From an environmental and administrative view-point, the permit system is attractive, as the fixed amount of permits warrants that emissions do not increase.

There are a number of concerns with regard to the impact that a trading system can have on the economic growth in a country:

- Economic growth leads to increasing permit prices.
- In a growing economy, a set quota for allowable emissions can, in principle, place a ceiling on the production of certain goods.
- A system, in which permits are given freely to existing enterprises, could prevent newcomers from entering a market.[10]

The degree to which growth will lead to an increase in permit prices depends on the marginal abatement costs of new entrants (or the new technology in existing firms). New entrants that do not emit greenhouse gases will not impact on the price. For example, producers of renewable energies would not be affected in a permit system for power plants. Rising prices for permits due to economic growth may lead to increased pressure on the government to relax the environmental goal and allow for more permits on the market. Increasing permit prices also raises the incentive for emitting greenhouse gases illegally.

The second point could only be true if there are no more permits for additional emissions or emission reduction possibilities available at a price, which would still allow the profitable production of the goods. It is clear that a comprehensive emissions trading system across sectors will limit the growth of those sectors, where greenhouse gas emissions are large and reduction possibilities are expensive. It does not, however, imply that the permit system would constitute a ceiling on economic growth altogether. If successful, the policy will provide an incentive for a restructuring of the economy or (power) sector. This implies that growth will be stronger in sectors which produce less greenhouse gas intensive products, while sectors with limited greenhouse gas abatement options might shrink or develop new abatement options.

If sectors with high greenhouse gas emissions move to locations outside of the carbon tax / emissions trading zone, a 'leakage' effect may result. This means that while emissions may be reduced inside the zone, they could be increased outside the zone. Such leakage has also been termed 'environmental capital flight'.[11]

When permits are grandfathered and no set-asides exist for new entrants, these might find entry costs too high to go ahead with entering in an established market. Implicitly, this could therefore hinder the restructuring and growth of an economy.

There are differing degrees of magnitude of this problem. For one, it affects some new entrants more than others. While a newcomer with the same technology as the incumbent might suffer discrimination, a firm with new technology and lower emissions during production is affected to a lesser degree. The permit system thus influences which type of new entrants is more likely to enter. Also, incumbents might in principle use permits as a strategic barrier to new entrants in their product market.

There are a number of design solutions in a grandfathered system to effectively address the issue of newcomers. Set-asides given away for free or at a low price to new firms or declining free distributions to old incumbents are conceivable ways to address the problem. In practice occasional auctions of set-aside permits are used to warrant the availability of permits to new enterprises in the market. In this case, however, a discrimination of the newcomers remains, as they have to purchase on an auction what incumbents received for free.

Instrument implementation

Implementing carbon taxes or emissions trading in practice requires consultation with relevant stakeholders. Within a country's government commonly the Ministry of the Environment would be charged with developing a carbon tax. This Ministry would typically develop a proposal with the help of stakeholder negotiations. Those stakeholders that will have to pay the tax – mainly industry – will negotiate hard for exemptions and reductions from a tax or for a larger emission quota allocation. Environmental advocates will argue for higher tax rates and smaller emission quotas. As the consumer of electricity and heat is often not as well organized as industry and the environmental lobby, governments will often find it easier to raise taxes for end-users.

In this context the phenomenon of 'regulative capture' becomes important. It argues that due to the close working relationship that regulated enterprises and the regulating authority will develop, enterprises have influence on standard setting, and may manage to convince authorities to impose less stringent standards (Fisher *et al.* 1996). Depending on the circumstances, this problem may be equally pronounced for carbon taxes and tradable permits.

Revenue generation

Market-based mechanisms can affect a regulator's budget in different ways. First, the implementation of a mechanism is costly as was already discussed above. Second, those mechanisms can become a significant contribution to a government's budget. Any tax revenue raised through a carbon tax will directly go into the government's budget. In the context of emissions trading, however, funds are only raised when permits are auctioned off.

There are two major rules for the allocation of emission permits to those participating in the scheme. Under a grandfathering approach, the permits are distributed for free at the beginning of a period.[12] Their allocation might be based on historic emission data and/or other criteria set by the policy maker. For example, if a firm's past contribution to CO_2 emissions were 10 per cent of all emissions that are considered for inclusion in a trading regime, then the firm would retain a share of 10 per cent of the emission right to be distributed.

Conversely, in an auction approach, the permits are sold by the policy maker to those who want to emit in a bidding process or auction. The re-distribution of permits among enterprises then happens in permit markets, which can take all forms of market organization. Permits can be traded, for example, at stock exchanges or through private auctions or brokers.

From a company's perspective, the choice of tax versus emissions trading system as well as the choice of emissions allocation mechanism under emissions trading is important, as it affects the company's operating costs. The cost that a firm faces under either regime is shown in Figures 6.3 and 6.4, where triangle 1 equals the abatement cost, that is the cost of reducing emissions through measures taken inside the company.

In a perfectly competitive market, the price $p*$ for permits will equal the tax level $t*$ set by the policy maker. Hence the abatement costs are the same in a permit or tax system, given that the emissions reduction that is to be targeted is the same. Area 2 depicts the (opportunity) cost of the emissions permits that the enterprise holds. Whether the cost is opportunity cost or actual expenditure will depend on the allocation mechanism chosen for permits.

In the case of free permit distribution to enterprises (Figure 6.3), the acquisition of permits does not reduce a firm's profits. However, using the permit to cover one's own emissions does put a rational price tag on the previously free emissions, because abatement efforts would allow the enterprise to sell these permits. In the case of an auctioning of all the emission rights by the government (Figure 6.4), area 2 represents the payment, which would be required from the enterprises.

Equally, in the case of a tax on emissions, area 2 would represent a payment from the enterprise to the government.[13] In this case 'it will make no difference to the polluter whether he pays t dollars in effluent charges per unit of his emissions . . . , or whether, instead, he pays that same t dollars per unit . . . for the purchase of the permit' (Baumol and Oates 1988: 58).

Thus a firm will always prefer the free allocation of permits, while the government's income is higher under a carbon tax or with auctioned permits. Figure 6.5 gives an indication of the significance of environmental taxes as part of the total tax revenue. In 2000, the contribution of environmental taxes was at about 5.5 per cent on average in OECD countries. In Korea and Turkey, environmental

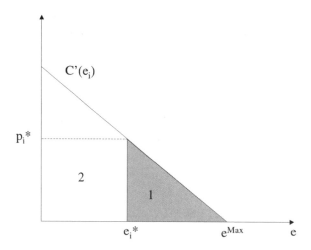

Figure 6.3 Grandfathering of permits.

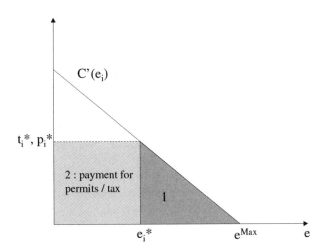

Figure 6.4 Auction of permits / carbon taxes.

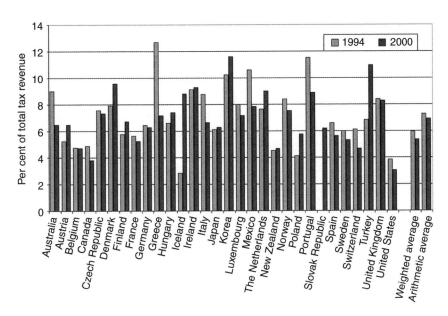

Figure 6.5 Share of environmental taxes as part of the total tax revenue in OECD countries.

Source: Organisation of Economic Cooperation and Development (OECD) (2003).

Note
The most important contribution of these revenues comes from the taxing of unleaded petrol.

taxes contributed more than 10 per cent to their year 2000 budget, and in Denmark, Iceland, Ireland, The Netherlands, Portugal and the United Kingdom revenue from environmental taxes exceeded 8 per cent.

There has been some debate on how the revenue from taxes is to be most usefully employed.[14] In order to be neutral to the remainder of the economy, the revenue may simply be injected as a lump sum into the government budget. Alternatively, part or all of the revenue raised may be transferred back to the firms as a lump sum. Such rules can help build support among industry for the implementation of carbon taxes in the first place. When re-injecting the money, care has to be taken on how the money is to be transferred.

If the transfer mechanism specifies the amount to be reimbursed at the same level as the amount paid by the firm, i.e. t^*e_i, all incentives to reduce emissions are lost. Another possible rule for the redistribution of funds is to give to each firm an equal share of the total revenue. Firms with comparatively small contributions to pollution will then make a net gain, while firms with a comparatively high contribution to pollution will make a net loss. Thus the incentive to reduce emissions is maintained. However, as with any type of transfers that are de facto subsidies, this system may give rise to abuse. For example, firms may be created that exist only on paper and do not emit any emissions, yet they could become eligible for the transfer payment.

Other approaches to tax recycling link the re-payments to criteria other than the level of emissions or the amount of the payment. This can, for instance, be done through reduced payments for social security or by reducing distortionary taxes (Fisher *et al.* 1996). Among the approaches discussed, a system of grandfathered permits is easier to implement because no recycling mechanism would be needed in order to reduce the political resistance of the affected enterprises. Instead, the issue of who receives the free permits is likely to become a bone of contention.

Designing carbon taxes and emissions trading schemes for climate change

In the design of a greenhouse gas emissions trading or carbon tax scheme very similar decisions have to be taken in order to define the framework within which trading is to take place. Decisions on the design of instruments are taken in response to the objectives that the instrument is to achieve. While the primary objective in the case of carbon taxes and emissions trading is to reduce greenhouse gas emissions, secondary objectives may include meeting additional objectives such as reducing other environmental problems, cost effectiveness, raising finances for the government's budget, keeping the administration of policy instruments simple, fairness to all stakeholders involved, or simply gaining experience with a specific policy tool.

Major design features that need to be decided upon both for taxes and emissions trading systems include:[15]

- Target groups:
  - Target gases;
  - Target sectors or participants;
- Administration of implementation:
  - Monitoring, reporting and verification system;
  - Authority supervising the scheme;
- Enforcement mechanism.

Coverage of target gases may be comprehensive and include all greenhouse gases, or it may focus only on one gas, frequently CO_2. For example, the Danish emissions trading scheme focuses on CO_2 alone. International emissions trading under Article 17 of the Kyoto Protocol, on the other hand, targets six greenhouse gases.

The coverage of target groups for taxes or emissions trading may also be changed over time. For example, the European Union's emissions trading scheme will initially cover energy supply, iron and steel, building materials, and pulp and paper corresponding to 51 per cent of the European Union's emissions. From 2006 the European trading scheme will be changed to include other sectors such as transportation and aluminium. The industry-led Ontario Pilot Emissions Reduction Trading (PERT) scheme in Canada focused initially (1996) on NO_X and VOC emissions, but in 1997 expanded to cover also CO, SO_2 and CO_2.

Participation in tax schemes is usually mandatory. Participation in emissions trading schemes can be both mandatory or on a voluntary basis. Examples for programmes that have run on a voluntary basis are the PERT scheme and the Greenhouse Gas Emissions Reduction Trading Programme (GERT). Both are Canadian programmes with multi-stakeholder processes that aimed at gaining experience with market-based instruments.

Administration of implementation of tax or trading schemes is the key to their success. Under both schemes responsibility for administering them will usually rest with a Ministry or government agency. That agency is then commonly charged with specifying acceptable approaches to measuring emissions and with specifying requirements for reporting emissions. The agency will furthermore set out verification procedures and powers, the processes by which taxes/permits are to be submitted, and govern enforcement procedures and penalties. Tax revenue will be raised through and accounted for by the usual channels of the Finance Ministry. Permit trades may be registered through a third-party registry.

Non-compliance with a tax or trading system is enforced through the normal judicial system. Commonly, penalties are imposed for the failure to pay taxes or the failure to have a sufficient number of permits for compliance. As long as the unit penalties of not complying with a tax or trading scheme exceed the tax rate and the permit price, and those penalties are credibly enforced, participants in either scheme retain an incentive to comply. If the permit price rises above the penalty rate, participants in the trading scheme will prefer paying the penalty instead of purchasing permits (or reducing emissions if that is more costly than paying the penalty). In the European Union's emissions trading scheme, the penalty will be €50 during 2005–2007 and €100 from thereon. In addition, allowances are lost equal to the excess emissions. With a permits price expected at €7, this penalty should be sufficient to create a satisfactory incentive for compliance.

Further decisions on design features are specific to the instrument emissions trading. They include:

- Distribution of permits:
  - Allowance system;
    - Cap and trade;
    - Baseline and credit/rate-based;
  - Allocation of permits;
    - Free distribution;
    - Auctioning;
    - Combinations of the above;
  - Opt-in and opt-out;

- Market functioning:
  - Permit life;
  - Price volatility;
  - Banking and borrowing.

In a system where the absolute level of emissions is capped, participants in the trading scheme are allocated a limited quantity of emissions permits which may be traded. Such a system is called a cap-and-trade system. An example for a cap and trade system with an absolute emissions cap is the Danish CO_2 Quota Act.

Alternatively, a credit may be given for a project that reduces emissions compared to a baseline. Such a system is called baseline-and-credit system. A related system is the rate-based system, where relative levels of carbon or energy efficiency have to be reduced. Examples for baseline-and-credit systems are the Clean Development Mechanism (CDM) and Joint Implementation (JI) under the Kyoto Protocol, or the PERT and GERT trading schemes in Canada. How baselines are measured is discussed in the chapter dedicated to baselines.

Under the UK trading scheme a system with an absolute target and a rate-based system were established in parallel. The rate-based system set a lower energy use per unit of production. Both systems are connected through a 'gateway', which is designed so as to avoid the targets in the absolute sector being watered down. Table 6.2 gives an overview of which trading schemes are based on absolute caps, and which are rate-based.

The policy maker also has to decide on which allocation method is to be chosen. Industry commonly argues for free allocation of permits while auctioning is desirable for the government as it raises revenue. For example, under the Danish CO_2 Quota Act, emission permits were grandfathered on the basis of 1994–1998 emissions with a preference given to central heat and power plants. In the United Kingdom, emission permits were free and the target determined in negotiated agreement. In Norway a system has been discussed whereby 84 per cent of the 1990 or 1998 emissions for industry would be allocated for free, and the remainder would be auctioned.

Opt-in and opt-out refers to the possibility that certain industry groups may decide to opt-in or opt-out of a trading scheme. This is often applied during the initial phases of a trading regime and in order to allow participants a smooth introduction into the scheme. The European Union trading scheme has such a provision during the first trading period from 2005–2007.

The validity of emission permits can differ. For example, the validity of temporal permits expires after a certain period of time. If no temporal restriction on the validity is imposed, then banking is allowed. This implies that a firm can utilize previously unused permits in subsequent trading periods. It can thus build up an account of unused permits from several 'vintages', which represent future emissions. Conversely, borrowing from future trading periods could be allowed. This means that a firm could pledge to cover current emissions with permits to be acquired in the future. When designing a trading scheme, decisions have to be made on whether permits may be banked or borrowed. While the banking mechanism has become a standard element in all greenhouse gas trading systems thus far, borrowing is not due to its possible negative impact on environmental goal achievement.

Finally, the preference for a particular design feature will depend on the political constraints as well as the actual design of the system. Decisions on such features are commonly subject to intense scrutiny through all stakeholders involved.

Existing carbon tax regimes

In practice, carbon taxes have only rarely been directly imposed on the measured emissions of CO_2 or other greenhouse gases, but on the carbon content of fuels. Mostly flat rates per fuel type have been adopted. Thus, taxes created in general fewer incentives to operate power plants such as to reduce greenhouse gas emissions but to substitute fuels with high carbon content with fuels of lower carbon content.

Carbon taxes have been implemented in Denmark, Finland, Germany, The Netherlands, Norway, Sweden and the United Kingdom.[16] Although these taxes have been named carbon taxes, they do not usually have a common tax base. For example, carbon taxes in Denmark and the United Kingdom are imposed on a per kilo Watt hour (kWh) basis on the consumption of electricity, carbon taxes in Denmark, Norway, Sweden and the United Kingdom are imposed on cubic metres (m^3) of natural gas consumed, and carbon taxes on unleaded petrol are imposed in Norway, Slovenia and Sweden.

In addition, there are many countries that have adopted taxes on energy consumption that act implicitly as a carbon tax without, however, being called a carbon tax. Moreover, the effectiveness of these carbon taxes not only hinges on the size of the tax rate but also on the modalities and rules for the recycling of the revenue of these taxes. These are commonly very complex, as they are the result of negotiations of all stakeholders, especially those firms who will be affected by the tax. Table 6.1 shows the levels of taxes imposed in the electricity sector in OECD countries, and how these taxes have been named in the various countries.

Wherever a tax has been imposed, tax reductions, exemptions or rebates have been negotiated for various sectors or technologies. In Sweden, a 50 per cent reduction of the CO_2 tax corresponding to €40 per tonne of CO_2 applies for the manufacturing industries. In Denmark tax rates vary by sector: a tax of €80 per tonne of CO_2 has to be paid for central space heating, €12 per tonne of CO_2 for light industrial processes, and €3 per tonne of CO_2 for heavy industrial processes. Norway's carbon tax is also subject to various exemptions and reductions. For example, Norway's pulp and paper industry and fish meal industry only pay 50 per cent of the tax on heavy fuel oil (Ekins and Barker 2001). Moreover, offshore oil production is fully exempt from carbon taxes.

Although the implementation of an international carbon tax has been discussed extensively, politically it has never been acceptable to a wide range of countries. Both the negotiation of a carbon tax rate at the international/regional level and the implementation of a carbon tax regime turned out to be too complex. Difficulties lie in deciding on a level of tax, on how the revenue would be used, and on how it should be re-distributed.

In 1992, the European Commission (EC) put forward a proposal for a European Union-wide tax on all energy products, except renewable energy sources (EC 1992). Half of the tax would have been based on the energy content, and half on the carbon content of fuels. After the EC proposal had been faced with severe opposition by the British Government it was eventually abandoned at the end of the nineties. The European Commission subsequently encouraged its member states to adopt carbon taxes at the national level (Cameron and Zillman 2001).

International greenhouse gas trading

Discussions of greenhouse gas emissions trading go back to the early 1990s to coincide with the negotiations and adoption of the UN Climate Change Conven-

Table 6.1 Taxes in OECD member countries levied on electricity consumption

Country	Tax	Tax rate (in €/kWh, except where indicated otherwise)
Austria	Energy tax	0.015
Belgium	Energy fee (low frequency electricity)	0.0013641
Denmark	Duty on CO_2	0.0134
Denmark	Duty on electricity (heating)	0.0673
Denmark	Duty on electricity (other purposes)	0.076
Finland	Excise on fuels (manufacturing sector)	0.0042073
Finland	Excise on fuels (rest of the economy)	0.0069
Finland	Strategic stockpile fee	0.0001262
Germany	Duty on electricity	0.0128
Italy	Additional tax on electricity, towns/ provinces (private dwellings)	Varies
Italy	Additional tax on electricity, towns/ provinces (industry)	Varies
Italy	Tax on electrical energy, state	0.003
Italy	Tax on electrical energy, state	0.0021
Japan	Promotion of power resource development tax	0.0041
The Netherlands	Regulatory energy tax (up to 10,000 kWh/year)	0.0601
The Netherlands	Regulatory energy tax (10,000–50,000 kWh/year)	0.02
The Netherlands	Regulatory energy tax (50,000–10 million kWh/year)	0.0061
Norway	Tax on consumption of electricity	0.0128
Spain	Tax on electricity	4.864%
Sweden	Energy tax on electricity (households)	0.0214
Sweden	Energy tax on electricity (manufacturing and commercial greenhouses)	0
Sweden	Energy tax on electricity (other sectors)	0.0151
Sweden	Energy tax on electricity (material permitted for abstraction > 200,000 tonnes)	0.0015
United Kingdom	Climate change levy (ordinary rate)	0.0069
United Kingdom	Climate change levy (reduced rate)	0.0014
United States	Delaware: Public utilities tax	4.25% of gross receipts

Source: OECD (2003).

tion. However, it was only after the adoption of the Kyoto Protocol in 1997 that policy makers began to seriously consider the implementation of a greenhouse gas emissions trading scheme, because its Article 17 adopted international greenhouse gas trading.

Indeed, agreement on the Kyoto Protocol negotiations could only be achieved through the adoption of provisions for trading greenhouse gas emissions internationally. The most important driving factor was the concern of the USA that they would not be able to implement sufficiently strong domestic policies to meet their 7 per cent emissions reduction target, and that they needed a cost-effective means of meeting their emissions reductions. The trading mechanisms adopted under the Kyoto Protocol are commonly referred to as 'flexibility mechanisms'.

Formally four flexibility mechanisms exist. First, Annex I Parties – those with binding emissions limitation targets – are allowed to meet their obligations jointly (Article 4, Kyoto Protocol) by entering into a formal agreement. The member countries of the European Union have entered into such an agreement (Cameron and Zillman 2001). Annex I Parties are furthermore allowed to transfer or trade emissions reduction units (ERUs) from projects undertaken within Annex I (Article 6). This project-based mechanism is commonly referred to as 'joint implementation'.

Under Article 17 of the Kyoto Protocol Parties are allowed to engage in the trading of their emission allowances. In addition, a form of joint implementation between Annex I and non-Annex I Parties using the Clean Development Mechanism (CDM) was defined in the Protocol (Article 12). The CDM allows emission reductions to be earned within a non-Annex I Party and used towards meeting an Annex I Party's commitment. An emissions reduction unit generated as part of the CDM is called 'certified emissions reduction units' (CER).

The 'flexibility mechanisms' in the Kyoto Protocol operate via 'assigned amounts' for emissions trading and Article 4 activities, ERUs for joint implementation, and CERs for the CDM. All these units are fully interchangeable and their accounting unit is tonne of CO_2 equivalent.[17] The 'assigned amount' of each Annex I Party is the amount of units that is allocated to this Party as part of its commitment under the Kyoto Protocol. Box 6.2 shows how the assigned amounts are calculated, and how they may be used to meet the target of 2008–2012.

The main rules for the operation of the flexible mechanisms were decided in 2000 as part of the Marrakech Accords. Further specification of methodologies for the CDM is undertaken through the Executive Board of the CDM and for joint implementation through the Supervisory Committee for Joint Implementation. These methodologies are largely concerned with the question of how baselines for projects can best be measured, and how emissions reductions once projected can be monitored.

The CDM Executive Board meetings are broadcast on the internet. All decisions on methods and projects can be accessed at the CDM website (http://cdm.unfccc.int). In parallel, the Meeting to the Parties to the Kyoto Protocol is further developing rules for international emissions trading, including on registries for trade. While the CDM became operational from 2000, joint implementation and international emissions trading will only operate from 2008. Nevertheless, few secondary market deals on the forward options have been struck.

Box 6.2 'The assigned amount'

The assigned amount is established under Article 3.1 of the Kyoto Protocol. It is calculated by subtracting the Kyoto Protocol emission reduction target from the base
year emissions of each Annex I Party. The base year for most countries is 1990.
Economies in transition were given more flexibility for choosing their base year,
because of the structural change in their economies in the early nineties. Any assigned
amount in excess of a country's 2008–2012 average emissions may be sold. Any
country with an assigned amount that is lower than its average 2008–2012 emissions
has to purchase extra emissions to meet their Kyoto target. A rule called 'commitment period reserve' assists countries in avoiding the sale of emission units much in
excess of what they will need to meet their Kyoto targets (Missfeldt and Haites 2002).

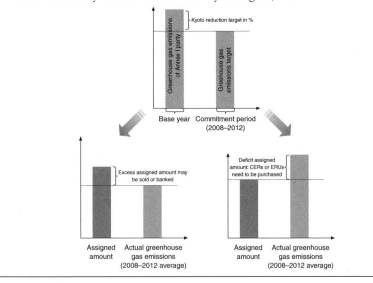

National and industry greenhouse gas trading

As part of countries' efforts to comply with their obligations under the Kyoto Protocol, and also to be able to fully participate in international emissions trading, a
number of national and industry systems have emerged. Table 6.2 gives an
overview of the schemes that have been implemented or are being considered.

The first scheme to be implemented was the Danish CO_2 Quota Act adopted in
1999, which targeted the CO_2 emissions from Danish power producers. The
scheme set a target to reduce emissions from 23 million tonnes in 2000 to 20
million tonnes by 2003, subtracting one tonne each year (Pedersen 2000, Jensen
2001). Since then, programmes have emerged in twelve different countries and the
European Union. In addition, four industry-led programmes have been established.

The United Kingdom Emissions Trading scheme was the second scheme to be
made fully operational at the national level. It is a voluntary programme, which

Table 6.2 Existing and emerging domestic trading regimes

Trading scheme	Participation	Status of systems	Scope of scheme	Start, end date	Absolute or rate-based limits	Emissions covered
Oregon	M	E	R	1997	A	CO_2 emissions, indirect reductions
Denmark	M	E	N	2001, 2003	A	CO_2 emissions
ERUPT	V	E	N	2000	R	Multiple gases, indirect reductions
United Kingdom	V(1)	E	N	2001	(4)	Direct and indirect CO_2 emissions
Australia	M	P	N	2008 (?)	A	Not yet decided
Canada	M	P	N	2008 (?)	A	All Kyoto gases under broad option
European Union	M	E	R	2005	A	Direct CO_2 emissions only
France	M(2)	P	N	2002	(5)	Direct CO_2, possibly indirect
Germany	M	P	N	2005 (?)	A	Direct CO_2 initially, expand to other gases
Norway	M	P	N	2008	A	All Kyoto gases
Slovakia	M	P	N	2005, 2008(6)	A(7)	Direct CO_2 emissions
Sweden	M	P	N	2005	A	Direct CO_2, possibly other gases
Switzerland	V	P	N	2008	A(8)	Direct CO_2 from fossil fuel combustion
PERT	V	E	I	1996	R	Direct and indirect CO_2, CH_4 and non-GHGs
BP	(3)	E	I	2000	A	Direct CO_2, CH_4
Shell	V	E	I	2000, 2002	A	Direct CO_2, CH_4
Chicago Stock Exchange	V	P	I	2002, 2005	A	All Kyoto gases

Source: Haites and Mullins (2001).

Note
M = Mandatory scheme; V = Voluntary scheme; E = Existing scheme; P = Planned scheme; N = National scheme; I = Industry scheme; R = (Sub-)Regional scheme; A = Absolute limits/emissions cap; R = Rate-based limits/credit baseline approach.
(1) Participation in the UK scheme is voluntary, but strong incentives exist to encourage participation.
(2) Participation in the French programme would be through voluntary agreements. In the event that a voluntary agreement could not be negotiated, the government could impose limits on firms.
(3) Participation is voluntary for BP, but mandatory for the operating units.
(4) The UK system has both absolute and rate-based participants.
(5) Both absolute and rate-based limits are proposed for the French system.
(6) A pilot phase would begin in 2005, the full programme would start in 2008.
(7) The allowances allocated would exceed their current emissions for most sources.
(8) The emission limitation commitment may be rate-based, but the allocation will be an absolute quantity based on projected output with the allocation adjusted ex post to reflect actual output.

provides strong financial incentives to join. For example, energy intensive sectors that accept a rate-based or absolute target receive an 80 per cent discount on the Climate Change Levy, which is the British carbon tax. Targets were negotiated with 40 industrial sectors, covering some 8,000 individual companies. The annual emissions reduction is estimated at 9.3 million tonnes of CO_2 equivalent by 2010. The first compliance period started on 1 January 2002. The market price for UK allowances in 2003 was around £2 per tonne of CO_2 equivalent.[18]

European Parliament adopted a European-wide scheme on July 2, 2003. The European Union Directive provides for the introduction of legally binding, absolute emission caps from 2005 for around 12,000–15,000 power stations and industrial plants with high levels of energy consumption. The Directive gives right to emission allowances that are grandfathered to the companies in accordance with the emission caps. The allocation is developed at the European Union member state level by means of 'National Allocation Plans'. The companies that are subject to European Union emissions trading these plants were emitting 1,681 million tonnes of CO_2 or 51 per cent of the European Union's CO_2 emissions, and 38 per cent of the European Union's six Kyoto gases in 1990.

The European trading scheme covers plants midstream rather than in a purely up- or downstream fashion. The following industries have been included: power and heat generation (in plants with a thermal input capacity exceeding 20 MW); mineral oil processing; coke ovens; metal processing; cement and lime production; other building material and ceramics; glass and glass fibres; and paper and cellulose. Minimum sizes apply, and initially only CO_2 emissions will be covered. After 2007, all Kyoto gases are to be included.

The total value of allowances to be traded has been estimated at €27 million for the period of 2005–2007. This figure could increase by more than 30 per cent if the accession countries join. For the period from 2005–2007, Member States could temporarily exclude, or 'opt-out' a number of installations in the plan. In mid-2003 estimates of carbon prices on the European market ranged around €7 per tonne of CO_2 equivalent (PointCarbon 2003). The non-compliance penalty is set at €40 per tonne of CO_2 until 2007. After 2007, the penalty will be raised to €100 per tonne of CO_2.[19]

One of the most successful industry-based programmes has been the one led by British Petroleum (BP). In 1998, BP had set itself a target of reducing its greenhouse gas emissions to 10 per cent below BP's 1990 level until the year 2010. In 2002, BP had met its target seven years ahead of schedule. A key instrument in bringing those reductions about was the company-wide greenhouse gas trading scheme, which was started in 2000.

Approximately 150 business units operating in 100 different countries are participating in the trade. As reflected in the fact that 40 business units account for approximately 80 per cent of BP's total emissions, business units varied greatly in their emissions. The trading programme was a cap-and-trade system in which CO_2 and methane were traded. To enable trading a data measurement and assurance process was launched, and abatement costing methodology developed. A registry tracked the emission trades. In 2000, a total of 2.7 million tonnes were traded at an average price of $7.6 per tonne of CO_2, and in 2001, a total of 4.5 million tonnes were traded at an average price of $36 per tonne of CO_2 (Akhurst et al. 2003).

Among the programmes that have been discussed at the national level in European countries such as France, Germany and Sweden, it is likely that the European Directive will replace those national programmes. Even Switzerland and Norway are considering joining the European trading scheme. The future of the Canadian and Australian schemes is somewhat uncertain. ERUPT (Emission Reduction Unit Procurement Tender) is a Dutch Government programme using the joint implementation mechanism to acquire tradable greenhouse gas units generated in host countries during the commitment period 2008–2012 as part of the Dutch obligations under the terms of the Kyoto Protocol.

Conclusion

Both carbon taxes and emissions trading are policy instruments that in the context of a perfectly competitive and transparent market setting are capable of bringing about desired levels of greenhouse gas emissions reductions at least cost. Carbon taxes provide greater certainty with respect to the price attached to emitting greenhouse gases than emissions trading, while emissions trading provides greater certainty regarding the capacity to meet the targeted emission reductions. To take advantage of both we noted that a combination of carbon taxes and tradable permits does not distort cost efficiency, and may improve on the environmental outcome as emissions reductions can be targeted with greater certainty.

The recent literature on technological change shows that the least cost property of emissions trading is not always maintained when strategic interaction of trading participants and the fact that firms may imitate patented technology is taken into account. While the environmental economics literature has thus grown somewhat sceptical that emissions trading is always the best approach to solve environmental externalities, its application in practice is blossoming.

The adoption of the 1997 Kyoto Protocol has led to the endorsement of international emissions trading under its Article 17. Since then national emissions trading schemes have developed mainly in Europe, and few industry-led scheme were also established. The most important market will, however, be the European Union's emissions trading regime, which is set to start in 2005.

In contrast to this, the idea of a supra-national carbon tax – although seriously debated in the early nineties – has not found practical implementation. At the national level, however, carbon taxes have been implemented mainly in European countries. Most taxes are linked to energy consumption rather than direct emissions of greenhouse gases. Moreover, many exemptions exist, and revenues from taxes may be recycled to industries.

The emerging trading schemes and the continuing environmental economics debates will provide scope for more research in the area of market instruments, in which hopefully some of the readers of this book will engage in the future to provide us with more answers to remaining questions.

Notes

1 Other global pollutants are those gases that destroy the ozone layer. They include CFCs. SO_2 and NO_X lead to acid rain. They are regional pollutants rather than global pollutants.

2 The Intergovernmental Panel on Climate Change, the international scientific body that brings together and evaluates the science of climate change world-wide, has put together a set of default values. For example, 1 terajoule (TJ) of combusted crude oil leads to 20 tonnes of carbon, 1 TJ of combusted natural gas (dry) leads to 15.3 tonnes of carbon, 1 TJ of combusted coking coal leads to 25.8 tonnes of carbon, and 1 TJ of combusted peat leads to 28.9 tonnes of carbon. These emission factors illustrate that among fossil fuels, natural gas is the most climate-friendly fuel. Tonnes of carbon are converted into tonnes of CO_2 by multiplying them with the factor of 3.67.

3 In fact there is a global organization of cities called ICLEI, under which cities world-wide have adopted emissions reduction targets as part of ICLEI's 'Cities for Climate Protection Campaign'. Five hundred local governments are participating, which represent 8 per cent of the global greenhouse gas emissions. Participating local governments have to establish an emissions reduction target, develop a local action plan, implement policies and measures, and monitor and verify results (ICLEI 2003).

4 Satterthwaite and Williams (1989) show that a sealed bid/sealed offer auction as conducted by the New York stock exchange reduces the possibility of market manipulation by individual sellers if a sufficiently large number of participants are in the market.

5 For more information about RECLAIM go to http://www.aqmd.gov/rules/reclaim/reclaim_home_page.html.

6 The US sulphur trading scheme has been qualified as one of the most successful tradable permit regimes, because 'environmental goals were achieved on time, without extensive litigation and at costs lower than projected' (Joskow and Schmalensee 1998).

7 The ranges for the prices in a fully competitive market are from $0 to $12.50 and for markets where market power is exercised from $1.10 to $30.20. Prices under perfect competition are consistently lower than those without competition.

8 See for example Downing and White (1986), Magat (1978) and Zerbe (1970).

9 The other factor contributing to this fuel switch was the deregulation of the railways, which made long-distance transport of low-sulphur coal affordable.

10 In a system where permits are exclusively and regularly auctioned the issue of new entry is not a problem. The only exception to this statement might occur in the case of market power.

11 For an empirical evaluation of this see Bruvoll, Faehn and Strøm (2003).

12 In a system with permanent permits, such free distribution happens only once when the system is introduced.
13 The question, if the impact on profits will be equal to the amount of the payment depends, however, on whether a tax is levied which can be deducted as cost before taxation, or whether it will increase the overall tax burden on the gross income of the firm.
14 See the review in Ekins and Barker (2001).
15 This section builds on Mavrakis and Konidari (2003) and UNEP/UNCTAD (2002). An excellent overview of design features in existing or developing emissions trading schemes is given in Haites *et al.* (2001).
16 Note that the British carbon tax is commonly referred to as the 'Climate Change Levy'.
17 Measurement in CO_2 equivalent means that all other gases, such as methane, are converted into carbon by using a conversion factor, which reflects their contribution to climate change relative to CO_2.
18 More information about the scheme can be found on its website http://www.defra.gov.uk/environment/climatechange/trading/ukets.htm.
19 More information about the trading Directive can be found at http://europe.eu.int/comm/environment/climat/emission.htm. A good overview of the EU trading scheme is given in Gagelman and Hansjuergens (2002).

Bibliography

Akhurst, M., Morgheim, J. and Lewis, R. (2003) 'Greenhouse gas emissions trading in BP', *Energy Policy* 31:657–663.
Baumol, W.J. and Oates, W.E. (1988) *The Theory of Environmental Policy*, 2nd edn, Cambridge: Cambridge University Press.
Bohm, P. (1998) 'Benefits of international emissions trading: theory and experimental evidence', Paper presented at the International Emission Trading Conference, Sydney, May.
Bruvoll, A., Faehn, T. and Strøm, B. (2003) 'Quantifying central hypotheses on environmental Kuznets curve for a rich economy: a computable general equilibrium study', *Scottish Journal of Political Economy*, 50:149–173.
Cameron, P. and Zillman, D. (eds) (2001) *Kyoto: from Principles to Practice*, Kluwer Law.
Cansier, D. (1998) 'Ausgestaltungsformen handelbarer emissionsrechte und ihre politische Durchsetzbarkeit', *Zeitschrift für angewandte Umweltforschung* 9:97–112.
Cramton, P. and Kerr, S. (1998) 'Tradable carbon allowance auctions: how and why to auction', Center for Clean Air Policy, March.
Crocker, T. (1966) 'The structuring of atmospheric pollution control systems', in H. Wolozing (ed.) *The Economics of Air Pollution*, New York: W.W. Norton.
Dales, J. (1968) *Pollution, Property, and Prices*, Toronto: University of Toronto Press.
Downing, P.G. and White, L.J. (1986) 'Innovation in pollution control', *Journal of Environmental Economics and Management* 13:18–29.
Ekins, P. and Barker, T. (2001) 'Carbon taxes and carbon emissions trading', *Journal of Economic Surveys* 15:325–376.
European Commission (EC) (1992) 'A Community strategy to limit CO_2 emissions and to improve energy efficiency', COM (92) 246 final, 1 June 1992, Brussels.

Feess, E. (1998) Umweltökonomie und Umweltpolitik, 2, überarbeitete Auflage. München.

Fisher, B.S., Barrett, S., Bohm, P., Kurdoda, M., Mubazi, J.K., Shah, A. and Stavins, R.N. (1996) 'An economic assessment of policy instruments for combating climate change', in Intergovernmental Panel for Climate Change: Climate Change, *Economic and Social Dimensions of Climate Change*, Cambridge: Cambridge University Press.

Fisher, C., Parry, I. and Pizer, W.A. (2003) 'Instrument choice for environmental protection when technological innovation is endogenous', *Journal of Environmental Economics and Management* 45:523–545.

Gagelman, F. and Hansjuergens, B. (2002) 'Climate protection through tradable permits: the EU Proposal for a CO_2 emissions trading system in Europe', *European Environment* 12:185–202.

Grubb, M. (1997) 'Technologies, energy systems and the timing of CO_2 emissions abatement', *Energy Policy* 25:159–172.

Haites, E. and Mullins, F. (2001) 'Linking domestic and industry greenhouse gas trading systems', Report prepared for EPRI, IEA and IETA.

Hanley, N., Shogren, J.F. and White, B. (1997) *Environmental Economics in Theory and Practice*, London: Macmillan.

Hargrave, T. (1998) US Carbon Emissions Trading: Description of an Upstream Approach. Center for Clean Air Policy. Washington, D.C., March 1998. Available at www.ccap.org.

Hauff, J. (2000) 'The feasibility of domestic CO_2 emissions trading in Poland', Risoe-R-1203. Online. Available at http://www.uneprisoe.org/EmTrading/ETPoland.pdf (accessed 29 September 2003).

Hauff, J. and Missfeldt, F. (2001) 'Emissions trading in Poland', ENER Forum 1, Integrating the Kyoto Mechanisms into National Framework, Krakow. Online. Available at http://www.eu.fhg.de/ENEREnerhome.htm (accessed 29 September 2003).

ICLEI (2003) Website: www.iclei.org.

Jensen, J. (2001) 'The Danish emissions trading scheme', ENER Forum 1, Integrating the Kyoto Mechanisms into National Framework, Krakow. Online. Available at http://www.eu.fhg.de/ENER/Enerhome.htm (accessed 29 September 2003).

Joskow, P. and Schmalensee, R. (1998) 'The political economy of market-based environmental policy: the US acid rain program', *Journal of Law and Economics* 41:37–85.

Jung, C., Krutilla, K. and Boyd, R. (1996) 'Incentives for advanced pollution abatement technology at the industrial level: an evaluation of policy alternatives', *Journal of Environmental Economics and Management* 30:95–111.

Kemfert, C., Haites, E. and Missfeldt, F. (2003) 'Can Kyoto Protocol parties induce the United States to adopt a more stringent greenhouse gas emissions target?', mimeo.

Magat, W.A. (1978) 'Pollution control and technological advance: a dynamic model of the firm', *Journal of Environmental Economics and Management* 5:1–25.

Mavrakis, D. and Konidari, P. (2003) 'Classification of emissions trading scheme design characteristics', *European Environment* 13:48–66.

Milliman, S.R. and Prince, R. (1989) 'Firm incentives to promote technological change in pollution control', *Journal of Environmental Economics and Management* 17:247–265.

Missfeldt, F. and Haites, E. (2002) 'Analysis of a commitment period reserve at national and global levels', *Climate Policy* 2:51–70.

Missfeldt, F. and Requate, T. (2001) 'From national emissions taxes to international emissions trading: the cases of Scandinavia and the UK', Discussion Paper No. 342. Department of Economics, University of Heidelberg.

Montero, J.P. (1997) 'Marketable pollution permits with uncertainty and transaction cost', *Resource and Energy Economics* 20:27–50.

OECD (2003) 'Environmentally related taxes database'. Online. Available at http://www.oecd.org (accessed 29 September 2003).

Pedersen, L.S. (2000) 'The Danish CO_2 emissions trading system', *RECIEL*, 9.

Pigou, A.C. (1946) *The Economics of Welfare*, London: Macmillan.

PointCarbon (2003) 'Viewpoint: the birth of the world's largest emissions market'. Online. Available at www.pointcarbon.com (accessed 29 September 2003).

Requate, T. and Unold, W. (2003) 'Environmental incentives to adopt advanced abatement technology: will the true ranking please stand up?', *European Economic Review* 47:125–146.

Satterthwaite, M.A. and Williams, S.R. (1989) 'Bilateral trade with the sealed bid k-double auction: existence and efficiency', *Journal of Economic Theory* 48:107–133.

Schwarze, R. (1997) 'Taxes versus tradeable permits for climate change policy: the case for new policy principles and criteria for a new field of environmental policy', Technical University Berlin, Discussion Paper No. 22.

Stavins, R.N. (1995) 'Transaction cost and tradable permits', *Journal of Environmental Economics and Management* 29:133–148.

Sterner, T. (2003) *Policy Instruments for Environmental and Natural Resource Management*, Washington, D.C.: Resources For the Future Press.

UNEP/UNCTAD (2002) 'An emerging market for the environment: a guide to emissions trading'. Online. Available at http://www.uccee.org (accessed 29 September 2003).

Westkog, H. (1996) 'Market power in a system of tradable CO_2 quotas', *The Energy Journal* 17:85–103.

Zerbe, R.O. (1970) 'Theoretical efficiency in pollution control', *Western Economics Journal* 8:364–736.

Żylicz, T. (1998) 'Obstacles to implementing tradeable pollution permits. The case of Poland', OECD, ENV/EPOC/GEEI(98)16. Paris.

Żylicz, T. (1999) 'The Chorzów project', unpublished manuscript.

7 Cost-Benefit Analysis and climate change

Nick Hanley and Dugald Tinch

Purpose of this chapter

Cost-Benefit Analysis (CBA) is used as a tool for policy and project analysis throughout the world. Attempts have been made to incorporate the environmental impacts of project/policies within CBA, in order to improve the quality of government and agency decision-making. Many technical problems persist, however, in applying CBA to environmental issues. In this chapter, we discuss the welfare economics foundations of CBA; go through the stages of a 'typical' CBA; review attempts at applying CBA to climate change and climate change policy; and discuss some general problems with CBA in the specific context of climate change. Our objectives are to explain what CBA is and how it can be used; and to illustrate its potentials and problems in the specific context of climate change.

The welfare economic foundations of Cost-Benefit Analysis

Cost-Benefit Analysis (CBA) is a decision-aiding tool which has some similarities with simple investment appraisal, but which is firmly based in the theory of welfare economics. Most importantly, this is true in the way that gains and losses are measured. For consumers, welfare effects are evaluated as changes in consumers' surplus, ideally measured using the exact welfare measures of compensating and equivalent variation (when quantities are allowed to vary) or compensating and equivalent surplus (when quantities are fixed to the consumer). For example, if an energy tax increases the price of electricity, we can estimate the welfare effect of this on the representative consumer by the fall in their consumers' surplus. This would be a measure of one cost of the policy in a CBA.

In environmental applications of CBA, we are often concerned with studying changes in the quantities of public goods, such as air quality or landscape quality.

Environmental resources possess the qualities of non-rivalness and non-excludability in varying amounts. For changes in a public good which are determined exogenously, we can use willingness to pay, or willingness to accept compensation, as money measures of these welfare amounts. For changes in producer welfare, CBA utilizes estimated changes in producer surplus (or quasi-rents), when prices change. Welfare impacts on production can, alternatively, be traced back to impacts on the owners of the factors of production (for example, change in land rents). We can also make use of the concept of opportunity costs, to assess the costs of using scarce resources for one purpose, in terms of the foregone benefits from allocating these resources to their (next best) alternative use.

The second way in which CBA is based on welfare economics is in terms of what counts as a benefit or cost. Since welfare economics evaluates alternative resource allocations in terms of relative effects on utility, so CBA includes as 'relevant' any impact on utility, bad or good, irrespective of whether it is reflected in market prices or not. Thus, reductions in air quality which reduce the utility of people living and working in a city are relevant costs, even though not all of this cost may be reflected in changes in market values.

Finally, CBA is tied into welfare economics theory in terms of the aggregation and comparison of benefits. Clearly, there will be very few policies or projects which impact on one individual only. Thus we need to be able to compare welfare changes across individuals. Also, it is somewhat obvious that all projects/policies will involve a mixture of gains and losses, thus that we need to be able to add up positive and negative impacts across individuals and compare them, in order to say something about the net impact on social welfare. Inter-personal utility comparisons from the point of view of social welfare are problematic, since we cannot assume that gains and losses of utility are equally socially valuable at the margin. Adding up compensating or equivalent variations for a policy may give us a net figure for gain or loss, but unless we know something about the social welfare function (SWF), it is hard to say anything about the overall effect on social well-being. The Bergson-Samuelson SWF is most commonly 'used' (in a thought-experiment kind of way) in CBA. Note, however, that the SWF is defined in terms of utility amounts, whereas empirically we work with money measures of these (such as willingness to pay). The weights used in a SWF based on money measures represent the relative marginal utilities of income of different groups or individuals in society. However, typically we do not know the empirical magnitudes of these parameters.

The somewhat pragmatic solution adopted by CBA has been to fall back on the sum of surplus changes and opportunity costs for a project, which may then be weighted to take account of distributional effects, for example by putting a higher weight on benefits accruing to poor groups. This weighting is especially likely to be done in applications on CBA in developing countries (see, for example, Brent 1990), but is much less likely to be done in developed countries. The use of the sum of money benefits and costs as a measure of the change in social welfare is based on the Kaldor-Hicks criterion, which asks: 'could the gainers compensate the losers and still be better off?' This criterion, proposed independently by Nicholas Kaldor and John Hicks in 1939 (Hicks 1939; Kaldor 1939), involves a comparison of benefits and costs as a measure of the net welfare effects of a policy/project. It effectively separates the issue of economic efficiency from that of the distribution of gains and losses.

Practically, the Kaldor-Hicks test implies comparing the sum of benefits across all those who gain, with the sum of costs across all those who lose, and seeing if this number is positive (in which case the proposal passes the CBA test) or negative (in which case it fails). Where benefits and costs accrue over time (the usual case), then discounting is typically used to add up impacts over different time periods. As Johanssen (2000) notes, there are many problems with the Kaldor-Hicks criterion from a theoretical viewpoint. However, it remains as the principle underlying theoretical support of why governments *should* undertake CBA analysis of potential policies/projects, since it is the only way in which we can talk about the CBA test as a measure of a project's potential contribution to social welfare.

In conclusion, CBA has strong links with welfare economics, but a somewhat shaky foundation in terms of inter-personal welfare impacts. The CBA process can be said to be a test of economic efficiency/inefficiency, but no strong conclusion can be then made about the net impact on social welfare. Distributional issues are usually kept separate. Acceptance of the Kaldor-Hicks criterion as a way of social decision-making also implies acceptance of a number of beliefs: these include comparability of gains and losses, that compensation is possible for all losses; and that ends are prioritized over means. Acceptance of CBA as a way of thinking about what society *should* do also means buying into the concepts of consumer sovereignty – that the only source of social well-being which we need to take account of is the well-being of individuals (i.e. there is no additional social 'good') and that consumers are the best judges of their own well-being (Randall 2002).

Stages of a CBA

How does one go about actually undertaking a CBA? The following structure provides a guide to some essential steps: for more details, see Hanley and Spash (1994).

Stage one: definition of project/policy

This definition will include: the reallocation of resources being proposed (for example the introduction of an energy tax) and the population of gainers and losers to be considered. The motive for the latter is to determine the population over which costs and benefits are to be aggregated. Often, it is a hard question to answer: issues of climate change can impact on the global population, but this is a hard scale at which to conduct analyses, and not the most relevant from a political economy viewpoint.

Stage two: identification of project/policy impacts

Once the project is defined, the next step is to identify all those impacts resulting from its implementation. Consider again the introduction on an energy tax. Stage two would include an estimate of all changes in the economy brought about by the tax (for example, a fall in energy use), and estimates of changes in emission levels for different pollutants (both air-borne and solid wastes).

Stage three: which impacts are economically relevant?

From the discussion on page 148, we know that from a welfare economics perspective, society is interested in maximizing the weighted sum of utilities across its members. These utilities depend, amongst other variables, on consumption levels of marketed and non-marketed goods. The former include a range of items from food to theatre visits, while the latter include fine views and clean air. The aim of CBA is to select projects and policies which add to the total of social utility, by increasing the value of consumables and nice views, by more than their opportunity costs. Thus, what are counted as positive impacts, which from now on will be referred to as *benefits*, will either be increases in the quantity or quality of goods that generate positive utility or a reduction in the price at which they are supplied. What we count as *costs* (that is negative impacts) will include any decreases in the quality or quantity of such goods, or increases in their price. These negative effects also include the using-up of scarce resources (inputs to production) in a project/policy.

The crucial point here, raised previously above, is that the environmental impacts of projects/policies are relevant for CBA so long as they either cause at least one person in the relevant population to become more or less happy and/or change the level or quality of output of some positively-valued commodity. For example, the environmental impacts of the energy tax could include implications for acidification of upland lakes, and changes in urban air pollution levels. The absence of a market for water or air quality is irrelevant in terms of the significance of impacts; although not in terms of how they are valued, as noted below.

Stage four: monetary valuation of relevant effects

In order for physical measures of impacts to be comparable, they must be valued in common units. The common unit in CBA is money, whether dollars, euros or yen. This use of money as the unit of account is merely a device of convenience, rather than an implicit statement that money is all that matters. Markets generate the relative values of all *traded* goods and services as relative prices: prices are therefore very useful in comparing impacts. The remaining tasks for the CBA analyst are then to:

1   predict real (i.e. relative) prices for value flows extending into the future;
2   correct market prices for imperfections in the economy, where necessary;
3   calculate prices (relative values in common units) where none exist.

Tasks 2 and 3 consist of adjusting market prices. In a perfectly competitive market, under certain assumptions, the equilibrium price indicates both the marginal social cost (MSC) and marginal social benefit (MSB) of the production of one more (or one less) unit of that good. This is because opportunity costs of production are given by the supply curve (given perfectly competitive input markets), whilst the demand curve is a schedule of marginal willingness to pay. Clearly there will be many cases, however, when the market price is a bad indicator of both MSC and MSB. If this is the case, *shadow* prices can be used to reflect true resource scarcity. Three cases can be distinguished: imperfect competition; government intervention in the market; and the absence of a market. If there is imperfect competition in a market, microeconomic theory shows that market price will not equal marginal cost in most cases. Government intervention drives a wedge between producer prices and marginal social benefits: this is most obviously the case in terms of agricultural production. Most Western governments support their agricultural sectors, and most do it partially by holding up prices above free market levels. In this case, then the net social value of output needs to be computed if a CBA is to accurately compare *social* costs and benefits.

The central focus of environmental applications of CBA, however, is the difficulty of placing a value on resources or services not traded in markets. In this case, there are a number of techniques available which seek to estimate the economic value of such goods, as set out for example in Hanley, Shogren and White (2001). For example, if a CBA is being conducted on investments in renewable energy, one impact is that less electricity is needed from alternative, fossil-fuel powered-generating stations. Fossil-fuel stations emit sulphur dioxide (SO_2) and nitrous oxides (NO_X), both contributors to acid rain. So one benefit of the nuclear station is lower acid-rain-causing emissions, and thus (on this measure) cleaner air. Estimates for such avoided external costs are clearly part of the CBA process in this case. When society chooses between alternative uses of scarce resources which impacts on human life as well, then this creates a need for shadow prices to be placed on avoided deaths, illnesses and non-fatal accidents.

Stage five: discounting of cost and benefit flows

Once all relevant cost and benefit flows that can be expressed in monetary amounts have been so expressed, it is necessary to convert them all into *present value* (PV) terms by discounting. Due to the productivity of capital and positive time preferences, future cost and benefits flows need to be converted into 'present values' to make them comparable with each other. This is achieved through the process of *discounting*. The present value now of a cost or benefit (X) received in time *t* with a discount rate of *i* is calculated as follows:

$$PV = X_t \left[(1 + i)^{-t} \right] \tag{7.1}$$

The expression in square brackets in equation (7.1) is known as a discount factor. Discount factors have the property that they always lie between 0 and 1. The further away in time a cost or benefit occurs (the higher the value of *t*), the smaller the discount factor. The higher the discount rate *i* for a given *t*, the lower the discount factor since a higher discount rate means a greater preference for things now rather than later. Discounting often has a profound impact on the outcome of a CBA analysis.

Stage six: applying the net present value test

The main purpose of CBA is to help select projects and policies which are efficient in terms of their use of resources. The criterion applied is the Net Present Value (NPV) test. This simply asks whether the sum of discounted gains exceeds the sum of discounted losses. If so, the project/policy can be said to represent an efficient shift in resource allocation, given the data used in the CBA. In other words, the NPV of a project is:

$$\sum_{t=1}^{t=T} (B_{t(1+i)}^{-t}) - \sum_{t=1}^{t=T} (C_{t(1+i)}^{-t}) \tag{7.2}$$

where cost and benefit flows are counted from year $t = 1$ to year $t = T$, and where *i* is the discount rate. The criterion for project/policy acceptance is: accept if the NPV > 0. Based on the Kaldor-Hicks criterion, any project passing this NPV test is deemed to be an improvement in social welfare.

An optional part of the seventh stage involves changing the weights in the NPV function. The NPV measure only works as a welfare change measure if we assume that the existing distribution of income is, in some sense, optimal (Johanssen 2000). This is because we do not know the correct marginal utilities of income with which to weight benefits and costs; whilst benefits and costs are also at least partly expressed in terms of willingness to pay, which depends not just on preferences but also on *ability* to pay. For these reasons, an optional stage which follows the NPV calculation is to examine the effects of different weighting schemes on NPV values. Climate change impacts may vary enormously in terms of income levels of effected parties (Fankhauser, Tol and Pearce 1997; Tol 2001). For example, rich consumers in the EU may be asked to forgo the benefits of cheaper energy in return for offsetting future damages due to flooding to very poor people living in Bangladesh. Climate change impacts can in principle be divided up according to which group in society they affect, groups being defined on income grounds alone.

The conventional NPV calculation implicitly puts an equal weight (equal to unity) on all these impacts. However, society might place more importance on each \$1 of impact on poor groups than on rich groups. This could be reflected in a different weighting scheme. One possible set of weights would be $w_i = (Y^*/Y_i)$, where w_i is the weight to be attached to impacts on group i, Y^* is mean household income across all groups, and Y_i is mean income within group i. This gives a higher weight to poorer groups than to richer groups, and the NPV formula becomes:

$$NPV = w_1B_1 + w_2B_2 + \ldots w_nB_n \qquad (7.3)$$

where B_n are discounted net benefits to group n. Table 7.1 gives a very simple illustration of the effects of re-weighting cost and benefit flows.

Re-weighting may seem like an attractive option, but there are severe problems. First, which weights should be used? Weights should probably also show the differential marginal impacts of changing incomes on utility, in which case our simple formula should also be a function of the elasticity of the marginal utility of income. Yet marginal utility of income weights are typically not known, and relative income is only one grounds on which to differentiate between groups (Azar and Sterner 1996). How should these groups be defined, and how easy is it to work out how much each group will be affected? As Pearce (2003: 14) has pointed out, 'any number of Social Welfare Functions can be postulated, each producing different weightings, and hence different overall climate damage figures'. Re-weighting cost-benefit outcomes is therefore a very tricky matter in practice.

Table 7.1 Climate change impacts by income group

Group affected	Unweighted impact discounted (\$ billion) (− a loss, + a gain)	Weighted impacts
G1 Low income	−2.4	−4.8
G2 Mid income	+1.1	+1.1
G3 High income	+2.3	+1.15

Stage seven: sensitivity analysis

The NPV test described above tells us about the relative efficiency of a given project, given the data input to the calculations. If this data changes, then clearly the results of the NPV test will change too. But why should data change? The main reason concerns uncertainty. In all ex ante cases of CBA, the analyst must make predictions concerning future physical flows (for example, sea level rise) and future relative values (for example, the value of agricultural land). None of these predictions is made with perfect foresight, and climate change predictions are clearly a very good illustration of the magnitude and multiple sources of uncertainty about the future. An essential final stage of any CBA is therefore to conduct sensitivity analysis. This means recalculating NPV when the values of certain key parameters are changed. These parameters will include physical changes brought about by a resource allocation, the marginal social values of these changes (or consumers and producers surplus values), the time period over which costs and benefits are considered, and the discount rate.

One intention here is to discover to which parameters the NPV outcome is most sensitive. For example, in appraising an energy tax where the NPV has been calculated as positive, by how much in percentage terms does the base rate of GDP growth have to rise before the NPV becomes negative? By how much do air pollution costs need to fall before NPV goes negative? What is the impact of changing the discount rate? The NPV result will often depend crucially on the choice of discount rate: this will certainly be so for issues with long-term effects such as climate change policy.

Applications of CBA to climate change and climate change policy

The nature of benefits and costs of climate change and climate policy

The 1990s saw a large amount of work carried out into adapting CBA techniques to the problem of climate change and to the design of climate change policy. All models included economic growth assumptions, estimates of abatement costs, emissions forecasts and damage functions relating to the effects of global warming.[1] However, there is much debate about alternative economic, ecological and climate scenarios. This section will identify some of the key results of CBA studies on climate change and how changing the elements included in the studies can have a major impact upon their results. Note that much work on *costs* of controlling the main greenhouse gases has been undertaken as a form of cost-effectiveness analysis, which involves taking as given specific targets for reductions in emissions, without questioning whether the benefits are commensurate.

For a useful supplementary view on the literature on the costs and benefits of greenhouse gas control, see Chapter 6 of Spash (2002).

We should also be clear about terminology here. 'Costs' are usually expressed as the costs of reducing emissions of greenhouse gases, and typically focus on carbon dioxide. These costs are usually a function of:

- the level of emission reduction;
- the timing of this reduction;
- which country/countries is/are responsible for the reduction;
- and how the reduction is achieved: for example, whether emission trading is allowed.

'Benefits' are typically thought of as avoided damages, although in some cases climate change can be beneficial to a country[2] or a sector, in which case some element of benefits will be negatively signed. Avoided damages are also country- and sector-specific, and depend on the accumulated *stock* of greenhouse gases in the atmosphere at any point in time. Damage estimates, and thus benefits of avoiding these damages, will additionally depend on assumptions about the degree of mitigating behaviour that economic agents are involved in, for instance, whether farmers switch crops to those better suited to the new climate (see, for instance, Abler *et al.* 2002), or whether additional flood defences are built.

Controlling climate change: cost and benefit estimates

Benefits: the benefits of avoided damages

Fankhauser and Tol (1996) summarize climate change costs from a number of studies. They show that estimates of marginal damages ranged from about US$5–125 per tC (tonne of carbon). They also showed that aggregated monetized damage due to climate change is estimated at 1.5 to 2.0 per cent of world GDP for a doubling of pre-industrial CO_2 (increase of 1.9–5.2 degrees C with 2.5 degrees C as best estimate IPCC 1991). These (estimated) damages are not evenly spatially distributed, the OECD losing 1.0 to 1.5 per cent of GDP and developing countries 2.0 to 9.0 per cent. Chapter 11 shows other regional disaggregations of damage cost estimates.

Pearce (2003) presents a recent summary, which shows that the estimates of damage have fallen over time to the extent that some improvement in world GNP is predicted by some studies (Table 7.2). Pearce himself settles on a best guess for marginal damages of $4–$9/tonne.

Tol and Downing (2000) suggest that early models and literature tended to be 'too pessimistic' and more recent models and literature tend to be 'too

Table 7.2 Aggregate social cost of global warming (% of world GNP)

	Pearce et al. *(1996)*	*Mendelsohn* et al. *(1996)*		*Nordhaus and Boyer (2000)*	*Tol (2002)*
	2.5°C	1.5°C	2.5°C	2.5°C	1.0°C
DCs	—	+0.12	+0.03	−0.5 to +0.4	
LDCs	—	+0.05	−0.17	−0.2 to −4.9	
World	−1.5 to −2.0	+0.10		−1.5	+2.3

Source: Pearce (2003).

Note
+ indicates a benefit, − a cost (damage).

optimistic'. This change in the estimation of the impact of climate change has occurred for a number of reasons. The simplest explanation is that those studies predicting a benefit from climate change do so for a lower temperature increase, which may be related to changing estimates of climate change impact. However, there are some other explanations for differences in estimates between studies.

ADAPTATION

Early studies did not allow for adaptation to climate change by the various individuals and societies. One example being the 'dumb farmer scenario'. Farmers were assumed in early studies not to change management practices as climatic variables change with obvious negative impact on yields and income. However, if farmers are expected to adapt they may be able to increase yields and move to more profitable crops (Mendelsohn *et al.* 1994; Abler *et al.* 2002). In a general study Plambeck and Hope (1996) find a marginal difference of US$11 per tC between a scenario with and without adaptation to climate change.

INCREASED UNDERSTANDING OF COMPLEX SYSTEMS

The General Climate Models and Regional Climate Models developed in order to identify patterns of climate change have been improved. For example emissions of Aerosols and SO_2 have been shown to reduce temperature increases through promoting cloud formation (Heal *et al.* 2002). Many early studies ignored the impact of CO_2 enrichment of crops and forestry. Also many sectors which may benefit from global warming such as summer recreational activities and citrus cropping were not included in earlier studies (Neumayer 1999). There is still much debate about the complexity of systems, Schultz and Kasting (1997) showed that improvement of models for CO_2 uptake has major impact upon policy proposals.

INTEGRATED ASSESSMENT

Early models tended to have 'one-way' linking between models where the results of one model become the inputs to another. Integrated Assessment has become a more common tool where a series of sub-models make up a single simulation framework (Linder *et al.* 2002). This approach introduces a series of multi-directional feedback loops which allow for the interactions in the climate change, economic, ecological and management decision models. Many studies have concentrated on the economic impacts of climate change in terms of agricultural productivity and sea level rise only. Integrated assessment gives a greater potential to include likely impacts on economic development and growth.

STOCK EFFECTS

Since damages relate to the stock of greenhouse gases, and since this stock is rising over time due to the lagged effect of past emissions, most studies show the marginal damage costs of carbon emissions as rising over time. For example, the Nordhaus and Boyer study cited above shows marginal damage costs rising from $6.4/t in 1991–2000, to $15/t in 2021–2030.

DISCOUNTING

Climate change occurs over long time spans so the choice of discount rate is obviously of great importance. Tol and Downing (2000) show how changing the pure rate of time preference can have a large impact on the results of studies (Table 7.3).

Table 7.3 The marginal cost of CO_2 and N_2O emissions ($/tC and $/tN$_2$O)

Model and discount rate (%)	World average CO_2	World average N_2O
FUND1.6 (pessimistic)		
0	109.5	11,547.1
1	73.8	7,079.0
3	37.0	3,234.0
FUND2.0 (optimistic)		
0	27.5	2,646.0
1	12.5	1,266.7
3	1.3	231.4

Source: Tol and Downing (2000).

Note
Emissions period 2000–2009. Costs discounted to 2000. Time horizon 2100.

The costs of reducing greenhouse gas emissions

Here, we mention a few studies, before looking at reasons for variations in estimates. The IPCC (2001) report values for the developed world ranging from US$20–$665 without trading of emissions permits and US$14–135 with trading. A range of costs from 0.19 to 2.02 per cent of GDP without trading and 0.05 and 1.14 per cent with emissions permits trading are reported, again only for developed regions. Dammes and Moore (1999) estimated UK marginal abatement cost to meet the Kyoto protocol at £45 tC, rising to £100/tC for a tougher 20 per cent target reduction. Other estimates may be found in Ekins and Barker (2002).

Factors driving differences in estimated costs include:

1   *Trading in carbon*: Tol (2001) amongst others has shown that introducing tradable emissions permits will significantly reduce the costs of GHG reductions (in terms of consumption losses). This occurs as it allows CO_2 emissions reductions where the marginal cost of abatement is lowest. Further evidence has been provided by Bohm (1999), who estimated that a jointly-implemented carbon emissions trading system applied across Sweden, Denmark, Norway and Finland could give a total saving in abatement costs of 48 per cent; and in the context of carbon taxes co-ordinated across Europe by Conrad and Schmidt (1998).

2   *Inclusion of secondary Benefits*: Reducing GHG emissions also leads to a reduction in other air pollutants which have costs associated with them, suggesting a higher level of abatement may be optimal (Ekins 1996).

3   *Modelling assumptions*: All estimates of the costs of reducing carbon emissions come from economic models. How these models are set up can influence the resultant estimates of (marginal) costs. The main three types of models used in this context have been dynamic optimization, computable general equilibrium, and macroeconomic simulation models (Ekins and Barker 2002). For example, the survey by Weyant and Hill (1999) shows a difference on predicted impacts of meeting Kyoto targets on GDP in Canada from -1.96 per cent to -0.96 per cent for exactly the same policy (tradable permits), depending on the model used. Within a given model type, ancillary assumptions also matter a lot to cost predictions. For instance, when a carbon tax is the policy instrument, whether revenues from the tax are recycled so that other taxes can be cut. In many studies, this shows a *negative* cost of reducing greenhouse emissions (that is, GDP is higher with a recycled carbon tax and lower carbon emissions, than without a carbon tax) – see, for instance, Barker and Kohler (1998).

Applying CBA to climate change: what are the key problems?

The preceding section on the application of CBA to climate change and climate policy shows up some of the many problems facing the CBA practitioner. These are presented below in a summarized form.

The valuation of non-market impacts

Many impacts of climate change such as species extinction and loss of human life are non-market impacts, which presents further difficulties for CBA analysis. Nordhaus shies away from attempting to value these impacts but rather arbitrarily adjusts the cost co-efficient used in DICE to account for omitted factors. Other studies have attempted to value such non-market impacts and have often found them to be of greater value than the traditionally estimated impacts on agriculture and sea level rise (Howarth and Monahan 1996).

However, there is considerable controversy on both the best way to obtain estimates of non-market values, and on how much reliance should society place on estimates so generated. Additionally, we might ask whether we are acting immorally by placing money values on changes in expected mortality or losses in biodiversity due to climate change. Pearce (2003) counters that decisions about what to do about climate change imply some judgment about *all* of the benefits of avoided damage, so that it is better to be 'up front' about such valuations. This is an argument in favour of seeking monetary values for non-market impacts of climate change, and one that many economists would agree with.

Ecosystem complexity

How can society accurately predict the effects of economic activity on complex ecosystems? Non-linearities and surprises may be expected in such systems, but CBA copes with such phenomena rather badly. Climate change involves impacts on multiple, interlinked ecosystems, which co-evolve with economic systems which both register and create damages. Ecosystem complexity can be seen as one example of uncertainty in CBA, and CBA does not cope very well with this, as we explain below.

Discounting and the discount rate

Climate change policy often involves costs to present generations yet benefits (avoided damages) to future generations. Lack of a climate policy could imply the opposite. Either way, costs and benefits are likely to be spread asymmetrically over a very long time period. Discounting means that a marginally 'cheaper' policy may be adopted today at the expense of large future benefits (Roughgarden and Schneider 1999).

The choice of discount rate is therefore crucial in using CBA to think about climate policy options. This, however, raises several important questions. First, *should* society discount future costs and benefits? Second, when costs and benefits stretch between generations, is the usual exponential type of discounting (as shown in equation 7.1) appropriate, or should we seek an alternative method, such as hyperbolic discounting or time-varying discount rates? Recent work by Weitzman (1998) suggests that discount rates should be lower for far-in-the-future costs than for nearer-in-time costs. Empirical evidence also suggests that people have different discount rates for different goods (e.g. Luckert and Adamowicz, 1993), with environmental costs being subject to lower rates, and lower discount rates for long-term costs/benefits than short-term ones. Finally, if we are uncertain about the time path of discount rates, then this can also have big impacts on net present values. For instance, Newell and Pizer (2003) show that, according to the assumption ones makes about the nature of this uncertainty, the present value of a marginal tonne of carbon emissions changes from $21.73 with a constant 2 per cent discount rate, to $33.84 under their preferred model of uncertainty: a 56 per cent increase in the present value of reducing carbon emissions.

Finally, does discounting violate the rights of future generations? Harrod, many years ago, described discounting as a polite expression for rapacity. It is certainly true that operating a 'maximize net present value' rule lays potentially heavy costs on future generations. Chichilnisky (1997) has recently pointed out that discounting is not even a necessity from the viewpoint of inter-temporal efficiency. However, this view would not be shared by all (Pearce, Barbier and Markandya 1990). For a recent summary of the literature on the environmental discount rate, see Sheraga and Sussman (1998).

Sustainability and CBA

CBA is concerned with the efficiency of resource allocation, whilst sustainability is an intra-and inter-generational fairness issue. This means that subjecting projects and policies to a CBA test is not a test of their sustainability. Climate change policies that pass the CBA test are thus not necessarily compatible with some definitions of sustainability. For example, they may allow irreversible losses in natural capital.

Un-compensatable losses

As was noted earlier, the Kaldor-Hicks compensation test which is the theoretic foundation of CBA assumes that losers can in principle be compensated. Yet if climate change imposes irreversible losses on future generations, would they be willing to exchange these for gains in consumption possibilities, if somehow they could be brought to a present-day negotiation table?[3] Perhaps not. In this case, the justification for CBA as a way of testing for potential improvements in social well-being is undermined.

Dealing with uncertainty

Consider the example of a CBA which addresses the environmental costs of climate change in terms of impacts on biodiversity in Scotland. Three situations regarding our knowledge of these environmental costs are possible. First, scientists may be unsure about what physical impacts climate change will have; this implies that not all 'states of the world', $\{s_1 \ldots s_n\}$, are known. Second, scientists may be able to identify all possible impacts, $\{s_1 \ldots s_n\}$, but not be able to identify the probability distribution of these states of the world. Third, all possible states of the world and their probability distribution may be known. Most treatments of *risk* in economics is concerned with the circumstances of the third case, but not of the first two. If we know all possible states of the world and their probabilities, then expected values can be estimated along with their certainty equivalents. These can then form part of a CBA. However, if either not all states of the world are known, or if their probabilities are unknown, then we face a situation of true, or hard, uncertainty. In this case, which is likely to describe most environmental management situations, then CBA must fall back on sensitivity analysis, which estimates net benefits under different, feasible states-of-the-world.

Dealing with uncertainty is one of the major problems for CBA of climate change. The time scales and complexity of the systems being studied are difficult to deal with and lead to uncertainty about the predictions from these models. Whilst the science of climate change and the likely impacts in terms of a positive or negative effect are understood there is still much uncertainty about the scale of these impacts, their probability and likely severity (Chapter 2 of this book; Howarth and Monahan 1996). The IPCC Third Assessment Report (2001) identifies five areas of uncertainty which are relevant here:

1 emission scenarios;
2 carbon cycle responses;
3 climate sensitivity to carbon cycle changes;
4 the regional implications of a global climate scenario;
5 the possible impacts on human society.

This shows that there is uncertainty about every element of climate change (Heal and Kristrom 2002)! The impact of doubling CO_2 identified by the IPCC (1991) is predicted to be a temperature increase of between 1.9 and 5.2 degrees C, a factor of three difference. A 1 degree C change in the Earth's mean temperature was related to the little ice age, which caused crop failures and freezing of the Baltic Sea between the fourteenth and seventeenth century; whilst a 5 degrees C temperature increase would result in a climatic regime not seen in over a million years (Howarth and Monahan 1996). Changes in extreme events and the impacts of these will also be important to real-world future trajectories. The IPCC has attempted to deal with uncertainty by identifying the degree of confidence in climate change predictions so future studies based on these predictions can take that uncertainty into account (Heal *et al.* 2002).

Faced with such uncertainty, can CBA still make a useful contribution to decision-making? Economists disagree. Some, such as Tietenberg (1998), say no. Others, such as Pearce (1998), say yes.

Conclusions

The preceding section closed by noting some very major problems in applying the CBA method to decisions over climate change. So should we therefore reject CBA in this instance as a way of informing social decision-making? Pearce (2003) has noted that every policy decision relating to climate change implies that an *implicit* cost benefit analysis of some form or another has taken place. The costs of a policy must be lower than the perceived benefits for it to be adopted and non-adoption indicates the costs are thought to be higher than the benefits. It therefore seems rational to suggest that decision makers should be informed by some quantifiable measure of the size of costs and benefits, rather than relying on implicit notions of what these costs and benefits are.

Economists do not in general argue in any case that CBA is the *only* piece of information that governments need to take on board (Arrow *et al.* 1998). CBA certainly allows for public preferences to enter into social decision-making in a quantified manner, and provides a useful filter for projects that are very wasteful of scarce resources. Society can still decide to implement such projects anyway if more pressing needs exist. Randall (2002) has formalized this idea by saying that CBA should only be decisive where nothing more important is at stake, for instance where ethical trump cards or Safe Minimum Standards are involved (Berrens *et al.* 1998).

CBA also identifies who gains and who loses from climate change and by how much. This can be in terms of which countries or regions stand most to gain and most to lose (see Chapter 11). Within a country, CBA can also show who gains and who loses from climate change policies such as carbon taxes, and by how much. Finally, CBA provides a way of structuring the debate about how best to respond to climate change, since it forces us to weigh up the advantages and disadvantages of alternative courses of action. That it is particularly difficult to do this in the context of climate change should not put us off trying to solve these problems.

Notes

1 For a summary of one of the most frequently used models (Nordhaus's DICE) see Roughgarden and Schneider (1999). Chapter 8 of this book focuses entirely on this modelling issue.
2 For instance, Frijters and van Praag (2001) claim this is the case for Russia.
3 For an interesting discussion of this point, see Norton (2002).

Bibliography

Abler, D., Shortle, J., Carmichael, J. and Horan, R. (2002) 'Climate change, agriculture and water quality in the Chesapeake Bay Region', *Climate Change* 55:339–359.

Arrow, K., Cropper, M., Eads, G., Hahn, R., Lave, L., Noll, R., Portney, P., Russell, M., Schmalensee, R., Smith, V.K. and Stavins, R. (1998) 'Is there a role for benefit-cost analysis in environmental, health and safety regulation?', *Environment and Development Economics* 2:196–201.

Azar, C. and Sterner, T. (1996) 'Discounting and distributional considerations in the context of global warming', *Ecological Economics* 19:169–184.

Barker, T. and Kohler, J. (1998) *International Competitiveness and Environmental Policies*, Aldershot: Edward Elgar.

Berrens, R., Brookshire, D., McKee, M. and Schmidt, C. (1998) 'Implementing the safe minimum standard approach', *Land Economics* 74:147–161.

Bohm, P. (1999) 'An emissions quota trading experiment amongst four Nordic countries', in S. Sorrell and J. Skea (eds) *Pollution for Sale: Emissions Trading and Joint Implementation*, Cheltenham: Edward Elgar.

Brent, R.J. (1990) *Project Appraisal for Developing Countries*, New York: University Press.

Chichilnisky, G. (1997) 'The costs and benefits of benefit-cost analysis', *Environment and Development Economics* 2:202–205.

Conrad, K. and Schmidt, F. (1998) 'Economic impacts of a coordinated versus and uncoordinated carbon dioxide policy in the European Union', *Economic Systems Research* 10:161–182.

Dammes and Moore (1999) *The Implications for the UK of an International Emissions Trading Scheme*, London: DETR.

Ekins, P. (1996) 'How large a carbon tax is justified by the secondary benefits of CO_2 abatement?', *Resource and Energy Economics* 18:161–187.

Ekins, P. and Barker, T. (2002) 'Carbon taxes and carbon emissions trading', in N. Hanley and C. Roberts (eds) *Issues in Environmental Economics*, Oxford: Blackwell Publishing.

Fankhauser, S. and Tol, R.S.J. (1996) 'Climate change costs: recent advancements in the economic assessment', *Energy Policy* 24:665–673.

Fankhauser. S., Tol, R.S.J. and Pearce, D. (1997) 'The aggregation of climate change damages: a welfare theoretic approach', *Environment and Resource Economics* 10:249–266.

Frijters, P. and van den Praag, B. (2001) 'The effects of climate change on welfare and well-being in Russia', in D. Maddison (ed.) *The Amenity Value of the Global Climate*, London: Earthscan.

Hanley, N. and Spash, C. (1994) *Cost-Benefit Analysis and the Environment*, Cheltenham: Edward Elgar.

Hanley, N., Shogren, J. and White, B. (2001) *An Introduction to Environmental Economics*, Oxford: Oxford University Press.

Heal, G. and Kristrom, B. (2002) 'Uncertainty and climate change', *Environmental and Resource Economics* 22:3–39.

Hicks, J.R. (1939) 'The foundations of welfare economics', *Economic Journal* 49: 696–712.

Howarth, R.B. and Monahan, P.A. (1996) 'Economics, ethics and climate policy: framing the debate', *Global and Planetary Change* 11:187–199.

IPCC (Intergovernmental Panel on Climate Change) (1991) *Climate Change: The IPCC Scientific Assessment*, Cambridge: Cambridge University Press.

Johannson, P.O. (2000) 'The microeconomics of valuation', in H. Folmer and G.H. Landis (eds) *Principles of Environmental and Resource Economics: A Guide for Students and Decision-makers*, Cheltenham: Edward Elgar.

Kaldor, N. (1939) 'Welfare propositions of economics and inter-personal comparisons of utility', *Economic Journal* 49:549–552.

Lind, R.C. (1995) 'Intergenerational equity, discounting, and the role of cost-benefit analysis in evaluating global climate change', *Energy Policy* 23:379–389.

Linder, M., Sohngen, B., Joyce, L.A., Price, D.T., Bernier, P.Y. and Karjalaien, T. (2002) 'Integrated forestry assessments for climate change impacts', *Forestry Ecology and Management* 162:117–136.

Luckert, M. and Adamowicz, W. (1993) 'Empirical measures of factors affecting the social rate of discount', *Environmental and Resource Economics* 3:1–22.

Mendelsohn, R., Nordhaus, W.D. and Shaw, D. (1994) 'The impact of global warming on agriculture: a Ricardian analysis', *The American Economic Review* 84:753–769.

Neumayer, E. (1999) 'Global warming: discounting is not the issue but sustainability is', *Energy Policy* 27:33–43.

Newell, R. and Pizer, W. (2003) 'Discounting the future: how much do uncertain rates increase valuations?', *Journal of Environmental Economics and Management* 46:52–71.

Nordhaus, W.D. and Boyer, J. (2000) *Warming the World: Economic Models of Global Warming*, Cambridge, MA: MIT Press.

Norton, B. (2002) 'The ignorance argument: what must we know to be fair to the future?', in D. Bromley and J. Paavola (eds) *Economics, Ethics and Environmental Policy*, Oxford: Oxford University Press.

Pearce, D. (1998) 'Economic development and climate change', *Environmental and Development Economics* 3:389–391.

Pearce, D. (2003) 'The social cost of carbon and its policy implications', *Oxford Review of Economic Policy*, forthcoming.

Pearce, D., Barbier, E. and Markandya, A. (1990) *Sustainable Development: Economics and Environment in the Third World*, Cheltenham: Edward Elgar.

Pearce, D., Cline, W., Achanta, A., Fankhauser, S., Pachauri, R., Tol, R. and Vellinga,

P. (1996) 'The social costs of climate change', in IPCC *Climate Change 1995: Economic and Social Dimensions*, Cambridge: Cambridge University Press.

Plambeck, E. and Hope, C. (1996) 'PAGE95: an updated valuation of the impacts of global warming', *Energy Policy* 24:783–793.

Randall, A. (2002) 'Benefit-cost considerations should be decisive when there is nothing more important at stake', in D. Bromley and J. Paavola (eds) *Economics, Ethics and Environmental Policy*, Oxford: Oxford University Press.

Roughgarden, T. and Schneider, S.H. (1999) 'Climate change policy: quantifying uncertainties for damages and optimal carbon taxes', *Energy Policy* 27:415–429.

Schultz, P.A. and Kasting, J.F. (1997) 'Optimal reductions in CO_2 emissions', *Energy Policy* 25:491–500.

Sheraga, J. and Sussman, F. (1998) 'Discounting and environmental management', in H. Folmer and T. Tietenberg (eds) *The International Yearbook of Environmental and Resource Economics*, Cheltenham: Edward Elgar.

Spash, C. (2002) *Greenhouse Economics: Values and Ethics*, London: Routledge.

Tietenberg, T. (1998) 'Economic analysis and climate change', *Environment and Development Economics* 3:402–404.

Tol, R. (2001) 'Equitable cost-benefit analysis of climate change policies', *Ecological Economics* 36:71–85.

Tol, R. (2002) 'Estimates of the damage costs of climate change: benchmark estimates', *Environmental and Resource Economics* 21:47–73.

Tol, R. and Downing, T. (2000) *The Marginal Costs of Climate Changing Emissions*, Amsterdam, Institute for Environmental Studies, Free University.

Weitzman, M. (1998) 'Why the far future should be discounted at the lowest possible rate', *Journal of Environmental Economics and Management* 36:201–208.

Weyant, J.P. and Hill, J.N. (1999) 'Introduction and overview', in *The Costs of the Kyoto Protocol*, *The Energy Journal*, Special issue: vii–xliv.

8 Economic modelling of global climate change

Warwick J. McKibbin and Peter J. Wilcoxen

Introduction

The current debate on greenhouse gas emissions is of fundamental importance for the future direction of the world economy. Carbon dioxide is the major greenhouse gas and a major source of carbon dioxide emissions is the burning of fossil fuels. Some people believe that not taking action to curb the rising emissions of greenhouse gases will be very detrimental for future generations. On the other hand there are those who believe that a fundamental shift in the economic structure of the world economy away from its current reliance on fossil fuels for energy production, will lead to substantial economic and social costs during a transition period that could last many decades.[1] Even if these costs are deemed to be worthwhile there is a continuing debate about how the burden of adjustment should be shared among countries. A crucial aspect of this debate is that most of the main issues are highly uncertain. Unfortunately policy decisions need to be made by governments and decisions need to be made by households and firms in making their future investment plans. It is important that these decisions are not made in an information vacuum.

Ideally in deciding on the appropriate course of action, policy makers would weigh up the benefits and costs of alternative policies both at the domestic level as well as globally. This is where global economic models have proven invaluable in providing both estimates of the costs as well as some indication of the range of uncertainties. Global economic models can and have been used to evaluate the implications of a range of global and domestic policy actions and clearly illustrate the interdependencies not only of greenhouse emissions but of policy actions in individual countries.[2]

Economic models are just one of many sources of information that can be brought to bear on the greenhouse problem. Like any model in any discipline, economic models are simplifications of reality. Nonetheless they do have a number of important advantages. Despite the range of criticisms and well-documented limitations of large-scale economic models, these models do provide information and basic insights that it would be folly to ignore. A key feature of using economic models to project future scenarios is that economists attempt to model the reactions of human beings based on observed empirical evidence. Incorporating human behaviour into any projections of the future is crucial. It is unhelpful to think of the world analogously as a balloon where each subsequent year is a re-scaling of the previous year. The world economy in 1997 is far from a simple scaling of the world in 1947 and it is unlikely that anyone in 1947 could have foreseen the world we now live in. Yet the current debate on greenhouse regularly involves speculation over horizons of at least 50 years into the future.

The purpose of this chapter is to give an overview of how economic models used for greenhouse policy are structured (with a focus on the G-Cubed model), what we have learnt from using the G-Cubed multi-country model of relevance to the greenhouse policy debate and finally to summarize evidence from models on the costs and benefits of the Kyoto Protocol.

The next section of this chapter gives an overview of how economic models can contribute to the greenhouse policy debate. We then give an outline of the key features of the G-Cubed multi-country model and how it has been used in the climate change debate (Appendix I gives more technical details of the model). The main insights from the modelling project are then summarized. Finally, we outline the results from a range of economic models in costing the Kyoto Protocol.

The role of economic models in the greenhouse debate

Economic models have an important role to play in the greenhouse debate because they embody knowledge, both theoretical and empirical, that has been accumulating for many decades. This is knowledge about the way individuals react to changing circumstances and the way these responses become manifest in various markets. Economic models are built around a range of identities, which hold independently of the assumed behaviour of individuals. If nothing else, this provides a consistency check on the wide range of assumptions that are involved in a question such as greenhouse policy. Within this structure, the behaviour of households firms and governments are then specified.

An economic model provides a framework for asking 'what if' questions about how economies respond to a change in a forcing variable whether it is a drought, an increase in OPEC oil prices or a domestic or foreign government policy change. These responses can be traced through the economy by modelling the behaviour of households, firms, government and institutions and how they inter-act in markets. However it is foolish to think we can use these models to predict the future beyond a few years with any precision. This is partly because of the simplicity of the models but also because the future is inherently unpredictable due to forces outside the model. The usefulness of these models is in asking questions about what the key driving variables will be in determining the future, as well as the effects of alternative policies on possible futures. In other words, the models help us understand how much a variable of interest is likely to change as a result of a change in a forcing variable. Models should be used as frameworks for thinking about the future; frameworks that are transparent and subject to empirical evaluation based on recent experience and observed empirical relationships.

Economic models provide a very effective way to move away from future analysis based solely on trend extrapolation. An example of why formulating policy based on extrapolation of trends can be a problem is clearly illustrated by the oil price shocks of the 1970s. In Bagnoli, McKibbin and Wilcoxen (1996) it is shown that GDP, energy use and carbon dioxide emissions for the United States and Japan rose in parallel from 1965 to 1973 (i.e. energy use per unit of GDP was relatively constant). When oil prices rose, however, energy use per unit of GDP began to fall significantly. During that period, in other words, energy use was growing substantially more slowly than GDP. In economic terminology, American and Japanese energy users substituted away from energy when oil prices where high; in ordinary language, they conserved energy.

We gain a couple of insights from this example that are crucial for thinking about greenhouse policy. One is that it is clear that economies can be highly responsive to changes in relative prices, even over fairly short periods of time. This response is reflected on the demand side through changes in consumption patterns and on the supply side through changes in the structure of economies. Second, it shows that extrapolative projections that would have been made in 1972 would very quickly be completely wrong because of significant unforeseen events. Thus any prediction of the future is clearly a conditional projection. Third, adjustment to surprises can be very costly (in terms of lost output) since in the short to medium term physical capital is difficult to move between sectors of the economy and workers cannot be retrained quickly. In the short run any sharp change in policy to quickly abate greenhouse gases is likely to be costly.

Economic models can play a very useful role but they need to be used carefully and form the core of a structured debate and not the source of definitive answers. They are particularly useful for analysing the myriad of issues arising in the debate on greenhouse policies because it is impossible to solve the many interdependencies without using a framework that captures these interdependencies transparently.

The ultimate usefulness of an economic model is not so much in the numerical magnitudes it produces (although these are very useful in placing debates in context) but in improving our understanding of the key underlying mechanisms that determine any set of numbers.

An overview of the G-Cubed multi-country model

The G-Cubed multi-country model was developed by McKibbin and Wilcoxen (1993a) and has been updated in McKibbin and Wilcoxen (1998). It is an intertemporal general equilibrium model. It combines the approach taken in the earlier research of McKibbin and Sachs (1991) in the McKibbin-Sachs Global model (MSG model) with the disaggregated, econometrically-estimated, intertemporal general equilibrium model of the US economy by Jorgenson and Wilcoxen (1990).

G-Cubed has been constructed to contribute to the current policy debate on environmental policy and international trade with a focus on global warming policies, but it has many features that will make it useful for answering a range of issues in environmental regulation, microeconomic and macroeconomic policy questions. It is a world model with substantial regional disaggregation and sectoral detail. In addition, countries and regions are linked through trade and financial markets. G-Cubed contains a strong foundation for analysis of both short run macroeconomic policy analysis as well as long run growth consideration of alternative macroeconomic policies. Budget constraints are imposed on households, governments and nations (the latter through accumulations of foreign debt). To accommodate these constraints households and firms are assumed to use the model to generate forecasts of future economic performance and use these projections in their planning of consumption and investment decisions. The response of monetary and fiscal authorities in different countries can have important effects in the short to medium run which, given the long lags in physical capital and other asset accumulation, can be a substantial period of time. Overall, the model is designed to provide a bridge between computable general equilibrium (CGE) models that traditionally ignore the adjustment path between equilibria and macroeconomic models that ignore individual behaviour and the sectoral composition of economies.

G-Cubed is still in the process of development but it is already a large model. In its current form it contains over 6,000 equations and 110 intertemporal co-state variables. The key features of G-Cubed are summarized in Box 8.1. The country and sectoral breakdown of the model are summarized in Box 8.2. The range of countries modelled to date include the United States, Japan, Australia, New Zealand, the rest of the OECD, China, oil exporting developing countries (OPEC), Eastern Europe and states of the former Soviet Union (EFSU), and all other developing countries (LDCs)) with 12 sectors in each region. There are five energy sectors (electric utilities, natural gas utilities, petroleum processing, coal extraction, and crude oil and gas extraction) and seven non-energy sectors (mining, agriculture, forestry and wood products, durable manufacturing, non-durable manufacturing, transportation and services).

This disaggregation enables us to capture the sectoral differences in the impact of alternative environmental policies.

A full theoretical outline of the model is contained in the Appendix. Here we will summarize the main behavioural assumptions in the model.

Box 8.1 Summary of main features of G-Cubed

- Specification of the demand and supply sides of economies;
- Integration of real and financial markets of these economies;
- Intertemporal accounting of stocks and flows of real resources and financial assets;
- There is extensive econometric estimation of key elasticities of substitution from disaggregated data at the sectoral level;
- Imposition of intertemporal budget constraints so that agents and countries cannot forever borrow or lend without undertaking the required resource transfers necessary to service outstanding liabilities;
- Short run behaviour is a weighted average of neoclassical optimizing behaviour and ad hoc 'liquidity constrained' behaviour;
- The real side of the model is disaggregated to allow for production and trade of multiple goods and services within and across economies;
- Full short run and long run macroeconomic closure with macro dynamics at an annual frequency around a long run Solow/Swan/Cass neoclassical growth model;
- The model is solved for a full rational expectations equilibrium at an annual frequency with a horizon of more than a century.

Each economy or region in the model consists of several economic agents: households, the government, the financial sector and firms in the 12 production sectors listed above. The behaviour of each type of agent is modelled. Each of the 12 sectors in each country in the model is represented by a single firm in each sector that chooses its inputs and its level of investment in order to maximize its stock market value subject to a multiple-input production function (defining technological feasibility) and a vector of prices it takes to be exogenous. For each sector, output is produced with inputs of capital, labour, energy, materials and a sector-specific resource. The nature of the sector-specific resource varies across sectors. For example in the coal industry it is reserves of coal, in agriculture and forestry/wood products it is land that is substitutable between these two sectors.

Energy and materials are aggregates of inputs of intermediate goods. These intermediate goods are, in turn, aggregates of imported and domestic commodities that are taken to be imperfect substitutes.

The capital stock in each sector changes according to the rate of fixed capital formation and the rate of geometric depreciation. It is assumed that the investment process is subject to rising marginal costs of installation, with total real investment expenditures in sector h equal to the value of direct purchases of investment plus the per unit costs of installation. These per unit costs, in turn, are assumed to be a linear function of the rate of investment. One advantage of using an adjustment cost approach is that the adjustment cost parameter can be varied for different sectors to capture the degree to which capital is sector specific.

Box 8.2 Overview of the G-Cubed model

Regions:
- United States
- Japan
- Australia
- New Zealand
- China
- Rest of the OECD
- Oil exporting developing countries
- Eastern Europe and the former Soviet Union
- Other developing countries

Sectors:
- Energy:
    - Electric utilities
    - Gas utilities
    - Petroleum refining
    - Coal mining
    - Crude oil and gas extraction

- Non-energy:
    - Mining
    - Agriculture, fishing and hunting
    - Forestry/wood products
    - Durable manufacturing
    - Non-durable manufacturing
    - Transportation
    - Services

Households consume a basket of composite goods and services in every period and also demand labour and capital services. Household capital services consist of the service flows of consumer durables plus residential housing. Households receive income by providing labour services to firms and the government, and from holding financial assets. In addition, they also receive transfers from the government. The household decision involves predicting expected future income from all sources (i.e. wealth) as well as current income. This information together with the relative prices of different goods and services then determine the pattern of consumption spending over time and the pattern of spending across the available goods.

It is assumed that the government in each country divides spending among final goods, services and labour according to the proportions in the base year input-output table for each country. This spending is financed by levying taxes on households and firms and on imports.

Households, firms and governments are assumed to interact with each other in markets for final goods and services, financial, and factor markets both foreign and domestic. The result of this interaction, given the desires of each economic entity, determine a set of relative prices that feed back into decision-making by the different economic agents.

In summary, the G-Cubed model embodies a wide range of assumptions about individual behaviour and empirical regularities in a general equilibrium framework. The complex interdependencies are then solved out using a computer. It is important to stress that the term 'general equilibrium' is used here to signify that as many interactions as possible are captured, not that the economy is in a full market clearing equilibrium at each point in time. Although it is assumed that market forces eventually drive the world economy to a long run steady-state equilibrium, unemployment does emerge for long periods due to different labour market institutions in different economies.

Key insights from studies using the G-Cubed model

Since 1992 the major strands of research into greenhouse policy with the model (and in most models in this area) have had two focuses. One has been on generating projections of the future evolution of the world economy and exploring the sensitivity of these projections to a variety of assumptions. The second focus has been on evaluating the impacts of a variety of policy changes on these projections. These two strands of research will be dealt with separately.

Baseline issues

In a study for the United Nations University, Bagnoli, McKibbin and Wilcoxen (1996) found that in a future horizon of 30 years, the assumptions about structural change are crucial for understanding the energy intensity of various economies. Using the model, the authors made two projections of the world economy from 1990 to 2020. The first projection assumed that all sectors in the economy experienced the same rate of technical change as the economy as a whole but this differed across economies with developing economies growing more quickly than developed economies. The second set of assumptions was that the differences in sectoral technical change followed the historical pattern scaled so that each economy had the same average economy wide GDP growth rate as in the first scenario. The result was a dramatically different degree of energy intensity in each representation of the world economy by 2020. Countries had approximately the same GDP growth rates in both scenarios (by assumption) but energy use was totally different. In the second scenario, economy wide energy per unit of GDP fell by around 1 per cent per year but this didn't reflect what energy modellers call 'autonomous energy efficiency improvement (AEEI)'. This purely reflected the changing structure of economies over time in response to relative price changes induced by different sectoral rates of technical change. Thus the carbon taxes required for carbon emission stabilization in the second scenario where close to 50 per cent less than those for the first scenario.

This study made the point that a simple projection of GDP growth was insufficient to determine the carbon emission path because it was what happened at the sectoral level that was important for future emissions and not the aggregate path of the economy. This is not to say that GDP growth is irrelevant but what matters is the source of that growth.

The other issue that emerged in this study and other related studies, is that the effect of small changes in growth over 20 or more years can have enormous effects on the levels of variables. Compounding is not a new discovery but the extreme range of possible outcomes from small changes in growth rates is always a sobering reminder of the degree of uncertainty we are dealing with. In particular there is a strong empirical basis to the argument that many economy variables have a unit root or a stochastic trend. If this is correct, or even approximately correct, then any standard errors we would calculate to give a statistical measure of our uncertainty of future projections would quickly approach infinity.

Policy issues

The G-Cubed model has been used for a range of studies of alternative greenhouse policies. Carbon taxes are examined in McKibbin and Wilcoxen (1993a, 1993b). These studies all highlight that a surprise carbon tax leads to a reduction in real output with the greatest losses occurring in the short run. In addition, any tax that aims at stabilizing carbon dioxide emissions at a constant absolute level would have to be continually increasing. The underlying baseline emissions of carbon dioxide rise into the indefinite future primarily due to population growth.

McKibbin, Ross, Shackleton and Wilcoxen (1999) show that the adjustment of capital flows are important for the impacts of climate policy. An increase in the price of energy inputs make goods produced using energy relatively more expensive in world markets. The conventional view is that the current account of a country would deteriorate as a result of a carbon tax. In McKibbin and Wilcoxen (1996a), we showed on the contrary that the current account could improve if the revenue from the tax was used to reduce the fiscal deficit. The rise in savings and fall in investment could easily lead to an improvement in the overall current account balance reflecting a capital outflow. The composition of the trade account would reflect the simple partial equilibrium reasoning but the economy wide general equilibrium effect could go the other way.

We also showed that the way in which the revenue from a carbon tax is used can have important consequences for the costs of the carbon abatement policy. If the revenue is used to reduce another tax in the economy, then the costs of abatement can be reduced. For example in the US if the revenue is used to reduce the fiscal deficit, there can be a fall in interest rates that stimulates economic growth and reduces the costs of the carbon abatement. This does not work in a small country like Australia because it is small in global capital markets and has very little impact on world interest rates. Nonetheless using the revenue to reduce taxes on capital can help to offset the negative effects of a carbon abatement policy in Australia.

The trade implications of environmental policy are the focus of papers by McKibbin and Wilcoxen (1993a, 1996a). These papers show that changes in environmental policy are unlikely to lead to major changes in trade flows through relocation of industry because the costs of environmental policy are generally small relative to the cost of relocating production facilities. This does not mean that environmental policies lead to small losses in economic output, but that the policies are unlikely to be fully offset by substitution towards goods that are not subject to the same environmental regulation. In the context of US policy for global warming the papers above have shown that the reduction in US emissions also reduces global emission except for an offset of around 10 to 20 per cent due to these substitution effects. A key insight from this research was that a significant part of energy use is for domestic transportation which is largely non traded and therefore is unlikely to move overseas.

As part of the Energy Modelling Forum/IPCC/UNU conference in Tokyo in March 1997, we found that we could not run many popular permit trading scenarios in the G-Cubed model because of the instability such a permit trading system caused in the global trade system. The main problem was the extent of stabilization proposed in the scenarios, which implied very high prices for emission permits. This resulted in wild fluctuations in real exchange rates as part of the process by which resources are allocated in the permit trading system. This has been discussed in McKibbin and Wilcoxen (1997). This suggests that there is a fundamental flaw in the global emission permit trading schemes frequently proposed (like that proposed under Kyoto). The problem is that permit trading systems would generate large transfers of wealth between countries. Supporters of a permit system regard this as an advantage because it would allow developed countries to compensate developing countries for reducing their emissions. Results from the G-Cubed model suggests that a plan such as this would put enormous stress on the world trade system (depending on the tightness of the emission targets, the extent to which the allocation of permits was different to the permits required to meet the targets and the marginal cost of abatement in different countries amongst other things). A developed country importing permits would see its balance of trade deteriorate substantially. This would lead to substantial volatility in exchange rates and would create distortions in the world trade system. Equally serious problems would be created for developing countries. Massive exports of permits would lead to exchange rate appreciation and a decline or collapse in traditional exports. In the international economics literature this is known as the 'Dutch Disease' or in Australia as the 'Gregory

Thesis'. It occurs because the granting of permits has an impact on the wealth of the receiving countries, which changes their consumption patterns and comparative advantage. These issues are generally ignored in the debate because permits are assumed to be the same as carbon taxes in the sense that the permit price is a uniform carbon tax across all countries. Once the wealth effects of the permit are taken into account, as they are in the G-Cubed model, the simplistic equivalence of a uniform carbon tax and an emission permit breaks down.

Results from a range of models on the cost of the Kyoto Protocol

The costs of policies that would limit greenhouse gas emissions are highly uncertain. The reason, in large part, is that baseline emissions are very difficult to predict.[3] The cost of reducing emissions to a target level depends heavily on how much they would have grown otherwise: the more quickly emissions grow in the absence of a policy, the larger will be the reductions needed to reduce them to a given target. Not only that, but reductions will have to be made sooner, and will hence be more expensive in present value terms, when baseline emissions are growing rapidly.

Many factors affect the baseline path of the world economy: the rates of population growth in different countries; the age structure, educational attainment and labour productivity of those populations; the rates of productivity growth within individual industries; the rates of convergence of developing country incomes and productivity to the levels prevailing in developed countries (or the lack of such convergence); OPEC's production decisions; new developments in the technology of fossil fuel extraction; technical progress in conservation and fuel efficiency;[4] the discovery of new fuel deposits and reserves; and even the degree of social and economic integration between countries. As a result, the economy is very difficult to predict over long spans of time and past attempts have generally been very far off the mark.[5] Plausible alternative assumptions about these factors can lead to vastly different emissions trajectories.

Even if the baseline path of the economy could be predicted perfectly, however, there would still be important uncertainties in calculating the cost of reducing emissions. Many key economic parameters are not known precisely. The scope of the problem can be conveyed by listing a few of these parameters: the short and long-term price elasticities of demand for different fuels; the rate at which the composition of household demands change as incomes rise;[6] the degree of substitutability between products from different countries; the intertemporal elasticity of substitution (which plays an important role in determining savings and capital formation); and the elasticity of labour supply. In addition, there is evidence that some inexpensive, efficient energy technologies already exist but are not currently used and the reasons why they have not been adopted are very poorly understood.[7]

A final factor that must be considered in computing the costs of a climate change policy are any indirect benefits it produces. Some of these may be environmental: a climate policy that reduces fossil fuel consumption may also lower conventional air pollutants, such as sulphur dioxide, oxides of nitrogen, carbon monoxide, particulates and volatile organic compounds (precursors of ground-level ozone). In some urban areas, these benefits could be substantial. Other benefits could be fiscal: if the climate change policy were a tax, for example, it would raise government revenue that could allow other taxes to be reduced. Such reductions could benefit the economy by increasing the supply of labour, or by stimulating investment and capital formation. This has become known as the 'double dividend' hypothesis and has spawned a considerable literature. However, the magnitude of any such effect is widely disputed and highly uncertain.

In spite of these uncertainties, a variety of studies have been done, most focusing on the short-term costs – through 2010 or 2020 – of one of two policies: reducing emissions to 1990 levels, or implementing the 1997 Kyoto Protocol.[8] Marginal costs are typically measured by calculating the carbon tax (a tax on the carbon content of fossil fuels) needed to achieve a particular emissions target. The results vary substantially across models. Table 8.1 shows the carbon taxes

Table 8.1 Carbon taxes needed in 2010 to achieve Kyoto targets (1990 US dollars per tonne of carbon)

Model	USA	Europe	Japan	CANZ
ABARE-GTEM	322	665	645	425
AIM	153	198	198	234
CETA	168	—	—	—
G-Cubed	76	227	97	157
GRAPE	—	204	304	—
MERGE3	264	218	500	250
MIT-EPPA	193	276	501	247
MS-MRT	236	179	402	213
Oxford	410	996	1,074	—
RICE	132	159	251	145
SGM	188	407	357	201
WorldScan	85	20	122	46
Administration	154	—	—	—
EIA	251	—	—	—
POLES	136	135	195	131
Mean	198	307	387	205
Standard deviation	92	270	273	100

Source: IPCC (2001), which draws heavily on Energy Modelling Forum 16, a multi-model evaluation of the Kyoto Protocol. The results of the study appear in a 1999 special issue of the *Energy Journal*.

needed in four regions; the US, Europe, Japan and CANZ (Canada, Australia and New Zealand) in order for each region to achieve its 2010 Kyoto emissions target without any international permit trading.

Figure 8.1 illustrates the range of these results. It shows the median tax for each region and has error bars indicating the 20th and 80th percentiles in the distribution of results. The models agree most closely on the US and CANZ carbon taxes but the range is still large: the gap between the 20th and 80th percentiles for the US is $153 and the gap between the smallest and largest results overall is $334. The results for Europe and Japan are much less certain: the gaps between the 20th and 80th percentiles for those regions are $314 and $379, respectively.

The effect of these taxes on each region's GDP in 2010 is summarized in Figure 8.2, which shows the median GDP loss for each region, along with the 20th and 80th percentiles of the distributions. In all regions, GDP losses are substantial but once again, the ranges of results are large.

Conclusions

Economic models have a valuable role to play in the policy debate on greenhouse gas abatement not because of the numbers they generate per se but because they can help understand the potential strengths, weaknesses and costs of alternative policies. They also give a picture of the range of uncertainty in both emissions projections and the cost of alternative policies, such as the Kyoto Protocol. There is also a range of economic models available, each of which can provide insights particular to the type of issue for which the model was designed.[9] It is unlikely that there will ever be an all-encompassing model that can answer every

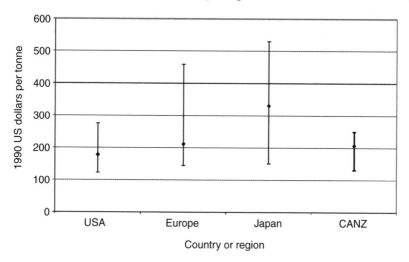

Figure 8.1 Median carbon tax needed in 2010 to achieve Kyoto target, by region (error bars show the range between the 20th and 80th percentiles).

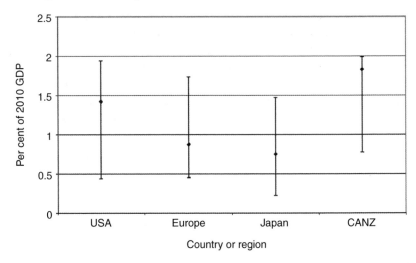

Figure 8.2 Median GDP loss in 2010 under Kyoto targets, by region (error bars show the range between the 20th and 80th percentiles).

question. For any given policy issue, a range of models should be used to give a range of insights and some measure of the range of possible quantitative outcomes for any given policy change. It is important that models be used sensibly. In the past, disenchantment with models has generally occurred because they were used to give the definitive answer to certain questions. It is inevitable that using models this way will be counterproductive because the future will never be as a model predicts because there are too many factors operating outside the model.

Economic models used properly provide a range of insights that are crucial for formulating policy. In fact in working with the G-Cubed model we have not only improved our understanding of the many complex issues related to climate change policy but we have also developed two proposals that we believe would allow the world to begin to address the issue of greenhouse gas abatement at low cost and with the flexibility required when there is so much uncertainty.

The first is the removal of subsidies to coal production and consumption globally as outlined in Anderson and McKibbin (2000). This paper found, using the G-Cubed model, that the distortions in global coal markets (particularly in Europe, Japan and China) if removed could reduce global carbon dioxide emissions by close to 8 per cent relative to those that otherwise would be experienced. This is close to the reduction in global emissions that would eventuate by 2010 if all Annex I countries targeted emissions to 1990 levels.[10] This research suggests that policies aimed at other goals such as trade liberalization can have important implications for greenhouse emissions and could be a useful step towards addressing the climate change issue.

In McKibbin and Wilcoxen (1997), we proposed an alternative policy to traditional permit trading systems that moves in the right direction of beginning to address the greenhouse problem but without causing the disruption a convention- ally advocated permit system could cause. It is an international agreement setting up a system combining emissions permits and fees at the national level.[11]

Research using the G-Cubed model suggests that no agreement based on country specific targets that ignore the differential nature of economies can emerge from the negotiations over the Kyoto Protocol. The political and eco- nomic implications of the Kyoto Protocol approach will prevent this. Until policy makers move away from explicit and unrealistic targets and timetables and towards uniformity in policy instruments that yields differential outcomes, it is difficult to believe that substantial progress can be made.

One of the lessons from modelling climate change policy is that negotiations should focus on formulating policies that minimize global economic cost and create the appropriate incentives for households, firms and governments to change their behaviour over time. These policies should also deal with the inher- ently uncertain nature of the greenhouse problem. The majority of debate and international negotiations since the 1992 Rio Summit have largely been com- pletely misplaced, focusing on explicit targets for emissions when the real issues of costs and sustainability of policies (both political and economic) have not been addressed. The models have shown where progress might be made on climate policy – it is up to the international negotiations to sensibly use this information.

Appendix I: A stylized two-country G-Cubed model

In this section a stylized two-country model is presented which distils the essence of the G-Cubed model and in particular how the intertemporal aspects of the model are handled.[12]

In this stylized model there are two symmetric countries (based essentially on US data adjusted to create symmetry). Each country consists of several economic agents: households, the government, the financial sector and two firms, one each in the two production sectors. The two sectors of production are energy and non-energy (this is much like the aggregate structure of the MSG2 model). The following gives an overview of the theoretical structure of the model by describ- ing the decisions facing these agents in one of these countries. Throughout the discussion all quantity variables will be normalized by the economy's endowment of effective labour units. Thus, the model's long run steady-state will represent an economy in a balanced growth equilibrium.

Firms

We assume that each of the two sectors can be represented by a price-taking firm that chooses variable inputs and its level of investment in order to maximize its stock market value. Each firm's production technology is represented by a constant elasticity of substitution (CES) function. Output is a function of capital, labour, energy and materials:

$$Q_i = A_i^o \left(\sum_{j = k,l,e,m} (\delta_{ij}^o)^{1/\sigma_i^o} x_{ij}^{(\sigma_i^o - 1)/\sigma_i^o} \right)^{\sigma_i^o/(\sigma_i^o - 1)} \tag{8.1}$$

where Q_i is the output of industry i, x_{ij} is industry i's use of input j, and A_i^o, δ_{ij}^o and σ_i^o are parameters. A_i^o reflects the level of technology, σ_i^o is the elasticity of substitution, and the δ_{ij}^o parameters reflect the weights of different inputs in production; the superscript o indicates that the parameters apply to the top, or 'output', tier. Without loss of generality, we constrain the δ_{ij}^o's to sum to one.

The goods and services purchased by firms are, in turn, aggregates of imported and domestic commodities which are taken to be imperfect substitutes. We assume that all agents in the economy have identical preferences over foreign and domestic varieties of each commodity. We represent these preferences by defining composite commodities that are produced from imported and domestic goods. Each of these commodities, Y_i, is a CES function of inputs domestic output, Q_i, and an aggregate of goods imported from all of the country's trading partners, M_i:

$$y_i = A_i^{fd} ((\delta_{id}^{fd})^{1/\sigma_i^{fd}-1)/\sigma_i^{fd}} + (\delta_{if}^{fd})^{1/\sigma_i^{fd}} M_i^{(\sigma_i^{fd} - 1)/\sigma_i^{fd}})^{\sigma_i^{fd}/\sigma_i^{fd} - 1)} \tag{8.2}$$

where σ_i^{fd} is the elasticity of substitution between domestic and foreign goods.[13] For example, the energy product purchased by agents in the model are a composite of imported and domestic energy. The aggregate imported good, M_i, is itself a CES composite of imports from individual countries, M_{ic}, where c is an index indicating the country of origin:

$$M_i = A_i^{ff} \left(\sum_{c = 1}^{7} (\delta_{ic}^{ff})^{1/\sigma_i^{ff}} M_{ic}^{(\sigma_i^{ff} - 1)/\sigma_i^{fd}} \right)^{\sigma_i^{ff}/(\sigma_i^{ff} - 1)} \tag{8.3}$$

The elasticity of substitution between imports from different countries is σ_i^{ff}.

By constraining all agents in the model to have the same preferences over the origin of goods we require that, for example, the agricultural and service sectors have identical preferences over domestic oil and imported oil.[14] This accords with the input-output data we use and allows a very convenient nesting of production, investment and consumption decisions.

In each sector the capital stock changes according to the rate of fixed capital formation (J_i) and the rate of geometric depreciation (δ_i):

$$\dot{k}_i = J_i - (\delta_i + n)k_i \tag{8.4}$$

Following the cost of adjustment models of Lucas (1967), Treadway (1969) and Uzawa (1969) we assume that the investment process is subject to rising marginal costs of installation. To formalize this we adopt Uzawa's approach by assuming that in order to install J units of capital a firm must buy a larger quantity, I, that depends on its rate of investment (J/k):

$$I_i = \left(1 + \frac{\phi_i}{2}\frac{J_i}{k_i}\right)J_i \tag{8.5}$$

where ϕ_i is a non-negative parameter. The difference between J and I may be interpreted various ways; we will view it as installation services provided by the capital-goods vendor. Differences in the sector-specificity of capital in different industries will lead to differences in the value of ϕ_i.

The goal of each firm is to choose its investment and inputs of labour, materials and energy to maximize intertemporal net-of-tax profits. For analytical tractability, we assume that this problem is deterministic (equivalently, the firm could be assumed to believe its estimates of future variables with subjective certainty). Thus, the firm will maximize:[15]

$$\int_t^\infty (\pi_i - (1-\tau_4)p^I I_i)e^{-(R(s)-n)(s-t)}ds \tag{8.6}$$

where all variables are implicitly subscripted by time. The firm's profits, π, are given by:

$$\pi_i = (1-\tau_2)(p_i^* Q_i - w_i x_{il} - p_i^e x_{ie} - p_i^m x_{im}) \tag{8.7}$$

where τ_2 is the corporate income tax, τ_4 is an investment tax credit, and p^* is the producer price of the firm's output. $R(s)$ is the long-term interest rate between periods t and s:

$$R(s) = \frac{1}{s-t}\int_t^s r(v)dv \tag{8.8}$$

Because all real variables are normalized by the economy's endowment of effective labour units, profits are discounted adjusting for the rate of growth of population plus productivity growth, n. Solving the top tier optimization problem gives the following equations characterizing the firm's behaviour:

$$x_{ij} = \delta_{ij}^o (A_i^o)^{\sigma_i^q - 1} Q_i \left(\frac{p_i^*}{p_j}\right)^{\sigma_i^o} \quad j \in \{l,e,m\} \tag{8.9}$$

$$\lambda_i = \left(1 + \phi_i \frac{J_i}{k_i}\right)(1 - \tau_4)p^I \tag{8.10}$$

$$\frac{d\lambda_i}{ds} = (r + \delta_i)\,\lambda_i - (1 - \tau_2)p_i^* \frac{dQ_i}{dk_i} - (1 - \tau_4)p^I \frac{\phi_i}{2}\left(\frac{J_i}{k_i}\right)^2 \tag{8.11}$$

where λ_i is the shadow value of an additional unit of investment in industry i.

Equation 8.9 gives the firm's factor demands for labour, energy and materials and equations 8.10 and 8.11 describe the optimal evolution of the capital stock. Integrating equation 8.11 along the optimum trajectory of investment and capital accumulation, $(\hat{J}(t), \hat{k}(t))$, gives the following expression for λ_i:

$$\lambda_i(t) = \int_t^\infty \left((1 - \tau_2)p_i^* \frac{dQ_i}{dk_i}\bigg|_{\hat{j},\hat{k}} + (1 - \tau_4)p^I \frac{\phi_i}{2}\left(\frac{\hat{J}_i}{\hat{k}_i}\right)^2\right)e^{-(R(s) + \delta)(s - t)}ds \tag{8.12}$$

Thus, λ_i is equal to the present value of the after-tax marginal product of capital in production (the first term in the integral) plus the savings in subsequent adjustment costs it generates. It is related to q, the after-tax marginal version of Tobin's Q (Abel 1979), as follows:

$$q_i = \frac{\lambda_i}{(1 - \tau_4)p^I} \tag{8.13}$$

Thus we can rewrite equation 8.10 as:

$$\frac{J_i}{k_i} = \frac{1}{\phi_i}(q_i - 1) \tag{8.14}$$

Inserting this into equation 8.8 gives total purchases of new capital goods:

$$I_i = \frac{1}{2\phi_i}(q_i^2 - 1)k_i \tag{8.15}$$

We assume that some firms use a 'backward looking' q to make their decisions. This backward looking q follows an error correction model towards the forward looking q.

$$\tilde{q}_{it+1} = \tilde{q}_{it} + \alpha_3(q_{it} - \tilde{q}_{it-1}) \tag{8.16}$$

We assume that firms based investment decisions partly on the forward looking q and partly on the backward looking $q(\tilde{q})$:

$$1_i = \alpha_2 \frac{1}{2\phi_i}(q_i^2 - 1)k_i + (1 - \alpha_2)\frac{1}{2\phi_i}(\tilde{q}_i^2 - 1)k_i \qquad (8.17)$$

So far we have described the demand for investment goods by each sector. Investment goods are supplied, in turn, by a third industry that combines labour and the outputs of other industries to produce raw capital goods. We assume that this firm faces an optimization problem identical to those of the other two industries: it has a nested CES production function, uses inputs of capital, labour, energy and materials in the top tier, incurs adjustment costs when changing its capital stock, and earns zero profits. The key difference between it and the other sectors is that we use the investment column of the input-output table to estimate its production parameters.

Households

Households have three distinct activities in the model: they supply labour, they save, and they consume goods and services. Within each region we assume household behaviour can be modelled by a representative agent with an intertemporal utility function of the form:

$$U_t = \int_t^\infty (\ln c(s) + \ln g(s))e^{-\theta(s-t)}\,ds \qquad (8.18)$$

where $c(s)$ is the household's aggregate consumption of goods and services at time s, $g(s)$ is government consumption at s, which we take to be a measure of public goods provided, and θ is the rate of time preference.[16] The household maximizes 0 subject to the constraint that the present value of consumption be equal to the sum of human wealth, H, and initial financial assets, F:[17]

$$\int_t^\infty p^c(s)c(s)e^{-(R(s)-n)(s-t)} = H_t + F_t \qquad (8.19)$$

Human wealth is defined as the expected present value of the future stream of after-tax labour income plus transfers:

$$H_t = \int_t^\infty (1-\tau_1)(W(L^G + L^C + L^I + \sum_{i=1}^{12} L^i) + TR)e^{-(R(s)-n)(s-t)}\,ds \qquad (8.20)$$

where τ_1 is the tax rate on labour income, TR is the level of government transfers, L^C is the quantity of labour used directly in final consumption, L^I is labour used in producing the investment good, L^G is government employment, and L^i is employment in sector i. Financial wealth is the sum of real money balances;

MON/P, real government bonds in the hand of the public; B, net holding of claims against foreign residents; A, the value of capital in each sector:

$$F = \frac{MON}{P} + B + A + q^l k^l + q^c k^c + \sum_{i=1}^{12} q^i k^i \tag{8.21}$$

Solving this maximization problem gives the familiar result that aggregate consumption spending is equal to a constant proportion of private wealth, where private wealth is defined as financial wealth plus human wealth:

$$p^c c = \theta(F + H) \tag{8.22}$$

However, based on the evidence cited by Campbell and Mankiw (1990) and Hayashi (1982) we assume some consumers are liquidity-constrained and consume a fixed fraction γ of their after-tax income (INC).[18] Denoting the share of consumers who are not constrained and choose consumption in accordance with the above equation by α_8, total consumption expenditure is given by:

$$p^c c = \alpha_8 \theta(F_t + H_t) + (1 - \alpha_8)\gamma INC \tag{8.23}$$

The share of households consuming a fixed fraction of their income could also be interpreted as permanent income behaviour in which household expectations about income are myopic.

Once the level of overall consumption has been determined, spending is allocated among goods and services according to a CES utility function.[19] The demand equations for capital, labour, energy and materials can be shown to be:

$$p_i x_i^c = \delta_i^c y \left(\frac{p^c}{p_i}\right)^{\sigma_c^o - 1}, \quad i \in \{k, l, e, m\} \tag{8.24}$$

where y is total expenditure; x_i^c is household demand for good i; σ_c^o is the top-tier elasticity of substitution and the δ_i^c are the input-specific parameters of the utility function. The price index for consumption, p^c, is given by:

$$p^c = \left(\sum_{j = k,l,e,m} \delta_j^c p_j^{\sigma_c^o - 1}\right)^{\frac{1}{\sigma_c^o - 1}} \tag{8.25}$$

Household capital services consist of the service flows of consumer durables plus residential housing. The supply of household capital services is determined by consumers themselves who invest in household capital, k^c, in order to generate a desired flow of capital services, c^k, according to the following production function:

$$c^k = \alpha k^c \qquad (8.26)$$

where α is a constant. Accumulation of household capital is subject to the condition:

$$\dot{K}^C = \int^C (\delta^C - n)K^C \qquad (8.27)$$

We assume that changing the household capital stock is subject to adjustment costs so household spending on investment, I^c, is related to $\int^c$ by:

$$I^c = \left(1 + \frac{\phi^c}{2}\frac{\int^c}{k^c}\right)\int^c \qquad (8.28)$$

Thus the household's investment decision is to choose I^C to maximize:

$$\int_t^\infty (p^{ck}\alpha k^c - p^I \int^c)e^{-(R(s) - n)(s - t)} \, ds \qquad (8.29)$$

where p^{ck} is the imputed rental price of household capital. This problem is nearly identical to the investment problem faced by firms and the results are very similar. The only important differences are that no variable factors are used in producing household capital services and there is no investment tax credit for household capital. Given these differences, the marginal value of a unit of household capital, λ_C, can be shown to be:

$$\lambda_c(t) = \int_t^\infty \left(p^{ck}\alpha + p^I \frac{\phi_c}{2}\left(\frac{\hat{J}_c}{\hat{k}_c}\right)^2\right)e^{-(R(s) + \delta)(s - t)} \, ds \qquad (8.30)$$

where the integration is done along the optimal path of investment and capital accumulation, $(\hat{J}_c(t), \hat{k}_c(t))$. Marginal q is:

$$q_c = \frac{\lambda_c}{p^I} \qquad (8.31)$$

and investment is given by:

$$\frac{J_c}{k_c} = \frac{1}{\phi_c}(q_c - 1) \qquad (8.32)$$

The labour market

We assume that labour is perfectly mobile among sectors within each region but is immobile between regions. Thus, wages will be equal across sectors within each region, but will generally not be equal between regions. In the long run, labour supply is completely inelastic and is determined by the exogenous rate of population growth. Long run wages adjust to move each region to full employment. In the short run, however, nominal wages are assumed to adjust slowly according to an overlapping contracts model where wages are set based on current and expected inflation and on labour demand relative to labour supply. The equation below shows how wages in the next period depend on current wages; the current, lagged and expected values of the consumer price level; and the ratio of current employment to full employment:

$$w_{t+1} = w_t \left(\frac{p_{t+1}^c}{p_t^c} \right)^{\alpha_5} \left(\frac{p_t^c}{p_{t-1}^c} \right)^{1-\alpha_5} \left(\frac{L_t}{\bar{L}} \right)^{\alpha_6} \qquad (8.33)$$

The weight that wage contracts attach to expected changes in the price level is α_5 while the weight assigned to departures from full employment $(\bar{L})$ is α_6. The above equation can lead to short-run unemployment if unexpected shocks cause the real wage to be too high to clear the labour market. At the same time, employment can temporarily exceed its long run level if unexpected events cause the real wage to be below its long run equilibrium.

The government

We take each region's real government spending on goods and services to be exogenous and assume that it is allocated among inputs in fixed proportions, which we set to 1996 values. Total government outlays include purchases of goods and services plus interest payments on government debt, investment tax credits and transfers to households. Government revenue comes from sales taxes, corporate and personal income taxes, and from sales of new government bonds. In addition, there can be taxes on externalities such as carbon dioxide emissions. The government budget constraint may be written in terms of the accumulation of public debt as follows:

$$\dot{B}_t = D_t = r_t B_t + G_t + TR_t - T_t \qquad (8.34)$$

where B is the stock of debt; D is the budget deficit; G is total government spending on goods and services; TR is transfer payments to households, and T is total tax revenue net of any investment tax credit.

We assume that agents will not hold government bonds unless they expect the bonds to be paid off eventually and accordingly impose the following transversality condition:

$$\lim_{s \to \infty} B(s)e^{-(R(s) - n)s} = 0 \qquad (8.35)$$

This prevents per capita government debt from growing faster than the interest rate forever. If the government is fully leveraged at all times, equation 8.35 allows equation 8.34 to be integrated to give:

$$B_t = \int_t^\infty (T - G - TR)e^{-(R(s) - n)(s - t)} \, ds \qquad (8.36)$$

Thus, the current level of debt will always be exactly equal to the present value of future budget surpluses.[20]

The implication of equation 8.36 is that a government running a budget deficit today must run an appropriate budget surplus as some point in the future. Otherwise, the government would be unable to pay interest on the debt and agents would not be willing to hold it. To ensure that this equation holds at all points in time we assume that the government levies a lump sum tax in each period equal to the value of interest payments on the outstanding debt.[21] In effect, therefore, any increase in government debt is financed by consols, and future taxes are raised enough to accommodate the increased interest costs. Other fiscal closure rules are possible, such as requiring the ratio of government debt to GDP to be unchanged in the long run. These closures have interesting implications but are beyond the scope of this paper.

Financial markets and the balance of payments

The eight regions in the model are linked by flows of goods and assets. Flows of goods are determined by the import demands described above. These demands can be summarized in a set of bilateral trade matrices which give the flows of each good between exporting and importing countries.

Trade imbalances are financed by flows of assets between countries. Each region with a current account deficit will have a matching capital account surplus, and vice versa.[22] We assume asset markets are perfectly integrated across regions.[23] With free mobility of capital, expected returns on loans denominated in the currencies of the various regions must be equalized period to period according to a set of interest arbitrage relations of the following form:

$$i_k + \mu_k = i_j + \mu_j + \frac{\dot{E}_k^j}{E_k^j} \qquad (8.37)$$

where i_k and i_j are the interest rates in countries k and j, μ_k and μ_j are exogenous risk premiums demanded by investors (calibrated in the baseline to make the model condition hold exactly with actual data), and E_k^j is the exchange rate between the currencies of the two countries.

Capital flows may take the form of portfolio investment or direct investment but we assume these are perfectly substitutable ex ante, adjusting to the expected rates of return across economies and across sectors. Within each economy, the expected returns to each type of asset are equated by arbitrage, taking into account the costs of adjusting physical capital stock and allowing for exogenous risk premiums. However, because physical capital is costly to adjust, any inflow of financial capital that is invested in physical capital will also be costly to shift once it is in place. This means that unexpected events can cause windfall gains and losses to owners of physical capital and ex post returns can vary substantially across countries and sectors. For example, if a shock lowers profits in a particular industry, the physical capital stock in the sector will initially be unchanged but its financial value will drop immediately.

Money demand

Finally, we assume that money enters the model via a constraint on transactions.[24] We use a money demand function in which the demand for real money balances is a function of the value of aggregate output and short-term nominal interest rates:

$$MON = PYi^\varepsilon \tag{8.38}$$

where Y is aggregate output; P is a price index for Y; i is the interest rate, and ε is the interest elasticity of money demand. The supply of money is determined by the balance sheet of the central bank and is exogenous.

Assessing the model

All models have strengths and weaknesses and G-Cubed is no exception. Its most important strength is that it distinguishes between financial and physical capital and includes a fully integrated treatment of intertemporal optimization by households, firms and international portfolio holders. This allows the model to do a rigorous job of determining where physical capital ends up, both across industries and across countries, and of determining who owns the physical capital and in what currency it is valued. Overall, the key feature of G-Cubed is its treatment of capital, and that is also what most distinguishes it from other models in either the macro, trade or CGE literatures.

G-Cubed also has other strengths. All budget constraints are satisfied at all times, including both static and intertemporal budget constraints on households, governments and countries. Short-run behaviour captures the effects of slow wage adjustment and liquidity constraints, while long-run behaviour is consistent with full optimization and rational expectations. In addition, wherever possible the model's behavioural parameters are determined by estimation, which is discussed further in Chapter 4 of McKibbin and Wilcoxen (2003).

Notes

1 For a summary of the debate in terms of economics, see Cline (1992); Nordhaus (1991, 1993) and McKibbin and Wilcoxen (2002b).
2 See for example Barnes *et al.* (1992); Bollen *et al.* (1999); Burniaux *et al.* (1991); CPB (1999); Jorgenson and Wilcoxen (1991); Manne and Richels (1992); Nordhaus (1992); Tol (1999) and Tulpule *et al.* (1999) for studies using the major global and country models.
3 Baseline emissions are the greenhouse gas emissions that would occur in the absence of a climate change policy (see Chapter 11 for a detailed definition).
4 This has been referred to as the 'autonomous rate of energy efficiency improvement', or AEEI, in the literature on the cost of reducing climate change. There is very wide disagreement about its magnitude.
5 A notorious example was *Limits to Growth* (Meadows *et al.* 1972), the predictions of which verged on apocalyptic.
6 That is, the degree of non-homotheticity in consumption.
7 See IPCC (2001), Chapter 5: 'Barriers, Opportunities, and Market Potential of Technologies and Practices'.
8 The Kyoto Protocol is discussed in greater depth in Chapter 5.
9 See the model references in footnote 2.
10 McKibbin, Pearce and Stoeckel (1994).
11 For a full exposition see McKibbin and Wilcoxen (2002a).
12 The reader is referred to Chapters 2 and 5 of McKibbin and Wilcoxen (2005) for greater detail.
13 This approach follows Armington (1969).
14 This does not require that both sectors purchase the same amount of oil, or even that they purchase oil at all; only that they both feel the same way about the origins of oil they buy.
15 The rate of growth of the economy's endowment of effective labour units, n, appears in the discount factor because the quantity and value variables in the model have been scaled by the number of effective labour units. These variables must be multiplied by $\exp(nt)$ to convert them back to their original form.
16 This specification imposes the restriction that household decisions on the allocations of expenditure among different goods at different points in time be separable.
17 As before, n appears in 0 because the model's scaled variables must be converted back to their original basis.
18 There has been considerable debate about the empirical validity of the permanent income hypothesis. In addition to the work of Campbell, Mankiw and Hayashi, other key papers include Hall (1978) and Flavin (1981). One side effect of this specification is that it prevents us from computing equivalent variation. Since the behaviour of some of the households is inconsistent with 0, either because the households are at

corner solutions or for some other reason, aggregate behaviour is inconsistent with the expenditure function derived from our utility function.

19 The use of the CES function has the undesirable effect of imposing unitary income elasticities, a restriction usually rejected by data. An alternative would be to replace this specification with one derived from the linear expenditure system.

20 Strictly speaking, public debt must be less than or equal to the present value of future budget surpluses. For tractability we assume that the government is initially fully leveraged so that this constraint holds with equality.

21 In the model the tax is actually levied on the difference between interest payments on the debt and what interest payments would have been if the debt had remained at its base case level. The remainder, interest payments on the base case debt, is financed by ordinary taxes.

22 Global net flows of private capital are constrained to be zero at all times – the total of all funds borrowed exactly equals the total funds lent. As a theoretical matter this may seem obvious, but it is often violated in international financial data.

23 The mobility of international capital is a subject of considerable debate; see Gordon and Bovenberg (1994) or Feldstein and Horioka (1980).

24 Unlike other components of the model we simply assume this rather than deriving it from optimizing behaviour. Money demand can be derived from optimization under various assumptions: money gives direct utility; it is a factor of production; or it must be used to conduct transactions. The distinctions are unimportant for our purposes.

Bibliography

Anderson, K. and McKibbin, W.J. (2000) 'Reducing coal subsidies and trade barriers: Their contribution to greenhouse gas abatement', *Environment and Development Economics* 5:457–481.

Armington, P. (1969) 'A theory of demand for products distinguished by place of production', *IMF Staff Papers* 16:159–176.

Bagnoli, P., McKibbin, W.J. and Wilcoxen P.J. (1996) 'Future projections and structural change', in N. Nakicenovic, W. Nordhaus, R. Richels and F. Toth (eds) *Climate Change: Integrating Economics and Policy*, CP 96-1, Vienna: International Institute for Applied Systems Analysis.

Barnes, D.W., Edmonds, J.A. and Reilly, J.M. (1992) 'Use of the Edmonds–Reilly model to model energy-sector impacts of greenhouse gas emissions control strategies', Washington, D.C.: Pacific Northwest Laboratory, mimeo.

Bollen, J., Gielen, A. and Timmer, H. (1999) 'Clubs, ceilings and CDM: macroeconomics of compliance with the Kyoto Protocol', *Energy Journal*, Special Issue: 177–206.

Burniaux, J.M., Martin, J.P., Nicoletti, G. and Martins, J.O. (1991) *GREEN – A Multi-Region Dynamic General Equilibrium Model for Quantifying the Costs of Curbing CO_2 Emissions: A Technical Manual*, Paris: Department of Economics and Statistics Working Paper 104, OECD.

Campbell, J. and Mankiw, N.G. (1990) 'Permanent income, current income and consumption', *Journal of Business and Economic Statistics* 8:265–279.

Cline, W.R. (1992) *The Economics of Global Warming*, Washington, D.C.: Institute for International Economics.

CPB Netherlands Bureau for Economic Analysis (1999) *Worldscan: The Core Version*, The Hague.

Dornbusch, R. (1976) 'Expectations and exchange rate dynamics', *Journal of Political Economy* 84:1161–1176.

Feldstein, M. and Horioka, C. (1980) 'Domestic savings and international capital flows', *The Economic Journal* 90:314–329.

Gordon, R.H. and Bovenberg, A.L. (1994) 'Why is capital so immobile internationally? Possible explanations and implications for capital taxation', mimeo, July.

Hayashi, F. (1979) 'Tobins marginal q and average q: a Neoclassical interpretation', *Econometrica* 50:213–224.

Hayashi, F. (1982) 'The permanent income hypothesis: estimation and testing by instrumental variables', *Journal of Political Economy* 90(4):895–916.

Intergovernmental Panel on Climate Change (2001) *Climate Change 2001: Mitigation*, Cambridge: Cambridge University Press.

Jorgenson, D.W. and Wilcoxen, P.J. (1990) 'Environmental regulation and US economic growth', *The Rand Journal* 21:314–340.

Jorgenson, D.W. and Wilcoxen, P.J. (1991) 'Reducing US carbon dioxide emissions: the cost of different goals', in J.A. Moroney (ed.) *Energy, Growth and the Environment*, Greenwich, CT: JAI Press.

Lucas, R.E. (1967) 'Adjustment costs and the theory of supply', *Journal of Political Economy* 75:321–334.

Lucas, R.E. (1973) 'Econometric policy evaluation: a critique', *Carnegie Rochester Series on Public Policy* 1:19–46.

McKibbin, W.J., Pearce, D. and Stoeckel, A. (1994) *Economic Effects of Reducing Carbon Dioxide Emissions*, Canberra: Centre for International Economics.

McKibbin, W.J., Ross, M., Shackleton, R. and Wilcoxen, P.J. (1999) 'Emissions trading, capital flows and the Kyoto Protocol', *The Energy Journal*, Special Issue: 287–334. Reprinted in *Economic Impact of Mitigation Measures*, The Hague: Intergovernmental Panel on Climate Change.

McKibbin, W.J. and Sachs, J. (1991) *Global Linkages: Macroeconomic Interdependence and Cooperation in the World Economy*, Washington, D.C.: The Brookings Institution.

McKibbin, W.J., Shackleton, R. and Wilcoxen, P.J. (1999) 'What to expect from an international system of tradeable permits for carbon emissions', *Resource and Energy Economics* 21:319–346.

McKibbin, W.J., and Wilcoxen, P.J. (1993a) 'The global consequences of regional environmental policies: an integrated macroeconomic, multi-sectoral approach', in Y. Kaya, N. Nakicenovic, W. Nordhaus and F. Toth (eds) *Costs, Impacts and Benefits of CO_2 Mitigation*, CP-93-2, International Institute for Applied Systems Analysis, Austria.

McKibbin, W.J. and Wilcoxen, P.J. (1993b) 'The global costs of policies to reduce greenhouse gas emissions', *Tokyo Club Papers* 6:7–40, Tokyo Club Foundation for Global Studies. Also Brookings Discussion Paper in International Economics #97, Washington D.C.: The Brookings Institution.

McKibbin, W.J. and Wilcoxen, P.J. (1996a) 'Environmental policy and international trade', in M. McAleer, S. Mahendrarajah and A. Jakeman (eds) *Modelling Change in*

Environmental Systems (forthcoming). Also Brookings Discussion Paper in International Economics #117, Washington, D.C.: The Brookings Institution.

McKibbin, W.J. and Wilcoxen, P.J. (1996b) 'The economic implications of greenhouse gas policy', in H. English and D. Runnals (eds) *Environment and Development in the Pacific: Problems and Policy Options*, Addison Wesley. Also Brookings Discussion Paper in International Economics #116, Washington, D.C.: The Brookings Institution.

McKibbin, W.J. and Wilcoxen, P.J. (1997) 'A better way to slow global climate change', *Brookings Policy Brief*, No. 17, June, Washington, D.C.: The Brookings Institution.

McKibbin, W.J. and Wilcoxen, P.J. (1998) 'The theoretical and empirical structure of the G-Cubed model', *Economic Modelling* 16:123–148.

McKibbin, W.J. and Wilcoxen, P.J. (2002a) *Climate Change Policy after Kyoto: A Blueprint for a Realistic Approach*, Washington, D.C.: The Brookings Institution.

McKibbin, W.J., and Wilcoxen, P.J. (2002b) 'The role of economics in climate change policy', *Journal of Economic Perspectives* 16:107–130.

McKibbin, W.J. and Wilcoxen, P.J. (2005) *Economics for an Interdependent World*, Washington, D.C.: The Brookings Institution, forthcoming.

Manne, A.S. and Richels, R.G. (1992) *Buying Greenhouse Insurance – The Economic Costs of CO_2 Emission Limits*, Cambridge: MIT Press.

Meadows, D.H., Meadows, D.L., Randers, J. and Behrens, W.W. (1972) *The Limits to Growth*, New York: Universe Books.

Nordhaus, W.D. (1991) 'The cost of slowing climate change: a survey', *The Energy Journal* 12:37–65.

Nordhaus, W.D. (1992) 'The DICE model: background and structure of a dynamic integrated climate-economy model of the economics of global warming', Cowles Foundation Discussion Paper No. 1009, New Haven, Cowles Foundation for Research in Economics, Yale University.

Nordhaus, W.D. (1993) 'Reflections on the economics of climate change', *Journal of Economic Perspectives* 7:11–25.

Tol, R.S.J. (1999) 'Kyoto, efficiency, and cost-effectiveness: applications of FUND', *Energy Journal*, Special Issue: 131–156.

Treadway, A. (1969) 'On rational entrepreneurial behavior and the demand for investment', *Review of Economic Studies* 36:227–239.

Tulpule, V., Brown, S., Lim, S., Polidano, C., Pant, H. and Fisher, B. (1999) 'The Kyoto Protocol: an economic analysis using GTEM', *Energy Journal*, Special Issue: 257–286.

Uzawa, H. (1969) 'Time preference and the Penrose effect in a two class model of economic growth', *Journal of Political Economy* 77:628–652.

9 The role of energy prices in global climate change

Brian S. Fisher and Mike D. Hinchy

Introduction

According to the Intergovernmental Panel on Climate Change, anthropogenic emissions of carbon dioxide are the most important single contributor to the risk of global warming. The bulk of anthropogenic emissions of carbon dioxide arise from energy consumption especially in the transport sector (motor vehicles) and electricity generation (coal fired power stations). Any economic policies such as taxes or subsidies that affect energy prices in market economies also affect energy consumption and, hence, carbon dioxide emissions and the risk of global warming.

Increasing concern about the risk of global warming has stimulated a great deal of research into policies that affect energy prices. There has been much research into the use of carbon taxes and related policy instruments that raise the price of energy sources based on carbon content to achieve national and global carbon dioxide emission targets. The use of energy is heavily subsidized in a number of developing countries while the domestic coal industry is subsidized in several countries in the European Union and Japan. Research has also been undertaken into the effect of the removal of these subsidies on global carbon dioxide emissions.

In this chapter research on the use of carbon taxes to achieve carbon dioxide emission targets is first reviewed. Research on the effect of the removal of energy subsidies is then discussed.

Carbon taxes

Partial equilibrium theory

Consider a profit maximizing price taking firm. The transformation function:

$$f(x_1, x_2, \ldots, x_1, e) = 0 \tag{9.1}$$

describes the technologically efficient input output options available to the firm (where a positive value for x_1 indicates an output and a negative value indicates an input) and e is the associated level of emissions.

It is assumed that a firm may adjust outputs and inputs to reduce emissions in one of three ways. First, 'tail end' cleaning technologies may be available (scrubber technologies) that will allow the firm to reduce the emissions associated with a given vector of outputs. Typically, such technologies will require the use of more of some inputs (and not less of other inputs) so that the total cost of producing the given output vector will be higher. Second, it may be possible to substitute lower emission for higher emission inputs (for example, natural gas for coal as an energy source) to produce the given outputs. If the initial vector of inputs were chosen optimally to produce a given vector of outputs such substitution will increase total production costs. Third, the use of some inputs resulting in emissions (and presumably some other inputs if they are not to be redundant) may be reduced resulting in a reduction in some outputs and net revenue (if the initial output input combination was optimal).

Suppose that a tax of t per unit of emissions is introduced. The problem of the firm is to maximize net revenue subject to equation 9.1. Forming the Lagrangean:

$$L = \sum_{i=1}^{n} p_i x_i - t.e - \lambda.f(x_1, x_2, \ldots, x_n, e) \tag{9.2}$$

where p_i represents the price of output/input i, the following first order conditions of interest are obtained:

$$\lambda.\frac{\partial f}{\partial e} = -t \tag{9.3}$$

$$\lambda.\frac{\partial f}{\partial x_i} = -p_i \qquad (i = 1, \ldots, n) \tag{9.4}$$

The shadow price, λ, may be interpreted as the price of an additional unit of emissions. The term, $\partial f/\partial e$, represents the marginal physical product of emissions. Thus, the term, $\lambda.\partial f/\partial e$, can be interpreted as the marginal cost of reducing emissions and is more commonly called the marginal cost of abatement. Equation 9.3 shows that the optimal level of emissions is determined by the condition that the marginal cost of abatement equals the tax rate.

The total cost of abatement is the difference between the net revenue of the firm when emissions are unconstrained and net revenue when emissions are constrained given that outputs and inputs are adjusted optimally in both situations. It would be expected that total costs of abatement would increase with the level of abatement (the smaller the value of *e*). Indeed, it would be expected that total costs would increase more than proportionately with the level of abatement. There are likely to be limits on emission reductions possible through scrubber technologies and substitution options. Once these limits are exhausted the firm has no option other than to reduce output. Thus, the marginal cost of abatement would be expected to increase with the level of abatement.

If all emission sources face a uniform tax on emissions and equate their marginal costs of abatement to the tax rate, marginal costs of abatement will be equalized across emission sources. This is, of course, the condition for the total costs of abatement to be minimized. Thus, as discussed in Chapter 8, a uniform tax on emissions is one of the policy instruments that uses market forces to achieve a least cost solution to the problem of achieving a given level of abatement. Since it is unlikely that the level of abatement resulting from a given tax rate will be known with certainty, some experimentation with the tax rate may be required to achieve the desired level of abatement.

Economy-wide studies

Two basic types of models known as 'bottom up' and 'top down' models have been used to study the impact of carbon taxes at the economy level. 'Bottom up' models contain detailed information about technological options in the energy sector but there is limited interaction with the rest of the economy. For example, in the simplest models, demand is totally unresponsive to changes in price. The model is solved simply for the least cost method of supplying a given quantity of energy. Imposing carbon taxes alters the contribution of different types of energy to the least cost supply. However, the total quantity of energy demanded remains fixed even though carbon taxes have altered the total cost of supply (and the supply price).

The assumption that demand is not responsive to price has been relaxed in more recent model developments. However, there is still much less interaction with other sectors of the economy than in 'top down' models. 'Bottom up' models are often solved using linear programming or non-linear programming techniques to minimize (discounted) energy system costs.

'Top down' models are usually computable general equilibrium (CGE) models and allow for more extensive interaction between different sectors of the economy. It is assumed that consumers make purchase decisions to maximize their welfare while firms make production decisions to maximize profits. All prices are variable and an equilibrium consists of a set of prices that ensures that demand for all goods is equal to their supply. Such models are usually solved using one of a number of methods for the numerical solution of a set of simultaneous equations. Modelling of technological options in the energy sector is much less detailed than in 'bottom up' models. Technological options are usually modelled based on a production function estimated from historical data where it is assumed that different inputs can be smoothly substituted for one another.

In a partial equilibrium framework, the costs of abatement are measured by the loss in net revenue for a firm. In general equilibrium models it is common to use a broader measure of the change in economic welfare. Abatement may alter the income of a representative consumer and change relative prices resulting in a change in the optimal consumption bundle. In some cases Hicksian equivalent variation has been used as a welfare measure but it has been more common to use the change in Gross Domestic Product (GDP) as a general purpose measure. Results from 'bottom up' models are often converted into a GDP equivalent form to allow comparison with the results from 'top down' models.

A general finding of both types of models is that the total cost of abatement, no matter how measured, tends to increase more than proportionately with the level of abatement. Such a finding is in line with theoretical expectations as discussed above.

It is also often found that 'bottom up' models yield lower welfare losses in attaining given abatement targets than 'top down' models. For example, to stabilize carbon dioxide emissions at 1990 levels, estimates from 'bottom up' models for a number of economies suggest a loss of GDP in the range of 0.5 per cent to 1 per cent. Estimates from 'top down' models for a given economy are usually somewhat larger although most estimates seldom involve more than a 2 per cent loss in GDP.

To understand the reasons for these difference in results, it is important to note that it is widely conceded that 'bottom up' models tend to be over-optimistic compared with observed performance about the speed of adoption of newer technologies in response to changes in relative costs. Such models do not appear to capture adequately the various sources of inertia that may slow shifts towards less costly technologies. These sources of inertia are probably better captured in 'top down' models since the speed of adjustment is based on historical estimates. On the other hand, the assumption in many 'top down' models that inputs can be smoothly substituted for one another can imply the use of unobserved technologies.

It also seems probable that some of the flow through effects of higher energy prices captured by 'top down' models but not by 'bottom up' models add to welfare losses. For example, higher energy prices will affect the relative prices of goods and services according to energy intensity resulting in changes in production patterns that may be a further source of welfare loss.

The strength of 'bottom up' models is in their technological detail and illustration of technological possibilities. 'Top down' models are probably better at capturing the relationship between economic aggregates, which would include economic welfare losses in response to imposing a carbon tax.

International repercussions

Theory

The economy level models considered in the previous section were closed models in the sense that any international repercussions of imposing carbon taxes were ignored. However, taking account of international repercussions may modify estimates of the size of the carbon tax and welfare losses incurred in achieving a given level of abatement. Policy proposals to reduce the risk of global warming involve simultaneous abatement by a large number of economies. In particular, the Kyoto Protocol proposes simultaneous abatement by the group of so-called Annex I countries that essentially consists of all developed countries (see Chapter 5). International repercussions of such simultaneous abatement could be of a considerable order of magnitude.

A basic theoretical point to make in considering international repercussions is that imposing a carbon tax to achieve an emission target alters the production possibility set for an economy. Some input output combinations that are techno-logically feasible may no longer be economically feasible since they violate the overall emission constraint implied by the carbon tax. The impact of a carbon tax on the production possibility set is analogous to that of negative technological progress.

A standard graphical device used to illustrate determining international equi-librium in a two good, two input, two country world involves the use of the pro-duction possibility sets for the two economies. If the production possibility set of either economy changes, the terms of trade change resulting in welfare changes in both economies. Since a carbon tax alters production possibility sets, changes in the terms of trade is an avenue for the international transmission of the effects of abatement.

If the overall international repercussions of abatement are to improve the terms of trade for an abating economy, welfare losses will be smaller than if the terms of trade were unchanged while the converse also applies. The terms of trade of non-abating economies may also be affected by abatement in Annex I countries. Impacts of Annex I abatement on the group of the Organization of Petroleum Exporting Countries (OPEC) and the possible response by OPEC has been a topic of special interest as discussed below.

Annex I abatement may also alter relative rates of return on capital in different economies resulting in changes in the pattern of international capital flows. Such changes in international capital flows may also result in welfare changes. In many studies it has been assumed that capital is not mobile internationally. It has been suggested that changes in international capital flows are likely to be related to changes in the terms of trade. Thus, results obtained under the assumption of no international capital mobility may serve as a reasonable first approximation to the more realistic case where capital is internationally mobile. Some support for this assumption is given by results from most of the few studies that have considered international capital mobility.

Empirical results

The international repercussions of abatement have been assessed with a number of models of the global economy using various regional aggregations. These models are exclusively 'top down' CGE models.

It is useful to consider simulation results for the international repercussions of single economies abating before turning to results for the more complex interactions that occur when a number of economies abate simultaneously. These results show that the large industrial economies of the United States, the European Union and Japan all experience an improvement in their terms of trade when they impose carbon taxes to achieve an abatement target. Such an improvement in the terms of trade reduces the welfare losses from abatement. These economies are net exporters of manufactures and net importers of fossil fuels. Carbon taxes result in higher energy prices that push up the prices of exported manufactures while reduced demand for fossil fuels results in lower import prices.

The Annex I economies that are net exporters of fossil fuels and net importers of manufactures, such as Australia and the former Soviet Union, suffer a deterioration in their terms of trade when they abate, which increases welfare losses. Domestic abatement reduces domestic demand for fossil fuels, which increases supplies to the export market, resulting in lower export prices and a deterioration in the terms of trade.

When all Annex I economies simultaneously abate (at the same individual levels as in the case just considered) it would be expected that combined welfare losses would be increased. Imposing carbon taxes would simultaneously reduce production possibilities in a number of economies, narrowing the scope to exploit gains from specialization through trade. Simulation results do confirm that the sum of losses in real GDP for all Annex I countries is larger under simultaneous abatement than under unilateral abatement.

There are two immediate factors that are apparent in explaining these increased welfare losses under simultaneous abatement. First, Annex I countries are significant importers of manufactures from other Annex I countries. Thus, simultaneous abatement by all Annex I countries raises the price paid for imported manufactures. Second, the fossil fuel exporting Annex I countries now face reduced demand in export markets as well as at home, resulting in lower fossil fuel prices. Of course, such lower prices are beneficial to importing countries and not all Annex I countries are worse off under simultaneous compared with unilateral abatement. However, collective welfare losses for the Annex I region are higher under simultaneous abatement than under unilateral abatement.

Non-Annex I impacts

The impact of Annex I abatement on non-Annex I economies is important for the economic welfare of non-Annex I economies. It is also important for the environmental effectiveness of Annex I abatement policies due to the problem of emission leakage. Emission leakage is said to occur when reduced emissions from Annex I countries are partly offset by increased emissions from non-Annex I countries. Results on these impacts are available from simulations with a number of models under various abatement strategies.

The main conclusion from these studies is that the impact of Annex I abatement on non-Annex I welfare is predominantly adverse. Combined non-Annex I welfare losses increase the more severe the level of Annex I abatement.

As discussed above, Annex I abatement results in a decline in the price of imported fossil fuels and a rise in the price of exported manufactures. The non-Annex I countries with the heaviest dependence on exported fossil fuels such as the Middle East and Indonesia suffer the greatest deterioration in their terms of trade and welfare losses under Annex I abatement. South Korea and Brazil are among the most favourably placed non-Annex I economies, being net importers of fossil fuels and net exporters of non-ferrous metal and iron and steel products. The latter products are highly emission intensive in production in Annex I economies and their price throughout the world rises markedly under Annex I carbon taxes. Under milder levels of Annex I abatement, such as that involved under the Kyoto targets, South Korea and Brazil and a few other non-Annex I countries have been found to experience mild welfare gains in various model simulations.

Emission leakage

Emission leakage is usually measured as 100 times the increase in non-Annex I emissions divided by the reduction in Annex I emissions. It may result from both the production of more emission intensive goods and the use of more emission intensive production techniques in non-Annex I countries. Production of more emission intensive goods may be for both own consumption and export to Annex I countries. More emission intensive production techniques may be adopted in response to lower prices for fossil fuels resulting from Annex I abatement.

Estimates of the degree of emission leakage vary widely among models. Estimates tend to be higher, the higher the elasticity of substitution assumed between imports and domestic production. The higher the elasticity of substitution the smaller the reduction in Annex I final consumption of emission intensive goods as greater substitution of non-Annex I for domestic production occurs. High elasticities of substitution also tend to result in larger declines in fossil fuel prices and greater use of emission intensive production techniques in non-Annex I countries. Nevertheless, there are some significant differences between estimates of emission leakage even among models with similar assumptions about the elasticity of substitution for reasons yet to be fully explored.

Resolving the issue of the most appropriate assumptions about elasticities of substitution between domestic production and imports involves some difficult problems. Commodities identified in CGE models are usually aggregates of many sub-commodities. Since the sub-commodity composition of a given commodity may differ significantly between countries the assumption of imperfect substitution between domestic production and imports for the aggregated commodity may often be reasonable. However, even if the initial estimate of the elasticity were appropriate it may not be appropriate for all of the simulation if in reality the sub-commodity composition of the aggregate would change markedly under the conditions assumed in the simulation.

It would be possible to reduce the extent of the above problem by working with more finely disaggregated commodities. However, the computational burden of solving CGE models tends to increase exponentially with the number of commodities. Furthermore, the need to ensure that the model is consistent with its database may constrain feasible values for elasticities of substitution. There is also the problem that under high elasticities of substitution it is possible in a simulation that a model may shift all of world production to one country.

A general finding of the various studies is that the degree of emission leakage tends to increase with the level of Annex I abatement. Such a result would be expected from the economy level non-linear relationship between total costs of abatement and the level of abatement. As the level of abatement increases and there is increasing reliance on output reduction relative to input substitution to reduce Annex I emissions, there would be stronger incentives for emission intensive production in non-Annex I countries. There would be increased incentives to displace Annex I production and to use emission intensive techniques due to lower fossil fuel prices.

The results discussed above are derived from models where it is assumed that an exogenously given rate of technological change is unbiased (that is, affects all inputs equally). In particular, it is usually assumed that there is an exogenously given rate of so-called autonomous energy efficiency improvement. It is also assumed that all world markets are perfectly competitive. These assumptions have been modified in a number of studies and the impact on model results is now considered.

The induced innovations hypothesis

The induced innovations hypothesis maintains that technological change is biased and that bias is related to movements in relative input prices. It is argued that the greatest profit opportunities exist for economizing on the use of inputs where relative prices have risen the most. Thus, technological change should be biased towards those inputs where relative prices have increased and biased away from inputs where relative prices have fallen.

Since a carbon tax would increase the relative price of energy, the induced innovations hypothesis implies that technological change would be biased towards economizing on the use of energy inputs. Although only the bias and not the overall rate of technological change is affected, simulation results show that the improvement in energy efficiency can significantly reduce welfare losses in meeting abatement targets. In fact, in some simulations of CGE models under the induced innovations hypothesis, welfare losses have been of a similar order to those obtained with bottom up models.

The difficulty with the induced innovations hypothesis is that attempts to test it using historical data have produced mixed results. Alternatives to the induced innovations hypothesis are that technical progress follows a path determined entirely by scientific and technological imperatives or that technical progress is a purely random process as evidenced by the number of 'accidental' discoveries. It may be objected that the extent to which scientific and technological imperatives are followed and the extent to which accidental discoveries are converted into working technologies will be influenced by profit opportunities. Nevertheless, it may be that there is sufficient randomness in the process of technical progress that it often makes it difficult to detect the patterns implied by the induced innovation hypothesis.

A related problem is that it is not simple to devise a conclusive test for the hypothesis given available data. Some of the most recent studies using more sophisticated methodologies have been relatively favourable to the hypothesis. However, it cannot be said that the hypothesis either receives overwhelming support or is decisively rejected by the weight of empirical studies.

OPEC response

Oil is probably the market where assumptions about the nature of world competition are most important in the context of climate change policies. The standard assumption in many CGE models of price taking behaviour by producers in the world oil market may appear questionable. In the past OPEC appears to have had some success in controlling production to influence the world price of oil. Nevertheless, in recent years a number of 'fringe' producers have emerged that have reduced OPEC's share of world oil production.

In various CGE model simulations of the impacts of Annex I abatement policies under the price taking assumption, the OPEC group of nations are usually found to suffer the largest welfare losses among non-Annex I countries. Such a result stems from the heavy dependence of OPEC nations on oil for export revenue. There clearly would be an incentive for OPEC to attempt to restrict production to force up prices to curb the loss in export revenue. However, the ability of OPEC to control prices may be limited by competition from fringe producers. To the extent that OPEC was successful in stemming the loss in oil revenue, it would reduce its own welfare losses and increase those of Annex I countries. Such a result follows since a favourable movement in the terms of trade for one group of countries represents a deterioration in the terms of trade for its trading partners.

The possible nature of an OPEC response to Annex I abatement has been studied mainly using models specifically constructed to examine this problem. It is usually assumed that OPEC seeks to maximize discounted net revenue from oil over some time horizon. The main finding is that while competition from the fringe reduces OPEC's market power, OPEC does have some power to stem the loss in oil revenue provided cartel discipline can be maintained. There would be incentives to break cartel discipline in a falling market. However, on the level of political economy, it has been suggested that Annex I abatement would be seen as a hostile act by OPEC and this could strengthen the resolve to maintain cartel discipline. Some have attributed the apparent greater cartel discipline shown by OPEC during 2000 and 2001 partly to the threat of abatement action by Annex I economies.

The most successful strategy for OPEC would be to expand the cartel to include the non-OECD fringe producers (some of the countries of the former Soviet Union and a number of developing countries). These countries would also suffer significant oil revenue losses under Annex I abatement and so have an incentive to join the cartel. It does not seem plausible to assume that OECD fringe producers could be induced to join the cartel given that most of these producers have received a high level of government assistance to increase production with the aim of weakening OPEC's market power.

While any successful OPEC cartel strategy would tend to increase welfare losses for Annex I countries, there would also be other side effects. One of these would be that the higher world price for oil would reduce the growth of consumption in non-Annex I countries and so reduce the amount of emission leakage.

The impact of possible OPEC strategies has not been studied using global CGE models mainly because many of the solution techniques used are not consistent with modelling the exercise of market power. Thus, all of the quantitative global ramifications of possible OPEC strategies have not been fully explored. This remains a challenge for future research.

Fossil fuel subsidies

Production and consumption of fossil fuels is heavily subsidized in many developing economies and a few developed economies. Subsidies are mainly directed at consumption in developing economies and production in developed economies. The major aims of subsidizing consumption of fossil fuels in developing economies appears to be to make energy cheaper for poorer households and to encourage economic growth with low cost energy. The major aim of subsidizing production in OECD countries appears to be (especially in the case of coal) to maintain local production and employment in the face of import competition.

The concept of subsidies used in the literature is broader than direct government payments to producers or consumers. Economic and environmental implications will follow from any government policies that lower the cost of energy production, raise the price received by energy producers or lower the price paid by energy consumers. All policies with such an effect can be regarded as forms of subsidies and so include restriction on exports, protecting markets for domestic production (through tariffs, quantitative restrictions on imports or requiring that some domestic buyers purchase from domestic producers at above import prices), interest subsidies, preferential tax treatment and so on.

There are some subsidies that may reduce the demand for fossil fuels and these have not been included in the studies of subsidies. In some countries household insulation is subsidized to reduce the demand for energy and, ultimately, fossil fuels. Furthermore, in some countries production of some types of non-fossil fuel forms of electricity generation is also subsidized.

To the extent that subsidies increase consumption of fossil fuels, removal of these subsidies would reduce carbon dioxide emissions. These subsidies may also have adverse effects on the efficiency of global resource allocation and their removal could also yield economic benefits.

Most research has been directed at attempting to quantify the size of existing subsidies. Efforts to analyse the impact of their removal has mainly involved partial equilibrium models. There is a clear need for a much more general analysis of the removal of subsidies where all the global ramifications are examined. Such an analysis may show that the reduction in carbon dioxide emissions may be less dramatic than it would appear from a partial analysis. For example, removal of consumption subsidies in developing economies may increase supplies of fossil fuels to export market resulting in increased emissions in other countries. It is also necessary in such an analysis to consider the types of alternative policies that might be introduced to replace subsidies. Subsidies have various policy aims and when the impact of replacement policies with similar aims is considered, the reduction in adverse environmental impacts may be less pronounced than would appear from a simple analysis of the direct removal of subsidies.

Methodology

The methodology used in nearly all studies of fossil fuel subsidies is known as the 'price gap' approach. Such a methodology is designed to create a basis for a first-order approximation to the impact of removal of subsidies on consumption of fossil fuels and associated environmental impacts. However, it will not capture all of the economic and environmental impacts associated with the removal of subsidies for reasons discussed below.

The basic idea underlying the price gap approach is that subsidies to producers and consumers lower end use prices, resulting in higher consumption levels. End use prices are compared with a reference price to measure the price gap. The reference price is intended to reflect the price that would prevail in a market undistorted by subsidies. In the case of traded goods, the reference price is taken to be the price prevailing in competitive world markets. In the case of non-traded goods, the reference price is taken to be equal to long run marginal costs. Estimates of average costs of production obtained from official sources are frequently used as a proxy for long run marginal costs. Once the price gap is estimated a first-order approximation to the change in domestic consumption from removal of subsidies can be calculated using estimates of the elasticity of demand.

As mentioned above, the price gap approach does not capture all of the economic and environmental impacts associated with assistance to domestic producers or consumers. For example, if domestic production were protected by a tariff, domestic prices may exceed the reference price and this would not be regarded as a subsidy under the price gap approach. It estimates a subsidy only if the domestic end use price lies below the reference price. Similarly, if domestic production were subsidized but domestic consumption were taxed there may be little difference between the domestic end use prices and the reference price. Nevertheless, removal of assistance to the domestic industry could have important effects on the location of production and the efficiency of global resource allocation. There also may be environmental impacts if, for example, production from deep coal mines in Europe with high methane emissions were replaced by production from open cut mines elsewhere with lower methane emissions.

The price gap approach was described as providing a basis for a first approximation to the consumption impacts of the removal of subsidies for two reasons. First, it fails to capture assistance that results in prices exceeding the reference price as discussed above. Second, the standard method of applying elasticities of demand to the estimated price gap is a partial equilibrium approach rather than a general equilibrium approach. For example, removal of subsidies will change real consumer income, resulting in changes in the demand for fossil fuels but these effects will not be captured. The price gap approach will also not capture economic and environmental impacts stemming from changes in the level or location of production.

General equilibrium modelling would provide the ideal approach to studying the removal of subsidies. To derive the maximum benefits from this approach it would be necessary to quantify all forms of assistance rather than infer assistance levels from estimated price gaps. The few general equilibrium studies that have been undertaken are discussed below.

In implementing the price gap approach, many additional assumptions have to be made where decisions by individual researchers may differ. One of the assumptions always reported is the exchange rate used to compare domestic and world prices. Some studies have used official exchange rates while others have used purchasing power parity rates. Purchasing power parity attempts to measure the relative cost of purchasing a given bundle of goods in different countries. Purchasing power parity rates may differ from official exchange rates mainly because the relative cost of purchasing non-traded goods may differ significantly among countries.

Estimates of the size of fossil fuel subsidies

In this section the results of the three major studies of the size of fossil fuel subsidies that have been undertaken will be reviewed. The first study, although somewhat dated, is valuable since the identical methodology was applied to produce estimates at two points in time that enables an estimate to be made of the trend in fossil fuel subsidies. Given that many somewhat arbitrary assumptions have to be made, estimates of changes in the size of fossil fuel subsidies are likely to be more reliable than estimates of their absolute size.

The relevant estimates are set out in Table 9.1. According to these estimates, the absolute size of subsidies was largest in Russia, China and Iran. The trend in the absolute level of subsidies was downwards in all countries between 1990–1991 and 1995–1996. Part of the reduction in the total level of subsidies was due to reduced subsidy rates. There were pressures from international organizations to reduce subsidies and more general competitive pressures resulting from a movement towards freer world trade. In the case of oil producers, budget problems and high debt-service ratios also contributed to the desire to divert oil from the domestic to export markets.

Part of the reduction in the total level of subsidies in some countries was also due to reduced domestic consumption of fossil fuels. Lower subsidies probably contributed to some of this reduction. The adoption of technologies more efficient in the use of fossil fuels was also probably a contributory factor.

The first study is also the only study that provides estimates of the size of fossil fuel subsidies in OECD countries. Although subsidies in the OECD were considerably smaller in absolute size than in the sample of non-OECD countries considered, they did not decline as rapidly as in the non-OECD countries. Subsidies to domestic coal production were the major source of fossil fuel subsidies in

Table 9.1 Estimated fossil fuel subsidies 1990–1991 and 1995–1996*

Country or group	Subsidy 1990–1991	Rate 1995–1996	Total subsidies 1990–1991	(1995 US$ million) 1995–1996	% GDP 1995–1996
Russia	45	31	28,797	9,427	1.5
Eastern Europe					
Bulgaria	54	29	2,003	733	7.05
Czech Republic	24	22	1,173	978	2.96
Hungary	13	16	548	560	1.47
Poland	50	18	4,653	1,692	1.97
Romania	54	37	4,743	1,876	7.24
Total	42	23	13,120	5,838	3.19
Asia					
China	42	20	24,545	10,297	2.42
India	25	19	4,250	2,663	1.06
South Korea	0	0	42	12	0
Thailand	10	9	524	459	0.37
Total	33	16	29,362	13,430	1.19
Oil producers					
Egypt	55	40	2,299	1,336	3.39
Indonesia	29	21	2,071	1,333	0.92
Iran	86	77	13,076	9,622	8.68
Mexico	32	16	5,403	2,271	0.66
Nigeria	60	38	928	592	1.87
Saudi Arabia	66	34	3,837	1,720	1.42
Venezuela	76	66	3,455	2,397	4
Total	56	42	31,067	19,272	2.26
Others					
Argentina	12	3	659	150	0.06
Brazil	26	0	2,193	11	0
South Africa	12	4	981	367	0.31
Total	17	2	3,833	528	0.06
OECD	—	—	12,453	9,890	0.05
Total	45	28	118,632	58,385	0.27

Source: World Bank (1997).

Note
* Estimates relate to subsidies on both production and consumption.

Table 9.2 Estimated fossil fuel subsidies in 1991*

Country	Total subsidies (US$ million)	% GDP
Former USSR	145,000	10–13
China	7,900	1.8
Poland	6,730	10.0
Czechoslovakia	2,100	6.0
Brazil	950	0.2
Venezuela	5,350	10.6
Mexico	2,150	1.0
India	6,800	2.3
Indonesia	5,100	5.0
Saudia Arabia	5,000	4.8
South Korea	2,750	1.2
South Africa	1,550	—
Egypt	3,350	10.7
Iran	11,400	8.0
Romania	1,400	3.7
Bulgaria	1,200	6.0
Total	209,660	—

Source: Larsen (1994).

Note
* Estimates relate to subsidies on both production and consumption.

OECD countries, especially in Germany, Spain and Japan. A number of reforms have subsequently been introduced in these countries.

The results from the second study, shown in Table 9.2, emphasize the sensitivity of results to different judgments by researchers about somewhat arbitrary assumptions. This study, like the first, is based on the price gap approach and uses official exchange rates. Significant differences in the estimated size of subsidies in 1990–1991 are apparent for China, probably Russia (given the difference in geographical coverage with the former Soviet Union) and several other countries such as South Korea. Nevertheless, there is agreement about the top three ranking countries and there are six common countries in the top ten rankings in both studies.

The third study is the most recent and is based on the most comprehensive data set. Results cover eight major subsidizing non-OECD economies and are reported in Table 9.3. This study uses the purchasing power parity approach for exchange rate conversions. There are seven common countries in the first and third studies. In comparing the subsidy rates for these countries in the first study at 1995–1996 with those in the third study at 1997 there are only a few percentage points difference for six of the countries. The largest difference occurs for

Table 9.3 Estimated fossil fuel subsidies 1997 and effect of their removal*

Country	Subsidy rate (%)	Reduction in CO_2 emissions (%)
China	10.89	13.44
Russia	32.52	17.10
India	14.17	14.15
Indonesia	27.51	10.97
Iran	80.42	49.45
South Africa	6.41	8.11
Venezuela	57.57	26.07
Kazakhstan	18.23	22.76
Total (8)	21.12	12.80

Source: International Energy Agency (1999).

Note
* Estimates relate to subsidies on both production and consumption.

China, with the subsidy rate estimated at 20 per cent in the first study and 11 per cent in the third. From the second study although subsidy rates are not reported, the total size of the subsidy suggests a subsidy rate considerably less than 11 per cent.

China appears to be a particularly difficult case for estimating subsidy rates. Different policies apply to different types of enterprises and there have been a number of policy changes. China is by far the largest carbon dioxide emitter among non-OECD countries with emissions about twice the level of those from Russia. Thus, any estimates of the global impacts of removing subsidies will be quite sensitive to estimated subsidy rates for China.

The third study also provides estimates of the reduction of carbon dioxide emissions resulting from removal of subsidies and these are reported in the third column of Table 9.3. These estimates are derived simply by applying the estimated own price elasticity of demand to the percentage change in price from removal of the subsidy to derive the percentage change in consumption of each fossil fuel. No account is taken of any general equilibrium repercussions or even the possibility of interfuel substitution which arises since price relativities among the different fossil fuels will be altered. Furthermore, no account is taken of the impact of any replacement policies that might be used to achieve some of the aims of subsidies. Thus, for reasons that will be developed below, these estimates should probably be taken as upper bounds on the reduction in carbon dioxide emissions that would result from removal of the subsidies.

The eight countries in Table 9.3 were responsible for 64 per cent of carbon dioxide emissions from non-OECD countries and 29 per cent of world emissions in 1997. The estimated reduction in emissions for the eight countries from the removal of fossil fuel subsidies translates into a 10.2 per cent reduction in non-OECD emissions and a 4.6 per cent reduction in world emissions.

General equilibrium analysis

The key issue that needs to be addressed in a general equilibrium framework is the effect of the simultaneous removal of subsidies in all countries. The basic issues can be brought out most clearly by splitting the problem into the effects of removal of OECD subsidies holding non-OECD subsidies constant and the effects of removal of non-OECD subsidies holding OECD subsidies constant. The combined effects of removal of subsidies in all countries can then be considered.

The first case to consider is the impact of the removal of OECD subsidies (holding non-OECD subsidies constant). If subsidies resulted in domestic prices being below import prices as suggested by the empirical evidence, the initial impact would be reduced domestic production and increased imports with the domestic price rising to the world price. The higher price would result in reduced domestic consumption. However, increased demand for imports would tend to further push up the world price resulting in a further decline in consumption in the importing countries. The higher world price would have both substitution and income effects. Reduced consumption would result from the substitution effect. The income effect results from the changes in the terms of trade for the importing and exporting countries. There would be a negative income effect in the importing countries that would tend to further depress consumption of fossil fuels. In the exporting countries, if the income effect were stronger than the substitution effect there could be increased consumption of fossil fuels. Overall, the removal of subsidies in the OECD countries would be expected to result in a decline in consumption in the subsidizing countries and either a decrease or increase in consumption in the exporting countries.

The second case to consider is the effect of the removal of subsidies in the non-OECD countries holding OECD subsidies constant. Assuming that subsidies result in prices in non-OECD countries below the world price, their removal would result in prices in those countries moving up to the world price. Domestic consumption would decline. There would be a diversion of supplies from these countries onto the export market that would tend to result in a lower world price. To the extent that demand in OECD countries was responsive to the world price in spite of the domestic subsidy arrangements, there could be increased consumption in the OECD. Overall, a decrease in consumption in non-OECD countries would be expected to result in an increase in consumption in OECD countries.

Putting together the effects of the removal of subsidies in both OECD and non-OECD countries, there would be increased demand for imports from OECD countries and increased supplies of exports from non-OECD countries. The relative strength of these shifts in demand and supply would determine the direction of movement in the world price. The change in consumption in both groups of countries would depend on where the final world price settled in relation to the subsidized price together with any income effects resulting from changes in the world price.

The above comments highlight the possibility of quite complex general equilibrium or second-order effects that, if sufficiently strong, could mean that there could be a considerable error in relying on the results of partial equilibrium analysis. It is an empirical issue to determine the strength of these general equilibrium effects. The only case that has been studied with general equilibrium models is the effect of the removal of coal subsidies where there have been two studies. One study was based on a large scale general purpose model that has been applied to a wide variety of policy problems. The other study was based on a smaller model that aims to capture the special characteristics of the world coal market.

The study based on the general purpose model found that general equilibrium effects were not sufficiently strong to greatly modify the results based on a partial equilibrium analysis. It was found that a phased removal of OECD coal subsidies and import restrictions on coal would result in a decline in global carbon dioxide emissions by 5 per cent by 2005. Such a decline occurred in spite of a slight increase in emissions in exporting non-OECD countries and Australia as a result of the income effect stemming from the improvement in their terms of trade.

The long-term economic welfare effects of removal of subsidies on the subsidizing nations were beneficial. Coal production was relocated to lower cost sources and capital was released from the domestic coal industry. Additional overseas investment at higher rates of return made possible by this release of capital raised gross national product in the subsidizing nations. Coal exporting nations also experienced an improvement in welfare.

The effect of the simultaneous removal of coal subsidies and export and import restrictions in OECD and non-OECD economies was also considered using the general purpose model. It was found that such removal would result in an 8 per cent reduction in global carbon dioxide emissions by 2005. An increased supply of exports from non-OECD countries had some effect in stimulating consumption in OECD countries but this was more than offset by the effects of the removal of subsidies in those countries. Long-term effects on economic welfare were beneficial for the liberalizing nations with a lower cost pattern of coal production established.

The only case considered in the coal market specific model was the effect of the removal of OECD subsidies and the results differ markedly from those obtained with the general purpose model. It was found that subsidy removal would reduce world carbon dioxide emissions by only 0.2 per cent although this result relates just to steaming coal. The crucial difference in assumptions between the models appears to be the degree of substitutability between imports and domestic production. In the general purpose model the so-called Armington assumption was made that domestic production and imports are imperfect substitutes. A much higher degree of substitutability is assumed in the coal specific model, where an integrated world market is assumed. Removal of subsidies results in a stronger supply response in the coal specific model so that there was a smaller increase in world price and decline in consumption. No results on impacts on economic welfare were reported.

As noted above, the elasticity of substitution between domestic production and imports also appears to be a key variable in explaining differences in model estimates of the degree of emission leakage. The higher the elasticity of substitution the greater the international repercussions of policy changes by any country.

Substitution between coal and other forms of energy is not permitted in the coal specific model whereas it can occur in the general purpose model. Introducing such substitution may tend to increase the decline in consumption in the coal specific model. Nevertheless, the central conclusion from the study is that removal of OECD subsidies is unlikely to result in a significant decrease in carbon dioxide emissions.

The difference in results between models warrants further study in an attempt to arrive at the most realistic set of assumptions about the properties of the international coal market. Results from the coal specific model highlight the potential significance of general equilibrium effects. It would be desirable to extend general equilibrium analysis to subsidy removal for other fossil fuels.

Alternative policies

The aim of subsidies in OECD economies appears to be mainly to support local employment and regional economies. If subsidies were to be phased out additional government finance might be devoted to structural adjustment assistance including retraining of displaced coal miners. Such expenditure would not be expected to have a significant longer term impact on the demand for fossil fuels.

In developing countries the usually cited aim of subsidies is to improve the real income of the poor. A number of studies have raised doubts about whether some subsidies actually achieve this aim. Some subsidies have been shown to have a regressive effect with most of the benefits going to middle and higher income groups. This is especially the case in countries where the poor are heavily reliant on biomass that is not traded in commercial markets. However, in Asia, subsidization of kerosene, which, is widely consumed by the poor, is probably a better targeted policy.

One possibility would be to replace energy subsidies with direct income transfers to the poor. To the extent that some of this additional income was spent on fossil fuels, the decline in consumption of fossil fuels would be less pronounced than implied by an analysis based on the assumption that no policies were used to replace subsidies.

Conclusion

Policies that target energy prices are likely to play an important role in any effort to combat global climate change. Although there has been much research into the impacts of possible policies there remain a number of unresolved issues and need for continuing research. There is long standing disagreement between proponents of bottom up and top down models about the appropriateness of assumptions and plausibility of results from the respective types of models. Welfare losses in both Annex I and non-Annex I economies may also be strongly influenced by the extent to which the induced innovations hypothesis is valid. The nature of any OPEC response may also have an important bearing on these magnitudes. Environmental effectiveness of Annex I abatement will depend on the uncertain degree of emission leakage.

In the case of removal of fossil fuel subsidies, the main uncertainty is the size of the second-order repercussions of such a move. It is possible that the reduction in global carbon dioxide emissions could be smaller than suggested by the analysis of first-order impacts.

Bibliography

Anderson, K. and McKibbin, W.J. (2000) 'Reducing coal subsidies and trade barriers: their contribution to greenhouse gas abatement', *Environment and Development Economics* 5:457–481.

Berg, E., Kverndokk, S. and Rosendahl, K. (1997) 'Market power, international CO_2 taxation and oil wealth', *The Energy Journal* 18:33–71.

Chavas, J., Aliber, M. and Cox, T. (1997) 'An analysis of the source and nature of technical change: the case of US agriculture', *Review of Economics and Statistics* 79:482–492.

Goulder, L. and Schneider, S. (1999) 'Induced technological change, crowding out, and the attractiveness of CO_2 emissions abatement', *Resource and Environmental Economics* 21:211–253.

International Energy Agency (1999) *World Energy Outlook: Looking at Energy Subsidies: Getting the Prices Right*, Paris: IEA.

IPCC (2001), *Climate Change 2001: Mitigation*, Cambridge: Cambridge University Press.

Larsen, B. (1994), *World Fossil Fuel Subsidies and Global Carbon Emissions in a Model with Interfuel Substitution*, Policy Research Working Paper 1256, Washington, D.C.: World Bank.

Light, M. (1999) 'Coal subsidies and global carbon emissions', *The Energy Journal* 20:117–142.

World Bank (1997) *Expanding the Measure of Wealth: Indicators of Environmentally Sustainable Development*, Washington, D.C.: World Bank.

10 Project-based mechanisms

Baselines, additionality and monitoring

Jane Ellis

Introduction

The Kyoto Protocol includes two project-based mechanisms: Joint Implementation (JI) and the Clean Development Mechanism (CDM). JI and CDM projects generate emissions credits,[1] and allow countries to offset domestic emissions with increases in carbon sequestration or emission mitigation activities undertaken in another country. These mechanisms provide flexibility as to where greenhouse gas (GHG) mitigation activities can be undertaken, and which GHGs can be reduced.

JI and CDM activities are intended to help achieve lasting emission mitigation in participating countries, either by increasing carbon sequestration, or by reducing (or limiting growth in) GHG emissions. While there are some differences between JI and the CDM, both JI and CDM projects have to show that the emission reductions or sink enhancements they generate are 'additional' to any that would occur in the absence of the certified project activity. In addition, CDM projects are also expected to help achieve sustainable development in the project-site country. The opportunity to offset higher cost domestic actions against lower cost emission reduction or sink enhancement activities elsewhere should help Parties to the Kyoto Protocol meet their emission commitments in an economically-efficient manner.

A quantitative indication of what greenhouse gas emissions (or sequestration) would have been in the absence of a project is needed to determine how many 'emissions credits' an individual JI or CDM project should generate. The level of GHG emissions or sequestration in the hypothetical 'what would have happened otherwise' case is referred to as a project's baseline. Actual, monitored greenhouse gas emissions (or sequestration) levels of the JI or CDM project are compared with the agreed baseline, and the difference between the two is the mitigative effect of the project, or the total credit amount.

According to the Kyoto Protocol, CDM and JI projects could start generating emission credits in 2000 and 2008 respectively. In order to be able to generate credits, the rules governing how JI and the CDM operate have to be agreed. Some of the relevant modalities and procedures were agreed at the 7th Conference of Parties (COP) to the Framework Convention on Climate Change (FCCC) and laid out in the Marrakech Accords.[2] This agreement includes how the mechanisms are supervised, what the requirements to participate in the mechanisms are and how emission mitigation activities are verified. These modalities and procedures are different for the different mechanisms.

Some guidance on how to assess additionality, set up emission baselines and monitor projects was also agreed at COP 7. However, instructions on how to set baselines are not written in easily understandable language, and are also internally inconsistent in places. They are also not detailed enough to provide sufficient guidance to project developers when assessing how to set up or monitor a JI or CDM project.

Undertaking project-based GHG mitigation activities in another country is one of several options open to Parties working to meet their emission commitments under the Kyoto Protocol. Other options include domestic emission reduction activities, domestic sink enhancement activities, and domestic or international emissions trading. The potential 'market' for and interest in CDM (and to a lesser extent, JI) projects depends both on the size of the gap between countries' or entities' emissions and emissions targets and on the relative cost of domestic and international mitigation activities.

JI and CDM projects could be important tools in helping countries to increase their levels of development and industrialization in an environmentally-friendly manner. They may therefore be initiated in small numbers, almost irrespective of the rules established to govern how such projects should operate. However, JI and CDM projects are likely to only be undertaken in significant numbers if they can be initiated relatively simply and quickly, run in a cost-effective manner, and generate competitively-priced emission credits.

In order for the credits generated from JI or CDM projects to be credible, the projects have to be additional, the emission baselines against which a project performance is compared need to be environmentally sound, and project monitoring needs to be rigorous. However, there are transaction costs associated with project approval and registering, baseline development and project monitoring. These add to the transaction costs associated with a project. If CDM/JI are to be successful and widespread, it is important that the purely CDM/JI-related transaction costs do not impose transaction costs that create too high a barrier to potential project developers and investors.

How additionality is assessed, baselines are calculated and projects is monitored is crucial in determining not only how many emission credits are generated by a particular project, but how much these emission credits cost. This chapter examines issues related to assessing a project's additionality, setting baselines, and monitoring and verifying the emission mitigation effect of projects. It also suggests means to achieve the appropriate balance between environmental integrity and practical feasibility.

What is 'additionality'?

According to the Kyoto Protocol, only projects that are 'additional', i.e. that result in GHG mitigation that would not have occurred otherwise, are eligible to generate JI or CDM emission credits. However, defining what is 'additional' is an elusive concept. Although much analytical work has been done on this subject over several years,[3] no easy answer or definition has been found – even for sector-specific analyses.[4]

There are in theory many different criteria that could be used to determine whether or not a project is additional. These include:

- Emissions (or environmental) additionality: whether the GHG mitigation project emits less (or sequesters more) than the non-project scenario.
- Investment additionality: whether the project requires additional investment that would not have occurred otherwise.
- Financial additionality: whether any public funding is additional to financial resources already dedicated to the host developing country for other purposes.
- Technological additionality: whether the project involves an additional influx of climate-friendly technology.
- Regulatory additionality: to ensure that a project introduced in order to meet changing regulatory standards (e.g. on pollution) is not counted as 'additional'.

Determining a procedure to assess whether or not a project is additional may be easier to determine for some types of additionality (such as environmental additionality) than others (such as investment additionality, where potentially confidential financial data and subjective financial requirements, such as rates of return, are needed). The focus here will be on environmental additionality, which is the only type of additionality required explicitly in the Marrakech Accords.

Part of the difficulties surrounding a definition of additionality is due to the potential that many GHG-friendly projects have for multiple advantages (i.e. GHG reductions could be an ancillary benefit of a project already planned. In such a case the project would not be 'additional' (although it would be difficult to prove that a project was set up for a non-GHG purpose). It is also due to the diversity of projects that could be undertaken to fulfil a specific need. For example, reducing emissions from electricity generation could be achieved via demand-side projects such as switching to more efficient or less carbon-intensive modes of electricity generation, or to 'supply side' projects that increase end use efficiency.

Many JI/CDM projects will have environmental, economic or social benefits at a local or regional level in addition to global GHG benefits. For example, a rural electrification project based on renewable energy sources can help improve the quality of life and facilitate the development of small-scale industries in a region. Fuel efficiency projects in the industrial or transport sectors can reduce local pollution and have substantial health benefits for the local population – as well as reducing fuel costs. Afforestation and reforestation (A/R) projects can help prevent soil erosion, and can also be used to generate food, fuel and income for the local population.

These non-GHG benefits of JI/CDM projects means that governments or entities may undertake such activities for non-GHG reasons. Thus, a fuel efficiency project initiated with the aim of reducing local pollution will not be additional, but the same project initiated in order to mitigate GHG emissions would be. In practice, what criteria could be used to distinguish these projects from one another?

This difficulty is compounded when considering the diverse economic and financial contexts and expectations of different potential investors in JI/CDM projects. Investors could be from the public or private sectors, and access to investment capital may be more or less easy. Private investors may require a higher return on their investment than public investors. These financial constraints mean that many GHG reduction projects will not be able to be undertaken under a business as usual scenario, even if these projects are economically attractive to investors.

Deciding whether or not an activity is 'additional' is rendered more complex by the fact that the answer may be different in different countries or regions. This may be for physical/geographical reasons (e.g. access to different energy resources), for economic and financial reasons, or for reasons related to differences in legislation, policy or culture between different potential project-site countries. For example, biomass use may be routinely initiated (and therefore not additional) in countries with a large and accessible forest resource and policies in place to promote its sustainable use. However, in areas in which no such incentives exist, a similar activity may be additional. If the definition of additionality means that all biomass projects everywhere can generate emissions credits, a large proportion of projects that go ahead could actually be free riders.

In fact, for many projects, whether or not it is assessed as 'additional' depends on how additionality is defined, which in turn may involve subjective decisions. The difficulty of determining what is additional is reflected in the decision texts agreed at COP 7, where the only clarification of what 'additionality' means is that a baseline should 'reasonably represent' the without-project scenario.

Assessing environmental additionality

Even determining the environmental additionality of a project may be subject to uncertainties, and seeming contradictions. For example, a project may be inherently climate friendly, such as generating electricity from wind power, or increasing the energy efficiency of an industrial process. But this climate-friendly project may have gone ahead in the absence of JI and CDM and in this case would not in principle be eligible for crediting. At the other extreme, a JI or CDM project may actually result in more GHGs being emitted than the pre-project scenario, but may still result in a smaller increase in GHG emissions than in a non-project scenario. Such a project would be considered 'additional' and eligible to generate emissions credits under JI or CDM. The Marrakech Accords would count both project types as 'additional'.

Determining objective criteria for environmental additionality may be complex, even for potential JI/CDM projects in the energy or industrial sectors.[5] Even within one project type there are frequently more than one plausible scenario that could be drawn up to indicate 'what would have happened otherwise'. These different scenarios may have very different GHG emission profiles. This is especially marked in energy-related projects. For example, electricity can be generated by a variety of fuels – ranging from carbon-free renewables and nuclear power to carbon-intensive coal. Heat can also be produced by burning carbon-neutral or carbon-intensive fuels. Different technologies using the same fuel can differ markedly in efficiency (and therefore in GHG emissions). How can it be determined objectively which would have been used at a particular project site when, for example, countries typically use a range of fuels and technologies to provide these services?

Thus, a project judged against one of the potential scenarios may be environmentally additional, whereas the same project judged against a different scenario may not. The Marrakech Accords allow project developers considerable leeway in choosing how to prove that their project is additional.

Complexity is increased when trying to assess additionality for afforestation or reforestation projects. This is because of many factors, including the difficulty of separating natural from human-induced effects; the naturally dynamic nature of forests, potentially complex feedback effects; site-specific influences on carbon uptake rates, and the importance of cultural and socio-economic effects in influencing patterns of land use.

Examining some on-the-ground projects undertaken during the pilot phase of 'activities implemented jointly' (AIJ) highlights the difficulties in determining whether a particular project is additional or not. All AIJ projects underwent project-specific assessments of additionality. However, the criteria on which additionality was judged was frequently not clear,[6] and in at least one case, a project that had already been initiated then claimed it was 'additional'. This has led to the additionality of some of these AIJ projects being questioned.

Questions have also been raised about the additionality of some of the more recent CDM-type projects being developed. In particular, low-carbon projects that would have gone ahead anyway (such as large hydro projects or biomass projects) would be likely to easily 'pass' any additionality screening if this was linked only to the relative performance of the project and the baseline.

Any determination of environmental additionality therefore needs to be flexible enough to allow truly additional projects to generate credits while at the same time reducing the likelihood of allowing non-additional projects (even if they are environmentally friendly) to generate credits. This is not easy, as the choice of baseline assumptions or methodologies that determine the different baseline levels may involve some degree of subjectivity.

Who determines whether a proposed project is eligible and additional?

Under the rules and modalities set up in the Marrakech Accords, there are various procedures and eligibility requirements, involving a number of different actors, that potential large-scale emission reduction projects need to 'pass' in order to be eligible for JI or CDM status.[7]

Some broad ground-rules on project types have been agreed at an international level. For example, the Marrakech Accords require Annex I Parties to refrain from using nuclear facilities to generate emissions credits. This essentially means that nuclear projects cannot qualify for JI/CDM status. The same Accord includes a technology-input requirement for CDM projects. This implies that projects such as those aiming to increase the use of currently available environmentally-friendly technology via education campaigns and increased information are unlikely to be acceptable as JI/CDM projects.

The government of the country in which the project is planned to occur ('host-country') has a key role. It needs to approve the project, and – for CDM projects – confirm that the proposed project assists in achieving sustainable development (SD). Different host countries may have very different views of which project types would assist in achieving SD. For example, a country that generates the majority of its electricity from coal, such as China, may consider that its sustainable development would be helped by a project installing a highly-efficient coal-fired power station. However, another country that relies almost exclusively on renewable energy to meet its electricity needs, such as Costa Rica, may have a different opinion of a similar proposed project. The wording of the Marrakech Accord is flexible enough to enable a particular project type to be judged as eligible for JI/CDM in one country but not in another.

The supervisory boards for each of the mechanisms are also involved indirectly in determining the additionality or not of a particular project (although the supervisory board for JI has not yet been set up). For example, the CDM's Executive Board needs to formally accept CDM projects.

'Operational entities' (OEs) also have a say in whether or not proposed CDM project activities are additional. The CDM's Executive Board can only register those project activities that have been independently validated as additional by an accredited OE. Comparing the baseline and expected emissions of a project will be an important – but not sole – aspect of this validation. Other additionality checks may also be needed, such as assessing the impact of environmental legislation or standards on the type or performance of projects. However, such further checks should be relatively simple, as whilst using them could help screen out non-additional projects, they may also increase the time and cost associated with establishing a JI or CDM project.

These provisions apply to large-scale emission reduction projects. There are other types of GHG mitigation projects that may require an additionality assessment. These include small-scale CDM projects and CDM projects that enhance carbon 'sinks' (i.e. forestry projects).

The Marrakech Accords also include a provision to simplify the additionality requirements for some small-scale projects that have a high likelihood of being additional, but for which CDM-process-related costs might be a barrier to implementation. The three project types to benefit from this streamlined procedure are renewable energy project activities with an output capacity up to an equivalent of 15 MW; energy efficiency improvement activities that reduce energy consumption by up to 15 GWh/year, and other project activities that reduce emissions and emit less than 15 kt CO_2e per year. Rules for the modalities of assessing additionality, baselines and monitoring for small-scale CDM projects are on a fast-track for development, although the intention of having them developed for COP 8 (end 2002) was not met.

As outlined above, determining whether or not a sink-enhancement project is additional may be more complex than for an emissions reduction project. The rules governing how the CDM should operate for land-use projects have not yet been developed, but should be done so by COP 9 (end 2003). This, combined with the fact that basic definitions – such as what constitutes 'afforestation', 'reforestation' and 'forest' – have not been agreed for potential JI/CDM projects, may reduce near-term interest in investing in forestry mitigation projects.

Some non-JI/CDM projects may also seek some sort of 'additionality' assessment. For example, although the US does not plan to become a Party to the Kyoto Protocol, it may nevertheless undertake project-based GHG mitigation actions abroad. In order to demonstrate that such projects did indeed result in GHG mitigation, such projects would need to be assessed as additional. Companies operating in Annex I countries that undertake projects as part of a company-based commitment to reduce, or limit growth in, GHG emissions may also need to pass some sort of additionality check.

Emission baselines[8]

The additionality of a project is quantified by comparing the project's level of emissions or uptake to that projected in the baseline. The difference between the two levels is the mitigation effect of the project. For JI or CDM projects, this difference provides the maximum amount of emission credits (ERUs or CERs) eligible to be transferred from one Party or legal entity to another. Baselines are thus essential for the assessment of potential CDM and JI projects by project developers. The level and validity period of the baseline determines how many credits a project will receive, and for how long. These will determine the revenue stream received from credits, and are thus of great interest to potential investors.

There are different ways to set up an emissions baseline. At one end of the spectrum they can be established so they apply to one project only ('project-specific'), and at the other end they can be developed for use in many projects ('multi-project' or 'standardized').[9]

Project-specific baselines evaluate emission reductions generated from one particular project (rather than a group of similar projects). These baselines are established by using project-specific assumptions, measurements, or simulations for all key parameters. Project-specific baselines may need to rely heavily on expert judgment to determine some key parameters, which may compromise the environmental credibility of such baselines if experts artificially inflate the value of these parameters.

Multi-project, or standardized, baselines seek to standardize emission levels or rates, and are designed to be applicable to multiple projects of a similar type. Individual projects would be measured against these baselines as part of the additionality test for these projects. If the project proved to be additional (i.e. emitted less or sequestered more than the baseline), the difference would determine how many credits the project would generate. Multi-project baselines may often be calculated based on assumptions about the emissions *rate* (e.g. g CO_2/kWh). Multi-project baselines can be highly aggregate and be applied to many projects, or fairly disaggregated and applied to a smaller range or number of projects.

Experience with calculating emission baselines has been gained during the pilot phase of 'activities implemented jointly' (AIJ).[10] The majority of emission baselines for AIJ projects were established on a project-specific basis. Analysis of such experience[11] has indicated that in the absence of detailed guidelines on how to set up an emissions baseline, the methodologies and assumptions used are often incomparable, inconsistent and not transparent. Therefore, although the AIJ pilot phase increased experience with, and work on, emission baselines in both donor and host countries, it did not provide clear, direct methodological lessons on emission baselines.

From a theoretical point of view, an ideal baseline would be:[12]

- environmentally credible, in order to ensure that credits reflect only 'additional' activities;
- simple and inexpensive to set up, in order to encourage investment in such projects;
- transparent, in order to facilitate validation of the project.

In practice, drawing up a baseline is likely to involve tradeoffs among these criteria.

After much debate over many years about which approach was preferable, the Marrakech Accords leave both options open (although the language of the Accords is – perhaps intentionally – confused on this point). The approach used to determine an emissions baseline for a JI or CDM project influences the project's transaction cost, transparency and administrative feasibility (including data, monitoring and reporting requirements) as well as, potentially, its environmental additionality.

Establishing credible multi-project baselines or assumptions is a complex, highly technical and time-consuming process, as the parameters that need to be taken into account when establishing multi-project baselines vary from sector to sector. However, using multi-project baselines will increase transparency and the comparability of projects. Using multi-project baselines is also likely to decrease the transaction costs associated with project development because one baseline can be used for many projects. This has led to much interest being expressed in their development, particularly by potential investors, as multi-project baselines can be developed without compromising the environmental additionality of projects. The different issues that need to be considered when standardizing emission baselines are considered below.

How can baselines be standardized?

Baselines could be standardized in several different ways. These include:[13]

- Standardizing absolute baseline levels, or benchmark values (e.g. for project type X, the baseline to be used is Y kg CO_2/tonne output).
- Methodologies that would apply to a group of projects (e.g. for project type P, the baseline should be equivalent to the average performance of similar recently installed equipment).
- Parameters that could be used in baselines that have both project-specific and standardized components (e.g. for project type N, total emissions equal A + B + C. C needs to be calculated using site-specific data, but methodologies for A and B are given).

Which form is most appropriate to use will vary according to the type of project that is being undertaken. Thus, defining project categories (i.e. grouping the different types of projects that can use one particular baseline) is in itself also an important step. Given the significantly different contexts in which JI and CDM projects are undertaken, it may also be that baseline values, methodologies or parameters should vary within a project category, depending on whether they are developed for JI or CDM projects.

Analysis carried out by the OECD and IEA[14] indicates a number of important parameters when assessing how to develop emission baselines for a particular project type. These parameters are also of crucial importance when determining what needs to be monitored, and include assessing:

- Where a baseline can be used and which data should be used to develop the baseline (e.g. should it be developed and used at the local, regional, national or international level?).
- How long a baseline can be used to assess the emission performance of a given project (i.e. the crediting lifetime of a baseline).
- Which gases and sources should be included in the baseline, and whether a baseline should be for an entire process or individual process steps (i.e. the project boundary).
- Which data assumptions are appropriate, and whether or not these data are available (e.g. should the baseline use data on average performances, performance of only recent similar projects or projections?).
- Which units the baseline should be expressed in (e.g. in terms of absolute emissions, such as t CO_2, or in terms of a rate,[15] such as t CO_2/GWh).

How long a project can generate credits for – the crediting lifetime of a project – is also important. However, this parameter has been defined by the Marrakech Accords. Many of the other important baseline parameters are interlinked. For example, the availability of data (including emission factors) may influence decisions on which gases and sources to include in a project boundary.

For some project types, such as energy-efficiency projects or industry-sector projects, determining the emissions baseline may need to be a two-step process. First, an 'energy baseline', e.g. energy 'saved' or GJ per tonne output, would need to be developed. This value would then need to be 'translated' into GHG values using fuel-specific emission factors or electricity baselines.

Project categories

The possibilities for standardizing baseline methodologies, parameters or values differ for different types of projects. If standardized baseline methodologies, parameters or values are developed, it will need to be defined to which project category they can be applied.

There has been limited experience to date with developing and then applying standardized baselines to projects. A 'top-down' baseline for the Estonian heating sector was developed for AIJ projects.[16] Retroactive analysis has also identified a selection of possible standardized baselines for similar projects in the Czech Republic.[17]

Baseline analysis[18] and input from experts[19] indicate that many different project types are possible, even within a particular sector. For example, 'greenfield' (new) industry projects in the cement sector may need to be judged against a different type of baseline than 'brownfield' (retrofit) projects in the same sector. Projects that change the inputs into a process, such as fuel switching projects in electricity generation, or scrap rather than virgin ore input into metal production, may need to be judged against something different still. Baselines for projects that aim to change the product mix produced e.g. by an industrial plant may also need to be different. Thus, because there are many different types of projects that can be undertaken in a particular sector, more than one baseline may need to be developed for that sector.

There may be significant variations in a likely baseline level even within one type of project, for example, depending on the size of the project and where it is carried out. Part of any definition on project categories will therefore need to involve determining what levels of variation in project type, baseline conditions (such as geographical location of the project) are acceptable. At present, little work has been done on this area.[20] Guidance is needed on how to develop project categories, and on how to assess whether a baseline developed for one project can be applied to another of a similar type.

Crediting lifetimes

The number of years for which a project can generate credits determines the number, and therefore the value, of credits generated by a particular project. However, defining the crediting lifetime for a project is difficult to estimate objectively. This is because lifetimes of JI/CDM projects in different sectors (and even within sectors) can vary widely. For example, industry projects may install equipment that lasts 50 years or more, whereas energy efficiency projects may increase use of technologies whose lifetime is less than a decade. In many cases there is no objective decision for the crediting lifetime for a particular category of projects.

Another difficulty of determining standardized crediting lifetimes is related to the length of time over which a JI/CDM project is additional. For example, if the value of JI/CDM credits results in a planned project being initiated sooner than originally planned, this project is not 'additional' over its whole lifetime.

Thus, while determining crediting lifetimes is important for the value of the project, influences the additionality of credits generated by the project, it is not necessarily based on objective criteria, and can vary substantially from site to site. It is in project developers' interest to maximize the crediting lifetime of a project (and, for CDM projects, it would not be detrimental for host countries to approve a CDM project with an artificially long crediting lifetime). Moreover, it would be very difficult to verify the choice of crediting lifetime.

Fortunately, one of the concrete areas of guidance in the Marrakech Accords (at least for emission reduction CDM projects) is on the number of years for which a project can generate emission credits. Two options were established:[21] either ten years (without the option to renew the baseline), or seven years, with the option to renew the crediting lifetime for an additional two seven-year periods.

Crediting lifetimes (or, indeed other modalities) of afforestation and reforestation projects were not established by the Marrakech Accords, but are planned to be addressed by COP 9 (end 2003). However, they may need to be longer – and potentially considerably longer – than crediting lifetimes for projects in the energy/industry sectors. This is because the benefits from A/R projects may accrue over longer periods of time than benefits from energy/industry projects. In addition, long crediting lifetimes may be needed for A/R projects to ensure that their potentially reversible benefits are indeed long-term.

Some potential crediting lifetimes for forestry projects could be established objectively, such as those that mirror the actual timing of carbon sequestration in a particular project. However, some regimes would need subjective choices on crediting lifetime, such as those that require carbon to be sequestered over X years before credits are allocated. The potential use of subjective criteria in determining how long a project should receive credits for can result in huge (e.g. over 100 year) variations in crediting lifetime.[22]

Data assumptions and availability

Data availability may also influence decisions on how a baseline should be defined and what sources to include in it. Obtaining the data needed to establish a baseline may be difficult, and even where data is available, it is not always reliable. For example, there can be large differences between nameplate capacity and actual output, and manufacturers' specifications of efficiency and actual efficiency. Moreover, data availability and reliability varies between different countries and sectors.

Monitoring project performance[23]

Before credits from projects can be issued to project developers (and therefore used for compliance with emissions commitments), the performance of the project needs to be monitored and verified. The primary purpose of monitoring project performance is to compare actual GHG emissions levels of the JI or CDM project with the previously agreed baseline. Once the project performance has been monitored and the associated emission reductions validated, the credits can be transferred to the project proponents.

The Marrakech Accords indicate that monitoring project performance is an essential part of the JI/CDM project cycle. Monitoring project performance will also be an essential component of determining effectiveness of other GHG mitigation projects, e.g. those undertaken under national or voluntary programmes. The Accords lay out the role of some actors in monitoring, and outline some items that need to be included in a monitoring plan. However, no methodological or management guidance on how to monitor projects is provided. While methodological guidance is likely to vary depending on the type of project undertaken, some centralized management/organizational guidance would be useful. If project developers and operators knew what the mandatory 'monitoring plan' should consist of, what aspects of the project need to be monitored, how they should be monitored, when and by whom[24] it could reduce the time and costs associated with project development. Monitoring guidance could therefore increase transparency, predictability and comparability of credit generation from projects. It could also increase the ease and reduce the costs of verifying emission reductions.

Developing a project's baseline and monitoring requirements are closely linked, so guidelines for project monitoring and baselines should be carried out in parallel in order to ensure consistency. For example, if a particular emissions source is excluded from a project's baseline, monitoring reductions in emissions from this source should not generate emission credits. Developing monitoring guidelines will also influence (or be influenced by) any guidelines on how to report and/or verify the impacts of greenhouse gas mitigation projects.

The requirement that a monitoring plan needs to be set up at the project design stage – when a baseline is also being determined – should help this. It should also facilitate the gathering of appropriate input data at little or no extra costs; for example by ensuring that meters are placed at appropriate locations.

Some lessons for project monitoring can be learnt by examining experience under the AIJ pilot phase. Perhaps the two most important are that clear instructions are needed if project monitoring is going to be carried out in a systematic and comparable fashion and that training project operators in monitoring the GHG-relevant aspects of a project is important.

Choosing a monitoring methodology

CDM project developers can choose which method they can use to monitor the performance of a project. In particular, work is underway to develop highly simplified procedures for some categories of small CDM projects.[25]

Despite the fact that different methods may lead to potentially different results, the ability to choose a monitoring methodology appropriate to the project is important. Ideally, project monitoring should provide an accurate picture of the GHG impacts of a project. However, the credits generated by a project are calculated by comparing the project's performance with the project baseline (which is by definition a hypothetical scenario, and may be subject to considerably more uncertainty than the project's emission performance). It may therefore be appropriate to make some trade-offs to ensure that monitoring costs are kept to a reasonable level, e.g. under 8 per cent of a project's total cost.

For example, the relative importance of different gases and sources can vary enormously, depending on the characteristics of the individual greenhouse gas mitigation project: while methane leakage may need to be monitored for landfill gas projects, it may not be significant for projects generating gas-fired electricity. It is more cost-effective if project developers are allowed to use simplified methodologies to monitor sources that are either small or relatively unaffected by the project.

Decisions by project operators on the precision with which a project's performance needs to be monitored can also have potentially significant effects on the cost of monitoring projects (Figure 10.1).

Fortunately, project developers will not have to start from scratch when developing monitoring methodologies for projects, as detailed guidance relevant to monitoring the benefits of greenhouse gas mitigation projects has been drawn up for other purposes. For example, the IPCC guidance on calculating emissions

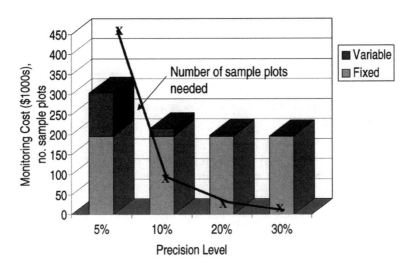

Figure 10.1 Influence of number of sample plots on the monitoring cost and precision level for the Noel Kempff project.

Source: adapted from Powell (1999) and Kadyszewski (2001).

inventories[26] can be used to calculate emissions from industrial processes or direct fuel use. The International Performance Measurement and Verification Protocol for energy efficiency projects[27] can be used to assess the electricity 'saved' by some types of energy efficiency projects. The WRI/WBCSD Greenhouse Gas Protocol for corporate accounting[28] also gives useful guidance as to what to include and exclude from project boundaries. These methods, as well as national or regional monitoring standards, can all be applied to some extent to calculating the impacts of JI/CDM projects.

Choosing the frequency of monitoring

CDM project credits can only be issued after a project has been monitored. Thus, the timing of credit issuance (and associated revenue) will be influenced by when, and how often, a project is monitored. The absolute cost of monitoring a project may also be influenced by the frequency with which a project is monitored. For example, significant economies of scale may be possible if less-than-yearly monitoring reduces the costs, such as travel costs, of verifiers (who may be based far away from the project site).

A project developers' decisions on the timing and frequency of monitoring can thus be influenced both by financial considerations and the inherent characteristics of different project types, as different types of projects will need to be monitored with different frequencies. For example, carbon uptake by an afforestation/reforestation project may need to be monitored less regularly than electricity generation projects. There will be a trade-off between the time/cost of frequent monitoring and reporting, and the time/cost needed to verify a project's emissions/enhancements.

Cross-cutting issues

Because of the inter-linkages between how a project baseline is defined, and what project monitoring needs to comprise, some issues are relevant both to baseline and monitoring development. For example, where to draw the project boundary is one of the crucial decisions in determining both a project's baseline and monitoring plan. Another is that of the balance between maintaining environmental integrity and reducing transaction costs associated with project development and implementation. There are also strong links between monitoring guidance, and guidance on reporting and verification.

Project boundaries

The Marrakech Accords require that each JI/CDM project 'shall' include a 'monitoring plan' as part of the project design document. Defining the boundaries of what needs to be monitored is a crucial step in setting up a plan to monitor the project's performance. In order to ensure that credits from projects credibly reflect GHG mitigation, they need to reflect what is included in a project's baseline, i.e. the pre-project (baseline) and post-project (monitoring) data should compare emissions/uptake from the same sources.

How a project boundary is defined is important, because it influences the environmental credibility of credits generated by the project and the costs of monitoring (through the effect of project boundary definitions on the number of sources that need monitoring). For example, monitoring the emissions from a zero-emitting project such as stand-alone renewable electricity generating projects is a trivial exercise, if the project boundary is drawn around the project site. However, if the project boundary includes emissions associated with preparing the project site, transporting equipment to the project site and operating the project, the complexity of monitoring operations increases.

In the Marrakech Accords, project boundaries for emission reduction CDM projects are defined as 'encompass[ing] all anthropogenic emissions by sources of greenhouse gases under the control of the project participants that are significant and reasonably attributable to the CDM project activity'.[29]

This definition of project boundaries therefore sets up a three-staged approach to defining project boundaries. Only emission sources that are significant *and* reasonably attributable *and* 'under the control' of the project participants need to be included in the project boundary. However, none of these key words are defined – although they are all open to interpretation. Further guidance will need to be more specific if it is to ensure consistent and comparable decisions by project developers on determining what project boundaries for baselines and monitoring JI/CDM projects should be.

Determining project boundaries is not necessarily a simple task.[30] GHG mitigation projects can affect many different sources and gases. This impact can be direct or indirect and can occur on the project site or external to the project site. For example, a project's fuel combustion, process emissions or sequestration are both on-site and direct. However, emissions associated with fuel transport to the project site, or electricity distribution from a project site are direct emissions, but occur off-site. Indirect on-site emissions could be caused by a change in operating characteristics of the project site (e.g. increased heating demand) or through preparation of the project site (e.g. flooding a site for hydro-generation or deforestation on the project site). Indirect, off-site effects can also include the effect that a project has on fuel demand and/or prices, or the GHG emissions generated by producing materials or equipment used on a project site.

The relative significance of sources of emission or mitigation can vary greatly by project type and during the life of the project. For example, the relative importance of different carbon pools can change during the growth of a forest.

Any guidance on how to set project boundaries would therefore need to be set up at a sectoral or project-type level, and would greatly improve the comparability of different projects in the same sector.

Comparisons of the detailed guidance on project monitoring drawn up by different bodies, e.g. for electricity or forestry projects (see Ellis 2002 for a detailed discussion) shows that different organizations give different recommendations on what to monitor, and when. These different recommendations reflect implicit decisions by different guidance developers of what is or is not a significant emissions/enhancement source that can be monitored cost-effectively.

Reducing the transaction costs associated with project approval

Countries and companies required to limit their GHG emissions can potentially do so by one of several means. They could invest in local (e.g. domestic or on-site) emission reduction activities, in domestic activities that aim to enhance carbon sequestration by sinks, they could buy emissions credits via domestic or international emissions trading schemes, or they could undertake project-based emissions in another country. Thus, undertaking JI/CDM projects is only one of several emission limitation options available.

During the AIJ pilot phase the main investment in projects came from governments, and approximately 120 projects, some of which were quite small-scale, were initiated in the first three to four years of the pilot phase. Thus, although there have been significant benefits from AIJ projects in terms of capacity building and awareness raising, the global GHG benefit has been small. If the mechanisms of JI and CDM are to play an important role in climate mitigation, many more projects, and therefore industry investment is needed.

However, the up-front costs associated with CDM or JI project development can be large, and can constitute a significant barrier to project investment, particularly for small projects where the total costs are relatively low. Thus, in order to become an attractive investment option, JI/CDM transaction costs will need to be kept reasonable and obtaining approval for JI and CDM projects will need to be straightforward. This is not likely to be an easy task, given the likely low value of carbon credits and the JI/CDM project cycle as laid out in the Marrakech Accords. Indeed, a lengthy project approval process combined with potentially low values for carbon credits could mean that transaction costs could actually be greater than the revenue from the emissions credits generated by a project unless it generates many thousands of credits over its lifetime.[31]

The most important transaction costs associated with project development (e.g. for the CDM) are likely to be those related to developing a baseline, developing and carrying out a monitoring plan, and verifying project performance. Some of these purely CDM or JI-related transaction costs, e.g. those

Table 10.1 Overview of CDM transaction cost estimates

Studies	Estimated CDM transaction costs	Assumptions
PWC (2000)	US$0.4m to $1.1m, i.e. representing between 2–23% of capital expenditures (e.g. in the case of 0.1 MW PV project, involving only 1 operational entity, CDM-related transaction costs amount to $387,000).	Total costs *over project cycle* (in 2000$). Range depends on project size and type and number and nature of operational entities involved.
Walsh (2000)	$40,000 (highly simplified project) to more than $80,000. Complex projects: $100,000 to $500,000. Subsequent annual reporting and occasional auditing costs: 10–20% of initial costs.	Includes *initial* costs of defining a CDM project, establishing the baseline, documenting project additionality, preparing registration forms, obtaining certification, government approval and submitting required documents. Assumes a blend of industrialized country and developing country professional fees.
EcoSecurities Ltd. (2000)	Total up-front costs: $57,000–$90,000. Monitoring and verification: $3,000–$15,000 per year.	Estimated costs of transacting a JI project, assuming JI requirements are similar to CDM project cycle.
PCF	Total costs: $200,000–$400,000.	Half of the amount for baseline work; half for verification/certification work throughout the project.
Martens *et al.* (2001)	Transaction costs for small-scale solar home systems projects range around 20% of the total CER revenues, using a standardized baseline and streamlined procedures.	Without the standardized baselines and streamlined procedures, project design costs could be almost three times higher and total transaction costs 50% higher.

Source: Bosi (2001).

related to developing a project's monitoring plan, will be incurred before a project can be approved, and can be significant – particularly for small projects (Table 10.1).

The Marrakech Accords lay out certain delays for CDM project development (e.g. to ensure adequate time is given for stakeholder consultation and project approval by the CDM's Executive Board). However, the actual process of project approval is likely to take longer than that laid out in the Marrakech Accord, particularly for a first JI or CDM project. If experience from the AIJ pilot phase and the Dutch ERUPT tenders for JI projects are representative, long delays (and associated opportunity costs) for project approval is also likely. The main factors behind such delays are institutional bottlenecks in the host country in the project approval process; uneasiness by the potential host country in signing away carbon 'assets'; and setting up a purchase agreement from the project output (e.g. a power purchase agreement).[32]

The transaction costs associated with developing individual JI/CDM projects can be reduced by various means, e.g:

*   Use of simplified and/or agreed procedures and modalities on determining the additionality, baseline, project boundary and leakage of a project. This can increase the transparency and consistency of projects as well as increasing the likelihood that projects will be approved and agreed by the project participants.
*   Having clear information on approval criteria and procedures for potential JI/CDM projects in different countries. This reduces the time and uncertainty associated with obtaining project approval from the host country. (However, it requires both government willingness to engage in JI/CDM projects, and work in designing and establishing institutions and procedures needed to screen, approve – and possibly also identify – potential projects).

All of these apart from the latter require a greater or lesser degree of up-front funding by someone other than the project developer.

There will also be on-going costs associated with monitoring and verifying CDM/JI projects. Being able to group (or 'bundle') baseline calculation, monitoring and/or verification of many similar projects could help reduce these costs.[33] A multi-project verification exercise[34] undertaken for 31 comparable Swedish AIJ projects estimates that multi-project verification activities could be 50–70 per cent cheaper than project-specific verification activities. Another study of potential CDM projects in India also indicated that bundling similar projects into groups of ten would 'turn several types of small-scale projects into viable CDM projects'.[35]

Conclusions

The Kyoto Protocol, agreed in 1997, allowed for emission reductions from project-based emission mitigation activities (CDM and JI) to generate credits which can be used to offset domestic emissions in Annex I countries. In order for the credits generated from JI or CDM projects to be credible, the projects have to be additional, the emission baselines against which a project performance is compared need to be environmentally sound, and project monitoring needs to be rigorous.

The Marrakech Accords, reached in 2001, laid out some general 'modalities and procedures' to help operationalize the CDM and JI. This included laying out the 'project cycle' that CDM and JI projects would need to follow to obtain emission credits and some guidance – for emission reduction projects – on how to assess additionality, set up emission baselines, and monitor projects. The Accords do not, however, include detailed methodologies for baselines or monitoring or general guidance for including afforestation or reforestation projects in the CDM.

Defining some sort of procedure or formula to indicate whether or not a project is 'additional' is not easy. This is because driving factors behind whether a project is developed in a more or less GHG-friendly manner can be significantly influenced by the policy, resource and financial context of a project's location and the aims, resources and financial context of the project developer(s). While some of these factors can be determined objectively, others are subjective and/or confidential.

The Marrakech Accords define 'additionality' in terms of the GHG performance of the project as compared to the baseline. CDM project developers also need to explain in the project design document why the project itself is not the baseline, e.g. why the project would not have gone ahead otherwise. This should reduce (but will not eliminate) the number of non-additional projects – free riders – that claim and/or generate emissions credits.

Because a project's baseline may play the dual role of identifying whether a project is additional and quantifying by how much, it is important that the baselines used for projects are credible. The Marrakech Accords allow project developers considerable leeway in deciding which methodology they can use to calculate the emission benefits of their project. This could result in project developers setting artificially high emission baselines, particularly for CDM projects where the host countries are not subject to emission commitments. However, the extent of 'gaming' (and resulting non-additional credits) should be limited by the option to use standardized baselines and the requirement for CDM baselines to be verified. Standardizing baselines can help to ensure consistency in the treatment of similar projects and would provide a high degree of transparency in baseline determination. Standardization could also, if developed by independent experts, limit the level of gaming/free riders and associated non-additional emissions credits.

Once up and running, emission mitigation projects need to be monitored in order to determine their actual emissions (or enhancements) and calculate the number of emissions credits they have generated. The Marrakech Accord's requirement that a monitoring plan needs to be set up at the project design stage will mean that monitoring considerations are included at an early stage in project planning. This should facilitate the gathering of relevant data at little or no extra costs by, for example, ensuring that meters are placed at appropriate locations. Ensuring that emission reductions are verified by an independent third party should also increase confidence in the validity of issued emission reductions.

Defining a project's boundary is important, as it will determine which emission sources should be included in a project's baseline, and which should be monitored. It therefore impacts both the number of credits a project can generate and the cost of baseline development and project monitoring. However, although not much detailed guidance exists on what to include and exclude from project boundaries, the different sets of guidance that have been developed are not on consensus. The Marrakech Accords indicate that the project boundary should include sources that are 'significant', 'reasonably attributable' to the project and 'under the control' of the project developer – but do not define any of these terms.

Thus, internationally-agreed texts such as the Marrakech Accords provide guidance, but not detailed instructions, for the project developer. There still remains much that project developers need to do to apply the guidance given to actual projects.

Recent development of CDM-type or JI-type projects, such as the World Bank's Prototype Carbon Fund (PCF) and the Dutch government's ERUPT programme have illustrated that CDM-related transaction costs are likely to be at least $100,000 for other than very simple first-of-a-kind projects. These costs are associated with calculating baselines, obtaining project approval and defining a monitoring and verification plan. JI-related transaction costs are likely to be somewhat lower, but still high. Reducing these costs is important in order to encourage interest and investment in credible CDM or JI-type projects, and to ensure that participating in JI or CDM projects increases, rather than decreases, the cost-effectiveness of using project-based activities to comply with a domestic emissions target.

There are several ways in which CDM/JI-related transaction costs can be reduced:

- Using standardized or simplified procedures to determine a project's baseline, boundary, and to monitor the performance of the project;
- Building on monitoring and/or emissions accounting methods already agreed (e.g. by the IPCC) rather than developing new methods;
- Setting out clear project approval and criteria (at both the host country and donor country level).

Progress is being made in all three areas, at both international and national levels. If the results of this work succeed in making credible emission mitigation projects an attractive investment option and significant numbers of such projects are initiated there is room for optimism that the project-based mechanisms could play a significant role in the international community's first steps towards a more sustainable future.

Notes

1 Emission credits from JI activities are called 'emission reduction units' (ERUs), and those from CDM project activities are called 'certified emission reductions' (CERs).
2 UNFCCC (2001).
3 See, for example, Carter (1997), Baumert (1998) and Michaelowa (1999).
4 See, for example, OECD/IEA (2000), Kartha *et al.* (2001) and Bosi *et al.* (2002).
5 See, for example, OECD/IEA (2000).
6 OECD (1999).
7 The Marrakech Accords also outline various requirements – such as having a national inventory system in place – that Parties have to meet in order to be eligible to participate in the mechanisms. These participation requirements are not dealt with further in this chapter.
8 This section summarizes a large body of analysis undertaken for the Annex I Expert Group (e.g. OECD/IEA (1999), OECD/IEA (2000) and UNEP/OECD/IEA (2001)) drafted for the most part by the author and Martina Bosi (IEA), and has benefited from the input of Jan Corfee Morlot, Jonathan Pershing, Stéphane Willems, other colleagues at the OECD and IEA as well as Fanny Missfeldt, Lasse Ringius, Jyoti Painuly and delegates to the Annex I Expert Group.
9 OECD/IEA (1999).
10 'Activities Implemented Jointly' was set up under the United Nations' Framework Convention on Climate Change, and was essentially a forerunner to JI and CDM with one important difference: AIJ projects were not allowed to generate emission credits.
11 See, for example, OECD (1999) and Schwarze (2000).
12 OECD/IEA (1999).
13 UNEP/OECD/IEA (2001).
14 OECD/IEA (2000).
15 A decision on whether to express baselines in terms of a rate or absolute emissions will affect the simplicity with which a baseline can be drawn up. For example, baselines expressed in terms of absolute amounts will need to be adjusted for the output from a project, while a rate basis baseline could be used for similar projects with varying output levels (i.e. the baselines would be expressed in tGHG per unit of output). Expressing baselines in rate terms may be desirable for greenfield projects in growing economies in order to take into account the development objectives and needs of developing countries. A rate-basis baseline would also work to avoid a project generating credits by simply being closed down. On the other hand, a rate-basis baseline might present particular challenges in the case of a country with absolute emission target, as the country's emissions might still grow, as a result of the JI projects – albeit at a lower rate.
16 Kallaste and Roos (2000).
17 Ernst Basler and Partners (1999).
18 See, for example, OECD/IEA (2000).
19 As summarized in UNEP/OECD/IEA (2001).
20 The Marrakech Accords do define three types of 'small-scale' CDM projects that can

qualify for fast-tracking. It was agreed at the second Executive Board meeting that these categories should be mutually exclusive.

21 UNFCCC (2001).
22 Ellis (2001).
23 This section draws from Ellis (2002).
24 Similar information will also be needed to quantify the effects of any project-based reductions within a national credit programme.
25 UNFCCC (2002).
26 IPCC/OECD/IEA (1997).
27 IPMVP (2000).
28 WBCSD/WRI (2001).
29 The definition for JI is similarly worded, although it also includes reference to removals by sinks.
30 See, for example, OECD/IEA (2000).
31 Bosi (2001).
32 Korthuis (2002).
33 However, in order for multi-project monitoring and verification to give credible results, the projects bundled together should be technologically similar, located in similar regions, have comparable baselines and monitor/report similar project indicators, e.g. DNV (2001a). In addition, the number of sample projects monitored should be statistically significant.
34 DNV (2001a) and DNV (2001b).
35 Factor Consulting and Management Ltd. (2001).

Bibliography

Baumert, K. (1998) 'The Clean Development Mechanism: understanding additionality', in *The Clean Development Mechanism*, draft working papers, CSDA/FIELD/WRI.

Bosi, M. (2001) *Fast-tracking Small CDM Projects: Implications for the Electricity Sector*, OECD/IEA Information Paper. Online. Available at http://www.oecd.org/env/cc/ (accessed 2003).

Bosi, M. and Laurence, A. with Maldonado, P., Schaeffer, R., Simões, A.-F., Winkler, H. and Lukamba, J.-M. (2002) *Road-Testing Baselines for GHG Mitigation Projects in the Electric Power Sector*, OECD/IEA Information Paper. Online. Available at http://www.oecd.org/env/cc/ (accessed 2003).

Carter, L. (1997) *Modalities for the Operationalization of Additionality*, prepared for presentation at UNEP/German Federal Ministry of Environment workshop on AIJ, Leipzig, March 1997.

DNV (2001a) *Multi-Project Verification of Swedish AIJ Projects: Verification Results and Documentation*, Report ER 10: 2001 prepared for the Swedish National Energy Administration.

DNV (2001b) *Multi-Project Verification of Swedish AIJ Projects: Methodology and Lessons Learned*, Report ER 9: 2001 prepared for the Swedish National Energy Administration.

Ellis, J. (2001) *Forestry Projects: Permanence, Credit Accounting and Lifetime*, OECD/IEA Information Paper. Online. Available at http://www.oecd.org/pdf/M00023000/M00023450.pdf (accessed 2003).

Ellis, J. (2002) *Developing Monitoring Guidance for Greenhouse Gas Mitigation Projects*, OECD/IEA Information Paper. Online. Available at http://www.oecd.org/env/cc/ (accessed 2003).

Ernst Basler and Partners (1999) *Swiss-Czech Cooperation Project 'Conversion of Heating Centers': Activities Implemented Jointly (AIJ) Study*, Study prepared for the Swiss Federal Office for Foreign Economic Affairs, Zurich.

Factor Consulting and Management Ltd. (2001) *Small-scale CDM Projects: Opportunities and Obstacles*. Online. Available at http://www.factorag.ch/pdf%20files/SUT%20Small-scale%20CDM%20Projects_Vol1_5-11-01.pdf (accessed 8 September 2003).

Kadyszewski, J. (2001) *Forestry Projects: How to Credit and Monitor*. Online. Available at http://www.iisd.ca/climate/cop7/enbots/nov5.html (accessed 8 September 2003).

IPCC/OECD/IEA (1997) *Revised 1996 IPCC Guidelines for National Greenhouse Gas Inventories*, IPCC-NGGIP.

IPMVP (2000) *International Performance Measurement and Verification Protocol Volume I*. Online. Available at http://www.ipmvp.org/info/downloads_2000.html (accessed 8 September 2003).

Kallaste, T. and Roos, I. (2000) *Top-down CO_2 Emissions Baselines for the Estonian District Heating Sector*, Swedish National Energy Administration, ER15: 2000, Eskilstuna.

Kartha, S. and Lazarus, M. with Bosi, M. (2002) *Practical Baseline Recommendations for Greenhouse Gas Mitigation Projects in the Electric Power Sector*, OECD/IEA Information Paper, OECD. Online. Available at http://www.oecd.org/env/cc/ (accessed 8 September 2003).

Korthius, A. (2002) Presentation at Szentendre workshop.

Michaelowa, A. (1999) 'Project-specific, benchmark, top-down approaches for baselines and additionality: a comparison', Paper prepared for the UNFCCC Technical workshop on Mechanisms, April 9–15 1999.

OECD (1999) *Experience with Emission Baselines under the AIJ Pilot Phase*, OECD/IEA Information Paper, OECD. Online. Available at http://www.oecd.org/env/cc/ (accessed 8 September 2003).

OECD/IEA (1999) *Options for Project Emission Baselines*, OECD and IEA Information Paper. Online. Available at http://www.oecd.org/env/cc/ (accessed 8 September 2003).

OECD/IEA (2000) *Emission Baselines: Estimating the Unknown*, Paris: OECD/IEA.

PCF (2000) *Learning from the Implementation of the Prototype Carbon Fund*, PCF Occasional Papers Number 1.

Powell, M. (1999) *Effect of Inventory Precision and Variance on the Estimated Number of Sample Plots and Inventory Variable Cost: The Noel Kempff Mercado Climate Action Project*. Paper prepared for the World Bank, Winrock International, Arkansas, USA.

UNEP/OECD/IEA (2001) *UNEP/OECD/IEA Workshop on Baseline Methodologies: Possibilities for Standardised Baselines for JI and the CDM. Chairman's Recommendations and Workshop Report*. Online. Available at http://www.oecd.org/env/cc/freedocs.htm (accessed 8 September 2003).

UNFCCC (2001) *The Marrakech Accords*.

UNFCCC (2002) *Indicative Simplified Baselines and Monitoring Methodologies for Selected Small-scale CDM Project Activity Categories*. Online. Available at http://cdm.unfccc.int/EB/Panels/meth/meth3anb.pdf (accessed 8 September 2003).

WBCSD/WRI (2001) *The Greenhouse Gas Protocol: A Corporate Accounting and Reporting Standard*. Online. Available at http://www.wbcsd.org (accessed 8 September 2003).

11 Developing countries and climate change

Anil Markandya and Kirsten Halsnaes

Introduction

At the very heart of the climate change debate is the question of developing countries: how they are impacted, what can be expected of them in way of response and what, if any, assistance should they get in dealing with the consequences of climate change. The countries themselves, without exception, take a strong view on the situation from an environmental justice point of view. They say that the present mess is largely the result of the GHG emissions generated by the industrialized countries in the course of the last 150 years.[1] It is unfair, therefore, to ask them to pay the price, either in terms of reducing their own emissions if that means reducing their rate of development, or in terms of undertaking expensive adaptation measures, without compensation from the industrialized countries, which they can ill afford in any event. This position is formalized in an economic context in the distribution of 'emissions rights'. If emissions of GHGs are to be restricted, how much should each country be allowed to emit? Developing countries take the view that such rights are equally shared by all individuals and the allocation should be on the basis of population. Of course that would mean that much more would be allowed to the 'population rich' countries and much less to the richer, but relatively less populated ones. This issue is expanded in the next section.[2]

In this chapter we aim to show how the tools of economic analysis can be used to shed light on the questions raised above. Of course, economics cannot answer ethical questions of who should have to bear the costs of climate change. But it can show us how to answer these questions in a way that is relatively efficient – i.e. uses the least amount of scarce resources. It can also help us understand the costs of actions better. The common man has a poor notion of what makes up such a cost. Financial and economic costs are confused and some costs are counted twice. Little distinction is made between present and future costs, and so on. So, by looking at the cost side carefully, economists can help reduce the areas of disagreement, of which many will remain in any event.[3]

The chapter is structured as follows; the present and projected share of GHG emissions of developing countries and what different allocation rules would mean in economic terms is considered first. The evidence on the possible impacts of climate change and what can be said on the impacts on developing versus developed countries is then reviewed. Next, we discuss how climate policies are determined, and the role of self interest in the negotiations. We then show how the Kyoto Protocol has responded to the climate change issues; in particular, how developing countries are included in the agreements. In this context, some mechanisms have been created and these are reviewed.

Allocating carbon rights

Table 11.1 provides the data on the recent levels of carbon emissions by region and on the population of the region as of 2000. We see that in that year the developed world was responsible for nearly half the emissions, the Former Soviet Union (FSU) and Eastern Europe (EE) for about 13 per cent and the developing world for the rest – around 38 per cent. The table also reveals that the developing world's emissions are growing fastest, whereas those of the FSU and EE are the slowest, with the developed world somewhere in between.

Now that carbon emissions are known to cause environmental damages (see Chapters 2 and 5 for a full discussion of this), the right to release them must be limited: what is more, limits were agreed on by many countries at Kyoto. As such carbon emissions become a scarce commodity and like all scarce commodities two questions are paramount: what is the price and who owns the rights to the commodity? In the case of carbon the answer to the first question is still a matter of debate: the 'current price' of carbon, which is either the implicit value of a tonne of carbon in valuing projects that reduce emissions of greenhouse gases; or the explicit value attached to a tonne of carbon in carbon trades. Such trades are now beginning to take place, in anticipation of a full agreement on carbon emission reductions. The second question is a matter of intense debate. For something like carbon emissions, which have previously been seen as a free good, and now as one that have global impacts, there is really no historic experience to draw on. One principle, based in some respects on natural justice, is to say that each human being is entitled to an equal amount of emissions rights, in which case these rights will be allocated on the basis of population. Table 11.1 shows what that will imply.

From Table 11.1 we see that the developed world would have to buy rights from the developing world, because *per capita*, its emissions are much higher than those of the developing countries. At a price of $5 per tonne of carbon, the net transfer would be about $11 billion from the developed countries and $1.6

Table 11.1 Emissions of carbon by region

Region	Mn. tonnes carbon				Millions	Mn. tonnes	Annual transfer $Bn. at		
	1990	2000	2020 (1)	% increase 1990–2020	Population 2000	Rights in 2000 on pop. basis	$5/tonne	$10/tonne	$15/tonne
North America	1,550	1,833	2,314	1.3	312.4	339	7.5	14.9	22.4
Western Europe	936	947	1,114	0.6	440.6	478	2.3	4.7	7.0
Industrialized Asia (2)	364	377	479	0.9	149.9	163	1.1	2.1	3.2
Total Developed	2,850	3,157	3,907	1.1	902.9	979	10.9	21.8	32.7
FSU and EE	1,290	827	1,024	−0.8	474.3	514	1.6	3.1	4.7
Developing Asia	1,065	1,659	3,377	3.9	3,083.4	3,344	−8.4	−16.8	−25.3
Middle East	229	323	555	3.0	295.2	320	0.0	0.0	0.0
Africa (3)	178	214	325	2.0	658.9	715	−2.5	−5.0	−7.5
Central & South America	174	251	629	4.4	515.7	559	−1.5	−3.1	−4.6
Total Developing	1,646	2,447	4,886	3.7	4,553.2	4,938	−12.5	−24.9	−37.4
Total	5,786	6,431	9,817	1.8	5,930.4	6,431	0	0	0.0

Source: IPCC (2001), Table 1.1.

Note
1 2020 figures are based on a business as usual assumption i.e. no action for climate change.
2 Includes Japan, Australia and New Zealand.
3 Refers to Sub-Saharan Africa.

billion from the FSU and EE to the developed countries. At higher prices the transfers would be proportionately higher. Over time, as emissions in the developing countries increase relative to those in the developed world, this transfer would decline.[4]

Needless to say, these transfers do not happen at present, as there is no agreement on property rights to carbon. If such an agreement could be reached, it is unlikely that a whole scale allocation of rights based on population would be acceptable, in spite of its appeal on grounds of equity.[5] One possibility is that developed countries would ask for some of the emissions rights to be 'grandfathered' – i.e. allocated to them on the basis that they have traditionally emitted them. In that case the allocation might be based on combination of current and population based emissions. One algebraic expression for this would be:

$$E_{it} = \left\{ \alpha . \frac{P_{i0}}{P_0} + (1 - \alpha) \frac{E_{i0}}{E_0} \right\} E_1 \qquad (11.1)$$

where:

E_{it} is emissions allocated to country 'i' in year t; E_{i0} is actual emissions of country 'i' in year 0; E_1 is total allowable emissions in year 1; P_{i0} is population of country 'i' in year t; E_0 is total emissions in base year; P_0 is total population in base year and α is the share of allocation based on population.

'0' is the base year for the calculations. It follows from equation (1) that if α was zero, any reduction would be equi-proportionate – i.e. each country would reduce emissions by the same proportion.[6]

The actual allocations that are emerging from the climate change negotiations are somewhat more muddled and cruder than the formula above would suggest. Countries are broadly classified in two groups: developing and developed; and developing countries have presently made no commitments to reduce emissions, while developed countries have some commitment to make a reduction relative to their 1990 levels, with the percentage reduction based on special factors – how carbon efficient their economy is, how dependent they are on coal, and on political power (see Chapters 3 and 9). We return to the actual mechanisms on p. 248.

What will the impacts of climate change be on developing countries?

The whole reason for undertaking reductions in emissions of greenhouse gases is that they will generate environmental, social and economic damages in the future. The most significant of these are those related to sea level rise, increased frequency of freak weather events, and to the health effects of increased vector borne diseases (e.g. malaria) and heat related cardiovascular and respiratory diseases (note, there will also be some benefits in places where increased temperatures reduce such impacts). There are also impacts on agriculture, forestry, water use, energy consumption etc., some of which will be positive. The scale of these damages is very difficult to estimate; the underlying physical models are still quite primitive and there is great uncertainty about future land use and population distribution, which will have significant effects on the damages caused by climate change. The other factor on which monetary estimates of the damages depend greatly is the discount rate (see Chapter 5). Typically, the models look far into the future and impacts start to get serious around 2030. After that they will continue to be relevant for one hundred years or more. At a high discount rate these damages become insignificant, as can be seen in Table 11.2. If we go from a 0 per cent discount rate to a modest 5 per cent rate, one estimate of total world discounted damage costs to 2100 falls from $500 trillion to $31 trillion. The reason is simply that a large part of the damages occur later in the period, and the discount rate has a major impact on their present value. To give an example, the present value of one million dollars of damages in 2053 is $600,000 at a 1 per cent discount rate (the calculation is $1/(1.01)^{50}$). At a 5 per cent discount rate, however, it is only $87,000 and a 10 per cent discount rate shrinks it to $8,500, or less than 1 per cent of the undiscounted figure.

Table 11.2 Net present value of climate change damages: 2000–2100

Discount rate	0%	1%	3%	5%	10%
Percentage by sector					
Sea level rise	57.8	61.1	68.6	75.1	82.1
Agriculture	2.7	2.4	1.5	0.7	−0.6
Extreme weather	33.5	30.1	22.7	16.3	9.5
Species loss	0.9	0.8	0.6	0.4	0.2
Health	5.2	5.6	6.7	7.6	8.7
Percentage by region					
OECD – America	0.3	0.3	0.3	0.3	0.3
OECD – Europe	0.5	0.5	0.5	0.5	0.4
OECD – Pacific	0.1	0.1	0.1	0.1	0.1
EE and FSU	−0.1	−0.2	−0.2	−0.2	−0.2
Middle East	6.9	6.9	6.6	6.2	5.5
C. and S. America	12.3	12.7	13.6	14.5	15.8
Developing Asia	48.4	48.1	47.9	48.5	50.6
Africa	31.7	31.7	31.3	30.2	27.5
Total in $bn. 1990 prices	519,500	248,800	74,400	31,800	10,100

Source: Eyre *et al.* (1997).

Table 11.2, which is based on the state of the research in 1997, gives the estimates of climate change on a business as usual assumption – i.e. that emissions continue to increase and no action is taken. In the event that emissions are significantly reduced these damages will fall, although there is enough change in the climate already built into the world's climate system to ensure a major impact along the lines indicated in that table. As we noted above these 'point' estimates can only be viewed as indicative, giving an idea, more or less of the order of magnitude of the damages.

As far as the developing/developed countries dimension of the problem is concerned, the most striking thing to note is how much greater damages are in the developing world. Over 90 per cent arise in the developing parts of Asia, Africa and Central and South America, with South and South East Asia being the most impacted. Indeed, the impacts on the rich regions in money terms is relatively very small – of the order of 0.1 to 0.5 per cent of the total. Most damages arise from sea level rise, followed by extreme weather and disease. Developing countries suffer most from all of these, partly because the physical impacts are greatest in their regions, and partly because of the large populations that are affected (especially in Asia).

The valuation of climate change impacts is highly controversial because it necessitates valuing impacts such as loss of life. In the environmental economics literature such values are derived based on individual willingness to pay (WTP) to reduce the risk of death. So if a group of 10,000 people has an average WTP of $100 to reduce the risk of death by one in 10,000, the group has a whole will pay one million dollars, for which they will gain a (statistical) reduction of one death in their group. Hence we say that the group has a *value of statistical life* (VSL) of one million dollars.

On this basis, it is obvious that the VSL for people in developing countries will be less than in developed countries. Estimates of damages from climate change which were based on this were roundly and angrily criticized by representatives from developing countries, who took exception to the view that people's lives were worth less if they came from India or China as opposed to the UK or USA (see again the discussion in Chapter 5). In Table 11.2 the valuations are not based on such distinctions. Instead, what has been done is to take an average value of life for all people, irrespective of their origins. The hypothetical group of 10,000 would then be made up of a representative sample of US, UK, Indian, Chinese and other nationalities and the WTP would be their average. This avoids the problem of making ethical judgments that people find offensive. Something like this is done at the national level as well – no road programme, for example, would take a different VSL for poor areas as opposed to rich areas when designing its safety features.

The state of valuation work relating to climate change is still very much in flux. New research suggests that the share of damages in developed countries may be higher (even without taking higher mortality and morbidity costs).[7] In any event the physical damages to developing countries remain significant, and certainly in physical units they are more important. As an example the most recent estimates from Tol and Heinzow (2002) estimate the number of life years of life disabled as a result of a one degree increase in global mean temperature is *negative* for the OECD, EE and FSU (i.e. people benefit in health terms from global warming), but amount to 207,000 for the Middle East, 229,000 for Latin America, 2,923,000 for developing Asia and 596,000 for Africa. These stark differences are important in understanding how climate change policies are determined, which we discuss below.

How are climate change policies determined?

Getting international agreement

So far we have seen that population rules for allocating emissions rights would favour developing countries – they have larger populations and lower *per capita* emissions. We have also seen that these countries are the ones who will suffer most if climate change is not avoided. So, what should be their position in any negotiations on carbon emissions and what kind of solution can we arrive at?

The first thing to note is that for any solution international agreement will be required, which means that countries will only participate if it is in their national interest to do so. That is why a solution in which rights were allocated according to population would not work. It would impose too high a cost on the developed countries, for whom the benefits are really very small, as given in Table 11.2. These very low values of damages, however, give a misleading impression if they are taken at face value. There is *huge uncertainty* surrounding the estimates, which means that mitigation action may well be justified on risk aversion grounds. For this reason all nations have some interest in reducing the damages, although it probably remains the case that it is more in the interests of developing countries to do so.

For the developing countries, the choices are also not that attractive. Even if they accept that they will suffer greatly from climate change, they are reluctant to commit to reducing their emissions because, they say, they need them to develop and reach the living standards of the presently developed countries. In the short run, this is probably correct. Table 11.1 shows that on a business as usual scenario emissions would grow at 3 to 4 per cent *per annum* in the developing world compared to around 1 per cent in the developed world. So a cap on their emissions, for example, would imply a greater sacrifice in terms of growth than in the developed countries.

In the long run, both developing and developed countries will have to take measures to address climate change. This can be seen most simply from the following data. At present developed countries emit around 4.3 tonnes of carbon per person, the countries of EE and FSU emit 2.2 tonnes per person and the developing countries emit half of that (1.1). If climate is eventually to be stabilized (and no one seriously doubts that it must) the target emissions *per capita* in 2100 must be around 0.3 tonnes per person, which is less than one-third of what developing countries are emitting today. This can only be achieved with a 'renewables transition' – i.e. a whole-scale shift out of using fossil fuels and a shift to renewable sources of energy. Fortunately this does not have to be achieved until about 2100, which means that the twenty-first century will have to make great changes to the way by which energy is obtained. A number of commentators believe that this is the real solution for everybody, and that investing in research and development for renewable energy will eventually result in the changes that are needed. Not everyone, however, is agreed that this is all we need. Unless emissions are reduced starting now, it is argued, the amount of damage over the next hundred years will be unacceptable and the price too high, especially in terms of human lives in developing countries.

On the face of it, then, the situation does not look so encouraging for an agreement based on mutual self interest. The developed world has little to lose from climate change and has the greatest emissions of carbon emissions, while the developing world has more to lose, but has relatively lower emissions and, it believes, a higher cost in curtailing future increases. Given this picture it is surprising that some agreement has emerged in the form of the Kyoto Protocol, albeit one that still has to be ratified by enough countries to come into force.

The reason some agreement has been reached suggests that all parties take a long-term view of 'self interest'. Some economists have suggested that an agreement can only be successful if no coalition of countries within it would find themselves better off by leaving and setting up outside the coalition.[8] It is hard to see how the Kyoto Protocol could possibly satisfy that definition at least if the term 'better off' is interpreted in a narrow sense. Given the information available, developed countries' narrow self interest would be not to sign an agreement limiting emissions, yet many have signed. That they have done so suggests they see the issue in wider terms. There is a fear that a world with climate change seriously hurting a large part of the population would not be viable or sustainable and would destroy the international order in a fundamental way. This cannot be in the interests of the developed countries as a group. An interesting paper, which argues along the same lines, is Jeppesen and Anderson (1998). It shows that introducing the ideas of commitment to environmental issues, and/or fairness, can greatly change the conclusions from the Barrett model, and can explain why International Environmental Agreements *do* get agreed on. Another reason one could mention here is issue linkage or meta-games: e.g. a developed country suffering a net loss under a climate agreement might still sign if this was necessary to realize net gains in some other negotiation. Getting countries to sign up with the Montreal Protocol is an example here.

This point, as made by Botteon and Carraro (1998), relates to the issue of public goods and the 'free rider', but goes beyond the claim made by economists that parties will try and get the public good for nothing. The argument here is that even if the net benefits of acting collectively are negative to one country it may still join if it believes this to be in its wider strategic interest. Free rider behaviour is less of an issue in international negotiations of this kind. Most countries understand the fallacy of 'Cournot-Nash' assumption – that if you do free ride others will continue to provide the collective action. Rather they take the 'Kantian' position, that if you do something which appears to be in your self interest others in a similar position would also do the same, in which case it would not be in anyone's interest.

In any event, some agreement has been hammered out for climate change. Broadly the key terms under the Kyoto Agreement are (see Chapter 9 for more detail):

- Industrialized countries agreed to reduce emissions by, on average, 5.2 per cent with respect to their 1990 levels by 2008–2012 (these 39 countries are referred to as Annex I). There are, however, differences between countries as to the level of reduction.
- No reduction commitment by non-Annex I countries (i.e. mostly developing countries).

At the same time, the Kyoto Protocol has obtained agreement on the importance of a number of 'flexibility mechanisms', which allow the 'reductions' in required emissions for the industrialized countries to be undertaken outside their borders. The three mechanisms are:

- Emissions trading between Annex I countries.
- Permission to transfer/acquire emissions from projects between Annex I countries (Joint Implementation or JI) (Article 6).
- Permission for Annex I countries to acquire emissions from non-Annex I (Clean Development Mechanism or CDM) (Article 17).

In the next section we will see why these flexibility mechanisms are in everyone's interest, a point taken up in Chapter 10.

Benefits from the use of the flexibility mechanisms

Flexibility and cost saving

The case for the use of flexibility instruments is very simple: they allow a given target reduction to be achieved at a lower cost than would be the case without them. This can be seen clearly in Figure 11.1, where the agreed annual reduction in carbon emissions is OA and the marginal cost curve for reduction is OR for the developing country and AP for the developed country. It is easy to see that the lowest cost for achieving this requires that reductions of OB be made in the developing country and AB in the developed country, irrespective of who is obliged to pay for the reductions. For example it may be the case that the developed country has the obligation and the developing country has no obligation (as in the Kyoto Protocol). If there were no flexibility, the whole reduction would have to be made in the developed country at a cost given by the area OPA, which exceeds the least cost by OEP. Indeed any restriction where the cuts have to be made (other than to say fortuitously that the developing country has to make a reduction of OB and the developed country AB) will result in a total cost higher than with flexibility.

Developing this example further, how could the least cost solution be attained? One way would be to allow trading in the rights to the reductions. The developed country, which has to make a reduction of OA would then go to the developing country and ask to purchase reductions equal to OB. For this it would

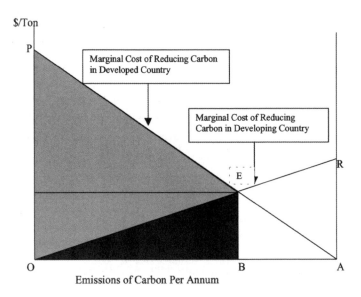

Figure 11.1 Costs of reducing carbon with flexibility.

make a payment. The minimum it would have to pay is the cost of making the reductions – the area OEB. The maximum it would pay is the cost of making the reductions at home – the area OPEB, or the sum of the light and dark shaded areas. The actual 'price' of carbon would then emerge somewhere in between those areas, each divided by OB.

It is also clear from the analysis that the developing country gains from the deal. Without it, no reductions would be made in that country and it would receive no payment. The former has what are known as ancillary benefits. Reducing carbon mostly involves reducing the use of fossil fuels, which are known to generate local pollutants that have detrimental health effects. In any event the payment is a windfall – it entails no cost to the developing country.[9]

The simplest way to achieve this would be to allow trading in emissions, the first of the flexibility mechanisms. One would have to ensure that the reductions actually did take place (the issue of verification) and that the reductions were genuinely in addition to any that would have happened anyway (the issue of the 'baseline' which determines the 'without project' emissions). Neither of these is easy, and indeed as we will see below it is not possible to have emissions trading

Table 11.3 Energy modelling forum main results: marginal abatement costs ($1990/tC)

Model	No trading				Only Annex I trading	Global trading
	USA	OECD-E	Japan	CANZ		
ABARE-GTEM	322	665	645	425	106	23
AIM	153	198	234	147	65	38
CETA	168				46	26
FUND					14	10
G-CUBED	76	227	97	157	53	20
GRAPE		204	304		70	44
MERGE3	264	218	500	250	135	86
MIT-EPPA	193	276	501	247	76	
MS-MRT	236	179	402	213	77	27
OXFORD	410	966	1,074		224	123
RICE	132	159	251	145	62	18
SGM	188	407	357	201	84	22
WORLDSCAN	85	20	122	46	20	5
ADMINISTRATION	154				43	18
EIA	251				110	57
POLES	136	135	195	131	53	18
Average	198	305	390	218	77	36

Source: IPCC (2001), Chapter 8.

with developing countries under the present Protocol targets. Mechanisms for organizing trading are, however, being worked out. Indeed a market for carbon is emerging and trades are taking place on exchanges in London and Chicago. 'Natsource', a trading firm, recently stated that the price had been as high as $16/tonne for CO_2 at the end of 2002 and there is an active market review available[10] even though the first commitment period is still five years away.

One should note that the gains from flexibility are likely to be substantial and that this is not merely a theoretical point. The Energy Modelling Forum conducted a coordinated modelling effort with nine global economic models that assessed the cost of meeting the Kyoto targets in 2010 given alternative assumptions about the use of flexibility mechanism that allows emission trading between industrialized countries, and with developing countries. Table 11.3 shows the marginal emission reduction costs given different scenarios for emissions trading.

The left part of the table shows the marginal emission reduction costs for USA, OECD-Europe, Japan and Canada/Australia/New Zealand (CANZ) assuming that these countries fulfil their Kyoto targets only by domestic actions. It can here be seen that the models generate an average across all models of around $200 for the US and as much as $400 for Japan. Industrialized countries of Europe and CANZ come out in between. The right part of the table shows that these marginal costs of emission reduction decrease significantly when flexibility mechanisms are introduced. With only Annex I trading the marginal cost is expected to reduce to around $77, while inclusion of developing countries reduces it further to around $36 (i.e. half). The cost savings from allowing trading are therefore great and as there is no environmental impact or other similar disadvantage associated with it, the case is very strong, at least for trade among Annex I countries. There is a problem, however, with developing countries, which we consider below.

The Clean Development Mechanism

Within the present arrangements it is not possible for developing countries to participate in emissions trading. As they have no target they will never be buyers of emissions rights and they cannot be suppliers as they do not have a target against which the supplies can be accounted. Between developed countries with targets, emissions trading has as a central feature the concept of an 'allowable emission unit'. Every traded emission unit has to be certified as coming from a target that has been imposed as part of the Protocol.

In view of this, and in view of the great savings demonstrated in Table 11.3 by allowing emissions reductions to take place in non-Annex I countries, the Protocol has developed the Clean Development Mechanism (CDM), which allows certified emissions reductions (CER) to be made in developing countries and to be credited against developed country targets under certain conditions. These are:

- The countries must be Parties to the Protocol.
- Their participation in the CDM must be voluntary.
- The country must establish a national CDM Authority to oversee the process.
- The projects should assist in creating sustainable development in the country in which they are implemented.

Examples of eligible projects are:

- End-use energy efficiency improvements.
- Renewable energy.
- Fuel switching.
- Agricultural reductions of methane and Nitrous Oxide emissions.
- Projects where carbon is stored or sequestered (e.g. by planting forests).

The rationale is that CDM should do what trading would do if it were possible to permit global trading. In practice it does not work out quite like that for the following reasons:

1   Emissions trading is more market efficient, as the commodity is well defined, prices are quoted openly and intermediaries are present to ensure arbitrage: i.e. that different markets and transaction options are informationally efficient. With CDM there is not the same degree of market efficiency. Each project is judged as a package with complex characteristics that could be unique.
2   There is a more direct involvement of the government through the National CDM Authority in deciding which projects are approved and which ones are not.

Both these factors make the CDM process more complex, costly and risky for the investor. A number of measures are being taken to reduce the impacts of these factors. National CDM authorities are becoming pro-active in identifying projects that could be of potential interest to investors, as are institutions such as the World Bank, Asian Development Bank, etc. The World Bank, for example, has a web site (www.worldbank.org/nss) on which detailed information for a range of projects are posted for 30 countries. The Asian Development Bank and UNEP have conducted studies documenting the amount of reductions possible, the cost per tonne from a range of projects, and other salient features of the options.

The Carbon Funds and CDM

Another important player in implementing the CDM is the Carbon Fund, set up by the World Bank. This is a financial instrument to which developing countries can offer carbon reductions projects. If agreed and approved, the projects are financed from the fund and the pool of reductions in carbon emissions credited to the investors in the fund. A schema of the transactions is shown in Figure 11.2. The fund was launched in 1999 with subscription of $145 million (fully paid) with 23 shareholders, mostly large energy companies. By 2001 it had built up a pipeline of over 45 projects with a total value of more than twice the capitalization. So far, the bank has participated in 26 projects with emission reduction purchases averaging $3 to $4 per tonne. Projects include a wind farm in Costa Rica, a hydroelectric project in Chile and reforestation of worn-out farmland in Romania. The fund also disseminates information on carbon trading through its website (http://prototypecarbonfund.org). The same website is also a very good source of information about the potential projects as virtually everything related to the project is accessible (excepting some confidential pricing information).

Essentially what the fund does is to act as an intermediary between investors in carbon credits and suppliers of credits. Investors also benefit from the risk reduction, which would exist if they invested in individual projects (which may fail for a variety of reasons). It also offers a verification and certification service, which is critical for projects in which the reductions will take place over a long period (ten years or more).

In practice the Carbon Fund has supported projects in which carbon reduction is only a part of the story. Examples of projects are rehabilitation of district

Figure 11.2 The prototype Carbon Fund.

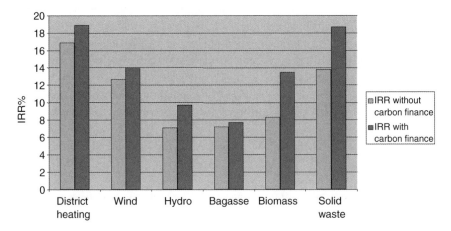

Figure 11.3 Impact of carbon finance on internal rate of return (IRR) for a sample of renewable efficiency projects.

Source: PCF.

heating, investment in wind farms, mini-hydro stations, getting energy from waste, bagasse,[11] etc. These projects would be difficult to finance in developing countries without some carbon finance because their rate of return is not high enough, given the risk and the fact that capital is very scarce in such countries. By selling the carbon credits, however, this return can be raised, as we see in Figure 11.3. Raising the rate of return by 2 to 5 per cent means that the project becomes viable.

The Carbon Fund is an innovative tool in finance and has had some teething problems but has shown that an instrument of this kind can contribute to implementing CDM projects. In fact, since this fund is fully subscribed, the Bank has now opened two new funds – the Biocarbon Fund and the Community Development Fund, which provide finance for projects that reduce carbon in developing countries while generating local benefits in terms of employment and poverty alleviation. The Community Development Carbon Fund will provide carbon finance to small-scale projects in poorer rural areas, while the BioCarbon Fund is a prototype fund to demonstrate projects that sequester or retain carbon in forest and agro-ecosystems and countries in transition. It will aim to deliver cost-effective emission reductions, while promoting biodiversity conservation and sustainable development. Both funds have a target size of $100 million.

CDM and sustainable development

The other issue with CDM projects is that they should contribute to 'sustainable development' (SD) in the countries in which they are implemented. This is a tall order as there is no clear set of indicators by which we can measure the achievement of this goal and opinions differ a lot as to what constitutes sustainable development. Work on the relationship between CDM and sustainability has been undertaken by Markandya and Halsnaes (2002) among others. It is not appropriate to discuss the concept of SD in any depth in this book (it needs a book on its own), but it is possible to provide an indication of what issues would need to be addressed in a CDM project if it is to contribute to sustainable development.[12]

The main concerns that CDM projects can impact on, and that have SD implications are:

- Improvements in the ambient environment by reducing air pollutants.
- Increasing incomes, reducing poverty and providing sustainable livelihoods for the people in the communities where projects are undertaken.
- Increasing the supply of clean energy to people who currently rely on fuel wood and crop residues, dung etc., which have health effects as well as causing deforestation in some cases (so health is improved and deforestation reduced).
- Providing training and capacity building in environmental management through project implementation in developing countries – an investment in human capital.
- Using the project as an engine of development and growth.

When assessing projects all these factors need to be considered. In itself this is not a problem; it is similar to the requirement for an environmental assessment and/or social cost benefit analysis for all public projects, which is standard practice in many industrialized countries. Indeed many countries now require a strategic assessment that addresses these sustainability issues directly.[13]

The key concerns that need to be addressed here are how to; evaluate projects with outcomes that do not convert into money units and; ensure that the process of evaluation does not become too complex and raise the 'cost of doing CDM business' too high.

Evaluating the projects with respect to environmental, social and indirect development benefits is not easy. The information that needs to be processed is complex but needs to be presented in a simple fashion to policy makers. In some cases the use of multi-criteria techniques may work and can be used. Typical indicators on which data will have to collected are:

- Energy intensity in sector where investment is made;
- Energy use per unit of output in project;
- Energy consumption per capita in affected group;

- Income inequality and poverty in affected groups;
- Emissions of air pollutants;
- Emissions of GHGs;
- Generation of solid waste;
- Intensity of use of forest resources as fuelwood;
- Rate of deforestation avoided;
- Mortality and morbidity rates in affected area;
- Unemployment rates in affected area.

The data would have to show the changes in these indicators as a result of the project, and for the whole period of the project. In general CDM projects have positive impacts on most indicators, but negative impacts could also arise, as for example when an electricity generator shifts to imported gas from domestic coal, reducing carbon emissions, but also increasing local unemployment and generating a decline in local economic activity.

The second issue of keeping the process simple and manageable is also important. Intermediaries such as the World Bank and other donors have an important role to assist national authorities undertaking the assessments. The requirements of the National CDM authority should take account of the capacity and resources of some of the project proposers. The idea is to make it possible for poor communities, for example, to be able to propose a project and get some assistance in preparing it in accordance with the requirements of the Mechanism.

Conclusions

In this chapter we have looked at climate change from the perspective of developing countries. Such countries have been, and remain, smaller emitters of carbon than the industrialized countries, yet they are the ones who will suffer more when the consequences of climate change are realized. The issue of which countries *should* have the obligation to make the reductions is not one that can be resolved in economic terms; all economics can do is to show the implications of different allocation rules, and that is what we have done.

Economics can also contribute to understanding what kinds of agreements are likely to be reached for a global public good such as carbon. Here the conventional 'free rider' model is not the best one to understand the degree of commitment that has been seen by the Parties. Rather, we need to understand national positions partly in terms of narrow self interest, and partly in terms of a wider sense of national interest, in which global sustainability has played some part. The Kyoto Protocol has to be seen in that light.

Economics can also contribute to understanding how to achieve the agreed reductions at least cost. Here the role of flexibility is critical, with emissions trading being the most effective as far as cost reductions are concerned. The potential gains from allowing trading between countries who have target reductions (the Annex I countries) are substantial. These gains would be even greater if developing countries could be allowed in the trading system, but that is not possible given that these countries do not have a target. Instead the CDM has been set up to allow developed countries to buy reductions from developing countries. This mechanism offers some important opportunities but it is still in its early stages of implementation. Some of the issues of implementation include those of verification and certification, as well as the riskiness of implementing projects in developing countries. Instruments to reduce these include 'securitizing' reductions through financial instruments such as the World Bank's Carbon Fund. Finally there is a need to keep the objective of CDM projects contribution to sustainable development in mind. Key indicators that need to be monitored for this are presented. At the same time the analysis of projects from this perspective has to be kept simple enough not to impose too high a cost on potential investors and some assistance with the assessment will need to be provided to small and medium sized potential suppliers of CDM projects.

Notes

1 See, for example, Agarwal and Narain (1991).
2 See IPPC (2001), Chapter 1, and Agarwal and Narain (1991).
3 For a discussion of the key issues relating to climate change and its socio-economic impacts see IPCC (2001).
4 These transfers are very large. To put them in perspective, annual official aid transfers to developing countries in 2001 were $52 billion and private flows about $3 billion (World Development Indicators 2003). There is also the issue of how the transfers would be made which is discussed later in this chapter.
5 It has even been argued that a population-based allocation provides an incentive to increase the birth rate and that it unduly favours countries that have not been successful in their population control policies.
6 One objection to grandfathering is that it favours those countries that have been profligate in their emissions. Countries like France and Japan, who have relatively carbon efficient economies complain that options for further reductions are limited and the rule discriminates against them.
7 See, for example, Tol *et al.* (2000).
8 See, for example, Barrett (1993). This definition is more than the classical 'free rider' although it is related to it. It includes the notion that the 'in group' may impose sanctions on free riders and the coalition that leaves has to be 'sustaining' – i.e. everyone in it must calculate that they are better off as part of that group than as a 'free rider' on their own. See Markandya and Mason (2001) for further discussion on this.
9 Of course any proper estimate of the costs of abatement in the developing country (the line OR) would have taken account of such ancillary or co-benefits. Indeed in

some cases the abatement cost could be negative, implying that the ancillary benefits exceed the costs of any investments to reduce the carbon emissions such as shifting to renewable sources or shifting to more efficient equipment. Some developing countries also argue that selling these carbon reductions now may mean that in the future, when targets are imposed on all countries, it will have to undertake reductions in emissions at a much higher cost. The analogy made is that of selling New York for a string of beans in the seventeenth century when it would have been better to hold on. In the case of carbon its relevance is debatable. Costs of future reductions will rise as the cheaper ones are undertaken first, but will fall as new lower cost renewable sources are divided. In any event the choice is that of the developing country – it can add a premium for certain reductions.

10 See, for example, www.pointcarbon.com.

11 Bagasse is the waste from sugar cane.

12 Some commentators argue that by adding a sustainability dimension to CDM, the Protocol will make it more difficult to implement carbon reduction projects in developing countries. This is correct, but it fails to recognize that projects with major social and environmental implications should be subject to scrutiny and disclosure on these issues, something that most countries are now implementing in other areas as well. The key is to keep it relatively simple and manageable.

13 For examples of an assessment of CDM projects in this framework see Markandya and Halsnaes (2002).

Bibliography

Agarwal, A. and Narain, S. (1991) *Global Warming in an Unequal World: A Case of Ecocolonialism*, New Delhi: Centre for Science and Environment.

Barrett, S. (1993) 'Self enforcing international environmental agreements', *Oxford Economic Papers* 46:878–894.

Botteon, M. and Carraro, C. (1998) 'Strategies for environmental negotiations: issue linkage with heterogenous countries', in N. Hanley and H. Folmer (eds) *Game Theory and the Environment*, Cheltenham: Edward Elgar.

Eyre, N., Dowring, T., Hoekstra, R. and Rennings, K. (1997) *Global Warming Damages*. Final Report prepared under contract JOS3-CT95-0002, ExternE Programme of the European Commission, Brussels, 1997.

IPCC (2001) *Climate Change 2001: Mitigation*, Cambridge: Cambridge University Press.

Jeppesen, T. and Andersen, P. (1998) 'Commitment and fairness in environmental games', in N. Hanley and H. Folmer (eds) *Game Theory and the Environment*, Cheltenham: Edward Elgar.

Markandya, A. and Halsnaes, K. (eds) (2002) *Climate Change and Sustainable Development*, London: Earthscan.

Markandya, A. and Mason, P. (2001) 'The essentials for allocating global environmental goods', in *The Economics of International Environmental Problems*, Kiel: Institute für Weltwirtschaft an der Universität.

Tol, R.S.J. and Heinzow, T. (2002) 'Estimates of the external and sustainability costs of climate change', in *GREENSENSE: Applied Intergrated Impact Assessment for the EU*, Report to the Fifth Framework Programmme of the European Commission, Brussels.

Tol, R.S.J., Frankhauser, S., Richels, R.G. and Smith, J.B. (2000) 'How much damage will climate change do?', *World Economics* 1:179–206.

Weyant, J. (1998) 'The costs of carbon emissions reductions', in W. Nordhaus (ed.) *Economics and Policy Issues in Climate Change*, Washington, D.C.: Resources for the Future.

World Development Indicators (2003) Washington, D.C.: World Bank.

12 The transition to renewable energy

Anthony D. Owen

Introduction

The twentieth century witnessed mounting public concern over the impacts of large-scale energy use on the environment, although many of these concerns had been evident in more localized areas for some hundreds of years. Anecdotal evidence indicates that air pollution had been a concern in England as early as 1352 when a ban was introduced on coal burning in London.

Historically, regulatory instruments have been the basic mechanism for enacting environmental policy throughout the industrialized world. Environmental quality has been seen as a public good that the state must secure by preventing private agents from damaging it. Direct regulation involves the imposition of standards (or even bans) regarding emissions and discharges, product or process characteristics, etc., through licensing and monitoring. Legislation usually forms the basis for this form of control, and compliance is generally mandatory with sanctions for non-compliance.

The proposal to impose taxes on pollution, whilst more recent, is also far from new, having been proposed at the turn of the last century by the famous British economist Professor Arthur Cecil Pigou as a means of reducing London's famous fogs (or smogs). Pigou observed that pollution imposed uncovered costs on third parties that were not included in ordinary market transactions. His proposal was to tax pollution by means of a so-called externality tax[1] in order to internalize within ordinary market transactions the damages caused by pollution.

Contemporary energy policy issues are dominated, directly and indirectly, by major concerns at both local and global levels of environmental degradation arising from combustion of fossil fuels. Even countries with relatively modest fossil fuel requirements, such as the poorer countries of Africa, Asia, and the South Pacific, could experience significant, if not catastrophic, consequences if the world's requirement for energy from fossil fuels does not abate within a relatively short time frame. Consequently, the economics of renewable energy technologies has a core position in energy policy formulation over the foreseeable future.

This chapter commences with a summary of the economics of environmental externalities. An overview of the methodology of life cycle analysis and its application to the energy sector to derive estimates of environmental externalities is then given. The implicit costs of externalities attributable to power generation (from both commercial and potentially commercial technologies) are then compared with the private costs that are generally passed on to the consumer. The analysis is then extended to the transportation sector.

Externalities

Definition

Externalities are defined as benefits or costs generated as an unintended by-product of an economic activity that do not accrue to the parties involved in the activity. Environmental externalities are benefits or costs that manifest themselves through changes in the physical-biological environment.

Pollution emitted by road vehicles and by fossil fuel power plants during power generation is known to result in harm to both people and the environment. In addition upstream and downstream externalities, associated with securing fuel and waste disposal respectively, are generally not included in power or fuel costs. To the extent that the ultimate consumer of these products does not pay these environmental costs, or does not compensate people for harm done to them, they do not face the full cost of the services they purchase (i.e. implicitly their energy use is being subsidized) and thus energy resources will not be allocated efficiently.

Externalities in a competitive market[2]

The impact of a negative externality is illustrated in Figure 12.1, which shows the competitive market for a good whose production generates damaging emissions. The demand curve (D) represents marginal private benefits arising from consumption of the good. It is assumed that the production process gives rise to negative externalities, such that marginal damages increase as emissions rise, resulting in an increasing gap between marginal private costs (MPC) and marginal social costs (MSC) of production. The socially optimal level of output is $0Q_S$ with a corresponding price $0P_S$. At this equilibrium position, the corresponding optimal level of environmental damage is $0E_S$. However, if the externalities of production are not 'internalized', equilibrium price and output would be at $0P_P$ and $0Q_P$, respectively. Thus the lower price has encouraged increased demand and, as a result, increased levels of environmental damage amounting to $E_S E_P$ above the optimal level.

The origin of an externality is typically the absence of fully defined and

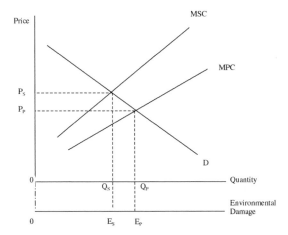

Figure 12.1 Impact of an externality.

enforceable property rights. However, rectifying this situation through establishing such rights is not always easy to do. In such circumstances, at least in theory, the appropriate corrective device is a Pigouvian tax equal to marginal social damage levied on the generator of the externality (with no supplementary incentives for victims).

Externality adders

In the context of energy markets, an 'externality adder' is simply the unit externality cost added to the standard resource cost of energy to reflect the social cost of its use. For power generation, the externality adder would generally be specified in terms of milli-dollars (1,000th of a dollar) per kWh (m$/kWh) or the equivalent in cents per kWh. For the transport sector the corresponding units would be m$/vkm (i.e. 1,000th of a dollar per vehicle kilometre) for passenger vehicles and m$/tkm (i.e. 1,000th of a dollar per tonne kilometre) for goods vehicles, or the equivalent in cents.

Pearce (2002) lists five uses for externality adders:

1   For public or quasi-public ownership of sources of electric power generation, the full social cost of alternative technologies could be used to plan future capacity with preference being given to that with the lowest social cost. Where electric power generation is privately owned, then regulators could use the full social cost to influence new investment, perhaps through an effective environmental tax.
2   Environmental adders can be used to estimate the appropriate level of environmental taxes. Although estimates of environmental adders have been

derived for a number of applications, examples of their actual implementation are few.

3   Environmental adders could be used to adjust national accounts data to reflect depreciation of natural resources and damage to the environment arising from economic activity, yielding so-called 'green' national accounts.

4   Environmental adders could be used for 'awareness raising'; i.e. to inform the public of the degree to which alternative energy sources have externalities that give rise to an economically inefficient allocation of resources.

5   Environmental adders might assist in determining environmental policy priorities.

The task of estimating the value of an externality adder involves a substantial commitment of resources and expertise in order to ensure credible information for policy purposes. In the context of the energy sector, a life cycle approach must be adopted in order to identify and quantify environmental adders associated with the provision of energy services. The approach also provides a conceptual framework for a detailed and comprehensive comparative evaluation of energy supply options (based upon both conventional and renewable sources). The methodology employed is the subject of the next section.

Life cycle analysis

When comparing the environmental footprints of alternative energy technologies, it is important that the power generation or combustion stage of the technology not be isolated from other stages of the 'cycle'. For example, fuel cells emit virtually no greenhouse gases (GHGs) in their operation. However production of their 'fuel' (hydrogen) from fossil fuels may involve increases in GHG emissions in excess of those that would arise from using current commercial fossil fuel technologies to meet the same level of energy requirements. To avoid such distortions, the concept of life cycle analysis has been developed.

Life cycle analysis (LCA) is based upon a comprehensive accounting of all energy and material flows, from 'cradle to grave', associated with a system or process. The approach has typically been used to compare the environmental impacts associated with different products that perform similar functions, such as plastic and glass bottles. In the context of an energy product, process, or service, a LCA would analyse the site-specific environmental impact of fuel extraction, transportation and preparation of fuels and other inputs, plant construction, plant operation/fuel combustion, waste disposal, and plant decommissioning. Thus it encompasses all segments including upstream and downstream processes and consequently permits an overall comparison (in a cost benefit analysis framework) of short- and long-term environmental implications of alternative energy technologies. Central to this assessment is the valuation of environmental externalities of current and prospective fuel and energy technology cycles. It should be noted, however, that only material and energy flows are assessed in a LCA, thus ignoring some impacts (such as supply security) and technology reliability and flexibility.

For the purpose of this chapter, life cycle analysis will involve the following methodological steps:[3]

• Definition of the product cycle's geographical, temporal and technical boundaries;
• Identification of the environmental emissions and their resulting physical impacts on receptor areas;
• Quantifying these physical impacts in terms of monetary values.

Traditionally, LCA has omitted the third of these steps and the final analysis has therefore been expressed in terms of just the biophysical impacts that can be quantified. The extension to include costing of these impacts is generally known as the 'impact pathway' methodology. Essentially, however, it can be considered as a specific application of LCA. This methodology formed the theoretical basis for the European Commission's ExternE study,[4] which was the first comprehensive attempt to use a consistent 'bottom-up' methodology to evaluate the external costs associated with a range of different fuel cycles. The main steps are illustrated in Figure 12.2.

Definition of the product cycle's boundaries

The first task is to identify, both in terms of activities and geographic locations, the various stages of the fuel/technology cycle. Each energy form is viewed as a product, and impacts are included for the actual pathway. The precise list of stages is clearly dependent on the fuel chain in question, but would include activities linked to the manufacture of materials for plant construction, demolition and site restoration as well as power generation. Other stages may also be appropriate, such as exploration, extraction, processing and transport of fuel, and the generation of wastes and by-products, and their treatment prior to disposal.

The extent to which the boundaries must encompass indirect impacts is determined by the order of magnitude of their resulting emissions. For example, in theory externalities associated with the construction of plants to make the steel that is used to make coal wagons to transport the coal to the power plants should be included in the power plant's LCA. In reality, however, such externalities are likely to have a relatively insignificant impact. In addition, externalities that pass into another product's boundaries must be excised from the analysis to avoid double counting. For example, the ultimate environmental externality of by-products of power generation that are fully utilized in another industry fall within the latter's life cycle as soon as product transfer occurs.

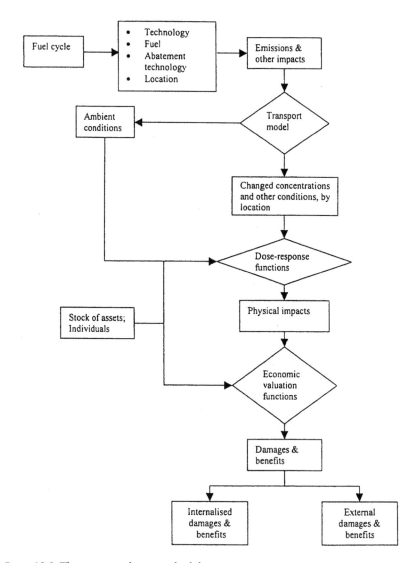

Figure 12.2 The impact pathway methodology.

Source: adapted from Sundqvist and Söderholm (2002).

For each fuel/technology cycle, boundaries are likely to vary, particularly in relation to upstream impacts, and consequently derivation of a 'generic' LCA for each technology may be unrealistic. For example, identical coal-fired power plants located in different areas of the same country may use coal from different sources (perhaps one uses imported coal, the other domestic), there may be variations in fuel quality or variations in atmospheric dispersion, or there may be differences in the sensitivity of the human and natural environment upon which fuel chain burdens impact. When different generations of coal-fired plants enter the analysis, use of a generic approach may lead to a further drop in precision. However, the increased precision achieved by deriving a site specific LCA for all projects may well be offset by the cost of such exercises. In reality, indicative or generic estimates may be unavoidable.

The system boundary will also have spatial and temporal dimensions. These will have major implications for the analysis of the effects of air pollution in particular. For many air pollutants, such as ozone and sulphur dioxide (SO_2), the analysis may need to focus on a regional, rather than local, scale in order to determine their total impact. For emissions of GHGs, the appropriate range is clearly global. Impacts must also be assessed over the full term of their effect, a period that may extend over many decades or even centuries in the case of emissions of GHGs and long-term storage of some nuclear waste products. This introduces a significant degree of uncertainty into the analysis, as it requires projections to be made of a number of variables that will form the basis of future society. Among these would be the size of the global population, the level of economic growth, technological developments, the sustainability of fossil fuel consumption, and the sensitivity of the climate system to anthropogenic emissions.

A generic 'chain' for coal-fired electricity generation is illustrated in Figure 12.3. Even from this simplified illustration, however, it is clear that the data requirements to undertake a LCA are formidable, particularly where sources in other countries have to be accessed. Data limitations and cost constraints will obviously combine to prevent a complete enumeration of the emissions of a given process. It is essential, therefore, that when this situation is reached the proportion left unaccounted should be clearly specified.

Identification of the environmental emissions and their resulting physical impacts on receptor areas

Environmental emissions (or burdens) from the energy sector that are capable of causing some form of impact can be identified in the following broad categories:

*   solid wastes;
*   liquid wastes;
*   gaseous and particulate air pollutants;
*   risk of accidents;
*   occupational exposure to hazardous substances;
*   noise;
*   others (e.g. exposure to electro-magnetic fields, emissions of heat).

All potential physical impacts of the identified burdens for all fuel chains must be

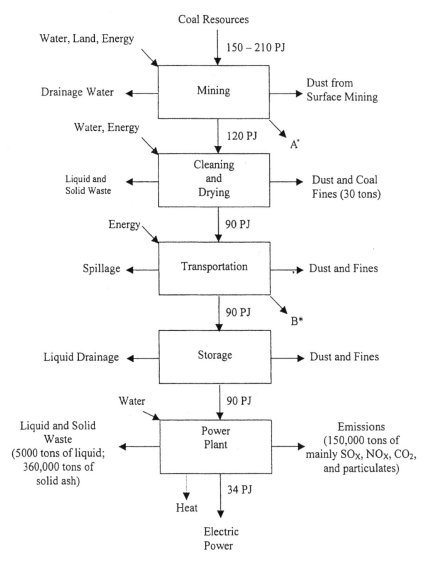

Figure 12.3 Coal-based electricity chain.

Source: Sorensen (2000).

Note
* These impacts pass into another product's boundaries.

analysed comprehensively. However, it is possible to produce several hundred burdens and impacts for the various fuel chains. Thus, for practical reasons, the analysis must concentrate on those that are considered to be non-negligible in terms of their externalities.

Some impact pathways may be relatively simple. For example, the construction of a wind farm will affect the appearance of a landscape, leading to a change in visual amenity. In other cases, the link between the burden, physical impact, and monetary cost is far more complex. In reality, much of the required data is either incomplete or simply does not exist. Thus any analysis is, of necessity, only partial.

Comparisons of alternative power generation technologies utilizing LCA are generally standardized as emissions per unit of energy produced (kWh) in order to allow for different plant sizes and capacity factors. However, the data used to quantify burdens is, to varying degrees, technology specific. For example, emissions of carbon dioxide (CO_2) in power generation depend only on the efficiency of the equipment and the carbon/hydrogen ratio of the fuel; uncertainty is negligible. Whereas emissions of SO_2 can vary by an order of magnitude depending on the grade of oil or coal and the extent to which emission abatement technologies have been adopted. As a general rule, one should adopt the most efficient technology currently in use in the country of implementation in order to compare environmental pollutants across different technologies.

Quantifying the physical impacts of emissions of pollutants requires an environmental assessment that ranges over a vast area, extending over the entire planet in the case of CO_2 emissions. Thus the dispersion of pollutants emitted from fuel chains must be modelled and their resulting impact on the environment measured by means of a dose-response function. Generally, for damages to humans, such functions are derived from studies that are epidemiological, assessing the effects of exposure to pollutants in real life situations.

The reliability of electricity production

The reliability of electricity production is also an important factor in ensuring compatibility of comparisons of alternative technologies.[5] With the exception of some biomass 'fuels', geothermal, tidal barrage and large scale hydropower, renewable energy supplies are intermittent and, to varying degrees, unpredictable.[6] To the extent that energy systems must be able to cope with these sources of fluctuations in output, additional system costs will be imposed. Circumstances may arise, therefore, where a LCA must be augmented by incorporation of the backup technology in the analysis. Clearly, if fossil fuel power generation provides this backup, the life cycle emissions of renewables must be augmented accordingly.

At very low levels of renewables penetration additional system backup costs would be negligible compared with generation costs, since variability would still be within normal tolerance levels for the system as a whole. Thereafter, higher levels of penetration would involve additional cost, since additional generation or electricity storage capacity would be required to meet peak demand if, for example, wind were unavailable. As a consequence, at a purely financial level, the value of intermittent generation should be less than that of conventional generation by approximately these additional costs.[7]

A potential solution to the problem is hydrogen storage. The excess of renewable electricity generated during off-peak periods could be stored as hydrogen using the process of electrolysis. This energy could then be retrieved, when necessary, by supplying the stored hydrogen to a fuel cell. Capacity would have to be sufficient to cover maximum demand when there was no wind, but any excess hydrogen could be used, for example, in the transport sector.

Quantifying physical damage in terms of monetary values

The many receptors that may be affected by fuel chain activities are valued in a number of different ways. For example, forests are valued not just for the timber that they produce, but also for providing recreational resources, habitats for wildlife, their interaction (both direct and indirect) with climate, the hydrological cycle, protection from soil erosion, etc. All such aspects should be valued in an externality analysis.

Commercial markets exist for a limited number of goods, e.g. crops, timber, buildings, etc., and consequently valuation data are easy to obtain. However, conventional markets do not exist for assessing damage from other impacts, such as human health, ecological systems, and non-timber benefits of forests. Alternative techniques have been developed for valuation of such goods, predominantly hedonic pricing, travel cost methods, and contingent valuation.[8]

The temporal valuation of the cost of emissions also raises the issue of the appropriate rate for discounting over generations.[9]

The costs of electricity generating technologies

Levelized electricity costs

Power plants are most frequently compared on the basis of their levelized electricity cost (LEC), which relates the discounted capital cost of the plant, its annual operating and maintenance costs and fuel prices to the annual production of electricity to yield a value in cents per kWh. The formula for calculating the LEC is simply the ratio of the present value of the plant's lifetime cost stream to the plant's annual energy output, namely:

$$LEC = \frac{\sum_t (I_t + M_t + F_t)(1 + r)^{-t}}{\sum_t E_t (1 + r)^{-t}} \qquad (12.1)$$

where:

I_t is capital expenditure in year t; M_t is operating and maintenance expenditure (including taxes) in year t; F_t is expenditure on fuel in year t; E_t is net electricity generation in year t; r is discount rate and Σ_t is the summation over the period including construction, operation during the economic lifetime, and decommissioning of the plant as applicable.

Renewable energy technologies that are, by their very nature, intermittent would incur fuel costs to the extent that backup capacity was used in order to maintain the desired supply of peaking power to the grid. At the margin, this may not incur additional investment costs. However, extensive use of intermittent renewables would require a capital expenditure and operation and maintenance costs for the backup technology to be pro rated into the LEC to allow for additional costs incurred in meeting peak supply.

Table 12.1 gives (indicative) levelized electricity costs (in Euro-cents/kWh) for electricity generation by the major renewable and non-renewable technologies. Both coal and gas exhibit a clear absolute cost advantage over the bulk of renewable technologies, although electricity generated by 'best performance' wind power has recently approached similar cost levels. Backup generation costs associated with the intermittency of renewables to ensure reliability of supply are not included. Thus on purely financial grounds (inclusive of all forms of subsidy), renewable technologies would, in general, appear to be non-competitive. The cost 'gap' has been narrowed significantly over the past two decades, a process that is expected to continue as reflected in projected cost levels for 2020 (Table 12.1). However, without significant policy actions to encourage enhanced levels of investment in renewable energy research and development, and purchasing incentives designed to deliver economies of scale in production, the gap is unlikely to be closed quickly enough to assist governments to meet their Kyoto Protocol (or other medium-term) commitments on global climate change initiatives in any major way.

The cost data presented in Table 12.1, however, give a misleading indication of the extent of the cost disadvantage of renewables:

- Unlike fossil fuel technologies, the efficiency of renewable technologies is generally very site specific. Thus, it would be expected that photovoltaics in the UK would incur a higher cost per kWh than countries located at lower latitudes. In contrast, coal and (to a lesser extent) gas fired power plants use a fuel that is internationally traded and therefore of similar cost (net of transport charges) throughout the world. Thus, comparisons should be made on the basis of 'optimal conditions' costs, rather than the full range that may incorporate old technologies, demonstration projects, or inappropriate siting decisions.
- Photovoltaics is generally 'delivered' as distributed electricity. Thus its cost should be compared with 'delivered' (i.e. inclusive of transmission and distribution costs) electricity from other sources, both renewable and fossil

Table 12.1 Cost of traditional and renewable energy technologies: current and expected
trends

Energy source	Technology	Current cost of delivered energy (Euro-¢/kWh)	Expected future costs beyond 2020 as technology matures (Euro-¢/kWh)
Coal	Grid supply (generation only)	3–5	Capital costs to
Gas	Combined cycle (generation only)	2–4	decline slightly
Delivered	• Off-peak	2–3	with technical
grid electricity	• Peak	15–25	progress. This
from fossil	• Average	8–10	may be offset by
fuels	Rural electrification	25–80	increases in the (real) price of fossil fuels.
Nuclear		4–6	3–5
Solar	Thermal electricity (annual insolation of 2,500 kWh/m^2)	12–18	4–10
Solar	Grid connected photovoltaics		
	• Annual 1,000 kWh per kW (e.g. UK)	50–80	~8
	• Annual 1,500 kWh per kW (e.g. Southern Europe)	30–50	~5
	• Annual 2,500 kWh per kW (e.g. lower latitude countries)	20–40	~4
Geothermal	• Electricity	2–10	1–8
	• Heat	0.5–5.0	0.5–5.0
Wind	• Onshore	3–5	2–3
	• Offshore	6–10	2–5
Marine	• Tidal barrage (e.g. proposed River Severn Barrage)	12	12
	• Tidal stream	8–15	8–15
	• Wave	8–20	5–7
Biomass	• Electricity	5–15	4–10
	• Heat	1–5	1–5
Biofuels	Ethanol (*cf.* petrol and diesel)	3–9 (1.5–2.2)	2–4 (1.5–2.2)
Hydro	• Large scale	2–8	2–8
	• Small scale	4–10	3–10

Source: adapted from ICCEPT (2002).

fuel. In Table 12.1, cost ranges for delivered electricity are also given.
Outside of rural electrification in developing countries the cost difference
still favours fossil fuel technologies, but the divergence is considerably
smaller than when delivery is ignored.

Figure 12.4 illustrates how electricity-generating costs for five technologies in the EU have declined since 1980 as the level of installed capacity has increased. The figure shows how technologies such as wind, solar photovoltaics, and biomass have had much steeper 'learning curves' than advanced fossil fuel technologies such as natural gas combined cycle (NGCC) and coal, giving the impression that their costs could ultimately be lower per kWh. It should be noted, however, that the axes are expressed in terms of units of exponential growth, thus effectively yielding a dimension-reducing transformation of the cost 'gap'. This transformation makes the historical cost of electricity from coal and gas technologies look relatively static, whereas in reality they are still declining, albeit at a relatively slow rate.[10]

Assessing the externalities of power generation

Environmental externalities of energy production/consumption (whether based upon fossil fuel combustion, nuclear power or renewable technologies) can be divided into two broad (net) cost categories that distinguish emissions of pollutants with local and/or regional impacts from those with global impacts:

- costs of the damage caused to health and the environment by emissions of pollutants other than those associated with climate change; and
- costs resulting from the impact of climate change attributable to emissions of greenhouse gases.

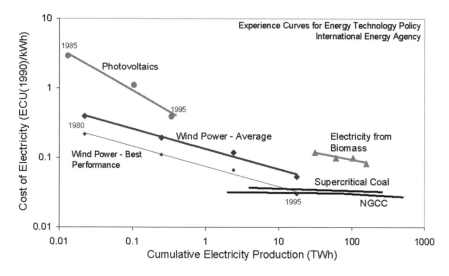

Figure 12.4 Electric technologies in EU 1980–1995.

Source: IEA (2000); © OECD/IEA, 2000.

The distinction is important, since the scale of damages arising from the former is highly dependent upon the geographic location of source and receptor points. The geographic source is irrelevant for damages arising from emissions of greenhouse gases.

Costs borne by governments, including direct subsidies, tax concessions, indirect energy industry subsidies (e.g. the cost of fuel supply security), and support of research and development costs, are not externalities. They do, however, distort markets in a similar way to negative externalities, leading to increased consumption and hence increased environmental degradation.

In order to address effectively these environmental matters, together with energy supply security concerns, radical changes in power generation, automotive engine, and fuel technologies will probably be required. Such changes must offer the potential for achieving negligible emissions of air pollutants and greenhouse gases (GHGs), and must diversify the energy sector away from its present heavy reliance on fossil fuels (and particularly gasoline in the transportation sector). A number of technologies, including those that are solar or hydrogen-based, offer the long-term potential for an energy system that meets these criteria.

However, a number of non-quantifiable policy objectives are also of significance in the planning of future technology options. Currently, the most important of these would appear to be the security of supply of energy resources and their associated transmission and distribution systems.

Pollution damage from emissions other than CO_2

This category refers to costs arising from emissions that cause damage to the environment or to people. These include a wide variety of effects, including damage from acid rain and health damage from oxides of sulphur and nitrogen from fossil fuel power plants. Other costs in this category include such factors as power industry accidents (whether they occur in coal mines, on offshore oil or gas rigs, in nuclear plant, on wind farms, or at hydro plants), visual pollution, and noise.

Among the major external impacts attributed to electricity generation are those caused by atmospheric emissions of pollutants, such as particulates, sulphur dioxide and nitrogen oxide (NO_X), and their impacts on public health, materials and crops. The impact of these atmospheric pollutants on forests, fisheries and unmanaged ecosystems are also important but have not yet been quantified. Emissions of SO_2 and NO_X have long range transboundary effects, which makes calculation of damages an imprecise exercise. Such calculations require measurement to be based upon the unique link between fuel composition, characteristics of the power unit, and features of the receptor areas. Thus estimated damage costs vary widely across countries. For example, for member countries of the

European Union (EU), estimated damage costs arising from power plant emissions of SO_2 range from ECU[11] 1,027–1,486/tonne for Finland[12] to ECU 11,388–12,141/tonne for Belgium (Table 12.2). Comparable US data, for those States where they have been derived, also exhibit substantial variability across States.

Estimated damages per tonne of pollutant for SO_2, NO_X, and particulates vary greatly because of a number of factors. Briefly these are:

- Vintage of combustion technologies and presence of associated emission-reducing devices such as flue gas desulphurization or low NO_X burners;
- population density in receptor areas for airborne pollutants;

Table 12.2 Damages of air pollutants (per tonne of pollutant emitted)

EU Country*	SO_2 (ECU)	NO_X (ECU)	Particulates (ECU)
Austria	9,000	9,000–16,800	16,800
Belgium	11,388–12,141	11,536–12,296	24,536–24,537
Denmark	2,990–4,216	3,280–4,728	3,390–6,666
Finland	1,027–1,486	852–1,388	1,340–2,611
France	7,500–15,300	10,800–18,000	6,100–57,000
Germany	1,800–13,688	10,945–15,100	19,500–23,415
Greece	1,978–7,832	1,240–7,798	2,014–8,278
Ireland	2,800– 5,300	2,750–3,000	2,800–5,415
Italy	5,700–12,000	4,600–13,567	5,700–20,700
The Netherlands	6,025–7,581	5,480–6,085	15,006–16,830
Portugal	4,960–5,424	5,975–6,562	5,565–6,955
Spain	4,219–9,583	4,651–12,056	4,418–20,250
Sweden	2,357–2,810	1,957–2,340	2,732–3,840
United Kingdom	6,027–10,025	5,736–9,612	8,000–22,917

US State*	SO_2 (US$)	NO_X (US$)	Particulates (US$)
California	4,558	9,266	4,682
Massachusetts	1,727	7,316	4,471
Minnesota	152	864	1,294
Nevada	1,744	7,600	4,672
New York	1,460	1,927	338
Oregon	0	3,556	3,048

Source: European Commission (1998) and EIA (1995).

Note
* EU data relate to 1995 and may be converted from ECU to US$ using the exchange rate applicable on June 30 1995 (ECU 1.33 = US$1.00). US data relate to 1992 (and have been converted from tons to tonnes). No attempt has been made to devise an inflationary factor to update these estimates. In this context, therefore, these estimates could be viewed as 'conservative' for later years.

- fuel quality (particularly coal); and
- mining and fuel transportation externalities (particularly accidents).

The major source of pollution is at the power generation stage for fossil fuels, whereas for renewables it tends to be during equipment manufacturing stages.

However, the damage estimates given in Table 12.2 are dominated by costs arising from human health effects, which are largely determined by the population affected (and hence the comparatively high damage values quoted in the table for the more densely populated EU countries). Estimation of health impacts is generally based upon exposure-response epidemiological studies and methodologies for placing a valuation on human life remain controversial.[13] Furthermore, countries that are sparsely populated, or populated in largely non-receptor areas, will tend to have relatively low health damage costs.

It is evident from the damage values contained in Table 12.2 that the country-specific nature of these estimates does not permit an 'average' European or US damages figure to be derived, and thus country (or regional) specific policies would be required in order to reduce existing damage levels. This could occur automatically if investment in new plant derived benefits from utilizing technological developments that further reduced pollutants, whilst existing plants could be retrofitted with improved technology as it became available.

The external damage costs of emissions of carbon dioxide

This category refers to external costs arising from greenhouse gas emissions from electricity generating facilities that lead to climate change with all its associated effects. This is a very contentious area, and the range of estimates for the possible economic ramifications of global climate change is considerable. Costs associated with climate change, such as damage from flooding, changes in agriculture patterns and other effects, all need to be taken into account. However, there is a lot of uncertainty about the magnitude of such costs, since the ultimate physical impact of climate change has yet to be determined with precision. Thus, deriving monetary values on this basis of limited knowledge is, at present, an imprecise exercise.

Table 12.3 gives life cycle CO_2 emissions (in tonnes per GWh) of the major forms of electric power generation. From this table it is clear that CO_2 emissions from coal and oil-based technologies far exceed those of the 'renewables' and are twice those of gas.

European external damage costs for electricity production

Table 12.4 gives cost ranges (in Euro-cents/kWh) for external costs associated with the range of electricity generation technologies for countries within the

Table 12.3 CO$_2$ emissions from different electricity generation technologies

Technology	CO$_2$ emissions (tonnes per GWh)			
	Fuel extraction	Construction	Operation	Total
Coal-fired (Con)	1	1	962	964
AFBC	1	1	961	963
IGCC	1	1	748	751
Oil-fired	—	—	726	726
Gas-fired	—	—	484	484
OTEC	N/A	4	300	304
Geothermal	<1	1	56	57
Small hydro	N/A	10	N/A	10
Nuclear	~2	1	5	8
Wind	N/A	7	N/A	7
Photovoltaics	N/A	5	N/A	5
Large hydro	N/A	4	N/A	4
Solar thermal	N/A	3	N/A	3
Wood (SH)	−1,509	3	1,346	−160

Source: IEA (1989).

Note
AFBC   Atmospheric Fluidized Bed Combustion.
BWR   Boiling Water Reactor.
Con   Conventional.
IGCC   Integrated Gasification Combined Cycle.
OTEC   Ocean Thermal Energy Conversion.
SH   Sustainable Harvest.

European Union. The ranges are often relatively large, reflecting variations in generation technology (and hence emission levels per kWh) and geographic location (and hence damage costs per kWh). To derive a 'representative' value, for each technology the median value of the lower bounds over all reporting countries was selected. The lower bounds should reflect optimal operating conditions and appropriate technology for each country. Taking the median value should minimize geographic and other country-specific factors influencing external costs.

These median lower bounds indicate that the external costs associated with coal technologies are three times those of gas and a very large multiple of those for renewable energy technologies. Combining these 'externality adders' with the lower bounds of the 'current' cost data given in Table 12.1 gives gas a marked societal cost advantage over all other modes of generation with the exception of wind and hydro.

If the 'environmental adders' were to be imposed upon expected future costs (Table 12.1), then it is clear that by 2020, under ideal operating conditions, many other renewables will become competitive with both gas and coal on the

Table 12.4 External costs for electricity production in the EU (range: Euro-cents/kWh)

Country	Coal and lignite	Peat	Oil	Gas	Nuclear	Biomass	Hydro	PV	Wind
Austria	3.7–15.0			1.1–2.6		2.4–2.5	0.1		
Belgium	3.0–5.5			1.1–2.2	0.4			0.1–0.3	0.05
Germany	3.5–6.5		5.1–7.8	1.2–2.3	0.4–0.7	2.8–2.9			0.1–0.2
Denmark	4.8–7.7			1.5–3.0		1.2–1.4			0.2
Spain	2.0–4.4			1.1–2.2		2.9–5.2			
Finland		2.3–5.1				0.8–1.1			
France	6.9–9.9		8.4–10.9	2.4–3.5	0.3	0.6–0.7	0.6		
Greece	4.6–8.4		2.6–4.8	0.7–1.3		0.1–0.8	0.5		0.25
Ireland	5.9–8.4	3.3–3.8							
Italy			3.4–5.6	1.5–2.7			0.3		
The Netherlands	2.8–4.2			0.5–1.9	0.7	0.4–0.5			
Norway				0.8–1.9		0.2	0.2		0–0.25
Portugal	4.2–6.7			0.8–2.1		1.4–1.8	0.03		
Sweden	1.8–4.2					0.3	0.04–0.7		
United Kingdom	4.2–6.7		2.9–4.7	1.1–2.2	0.25	0.5–0.6			0.15
EU range	1.8–15.0	2.3–5.1	2.6–10.9	0.5–3.5	0.25–0.7	0.1–5.2	0.03–0.7	0.1–0.3	0–0.25
Median Lower Bound	3.85	2.8	3.4	1.1	0.4	0.7	0.2	0.1	0.125

Source: adapted from European Commission (1998).

basis of the societal cost of electricity production. Such a comparison is fraught with difficulties, however, as the external costs per kWh associated with both emissions of pollutants and climate change in 2020 are likely to differ significantly from those given in Table 12.4. To a large extent differences will depend upon the success or otherwise of GHG abatement programmes over the same period. A decline in damage costs arising from emissions of non-GHGs can also be expected to occur as a consequence of continuing improvements in emission-reduction technology and retirement of older plants.

Energy subsidies

Support that lowers the cost of power generation can take many forms, including support to the use of inputs (e.g. water, fuels, etc.), public financing at interest rates below the market value, tax relief on corporate income, lump sum support to fixed capital investment in research and development, etc. Examples include the exemption of government-owned electricity generators from corporate income tax payments (increasing the relative after tax rate of return compared with electricity generation by private enterprises) or the provision of loans at interest rates below market rates, or over repayment periods in excess of market terms (which favour capital intensive energy forms, such as nuclear and coal, and encourages over-investment).

Figure 12.5 illustrates the impact of a subsidy of s cents per unit on a commodity (e.g. electricity). In the absence of a subsidy, equilibrium involves the supply of $0Q_0$ units of electricity at price $0P_0$ per unit. Upon introduction of a per-unit subsidy, the price (including the subsidy) paid by consumers falls to $0P_C$. $0P_U$ is now the price that the utility receives. In this illustration the benefits of the subsidy are shared about equally between the consumer and the utility. In the presence of the subsidy, demand increases to $0Q_1$ with a corresponding increase in environmental damage. In general, the 'benefit' of a subsidy accrues mostly to consumers if the ratio of the price elasticity of demand to the price elasticity of supply is small, and mostly to the producers if it is large.

In terms of consumer and producer surpluses, consumers' gains amount to the area denoted by (D + E + F) and producer gains to the area denoted by (A + B). Therefore both are better off with a subsidy in place. However, the government (or the provider of the subsidy) must pay out a total subsidy equivalent to the area (A + B + C + D + E + F). Thus there is a net welfare loss to society as a whole amounting to the area C.

Energy subsidies are particularly prevalent in developing countries, where energy prices typically contain a 'social' subsidy to enable the poor to receive basic lighting services. Perhaps the most extreme case of energy subsidies in the developed world involves the nuclear power industry, where various OECD governments subsidies the industry's fuel supply services, waste disposal, fuel

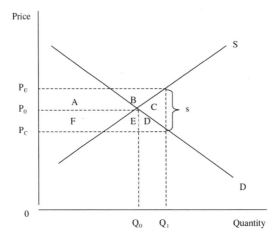

Figure 12.5 Incidence of a subsidy.

processing, and research and development. In addition, they also limit the liability of plants in case of accident, and help them clean up afterwards.[14]

Costs associated with energy subsidies world-wide and their ultimate impact on global emissions of CO_2 is the subject of Chapter 9.

Internalizing the externalities of electricity production

At least in theory, the most efficient process for imposing the 'polluter pays principle' would be to internalize as many of the environmental externalities of power generation as possible. Using the marketplace would permit energy producers and consumers to respond to such price signals in the most efficient and cost-effective way.

However, it should be emphasized that only external damage costs associated with emissions from fossil fuel combustion have been considered explicitly in these calculations. Those associated with other forms of power generation, security of supply considerations and with energy subsidies must also be incorporated into the analysis in order to achieve a reasonable balance across the range of power generating technologies, both renewable and non-renewable. For example, without such action nuclear power, with its negligible level of CO_2 emissions per kWh, would possess a marked competitive advantage over all other technologies (with the exception of some hydro systems), both renewable and non-renewable. However, as noted earlier, costs associated with emission of pollutants other than CO_2 are very variable and tend to be site-specific.

Once monetary values have been derived to reflect the external costs of differing technologies, the next step is to devise a mechanism for 'internalizing' them into market prices. In theory, an energy tax would represent a relatively straightforward solution, although the practicalities of its imposition would be fairly complicated. The tax would be required to be imposed at differential rates, depending upon the total estimated damages resulting from the fuel in question. A simple carbon tax alone, for example, would not impose any cost on the nuclear power industry. The tax would also have to be imposed by all countries, to ensure that the competitiveness of their industries in global markets was not compromised. The resulting tax revenue would also have to be distributed in such a way that implicit energy subsidies were not (re-)introduced. Finally, the worst of any social impact of energy taxes on poorer sections of society would have to be offset to ensure that the tax burden was not disproportionate in its incidence.

An alternative approach to the problem of reflecting external costs, and one that would possibly cause less economic disturbance, would be to introduce 'environmental credits' for the uptake of renewable energy technologies. Examples are currently commonplace. However, such credits do not 'internalize' the social costs of energy production but rather subsidize renewables. In addition, the taxpayer pays the subsidy and not the electricity consumer, thus rejecting the 'polluter pays principle'.

Renewable energy technologies are characterized by relatively high initial capital costs per MW of installed capacity, but very low running costs. This characteristic can make renewable technologies financially unattractive compared with traditional fossil fuel derived power using traditional project evaluation techniques based upon the anticipated life of the electricity generating facility (say, 30 years), due to discounting.[15] However, in terms of an economic/environmental evaluation, the relevant time frame should be set by the date at which all of the consequences attributable to the project had ceased to exist. In the context of CO_2 emissions from fossil fuel power stations this period could exceed 100 years, and in the case of spent-fuel storage for nuclear plants many centuries. Further, it is likely that the value of emission reduction will continue to rise into the future given projected world population growth, economic growth, and the subsequent difficulties in meeting global climate change agreements. In this context, the rate of discount is crucial in assessing the relative cost and benefit streams of alternative energy technologies in the context of intergenerational equity.[16]

The road transport sector

The road transport sector emits (directly or indirectly) a similar range of pollutants to the electric power sector. However, the resulting impacts are not directly comparable. Power station emissions are generally from high stacks in rural areas. In contrast, road transport emission sources are more diverse, invariably closer to ground level and frequently in urban areas. In addition, alternative (non-oil-based) road transport fuels are not commercially available and therefore the large-scale use of 'renewable' technologies is not currently a technologically feasible option. Nevertheless, consideration of environmental externalities of road transport fuels would provide an order of magnitude for calculation of environmental adders for the purpose of fuel taxation policy.[17] Ultimately this may provide the financial incentive for development of 'renewable' transport fuels, in conjunction with hydrogen and fuel cell technology.

Concerns over the health impacts of small particle air pollution, climate change, and oil supply insecurity, have combined to encourage radical changes in automotive engine and fuel technologies that offer the potential for achieving near zero emissions of air pollutants and GHG emissions, and diversification of the transport sector away from its present heavy reliance on gasoline. The hydrogen fuel cell vehicle is one technology that offers the potential to achieve all of these goals, if the hydrogen is derived from a renewable energy resource.

Fuel cells convert hydrogen and oxygen directly into electricity. They have three major advantages over current internal combustion engine technology in the transport sector:

- Gains in energy efficiency. 'Well to wheels' efficiency for gasoline engines averages around 14 per cent, for diesel engines 18 per cent, for near-term hybrid engines 26 per cent, for fuel cell vehicles 29 per cent, and for the fuel cell hybrid vehicle 42 per cent.[18] Thus, up to a three-fold increase in efficiency is available relative to current vehicles.
- Near-zero emissions of GHGs.
- Very low emissions of local air pollutants. Irrespective of the fuel, fuel cells largely eliminate oxides of sulphur and nitrogen, and particulates. All of these pollutants are associated with conventional engines.

In order to compare competing transport technologies on a basis that includes the cost of externalities as well as private costs, the societal life cycle cost of each technology must be calculated.

Fuel cell buses

Prototype fuel cell buses powered by liquid or compressed hydrogen are currently undergoing field trials in North America, while the European Commission is supporting the demonstration of 30 fuel cell buses in ten cities over a two-year period commencing in 2003.

There are a number of reasons why hydrogen (in compressed form) would appear to be a likely option for large vehicles, such as buses:

- they return regularly to a depot thus minimizing fuel infrastructure requirements;
- they are 'large', thus minimizing the need for compactness of the technology;
- in urban areas, low or zero emissions vehicle pollution regulations will assist their competitiveness as compared with diesel-powered buses;
- subsidies may be available from urban authorities in order to demonstrate urban pollution reduction commitments;
- they avoid pollution problems specifically related to diesel buses;
- they operate almost continually over long periods, thus making fuel-efficient technology more attractive.

Hörmandinger and Lucas (1997) have investigated the life cycle financial and economic cost of fuel cell buses utilizing hydrogen as fuel. They assessed the costs that a private operator would face in running a fleet of fuel cell powered buses, inclusive of a new fuel supply infrastructure, compared to those of a fleet of conventional diesel powered buses of similar performance. Given the presence of economies of scale in the production of hydrogen, they concluded that the fuel cell bus would be marginally more competitive than its diesel counterpart. Extending the analysis to societal life cycle costs, the analysis favoured the diesel option. Adding in the cost of environmental externalities led to a significantly greater increase in the cost of the diesel, as opposed to the hydrogen, bus. However, this was more than offset by the removal of the excise duty on diesel.

The Hörmandinger and Lucas base-case model assumed a fleet of just ten buses, operating over a 20-year time horizon and travelling 200 km a day, seven days a week. The central hydrogen reformer plant, using natural gas feedstock, and the refuelling station were based upon currently available technology. Both were exclusively for the use of the bus fleet. The cost of the fuel cell stack was set at $300 per kilowatt, and it was assumed that it would be replaced every five years. Although this cost was rather low by 1997 standards, the authors speculated that it would be reasonable for their assumed time frame (five to ten years in the future). The fuel cell buses were assumed to be of the same weight (without the power train) as the diesel buses. The cost of the tank for on-board storage of compressed hydrogen represented one of the major uncertainties of the model, since the technology is still under development.

Sensitivity of results: private costs

The annualized life cycle private costs, using a discount rate of 15 per cent, showed that the fuel cell bus was from 23 per cent (large bus) to 33 per cent (medium sized bus) more expensive than the diesel bus. The difference was due to both the provision of fuel and the initial cost of the investment.

A sensitivity analysis indicated that the medium size fuel cell bus reacted to changes in the base case parameter values in a similar way to its larger counterpart. The most important parameter with regard to impact on life cycle costs was the discount rate. However, although variations in the discount rate had a major influence on the individual life cycle costs of both technologies, since their investment and running cost profiles were very similar, their relative costs remained fairly static. For large buses, a drop in the discount rate from 15 per cent to 8 per cent reduced the cost differential from 23 per cent to 19 per cent.

Fleet size was found to be an important parameter, since the on-site production of hydrogen was subject to significant economies of scale. Thus an increase in fleet size from 10 to 25 gave the fuel cell bus a marginal cost advantage over the diesel alternative.

Price variations of feedstock (gas) had a relatively minor impact on bus costs, since it was a relatively minor cost component of the hydrogen reformer plant investment and operating costs. However, the diesel bus was much more sensitive to fuel cost increases. In the base case, an increase of 80 per cent in the price of diesel would remove its cost advantage.

As might be expected, the size and cost of the fuel cell stack was critical, although not compared with the costs of the reformer. Note that if hydrogen could be 'delivered' in the context of a hydrogen economy, then it is likely that reforming cost in the context of this example would be greatly reduced.

Sensitivity of results: societal costs

The societal cost of life cycle emissions involved augmenting the private costs by the damage costs arising from the environmental externalities created by the two options, and removal of the excise duty (56 per cent of the price) from the diesel fuel in the calculations. A lower discount rate of 8 per cent was also imposed, to reflect societal rather than private expectations.[19]

Externality costs were based upon previous studies of estimated damages arising from comparable emissions from the electricity and transport sectors. This transfer of results may not be appropriate if the characteristics of the exposure-response relationship differ from those of the reference studies. This is because in urban areas exposure to emissions from fossil fuel combustion in vehicles involves higher concentrations of pollutants than in rural areas due to the close proximity of emission and receptor points. However, even taking social costs at the higher end of the range only gave fuel cell buses a marginal benefit over their diesel counterparts.

A number of other social benefits were not quantified. In the context of this particular application their impact would have been extremely small. However, widespread adoption of fuel cell buses would have reduced other forms of local urban pollution from diesel buses (such as fuel spills and noise) and would have provided enhanced levels of security of domestic fuel supplies.

It is important to note that the GHG emission reduction benefits of hydrogen in the Hörmandinger and Lucas model were based upon the use of natural gas as feedstock, with no CO_2 sequestration. As a higher cost alternative, utilizing electricity generated from renewable sources to produce the hydrogen or adopting CO_2 sequestration with natural gas as the feedstock would have produced near zero fuel-cycle GHG emissions and consequently significantly greater societal benefits for the fuel cell buses. In this context, however, it is important that energy from renewable resources is 'additional' to that which was currently being generated. Simply utilizing existing renewable resources and making up the shortfall elsewhere from fossil fuels would not have contributed towards a net reduction in global GHG emissions.[20]

Fuel cell cars

Ogden *et al.* (2004) have estimated the societal life cycle costs of cars based upon alternative fuels and engines. Fifteen different vehicles were considered. These included current gasoline combustion engines and a variety of advanced lightweight vehicles: internal combustion engine vehicles fuelled with gasoline or hydrogen; internal combustion engine/hybrid electric vehicles fuelled with gasoline, compressed natural gas, diesel, Fischer-Tropsch liquids or hydrogen, and fuel cell vehicles fuelled with gasoline, methanol or hydrogen (from natural gas, coal or wind power). The analysis assumed a fully developed fuel infrastructure for all fuel options and mass production of each type of vehicle. This permitted all vehicles to be compared on the basis of their individual cost of construction, fuel costs, oil supply security costs and environmental externalities over the full fuel cycle. All costs were expressed net of direct taxes and subsidies, and all fuel costs were assumed to remain constant (in real terms) over the life cycle of all vehicles.

The present value of total societal life cycle costs, excluding external costs, favoured current and advanced gasoline cars (Table 12.5), with fuel cell vehicles being upwards of 60 per cent more expensive. This imbalance was reversed when lifetime air pollutant and GHG emission damage costs were included (Table 12.6). Now, hybrid vehicles utilizing traditional fossil fuels held a significant cost advantage over their fuel cell counterparts. It was only the introduction of an Oil Supply Insecurity (OSI) cost, that was intended to measure the cost of ensuring oil supply security from the Middle East, that those fuel cell vehicles based upon hydrogen (derived either from renewables or from fossil fuels with carbon sequestration) became competitive.[21]

In a sensitivity analysis, higher values attached to the environmental externalities, as might be expected, favoured the fuel cell vehicles and particularly those fuelled by hydrogen derived from fossil fuels with CO_2 sequestration.

Table 12.5 Projected base case societal life cycle costs for automobiles with alternative fuel/engine options

Technology	Present value: Lifetime fuel costs	Retail cost: Drive train and fuel storage	Cost of aluminium frame	Present value: Total private life cycle costs	Present value: Lifetime cost of externalities	Present value: Total societal life cycle costs
Current gasoline SI ICEV	2,828	2,837	0	5,665	6,723	12,388
Advanced lightweights ICEs						
Gasoline SI ICEV	1,674	2,837	936	5,448	3,579	9,026
H_2 (NG) SI ICEV	3,381	2,837 + 2,500	936	9,654	1,270	10,924
Advanced lightweights ICE/HEVs						
Gasoline SIDI ICE/HEV	1,316	2,837 + 1,342	936	6,432	3,015	9,446
CNG SI ICE/HEV	1,552	2,837 + 1,556	936	6,881	1,160	8,040
H_2 (NG) SI ICE/HEV	2,823	2,837 + 2,780	936	9,376	1,081	10,457
Diesel CIDI ICE/HEV	996	2,837 + 1,863	936	6,632	2,809	9,441
FT50 (NG) CIDI ICE/HEV	1,058	2,837 + 1,863	936	6,694	2,253	8,947
Lightweight fuel cell vehicles						
Gasoline FCV	2,009	2,837 + 5,097	936	10,879	3,243	14,122
Methanol (NG) FCV	2,238	2,837 + 3,220	936	9,231	916	10,147
H_2 (NG) FCV	2,169	2,837 + 2,459	936	8,402	736	9,138
H_2 (NG) FCV w/CO_2 seq.	2,411	2,837 + 2,459	936	8,644	225	8,869
H_2 (coal) FCV	2,200	2,837 + 2,459	936	8,432	1,247	9,679
H_2 (coal) FCV w/CO_2 seq.	2,435	2,837 + 2,459	936	8,667	314	8,981
H_2 (wind electrolytic) FCV	3,394	2,837 + 2,459	936	9,626	182	9,808

Source: modified from Table 1 of Ogden et al. (2004).

Note

AP: air pollutants; CIDI: compression-ignition direct-injection; CNG: compressed natural gas; CO_2: carbon dioxide; FCV: fuel cell vehicle; GHG: greenhouse gas emissions; H_2: hydrogen; HEV: hybrid electric vehicle; ICE: internal combustion engine; ICEV: internal combustion engine vehicle; NG: natural gas; OSI: oil supply insecurity; SI: spark-ignition; SIDI: spark-ignition direct-injection.

Table 12.6 Projected base case life cycle costs for externalities of automobiles with alternative fuel/engine options

Technology	Externalities			Present value: Lifetime cost of externalities
	Present value of lifetime costs			
	AP	GHG	OSI	Original
Current gasoline SI ICEV	2,640	1,429	2,654	6,723
Advanced lightweights ICEs				
Gasoline SI ICEV	1,162	846	1,571	3,579
H$_2$ (NG) SI ICEV	524	746	0	1,270
Advanced lightweights ICE/HEVs				
Gasoline SIDI ICE/HEV	1,097	683	1,235	3,015
CNG SI ICE/HEV	644	515	0	1,160
H$_2$ (NG) SI ICE/HEV	458	623	0	1,081
Diesel CIDI ICE/HEV	1,150	590	1,069	2,809
FT50 (NG) CIDI ICE/HEV	1,122	596	535	2,253
Lightweight fuel cell vehicles				
Gasoline FCV	338	1,019	1,886	3,243
Methanol (NG) FCV	248	668	0	916
H$_2$ (NG) FCV	257	479	0	736
H$_2$ (NG) FCV w/CO$_2$ seq.	119	106	0	225
H$_2$ (coal) FCV	366	881	0	1,247
H$_2$ (coal) FCV w/CO$_2$ seq.	215	99	0	314
H$_2$ (wind electrolytic) FC	68	114	0	182

Source: modified from Table 1 of Ogden *et al.* (2004).

Note
See Table 12.5.

Conclusions

This chapter has considered the economics of renewable energy technologies through the quantification in financial terms of the externalities of electric power generation, according to a range of alternative commercial and almost-commercial technologies, and externalities associated with gasoline and diesel in the transport sector.

In the stationary power sector, it has been shown that estimates of damage costs resulting from combustion of fossil fuels, if internalized into the price of the resulting output of electricity, could clearly render a number of renewable technologies (specifically wind and some applications of biomass) financially competitive with coal-fired generation. However, combined cycle natural gas technology would clearly have a marked financial advantage over both coal and renewables under current technology options and market conditions. Further, over the next two decades, the cost of renewable technologies (particularly those that are 'directly' solar-based) is likely to decline markedly as technical progress and economies of scale combine to reduce unit generating costs. Incorporating environmental externalities explicitly into the electricity tariff would serve to hasten this process.

The principle of internalizing the environmental externalities of GHG emissions (and other pollutants) resulting from power generation is of global validity. Whether this is achieved directly through imposition of a universal carbon tax and emission charges, or indirectly as a result of ensuring compliance with Kyoto targets and other environmental standards, a similar result is likely to be achieved; i.e. a rise in the cost of power generation based upon fossil fuel combustion and a relative improvement in the competitive position of an increasing range of renewable energy technologies.

We have noted that incorporation of environmental externalities into the costs of fossil fuel combustion still renders the bulk of renewable energy technologies non-competitive. However from a fuel security viewpoint they bring significant additional advantages that are not generally quantified. For most renewable energy technologies supply comes from 'local' sources, although it may be erratic in some cases. Conversely, fossil fuels must be transported to their point of combustion, sometimes over large distances, thus raising issues of security of supply lines. While the supply security 'premium' will differ for different fuels and different end uses, clearly for gasoline use in the transport sector the availability of alternative fuels would deliver a substantial premium.

Renewable energy technologies should also expand their presence in niche markets, particularly in the context of distributed generation.[22] Although their capacity is usually small, distributed generation technologies account for a significant proportion of total power supply in many parts of the world. Most distributed generation systems in commercial operation today consist of diesel and natural gas reciprocating engines and gas turbines. These are also likely to dominate in the short term. However by 2020 it is anticipate that fuel cells, as their costs fall, are likely to emerge as the primary distributed generation technology.[23] To the extent that hydrogen for the fuel cells is derived using renewable energy technologies, then this would represent a further step towards the hydrogen economy.

The current interest in a 'Hydrogen Economy' derives from the fact that, at this stage of human development, hydrogen is being regarded as the ultimate 'fuel'[24] for the twenty-first century, and beyond. Provided it is derived from renewable energy sources, when used with fuel cells it has near-zero emissions of both local pollutants and GHGs. Further, all of a country's hydrogen requirements could be produced from domestic sources, thus removing supply security concerns of fuel importation and the costs of holding stockpiles. Finally, fuel cells and hydrogen can be used for distributed power generation, thus avoiding centralized electricity generation and transmission costs and their associated environmental externalities.

Notes

1 Also known as a 'Pigouvian' tax.
2 Consult Baumol and Oates (1988) for a comprehensive coverage of environmental externalities.
3 These steps describe a 'bottom up', as distinct from a 'top down', methodology for life cycle analysis. Top-down studies use highly aggregated data to estimate the external costs of pollution. They are typically undertaken at the national or regional level using estimates of total quantities of emissions and estimates of resulting total damage. The proportion of such damage attributable to certain activities (e.g. the transport sector) is then determined, and a resulting monetary cost derived. The exercise is generic in character, and does not take into account impacts that are site specific. However, its data requirements are relatively minor compared with the 'bottom up' approach. The latter involves analysis of the impact of emissions from a single source along an impact pathway. Thus all technology data are project specific. When this is combined with emission dispersion models, receptor point data, and dose-response functions, monetized values of the impacts of specific externalities can be derived. Data requirements are relatively large compared with the 'top down' methodology, and therefore omissions may be significant.
4 The European Commission (EC) launched the project in collaboration with the US Department of Energy in 1991. The EC and US teams jointly developed the conceptual approach and the methodology and shared scientific information for its application to a range of fuel cycles. The main objectives were to apply the methodology to a wide range of different fossil, nuclear and renewable fuel cycles for power generation and energy conservation options. Although the US withdrew from the project, a series of National Implementation Programmes to realize the methodology for reference sites throughout Europe was completed. The methodology was extended to address the evaluation of externalities associated with the use of energy in the transport and domestic sectors, and a number of non-environmental externalities such as those associated with security of supply. Krewitt (2002) has provided a critique of the evolution of the methodologies used in the ExternE analyses.
5 Gagnon *et al*. (2002) address this issue at length.
6 For example, tidal energy is completely predictable whereas both solar and wind energy have lower levels of predictability.
7 The costs to the system of coping with unpredictable intermittency in the UK have been explored by Milborrow (2001).
8 A detailed explanation of these techniques, with practical examples, is given in Part III of OECD (1994).
9 Philibert (1999) summarizes the options available for discount rate determination in the context of intergenerational environmental damages. See also Weitzman (2001) for an innovative approach that reduces the discount rate over long time horizons.
10 This transformation also reduces the variability of observations around the estimated individual time lines. Hence the apparent high degree of 'fit' to the data points. The

results of any extrapolation of these trends should, therefore, be interpreted with great care.

11 The European Currency Unit (ECU) was conceived in 1979 as an artificial 'weighted' European currency. It was replaced by the Euro, the single European currency, on January 1, 1999.

12 The data for Finland reflect the sparsely populated nature of the country, the fact that significantly levels of pollutants fall into the sea, and an underestimate of damages due to lack of data from Eastern European receptor points.

13 See Aunan (1996) for a survey of exposure-response epidemiological studies. Pearce (2002) raises questions regarding the appropriateness of the ExternE methodology used to derive these monetary estimates of health impacts.

14 For example, the Price-Anderson Act limits the liability of the US nuclear electricity generating facilities in the event of an accident. Without this crucial federal legislation/subsidy it is unlikely that the US nuclear power industry could purchase full indemnity in the commercial insurance marketplace.

15 See Chapter 7.

16 *Ref*: Philibert (1999) and Weitzman (2001).

17 The interested reader is referred to Delucchi (2002) and European Commission (1997) for such calculations.

18 Fuel cells can more than double the efficiency of an ICE, but energy used in making and storing hydrogen offsets these gains to the benefit of fuel cell hybrid vehicles.

19 In the context of climate change damages arising from emissions of GHG this discount rate could still be regarded as unreasonably large.

20 In fact, such a practice could actually increase net emissions of CO_2. This is because 1 GWh of electricity provided from renewable resources avoids 972 tonnes of CO_2 if it replaces coal-fired generation. If the same 1 GWh were used to produce hydrogen by electrolysis for use in a fuel cell vehicle to replace a gasoline hybrid vehicle the avoided CO_2 emissions would amount to 390 tonnes. Although this comparison ignores the intermittent nature of some renewable energy technologies, which could lead to significant levels of power 'spillage', the gap is nevertheless considerable.

21 Owen (2004) discusses the validity of the OSI measure used in Ogden *et al.* (2004).

22 Distributed generation technologies produce power on a customer's site or at the site of a local distribution utility and supply power directly to the distribution network at distribution-level voltages.

23 IEA (2002).

24 Hydrogen, like electricity, is not a fuel but is an energy carrier.

Bibliography

Aunan, K. (1996) 'Exposure-response functions for health effects of air pollutants based on epidemiological findings', *Risk Analysis* 16:693–709.

Baumol, W.J. and Oates, W.E. (1988) *The Theory of Environmental Policy*, 2nd edn, Cambridge: Cambridge University Press.

Delucchi, M.A. (2002) 'Life-cycle analysis and external costs in transportation', in IEA/NEA, *Externalities and Energy Policy: the Life Cycle Analysis Approach*, Paris: NEA/OECD.

Energy Information Administration (EIA) (1995) *Electricity Generation and Environmental Externalities: Case Studies*, Washington, D.C.: US Department of Energy.

European Commission (1997) *External Costs of Transport in ExternE*, Brussels: European Commission.

European Commission (1998) *ExternE – Externalities of Energy*, Brussels: European Commission.

Gagnon, L., Belanger, C. and Uchiyama, Y. (2002) 'Life-cycle assessment of electricity generation options: the status of research in year 2001', *Energy Policy* 30:1267–1278.

Hörmandinger, G. and Lucas, N.J.D. (1997) 'An evaluation of the economics of fuel cells in urban buses', *International Journal of Energy Research* 21:495–526.

Imperial College Centre for Energy Policy and Technology (ICCEPT) (2002) *Assessment of Technological Options to Address Climate Change. A Report to the Prime Minister's Strategy Unit.*

International Energy Agency (IEA) (1989) *Environmental Emissions from Energy Technology Systems: The Total Fuel Cycle*, Proceedings of IEA/OECD Expert Seminar, Paris, 12–14 April.

International Energy Agency (IEA) (1999) *World Energy Outlook, Looking at Energy Subsidies: Getting the Prices Right*, Paris: OECD/IEA.

International Energy Agency (IEA) (2000) *Experience Curves for Energy Technology Policy*, Paris: OECD/IEA.

International Energy Agency (IEA) (2002) *World Energy Outlook 2002*, Paris: OECD/IEA.

Krewitt, W. (2002) 'External costs of energy – do the answers match the questions? Looking back at 10 years of ExternE', *Energy Policy* 30:839–848.

Milborrow, D. (2001) *PIU Working Paper on Penalties for Intermittent Sources of Energy*, London: The Cabinet Office.

Ogden, J.M., Williams, R. and Larson, E.D. (2004) 'Societal lifecycle costs of cars with alternative fuels/engines', *Energy Policy*, 32:7–27.

Organization for Economic Cooperation and Development (OECD) (1994) *Project and Policy Appraisal: Integrating Economics and Environment*: Paris, OECD.

Owen, A.D. (2004) 'Oil supply insecurity: control versus damage costs', *Energy Policy*, forthcoming.

Pearce, D. (2002) 'Energy policy and externalities: an overview', in IEA/NEA *Energy Policy and Externalities: The Life Cycle Analysis Approach*, Paris: NEA/OECD.

Philibert, C. (1999) 'The economics of climate change and the theory of discounting', *Energy Policy* 27:913–927.

Sorensen, B. (2000) *Renewable Energy: Its Physics, Engineering, Environmental Impacts, Economics & Planning*, 2nd edn, London: Academic Press.

Sundqvist, T. and Söderholm, P. (2002) 'Valuing the environmental impacts of electricity generation: a critical survey', *The Journal of Energy Literature* VIII:3–41.

Virdis, M.R. (2002) 'Energy policy and externalities: the life cycle analysis approach', in IEA/NEA in *Energy Policy and Externalities: The Life Cycle Analysis Approach*, Paris: NEA/OECD.

Weitzman, M.L. (2001) 'Gamma discounting', *The American Economic Review* 91:260–271.

Index

assistance rules 42–3; institutions and procedures 40–2; joint implementation 47–8, 80–2; objective and principles 36–8; reporting and review 45–7; substantive commitments 38–40; technology transfer 43–4; voting rule 41–2; vulnerable countries 44–5, *see also* Kyoto Protocol

United States 67–8; Clean Air Act 115; withdrawal from Kyoto 37–8, 54, 67, 90

Unold, W. 126

validity of permits 135
value of statistical life (VSL) 244
Victor, D. 109

wavelengths 13
Weitzman, M. 160
welfare economics 147–9
welfare losses 198–9
Westkog, H. 123–4
White, B. 151
Wigley, T.M.L. 10–11
Wilcoxen, P.J. xvi, 166–92
willingness to pay (WTP) 244
World Bank 251, 255

Yellen, J. 88

Zillman, D. 136
Zylicz, T. 116